KLEE PRESS

PROJECT MANAGEMENT FOR MUSICIANS

RECORDINGS, CONCERTS, TOURS, STUDIOS, AND MORE

JONATHAN FEIST

Berklee Press

Editor in Chief: Jonathan Feist
Vice President of Online Learning and Continuing Education: Debbie Cavalier
Assistant Vice President of Berklee Media: Robert F. Green
Dean of Continuing Education: Carin Nuernberg
Editorial Assistants: Dominick DiMaria and Sarah Walk
Cover Designer: Jamie de Rooij

Drawings © 2013 by Mark Addison Kershaw. All rights reserved.

ISBN 978-0-87639-135-8

1140 Boylston Street
Boston, MA 02215-3693 USA
(617) 747-2146

Visit Berklee Press Online at
www.berkleepress.com

DISTRIBUTED BY

HAL•LEONARD®
CORPORATION
7777 W. BLUEMOUND RD. P.O. BOX 13819
MILWAUKEE, WISCONSIN 53213

Visit Hal Leonard Online at
www.halleonard.com

CONTENTS

ACKNOWLEDGMENTS

Many people assisted in creating this book, and I am very grateful for their time and efforts. First and foremost is Debbie Cavalier, vice president of online learning and continuing education at Berklee College of Music. Besides being a great advocate for my creating this body of work, she has been an extraordinary manager to me for an astonishing number of years, and is among the smartest, kindest, and most gifted people that I know. I am also grateful for the existentialist support, faith, and inspiring role modeling of Jeff Schroedl, vice president pop and standard publications at Hal Leonard Corporation, and Dave Kusek, vice president emeritus of Berklee Media.

This project was deeply informed by many musicians and other professionals who granted me extensive interviews about how they manage projects in the music industry and beyond. First, to those who permitted me to videotape our conversations for use in my Berkleemusic online course covering this material, my sincerest appreciation goes to Elizabeth DeVore, Mike King, Dana Levit, Emily Peal, Anne Peckham, Bob Sinicrope, and Jerry Slavet. Critical content and/or production assistance was provided by Boriana Alexiev, Dominick Dimaria, Craig Reed, Jackie Muth, and Sarah Walk. Indispensable conversations, content insights, and contributions of samples, artwork, and stories came from Alan Bargfrede, Jay Barnes, Mitch Benoff, Lee Feist, Brent Frei, Isaac Ho, Thaddeus Hogarth, Bob Hubert, Pete Jackson, Mark Kershaw (Addison), Aaron Larget-Caplan, Matt Marvuglio, Michael Markus, David Patterson, Elliot Scheiner, Charys Schuler, Frank Shirley, and Joe Stump. Enormous thanks to guest editors/peer reviewers Steven Feist, Don Gorder, Susan Lindsay, Rajasri Mallikarjuna, Carin Nuernberg, Claudia Obser, and Roseanne Saalfield, all of whom I asked to review this text because they are so brilliant. And there are so many others, from my authors and colleagues at Berklee College of Music and Hal Leonard Corp., to the accommodating folks at From the Top, Smartsheet, and the Project Management Institute, to my whip-smart students, to my long-suffering friends and family. Several of you should be listed multiple times, here.

My most profound thanks, though, go to my extraordinary wife Marci Cornell-Feist, who besides being a delightful life partner has been a continuing inspiration for how to conduct business at the highest possible level of quality. Observing her imagine, launch, run, and develop The High Bar, and mentor hundreds of other organizations, over the years, has provided me with lesson upon lesson about how good work actually gets done, revealing the grisly details of how to maintain high professional standards in spite of what the world tends to throw our way. Much as she teases me for my monomania regarding project management, there is no denying that a great number of the better ideas discussed herein can ultimately be traced back to her.

I've tried to credit all concepts herein to the original sources, but many of these techniques and practices have become somewhat folkloric in origin, and their actual inventors were sometimes elusive to me, for whatever reason. It is likely that some additional crediting of concepts here would be appropriate. My apologies for any oversights. Contact Berklee Press if you spot any such omissions or other issues, and we'll address them in future printings.

This book is dedicated to my two favorite projects: Merlin and Forrest.

PREFACE

Musicians aspire to do an endless number and variety of projects. We record albums, perform concerts, and create nonprofit organizations. We construct instruments, develop practice regimens, form bands, play gigs, and go on tour. We build recording studios and develop concert series. We write songs, compose film scores, and commission new music. We set up teaching studios, create education programs, author method books, and produce musical theater shows. And we're often chipping away at several of these projects simultaneously.

Meanwhile, we raise families, pursue education, maintain houses, volunteer in the community, keep chickens, and sometimes have full-time jobs, often in other fields entirely.

It is an enormously complex and ambitious lifestyle. Our intentions are grandiose, and the roads towards fulfilling them are often long and winding.

Some musicians have managers who handle their logistics. Those who find themselves in the role of project manager (producers, studio owners, executives, and sometimes the artists themselves) have various degrees of actual training in the craft. Increasingly, musicians are acting independently, handling the business as well as the art, but making up as they go along the methods for how they hope to get their work done. Thus, the complexity of the musician's life is also increasing.

So, it's useful for pretty much everyone working in the music industry to have some project management skills. The ability to complete a project is among the core skill sets for any professional, though relatively few have actually studied project management. But it is effective project management that actually gets projects done, or done the way we hope.

What we can claim to have accomplished is based on what we finish, not on what we start. Setting projects in motion is relatively easy. Completing them is far more difficult. It is our history of completed projects that defines us professionally, though, not our history of started projects. Read any bio or résumé. Successful projects stand out as some of our life's most significant milestones, and we don't get partial credit for works in progress.

The goal of any musician's journey is to create a body of work that best represents our unique worldviews and gifts. That means serially completing projects, and we hope that each is better than the last.

This book is about completing visions. By adding a layer of organizational scaffolding around your work, you can keep it on track, maintaining the visionary focus while keeping it within budget, and on a time frame that will optimize its possibility for success. This meta-work surrounding the lifecycle of any defined work is called project management. There are various degrees of it, depending on the project's complexity, but the principles are scalable. The quality of a project's management often determines its success.

Good project management is the guardian angel of your life's work. Bad project management is its jailer. When done right, it points to the sun for inspiration, grips your hand to pull you higher, and watches your back as you wander treacherous paths. When done with insufficient attention, it distracts you and wastes resources. Determining an appropriate amount of management isn't always obvious, and so in this book, I will try to point you towards many tools and provide guidance regarding when they are most helpful.

By the end of this book, you will be able to:

- analyze visions, great and small, and develop effective and efficient systems that will bring these visions into existence

- use road-tested, research-based project management tools, such as work breakdown structures and critical time paths, as you work to fulfill your articulated vision and scope, so that all your efforts help you fulfill your goals—without creating unhelpful bureaucratic distractions

- accurately predict and manage a project's resources and timeline

- mitigate risk to budget, timeline, scope, and quality level

- manage teams effectively, monitoring their progress, keeping the work on track, avoiding risk, and recovering from inevitable bumps in the road

- organize work flow, synchronizing all efforts to be in support of the ultimate project vision

The examples in this book are based on real events in the music industry, often my own experience in publishing books, recordings, and videos for Berklee Press. There are also a lot of stories here from my colleagues in the music industry. At times, details are disguised. I might describe a tuba player in a ballet orchestra when the real story happened to a mandolinist in a bluegrass group—particularly if the tuba player did something bone-headed! When I give sample budgets or other sensitive information, the numbers portrayed are made up, to protect people's privacy. The main point of the illustrations is preserved, though, despite the variances from reality. Just consider the stories herein historical fiction, and you'll be mostly right.

I hope that the strategies and concepts presented here will help you to accomplish great works.

CHAPTER 1

What Is Project Management?

In this chapter, we will take a global view of project management. We will examine what a managed project looks like, the different major phases of a project's lifecycle, and an evolutionary path for how we can improve at managing our projects.

OBJECTIVES

By the end of this chapter, you'll be able to:

- define the essential concepts and terms of project management, and understand what project management is and when to use it

- identify how formal project management helps you accomplish more, faster, better

- identify the community of people involved in a project and how their roles fit together

- organize projects into their critical phases: initiation, planning, execution, monitoring and controlling, and closing

- understand different levels of project management capability and recognize the skills that will make you more effective

INTRODUCTION TO PROJECT MANAGEMENT

Project management is the process of deliberately implementing a vision. It is a strategic approach to accomplishing articulated goals in which you take control of all details, coordinate all moving parts, organize all components, and systematize all activities, working methodically to produce the desired outcome so that everything that occurs is in service to the overarching vision.

A *project* can be formally defined as a temporary endeavor undertaken to create a product, service, or result. This is the working definition currently used by the Project Management Institute, an organization devoted to researching and articulating best practices on how to manage projects. (Their publication, *The Project Management Body of Knowledge Guide*, or "PMBOK," is a highly recommended reference for all project managers.)

- *Products* are tangible, like albums, tours, businesses, marketing campaigns, books, performances, and recording studios.

- *Services* are systems, like Q/A criteria for mastering recordings, curriculum for students, or organizational procedures for how a team of ushers will run a concert.

- *Results* are new conditions or scenarios that are brought about, such as replacing an orchestra's conductor or reinvigorating a nonprofit board.

The lines blur. Most projects that musicians undertake are products.

In all cases, there's a clear goal and thus an identifiable ending or completion point for when that vision is fulfilled. That projects officially and inarguably "end" distinguishes projects from business as usual. "Business as usual" is the continual flood of regular stuff that comes into our lives and gets processed. Its management has more to do with ongoing systems than assessable final outcomes. Practicing your guitar and processing email are business as usual. They are general work that you continually process or maintain, rather than strategic building blocks that clearly help you move towards accomplishing a singular goal. However, a concert is a project, because it has a completion point when the vision is fulfilled.

An album is a project. A song is a project. "Playing drums" is a little vague, as far as what project managers like to formally call a "project." Where does it begin? How do you know that it has ended? How can you assess whether it is successful? But "a curriculum of study that will help you become a better drummer" might be a project, as long as there is a point at which the effort ends, perhaps in fulfillment of some previously planned assessment criteria. The completed curriculum then supports business as usual, which is the daily grind of actually practicing within those parameters.

You'll find refinements of this definition, in the world of formal project management. Some project management gurus find it convenient to think of projects as having more than two steps and requiring more than two minutes to execute. Some writers emphasize that projects require complex work from multiple disciplines. Fine. The key point is that we're creating something, we have a vision of the end result, and we want to create a clear strategy for how to make that vision come about.

A project might be establishing a teaching studio or building a recording studio. It's not really "running" either of these endeavors; that's more a maintenance or general management activity—business as usual, not a project. Many of the techniques we will discuss will also help in those ongoing activities. We'll look at some techniques for hiring people, for example, and those strategies will work for adding someone to your project team or for a permanent position in your organization. But what we're really looking at here are goals that begin and end, and have higher stakes than making your lunch or tuning your mandolin.

PROJECT INDEX

When you're pondering the definition of "project," it's natural that you'll start itemizing the many projects currently on your mind. This thought process easily becomes an existentialist question about who you want to be, and what you want to accomplish in life. Your projects are a reflection of your self—though they are not actually who you are. Projects are your footprints, not your feet. Still, though, their success feeds into our sense of self worth, and we might set a lot of projects in motion in our lives as musicians.

As a result, the musicians that I've known, and maybe everyone else too, all seem to be on the brink of exploding with countless projects—both music-related and otherwise. Collectively, this cloud of projects can take on an aura of uncontrollability and a feeling that there is just too much to do in life.

A helpful first step towards gaining control over this cacophony is to create a life project index, itemizing all that you are trying to do, ordered by priority. This is a document that is a few pages long, which lists and roughly organizes the projects you want to do. You can then methodically advance your work, referencing this list every day to see what you need to move forward.

There are three steps to developing a life project index: list, categorize, prioritize.

1. **List.** Do a "mind dump," listing everything on your mind that could be a project, in any dimension of your life. Remember, a project is a temporary endeavor that results in a product, system, or result. That's pretty open! Basically, write down any tangible chunk of work that you feel that you want to control. To start, itemize your projects without judgment: good ideas, bad ideas, current ideas, future ideas, urgent ideas, ideas that you know you will probably never do—whatever. Try to phrase them as tangible deliverables—nouns, indicating bodies of work that you have to accomplish. However, if you need to phrase some items as actions, that's okay.

   Spring concert

   Article for magazine

   Become conversant in French

   Asparagus patch

   Basement termite problem

   Pub gig

   …(and many more)

Whether you have dozens or hundreds of projects on this list, try to be thorough in your itemization. Get them all down, into the index, so that they are not still rattling around in the back of your head, making you feel that there's something you should be doing but can't put your finger on what it is. You want all your work to be evident. Exhaust yourself, listing them. Typing them in a computer file will let you edit and move them around more easily, but using a notebook while you're on the beach could work okay too.

2. **Categorize.** Perhaps after a break, look at your long list again, and start arranging your projects into categories that correspond with the different dimension of your life. For example, you might have category headers for work, house, garden, music performances, writing, relationships, animals, health, machines, hobbies, community service, personal finances, or more. Categorize all your projects. You might use a separate page (or set of pages) for each category.

   Work
   Spring concert
   Pub gig
   Article for magazine

   House/Garden
   Asparagus patch
   Basement termite problem

   Hobbies
   Become conversant in French

3. **Prioritize.** When your list is organized by categories, it's time to rank the projects by how urgently they need your attention. For each project, first decide whether you are going to actually commit to doing it, to definitely not ever do it, or perhaps to consider doing it someday but not anytime in the near future.

   - If you're not really going to ever do it, delete it from your list and agree to yourself that you're done thinking about it. It's just not feasible, given the other demands on your time.

   - If you might do it someday, create a "Back-Burner Projects" list (or what efficiency guru David Allen calls a "Someday/ Maybe" list), and store it there. Revisit that list now and then to see if your priorities change. Maybe, you'll upgrade something on that list to be a current project. Or not. It's on the back burner, keeping warm, while more critical projects cook along, front and center.

- If you're definitely going to do it, write the time frame of when, and then write the very next thing you need to do to move it forward. Also indicate how long you think that task will take.

Organize your final set of project lists with the urgent ones on top, followed by less urgent ones lower down. Charts make it clear, and it is worth learning how to do them in a program such as Microsoft Word or Excel, and also how to easily sort or drag the rows around to reflect your changing priorities. Add columns for priority, next action, and completion date. For priority, you can use a code system like 1=ASAP, 2=This Week, 3=Not Urgent, W=Waiting for someone else to do something before the project can move forward.

WORK

Priority	Project	Next Task	Duration (Hours)	Project Completion Date
1	Article for magazine	brainstorm topics	1	6/1
2	July 4th Concert	decide on final program (6/4)	2	7/4
W	Pub gig	pub owner will send contract	1	9/1

FIG. 1.1. Life Project Index: Work Projects

You can then maintain this set of lists as the central index into your life's work—what you need to do with your time to move your priorities forward. Take great delight in moving projects from your current lists to your back-burner list—or even just deleting them entirely. The more your lists reflect your priorities, the more helpful they will be.

Every morning, scan the index, and work at pushing your top priority projects forward. Likely, Monday through Friday, you'll spend most of your time on your work projects. On weekends, you might spend more time perusing what needs to be done in the garden. Once a week, read the whole document in detail.

We will see a great many refinements of this process throughout this book. For example, you can have a page or a folder of additional information for each project. But starting with a mind dump like this and then maintaining a working index is healthy and grounding, and it will give you a sense of control. You might redo the index every few months, or once a year, when you want to clear your head and take a fresh look at what's on your mind and assess what projects you really want to do. It's a good birthday or New Year's ritual.

Try it. Many people find that producing a life project index like this reduces stress. Some find that it increases stress. In either case, it is a good reality check, and working from this index gives you a realistic assessment of what's going on in your life.

This is your big picture. Once all of your projects are listed in this system, it is time to manage individual projects, end to end. Let's explore what that looks like by tracing the lifecycle of one specific project we did here at Berklee Press, envisioned by guitarist Thaddeus Hogarth.

A MUSICIAN'S PROJECT

Thaddeus Hogarth has a career typical of many contemporary musicians. He's an exceptional guitarist, with a killer band that frequently performs and tours. He teaches at Berklee College of Music, both on campus and online. He writes a blog and does a lot of recording. He even helps develop new gear.

In other words, his work is eclectic, filled with many kinds of projects.

After he finished authoring his popular Berkleemusic online course, *Funk/Rock and R&B Guitar Soloing,* Thaddeus was looking for another project to do, and so he found his way to my office at Berklee Press. Thaddeus thought he'd write a book on similar material. I thought that was a great idea.

Let's consider our overall process in how we made his project idea become a reality, organized as project lifecycle phases, which we will explore in more depth later this chapter.

Photo by Michael Sparks Keegan

THADDEUS HOGARTH

Initiating

Our first step was to talk about his imagined book and refine his vision of what it could be. This began the initiating phase of the project, where ideas are first set in motion, and the possibility for doing the project is initially explored. Thaddeus's thoughts clarified into a concept for a book that we'd call *Funk/R&B Guitar*. As we talked more, he got more specific. The book would be 96 pages long, with a CD of play-along tracks and technical demonstrations. Thaddeus wrote out a tentative table of contents and clarified that the book would actually support his online course as a textbook, as well as being a standalone product.

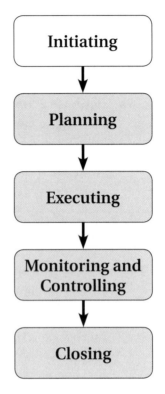

FIG. 1.2. Project Lifecycle: Initiating

In the initiating stage of a project's lifecycle, the vision gets articulated and the planned components get itemized and described. We created a document, often called a project charter, which is an articulation of its proposed scope (see chapter 2). That document was used to convince various decision makers that the proposed book was worthy of our publication.

They eventually said yes! So, I coordinated with our business team to draft a contract, which was circulated among a number of people who have to approve such things, before offering it to the author. Then we sent the contract to Thaddeus, and he cheerfully signed it.

Officially deciding to embark on the project marks the end of the initiating stage of the project's lifecycle.

Planning

Once the project charter was approved, we started planning how the project would go. The project charter (the document that articulated our planned scope, used for gaining project approval) had now evolved into a dynamic central component of our project plan, called the scope statement. Because it was the articulation of the vision that was formally accepted and contracted, we held it as a relatively fixed metric of what the ultimate book should be. Careful planning helped to ensure that the work to come on this project would conform to the accepted scope.

We knew that we wanted to release the book for the NAMM trade show in January, and so we had to consider the calendar, first of all. Certain tasks in this kind of project take a relatively predictable amount of time to complete (e.g., printing and boxing copies for shipment nearly always takes three weeks), while others are a little harder to pin down (e.g., required authoring time can vary a lot). By using various tools and tricks that you will learn throughout this book, we came up with a schedule that would result in us meeting that deadline. We were given a certain budget to produce the book's accompanying play-along CD, and Thaddeus found musicians and a studio that would be appropriate for that.

Project management software can be really helpful in doing this kind of planning work, as well as actually facilitating communications between everyone involved as the project unfolds. Figure 1.3 is an example from Smartsheet, an excellent cloud-based project management tool, which you can try for free at www.smartsheet.com. I use Smartsheet for many examples in this book because it offers a good balance of power and ease of use, as well as being compatible with many kinds of computers. We'll look at many of Smartsheet's features shown here throughout the book, but it's essentially an itemization of work and mechanisms for tracking it.

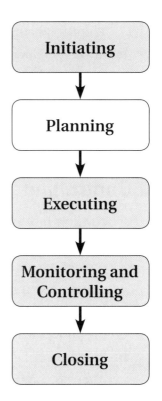

FIG. 1.4. Project Lifecycle: Planning

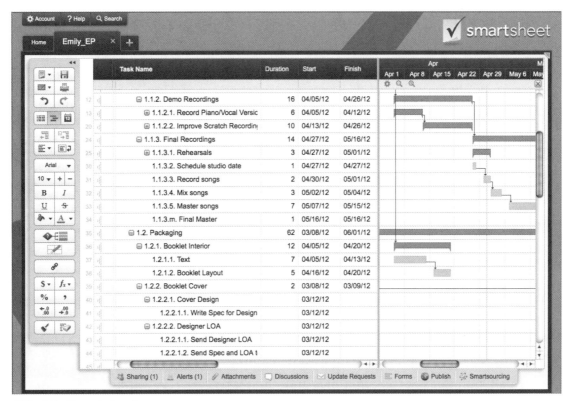

FIG. 1.3. Smartsheet

Planning is the second stage of project management. It concludes when the plan looks effective enough to adequately support the creation of content, though there is often a cyclical relationship between planning, execution, monitoring, and controlling.

Execution, with Monitoring and Controlling

Once the planning was all set, Thaddeus started creating the content. He wrote a draft, I edited it, and we passed it back and forth a few times, tightening it up. We rendered his music notation in the software program Finale, with the help of some other people on the project team. Then, when it was all set, he and his band recorded his CD. Because the project was planned so carefully, minimal changes were necessary to the text after the CD was done. We checked the master carefully and confirmed that the grooves were burning hot, as well as pedagogically on target. We checked the notation against the recording and edited, proofread, and otherwise reviewed every word, note, and graphical element.

Then, it went into graphic design. Various proofs were routed to various parties (notation engravers, proofreaders, Thaddeus, me, the production manager, etc.) for review. I art-directed a graphic artist to help her come up with a suitable cover design, with various rounds of drafts circulated to various decision-makers for feedback, and then revision. Marketing text was drafted for the back cover, which included quotes from various guitar luminaries saying how great the book was, which they knew because we sent them draft copies of the manuscript and CD to review. All these pieces cycled through content creators and various editors and other types of reviewers, and then back to the creator for new and improved iterations.

In all, hundreds of computer files and thousands of sheets of paper were circulated among dozens of

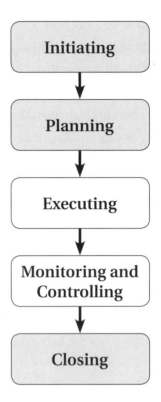

FIG. 1.5. Project Lifecycle: Executing, with Monitoring and Controlling

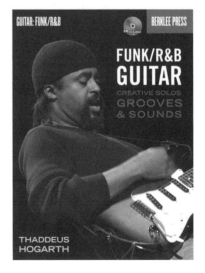

FIG. 1.6. *Funk/R&B Guitar*

people. Then finally, the book was printed, boxed up by robots, and shipped to stores worldwide. Some came to my office, too. It looks like figure 1.6, and it sells like hotcakes.

This was the *executing* stage of a project's lifecycle, where the content gets created. While it's being executed, the work is being monitored and controlled. In formal project management circles, those phases are often considered separately, though they often occur simultaneously. These phases end when the project's vision is realized.

Closing

Now a published author, Thaddeus went merrily on his way, whistling a happy author's tune as he prepared a little wheelbarrow that he'd use to haul his massive royalties all the way to the bank. He was done. But my own project management tasks were still rolling! Copies of the book had to be circulated to various places: the Berklee library, the guitar department, those luminaries on the back cover, the customer service team's bookshelf, the Library of Congress, and so on. The digital files for the book were archived in multiple locations. Obsolete drafts were recycled. Paperwork was completed. Web pages were developed for it on the Berklee Press and Hal Leonard websites, and sales and customer service agents were given summaries, explaining its purpose, so that Thaddeus's book could become their project, not mine.

These are all tasks in the closing phase of a project's lifecycle. And that, in a nutshell, is what project management looks like for publishing a book/CD about music.

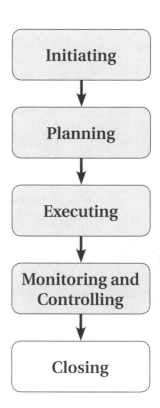

FIG. 1.7. Project Lifecycle: Closing

THE PROJECT MANAGER'S FUNCTION

The project manager's job is to guide the project through these phases and make sure that it turns out as well as possible given the various constraints put upon it. The usual factors that limit a project's quality are money, time, and defined scope (sometimes referred to as "features"). There's the old joke, "You can have it good, fast, or cheap. Pick any two."

The Triple Constraint

The classic diagram that illustrates this is called the *triple constraint.* If one dimension increases or decreases, the others must also change to compensate.

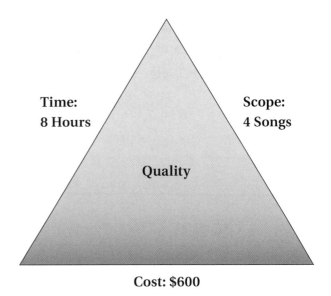

Say a recording studio charges $600 for eight hours of work. We want to record four songs, and we know that we can record one song in two hours, so we have a solid plan. In that case, the triangle is nice and balanced. Metaphorically speaking, that equilibrium is the quality we want.

FIG. 1.8. Triple Constraint

If one of the factors changes, such as that we wind up spending six hours on the first song because we're trying to get an intricate guitar solo exactly right, then our triangle will get a little bent out of shape, putting pressure on the other constraints. Now, we have just two of the eight hours we had scheduled to record three songs, and we expect to need six more hours (twelve total). To return to balance, we need to increase what we spend, decrease the number of songs we record, or rush through recording the remaining songs, likely decreasing their quality. Otherwise, we get a lopsided triangle like in figure 1.9, and we certainly don't want that.

FIG. 1.9. Changing Constraints (a) Time; (b) Features

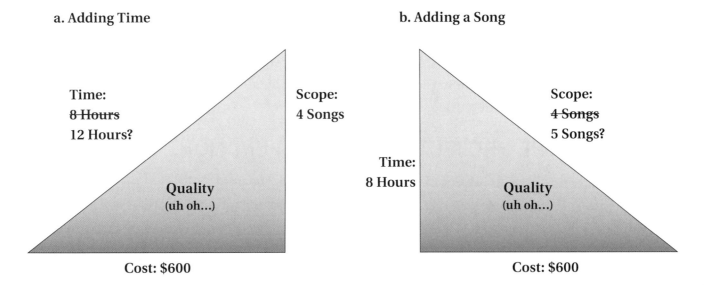

If we decide to add a song (increase scope, see figure 1.9b) or fail to raise enough money to fund it (decrease cost), we'll have a similar out-of-whack circumstance.

To avoid such a situation, we must step in before the project gets out of hand. That's the purpose of project management. If half an hour into that recording session, someone says, "We're moving too slowly; let's simplify what we're doing on this song, for now, and come back to it later if we have time," that might correct the project's course before it's too late.

There are other potential constraints too, besides cost, time, and scope: risks, human resources, team motivation, weather, legal regulations, geography, gear on hand, etc. So, a constraint is anything that defines the parameters of what the project can be. The project manager needs to understand and navigate around them.

TASKS/ACTIVITIES, PROJECTS, PROGRAMS

As we saw earlier with Thaddeus and his book, the overall process of project management is to get a good vision, figure out what work needs to happen in order to realize that vision, develop some strategies to get the necessary work done, and then implement those strategies effectively, while monitoring progress and updating strategies as needed. Tidy things up when you're done.

One of our great challenges is in matching appropriate management to our business at hand. Sometimes, you need to stop wringing your hands about process and simply sit down and work! In other circumstances, you need to closely manage what is happening in very precise detail.

The business of getting a project done can be considered as a progression of phases of types of work. Simple activities, just one step towards getting the project done, are called "tasks." A project is made of multiple tasks. If you like splitting hairs, depending on whom you ask, an "activity" is a type of task that might recur, or a generic "chunk of work," which might be broken down into tasks. So, you could say, a project would be playing a gig. A task is creating the set list. An activity is rehearsing. But you'll see variations in how these different terms are handled across different project management cultures, as well as between different project management software products, so we can't be too dogmatic here.

Several related projects that form a larger whole comprise a *program*. A music festival, for example, might be a program consisting of multiple performances, while each performance is managed as a discrete project.

Similar to a "program" is a "portfolio," which is a collection of projects that are less closely related but also grouped together as a logical unit. A record company might release a portfolio of a certain number of albums per year. They are related in that as a group, they accomplish a business objective, such as a necessary number of new annual releases in order to be profitable. Perhaps across an annual portfolio of albums, the record company aims for a balance of musical genres (30 percent rock, 30 percent R&B, 30 percent country, ten percent other), but one album doesn't directly influence another. The individual recordings are projects—tangible deliverables, according to a spec. Perhaps, the way the portfolio is managed is like a project in itself, with the albums as components. An A&R (artist and repertoire) agent responsible for producing twelve albums a year might have to coordinate certain aspects between them, like when to schedule the same studio to suit multiple projects in the portfolio. But the deliverables and interrelated nature are what distinguish these similar terms.

The following chart shows the relationships between these different terms. The bird-foot shaped lines show the one-to-many relationship between the types of elements. You can see, portfolios can contain multiple projects or programs (e.g., all concerts include specific concert series). In other scenarios, programs could contain multiple portfolios or projects (e.g., a university music program could include all student conductor portfolios).

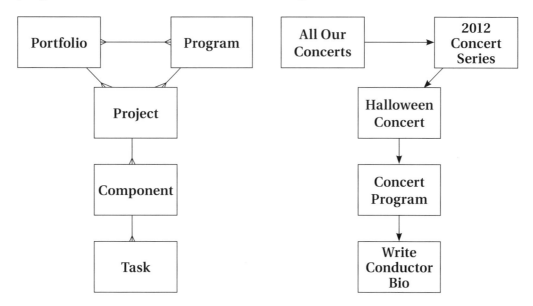

FIG. 1.10. Levels of Deliverables

What to call a "project" is often subjective; you can projectize practically anything. The portfolio manager (e.g., a concert hall's music director) could see the 2012 portfolio as a sort of project, with the set of new concerts as the deliverables. A conductor could see the Halloween concert as a project. A writer could see the conductor bio as a project. Or, looking down the line, smaller projects might be considered "components" of larger projects. At some point, though, you stop planning and managing and wordsmithing, and some-body starts creating content.

STRUCTURES, CONCEPTS, AND TOOLS

There are various theoretical tools associated with clarifying a project's necessary work and getting it done: charts, checklists, concepts, reporting systems, and so forth. Some critical tools are normal and everyday, and using them will strike you as common sense. Checklists, for instance. Other tools are pretty clever and specific, and if you haven't run across them before, they might stop you in your tracks and change the way you look at the world: critical time paths are one such example (see chapter 5). We will look at all these things in great detail throughout this book. But the overall mindset of striving towards complete systemization of work is the impor-tant thing here, more so than any individual project management tool.

Many types of software can assist in managing projects. Software can help you delegate tasks, build schedules, coordinate deadlines, draw flow charts, manage budgets, and generally facilitate workflow. Some products are optimized for groups, others for individuals.

Larger organizations sometimes have their own proprietary project management systems, maintained by an in-house technical staff. There are also programs you can buy or get for free: Smartsheet, OpenProj, Microsoft Project, OmniProject, Basecamp, Evernote, and so on. Some programs on your computer right now might have project management function-ality: Mail, Outlook, Entourage, Oracle Calendar, etc. And standard soft-ware products (Word, FileMaker, Excel, Quicken, PowerPoint, etc.) are very helpful for use in certain aspects of projects.

Dedicated project management software can make certain dimensions of this work much easier. Of course, people have been managing proj-ects for thousands of years without software, and many people continue to use paper and pen, but I recommend exploring some of these tools. As mentioned, in this book, I will be illustrating some project management concepts using Smartsheet. You can download a free trial version of it from www.smartsheet.com.

You can certainly develop your own paper system, without software, to manage your projects, and it might work just fine—perhaps even be your best option, as it avoids some of the complexity and reliance on technology that comes with software. There is much to be said for first learning to manage projects with a pencil and paper, and then using software tools to expand your efficiency once you are comfortable with the essential principles, rather than immediately becoming enslaved to technology and its learning curves, vulnerabilities, and so on. Your system has to be easy and friendly, to be useful. Otherwise, you won't actually use it, so what good is that?

A basic principle, then, is to only use management tools that are actually helping you get the work done. When you're in the field (i.e., not in an abstract environment, like reading a book or taking a course) and considering using a project management tool of any kind, consider whether what you're doing seems like busywork. Do you expect that what you've just created will actually just rot in a file cabinet, as opposed to it being an efficient tool that will keep your train on its tracks? If so, don't use it. The goal is to produce more and better music (ideally, at a financial profit), not just to engage in "the right" specific project management practices because some book recommends them. You need tools and techniques that are actively useful for you. Changes to your routine have to be clearly worth it, as the added complexity to your approach could leave you vulnerable to new problems creeping in, which defeats the purpose. Using systems half-heartedly can introduce risk.

PROJECT MANAGERS VS. MUSICIANS

Many musicians seem to be naturally hyper-organized. However, the opposite is certainly the more common stereotype, if not the reality. True or not, one of the challenges of introducing formal project management into endeavors of art, such as music, is that there is a kind of cultural aversion towards the structure and accountability of a managed circumstance, among many musicians.

Formal management can come across as an overbearing buzz kill, rather than a critical means towards success. What is perceived in other industries (software development, construction, engineering, manufacturing, etc.) as helpful clarifications and productivity enhancement tools can come across to musicians as challenging their competency, or forcing their creative spirit into a confining world of disposable widget manufacturing, rather than the potential transcription of divine inspiration, which is ultimately what motivates so many of them/us. Musicians measure success differently than workers in other industries do. The ultimate question for musicians is often not so much "Is it within budget, on time, and according to scope?" as it is "Does it groove?"

This orientation often helps artists to achieve extraordinarily great accomplishments, replete with a magic that might seem to defy ordinary human capability. However, it also frequently leads to a lack of cohesion regarding content. Mission drift is awfully common in our profession, where leaning towards inspiration and magic are so common—so basic to what we do. For example, a set list's continuity becomes compromised by an impulsive decision to go a little too far "outside" the genre than is actually best for the gig. A tour is made too long and too inconvenient because of a creative detour that wasn't strategically considered, and so the tour's end becomes a slog, rather than a euphoric finale. Not to mention the various cliché impulses that derail musicians' careers.

Perhaps, these digressions particularly plague those of us in any of the arts because our hands are so close to the intangible, and many artists are reluctant to risk a psychic or spiritual disruption that could result in distance from the muse. Explaining it would spoil it. Similarly, though, there is an aversion towards the process of tangible assessment of results. Artists tend to judge success intuitively, more than empirically. This sometimes comes across as a lack of organizational capability, but considering the complexity of a typical musical endeavor (concert, album, etc.), this doesn't seem to be a fair characterization. More likely, it is an indication of the different success metrics musicians hold than what are easily apparent to others.

Still, though, the art needs to conform to some parameters of reality, if the singing is to result in sufficient supper, and to counter this natural tendency towards vague success metrics, somehow, the music project manager needs to keep the work aligned with the business goals of the project, without sacrificing any divine chains of command that might be competing for the artist's attention.

If we project managers can find such a place, and adapt some of the principles of project management into the realm of art, we can help everyone in the project community arrive at better results. Efficient attention to details can reduce the pain of managing logistics and reduce the risk that certain complex endeavors result in fiasco—not to mention, improving the quality of the music itself, as well as its profitability. The trick, often, is in how we present these tools to the musicians we work with.

As we look at using these tools to help improve our effectiveness at our own work, and at the work of those around us, it's important to keep this cultural divide in mind.

Many artists will prefer to just "wing it," when doing their work. *Winging it*—acting reactively to the circumstance before you, rather than strategically planning it out first—is the opposite of project management.

Sometimes, just winging it works fine. Painstaking management is appropriate when the possibility of failure is of great enough inconvenience to be of concern. When you make a sandwich or tune your trombone, you don't really need a formal project management approach. If you mess up, you might enjoy your lunch less, or you might need to stop playing and retune. These aren't dire consequences.

Sometimes, projects of the same type might either be better with a methodical project management approach or with a just winging it approach, depending on the circumstance, risk vs. consequence, and the experience level of who is undertaking it. If you are writing a song for fun, where there is no deadline, just winging it might be fine. However, if you are writing a commercial song for a deadline next Friday, and you won't get paid and everyone will hate you unless what you produce is a dead ringer for a Tom Waits tune, then a more methodical approach might serve you better. That said, if you write songs for deadlines every Friday, very minimal project management might be okay. It depends.

More complex projects, particularly those with commercial intentions, generally call for some deliberate management, but this is a subjective call. If you're completely in command of a process and can reliably control all its details, then sufficient project management techniques might be already ingrained into your fingers and your brain, and trying to adopt different tools might not have sufficient benefit—and even, increase risks. But what is considered easy will vary between people. If you've never collaborated on writing a jingle before, you will likely want to follow some sort of plan. If you've written three hundred jingles with your partner, and today is just another day, you might not bother and just wing it.

USING PROJECT MANAGEMENT

There are different approaches and systems to making sure things go right. Software developers have their approaches, and architects have different ones. Some project management approaches have names: GTD, Scrum, Traditional Project Management, Six Sigma, Agile Development, and countless others. Project management software often comes with its own recommended tips for use. While many approaches claim to be major revolutions in project management theory, they all share fundamental similarities, with various differences and refinements to suit various activities and business goals. We'll look at a few of these different types of "project lifecycle models" later in this chapter.

Being aware of any of these efficient management practices will lead you to use them more often, and thus create greater efficiency in your work, even for projects that are low stakes.

The major factor to weigh, when determining how much formal management to bring to a project, is what the risk and consequences are for failure. The more dire the consequences, the more formal approaches to completing the project become appropriate. One aphorism that project managers like to say is "Project management is risk management." That one is always a hit at cocktail parties. That's what it's about, though. The more closely you manage how a project unfolds, the more you can reduce the chances that the project will fail or fall short, in some way. You provide its best chance of achieving its highest aspirations.

As you become more familiar with some of these management practices, you might find some relatively sophisticated tools creep into your everyday activities that are simple enough not to need a formal approach. For example, one key to getting things done is trying to have as much stuff happening concurrently as you can control. If this concept is new to you, mastering it could really change your life. But you probably already do it intuitively. Perhaps, you routinely wash a few dishes while you make coffee. That's a fairly critical principle of project management.

Project management is liberating. It systematizes all the non-magic, and reduces the anxiety level that inattention to detail can generate. It is simply a pathway to being organized and productive.

Project management isn't rocket science, but it is what makes rocket science possible.

For more information on project management, take a look at the Project Management Institute. It has a lot of good information and useful tools. You can even become a certified project manager, if you like. Probably, though, you're more interested in completing music projects than you are in the abstract science of project management, fascinating as it might be.

Herein, I'll try to find the balance of teaching the formal tools of project management, but in the context of completing music projects in the messy world we live in, rather than as a tidy and abstract science.

THE PROJECT TEAM/COMMUNITY

Let's clarify what a project's supporting structure looks like.

Project Manager

The person responsible for getting the project done is the *project manager*. The project manager plans the project strategy and then monitors (and encourages) its progress. He or she keeps the set of project specs: the definition, the objectives, the resources, and so on, all tied up with a red ribbon called the project's "scope statement." When someone proposes a change to the project scope, the project manager sharpens his or her pencil, looks deeply into how the proposed modification relates to current resources, and coordinates the process of figuring out whether or not to accommodate the change. If the change is approved, the project manager updates the scope statement and figures out how to incorporate the change into the work plan. Ideally, all proposed changes of scope go through the project manager: one person. Multiple people charged with protecting the scope can cause confusion, so that is to be avoided. Too many chefs spoil the pie.

Project Sponsor

The *project sponsor* is the person who controls the project's funding, and therefore, its existence. It might be a client, or it might be an executive, or a group, such as a board of trustees. Besides the project manager, the project sponsor will be among the key advocates. The sponsor might hire (or fire) the project manager.

Content Visionary

A *content visionary,* such as a performing artist, writer, or teacher, might be the heart and soul of a related project, but he or she is still just one member of the team required to fulfill the vision. Often, a content visionary will come to an organization (record label, publishing company, school, etc.) to pitch a project idea. The company will then pay for the idea's production, including the visionary's services. Usually, though not always, the decision to sign the visionary is done in the context of great faith that the visionary will bring it to a successful conclusion. However, some visionaries require more close management (and supporting work to make their contribution seem meaningful) than others....

A term of art that is common, though perhaps a little condescending, is to call the artist or writer the "talent." But we want everyone to be talented on our project team.

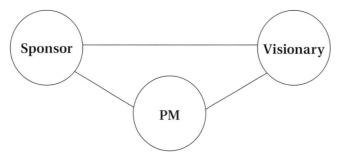

FIG. 1.11. Project Team Trio

These three roles—project manager, sponsor, and visionary—make up the tightest unit in the team. It's the executor, the money, and the idea guy. Sometimes, you might have multiple people performing some of these roles, particularly the sponsor or visionary. Independent artists often perform two or three of these roles themselves.

Outside this molecule, we have ever-expanding circles of intersecting parties. There may be some core supervisors and administrators standing close in the wings behind the project sponsor, such as the sponsor's boss and other sponsors of other projects within the organization that might be in competition for resources. Then, there will be other content creators besides the visionary: graphic designers, other musicians, engineers, book packagers, and so on. Some will be core team members, and others will have only tangential participation.

Supervisors and Administrators

There might be a layer of overseers above the project manager who set and approve the scope and make sure that the project manager is doing his or her work. They might be superiors at a record label, or school, or publishing company, or church, or other organization. It might be a staff supervisor or a board of trustees. These people are stakeholders in the project and might have a controlling interest in its destiny. If the project manager is an independent artist, this layer will likely be absent: no gallows, but no safety net either.

Content Team

The project manager works alongside a number of other people in a supervisory role. That doesn't mean that the project manager is "superior" to those doing the other work. Hopefully, though, everyone accepts that it's the project manager's job to keep things on track, and for the project to succeed, they need to do what the project manager says. Without that faith, you've got a dysfunctional system, and the project is likely doomed. The core people working for the project manager comprise the "project team." It can include performing musicians, arrangers, sound engineers, directors, concert promoters, graphic designers, accountants, CD replication companies, interns, ushers, stage hands, random volunteers, and so on. Some will be more "core;" others might be considered more "extended" team members. There might be a structural hierarchy that formalizes the manager's organizational superiority over the team members. The relationship might be one of client to vendor, or else the relationship might be more peer-to-peer. Sometimes, the manager even needs to delegate work to a superior in the organization. However it is set up, the project manager has to coordinate their work.

Other Stakeholders

The term "stakeholders" is often used to mean all of the above: the whole project community—even beneficiaries of the project, such as fans, customers, readers, and students, who might not have direct input into the project's direction but stand to benefit from the project. A fan who buys a ticket is a factor in the concert. If the concert gets cancelled, the fan will want a refund, and that will thus become part of the necessary work. So, everyone with an interest in the project's outcome could conceivably be called a stakeholder.

This diagram shows a wider view of the project team, which is sometimes called a *project community*, in this all-inclusive form. The core team includes the members closest to that central triumvirate.

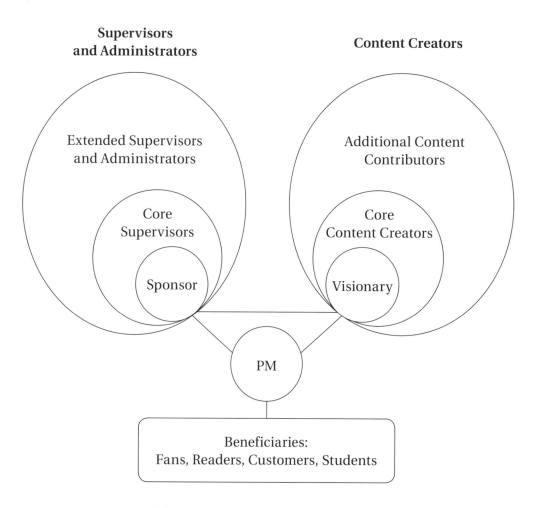

FIG. 1.12. Extended Project Community

Project Manager's Role

The project manager keeps the clipboard that contains various checklists, schedules, and other project management documents, and holds carrots, waves sticks, nips at everyone's heels, and is captain of the cheerleading squad. In essence, the project manager holds the spec, pesters the team to do what they are supposed to do, reports to the bosses on progress, and often, also contributes to the actual content (technically violating best project management practice, but behold the world we live in).

Project managers are bureaucrats, supervisors, and peons. We might wear the hats of fundraiser, evangelist, subject matter expert, timekeeper, therapist, backup musician, ghostwriter, babysitter, guru, legal consultant, party enabler, driver, visionary, tour guide, scapegoat, talking head, pinch hitter, janitor, nag, good cop, bad cop, best friend, nemesis, and more, all within the course of the same afternoon!

The ultimate goal is the implementation of the vision. The business is in managing the many risks that pressure towards the derailment of this vision. The manager gets the job done by designing and implementing on-target strategies and informative monitoring mechanisms.

It is often an enormously complex task. Buckets of money and people's life's work might be at stake. And it's so common for people in the music industry to just "wing it," rather than approach it methodically. That adds both stress and risk that can be mitigated.

Fortunately, much about project management is intuitive. Vision inspires strategy that guides implementation. If that's a clear path, and nothing too horrendous happens, the project will end in success.

Vision/Project Manager Relationships

The *project vision* is the articulation of what we are trying to accomplish. In the music industry, there are five common relationships between the project vision and the project manager.

- **Visionary as project manager.** This becomes increasingly common, as the model of indie artist becomes increasingly ubiquitous. The artist dreams something up and then makes it happen.

- **Artist's manager or producer as project manager.** The artist hires someone to "manage" the business side of things, including the projects that get created.

Band managers and producers often fulfill the role of project manager. It might be an ongoing or project-specific relationship with the artist.

- **Record label/publisher staff manager.** An artist dreams up a project, signs a contract with a corporation that will make it happen, and then is assigned a staff project manager to implement the vision. The artist might not have a relationship with the project manager before this project begins.

- **Corporation-generated vision.** A corporation's executive or board dreams up a project concept that they want to exist, often in response to market surveying. The staff project manager makes it happen, including finding an appropriate artist to breathe life into the manufactured vision.

- **Client as visionary; artist or band manager as project manager.** A wedding band, for example, takes explicit direction from a client, as does a writer of advertising jingles. The client is intimately involved in the work scope, even though they might not know anything about music.

Project management done by independent artists differs a bit from more corporate types of project management in that, so often, the project manager is also the visionary. This has some repercussions, in terms of getting the job done. On one hand, there's a built-in passionate advocate in the process who will work long hours and strive for a high level of quality. On the other hand, there's a lack of objectivity and cool-headed practicality and technical management experience, regarding the business of getting the project done. And there might be psychological baggage involved. That doesn't necessarily mean that artists should or shouldn't manage their own projects, though "best practice" in the wide world recommends separating the project management and content creation roles. Understanding the issues informs us of the risks regarding which path to take, and hopefully mitigates some of the risk: stress, missed deadlines, blown budget, burnout, and so on.

Somehow or another, though, the project vision is described. The quality of this definition is intrinsic to the project's success. This articulated vision becomes the critical reference point that keeps the project on track. Success is based on whether or not the vision was accomplished. Period. The vision is the definition of the project's success.

Only by clearly articulating a project's goals and specifications will you know what resources are required to complete it. Controlling the relationship between a project's requirements and the resources available is critical to the project's success. The requirements can only be understood by clearly defining the project's parameters. Getting this project definition exactly right is often half the battle.

CHOOSING A PROJECT LIFECYCLE MODEL

There are many possible conceptual models for how projects should be structured—perhaps almost as many as there are project managers with a hankering to publish books! Some models integrate market research, others require extensive quality control testing, and others facilitate much faster processes for testing multiple versions of the product.

Grand food fights are fought over which project management approach is the best, and YouTube has no shortage of videos proclaiming the benefits and deficits of whatever flavor is new this week. Each new version is a rebellion by oppressed workers against incompetent management. The vitriol runs high. T-shirts get printed.

Which approach you'll ultimately settle on will depend on your specific work, temperament, and organization. If your goal is to write a symphony and your priority is to articulate a vivid concept in your imagination, integrating user testing and feedback into your process might drive you crazy and inspire you to give up music altogether. If your goal is to create a community music school, market testing could be a very critical factor in your project's success. And if you are building an iPhone app, you'll want an iterative software development process that helps you get something to market fast—even if it isn't perfect. That's a different mindset than what you need when composing a symphony, where you really want the outcome to be very polished and perfect.

Some questions you might ask, when trying to figure out what approach you'll use:

Who owns the project? If you are creating something for a client or a superior at your organization, you will manage it differently than if you are implementing your own vision.

Do you want the people building the project to have creative input into it? If you're working with a rhythm section of exceptional musicians, you might want to capture their insights. If you are leading a choir of six-year-olds, you might opt for a more tyrannical role.

What is your goal: sales, art, or communication? All are valid. Each requires a different mindset and mechanisms to achieve success. For example, if your goal is high sales, then you might integrate a market research/evaluation/re-imagination cycle into the lifecycle, after short bursts of content creation, to confirm that what you are developing is saleable. Alternatively, if your primary goal is creative expression, you might instead want an extensive period of uninterrupted writing and refinement, before anyone is brought in to assess the work.

In many cases, you might only get a small improvement by choosing one project management approach over another. If you're running projects with millions of dollars of investment, or where lives are at stake, it's worth investing a lot in finding the precisely correct model. Regular agile vs. scrum (a specific king of agile) might make a meaningful difference, there. And if you start out really dysfunctional and then painstakingly implement an effective solution, you might similarly see a dramatic increase, no matter what approach you choose.

In my opinion, though, the rest of us shouldn't get inferiority complexes, based on exactly what model of project management we are using, unless there is some specific problem we're trying to address. There are many ways to manage projects successfully, and using common sense to expand your chosen path generally helps lead you to a positive result. Throughout the book, I'll suggest some general approaches and proven tools, and many will be relevant to your work.

Let's look at a few models.

Types of Lifecycle Model

A project's lifecycle generally follows a predictable, definable progression of stages of activities. You think about it, you do it, and then you clean up your mess. More formally, these lifecycle stages are concisely referred to as planning, execution, and closure.

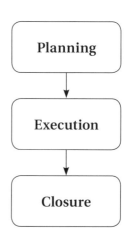

FIG. 1.13. Essential Phases

Here are some of the different models of project management approaches you will find:

Some projects have an awful lot of planning. This might be because they are very complex, because the people involved have a lot of concerns that must be figured out, or because they are too chicken to actually get around to doing anything substantive. The "right" amount of planning is a subjective call.

Other projects, or models for project management, have less planning. Often, if someone has a lot of experience doing the type of project being undertaken, there's less planning necessary/completed, whether or not that's a good idea. In truth, figuring out how much to trust your own life experience is among the great challenges of the human condition. Often, though, experience is a fair trade for explicit planning. If you know what you're doing, and you're not working with anyone else, it might not be fruitful for you to spend the time to write out a detailed project plan.

Similarly, some models are characterized by an expanded emphasis on execution, and spend more time there, incorporating prototyping, user testing, market research, multiple-release versions, and so on. This means an expanded execution phase—more of a learning-by-doing approach.

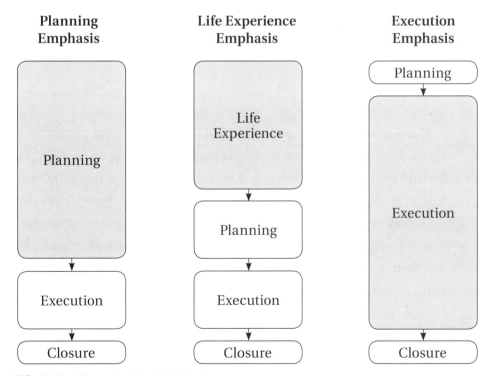

FIG. 1.14. Lifecycle Model Variations

Other types of project management might break down these steps into multiple sub-phases or configurations. Here is actually a much-maligned paradigm, called a "waterfall model," because one phase flows into another and there's no turning back.

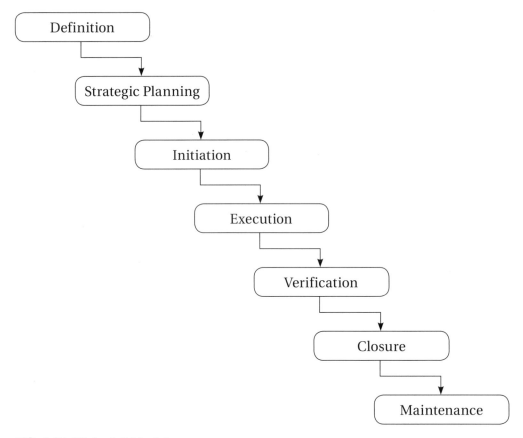

FIG. 1.15. Waterfall Model

The problem? It's not self-reflective. The plan or specs can't be altered in this model after execution begins. If you're producing a CD using this model and find that one of the songs just sounds awful when the band gets into the recording studio, there might not be a way to give it the attention it needs to bring it up to snuff, with the clock ticking. You might need to decide to either omit it, perhaps leaving a gaping hole, or put it on there anyway, warts and all, which will then compromise the project's quality—all because the project management approach being used was too rigid and prescriptive.

This next model builds some self-reflection into the scheme, which can facilitate better possible recovery from setbacks. After some initial planning, the project goes into a cycle of iterations, which are then examined and improved. For example, a recording built in accordance with this approach might involve a set of informal "scratch tracks"—cheap, simple, demo recordings—that get reviewed by everyone with a stake in the project before the actual formal recording session is undertaken. So, if a song stinks, it gets yanked or improved before the decision is made regarding the final set of tunes to be on the CD. This is based on the "lean startup" model, which is based on "lean manufacturing" (originating in the automotive industry, at Toyota), which is based on the Deming Cycle (Plan > Do > Check > Act [repeat]), which is based on the scientific method (Hypothesize > Experiment > Evaluate). Variations on a theme.

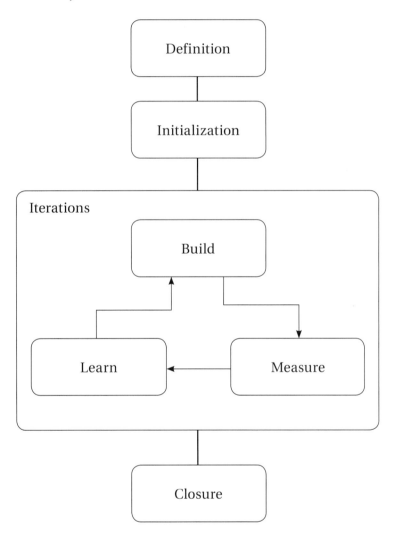

FIG. 1.16. Lean Project Management

Similarly, figure 1.17 shows the "agile development" model, currently popular among software engineers, breaking it down into the stages of analysis, design, implementation, testing, and evaluation (ADITE), and constantly cycling them through all stages of the project, which consists of a series of small *sprints*—relatively small, manageable chunks of work, rather than a single grandiose effort. This approach involves a great deal of team discussion and re-evaluation during the project lifecycle, which makes it very adaptable to changes in project scope. If a competitor releases a similar product before you release yours, this model might let you find a new twist on what to do, and change directions relatively easily and quickly. Work here happens in small bursts, and it gets verified and reality-checked with great frequency. Is this degree of second-guessing useful for music projects? Perhaps, in some circumstances. Then again, it can sometimes be a buzz kill, like when an individual visionary is trying to capture the magic of an abstract narrative.

Agile Model

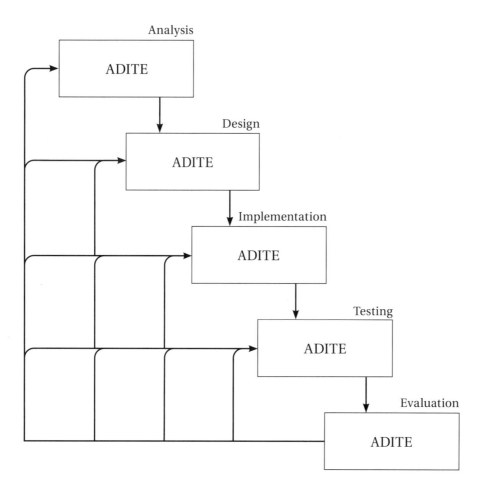

FIG. 1.17. Agile Development

One could argue that all of these project management lifecycle models are derived from the scientific method: Hypothesize, Experiment, Evaluate. Plan, Execute, Analyze. Build, Measure, Learn. Rinse and repeat. The cycle has been repackaged and rebranded since it was first documented in the Middle Ages, continually picking up new tricks and refinements along the way. There is no right or wrong way to approach projects, and knowledge of the various ways events might unfold can help you customize the management style to the work before you. Flexibility can enable resilience, but it can also be more chaotic. Somewhere, there is a balance to be found.

Phases of Lifecycle

The Project Management Institute organizes project lifecycles into five phases, which we've already seen. They probably know best.

- **Initiating.** Choosing the project. Focusing the vision of what the project is, and defining its objectives/deliverables and scope (features, quality level, budget, and time frame). Project acceptance is a part of this, and the process of getting it accepted tends to refine what the project will be. The initiating phase concludes when the project is accepted.

- **Planning.** Developing strategies for how to implement the defined vision, particularly regarding timing and schedule. Planning can safely transition into execution when the plan seems stable and complete enough to permit expending resources to do the work without there being excessive risk.

- **Executing.** Completing the tasks that will fulfill the objectives of the project vision. Execution is complete when the project vision is realized.

- **Monitoring and Controlling.** Analyzing/redirecting execution progress, resource usage, and quality, and revising the scope as necessary. These phases are close companions to execution, and help determine that the project vision has been sufficiently realized.

- **Closing.** Finishing all loose ends, such as open contracts, and then preparing the completed project for the next phase of its lifecycle. Closing concludes when all required tasks have been completed and the project manager can stop work on the project.

How much time and effort goes into each phase depends on the complexity of the project. Arguably, all these stages happen whenever you do anything—even when you're just "winging it." So, for a simple task, such as tuning a guitar, you might be just going through the stages mentally or intuitively, rather than deliberately, but they are still active:

- **Initiating.** Decide that you need to make this guitar play in tune. Articulate that each of six strings needs to sound in tune individually and all together as a set, and that the tuning process needs to be completed within three minutes.

- **Planning.** Determine that the best approach is to use an electronic tuner on each individual string, and then check them all by using your ear, sounding unisons on adjacent strings. No formal project management tools, expenditure of resources, or written documentation is necessary.

- **Executing.** Play each string, check the pitch with an electronic tuner, and then turn the peg to adjust it.

- **Monitoring and Controlling.** When the individual strings are tuned, play a few chords to test its overall intonation. Check the time after tuning every two strings to make sure you're on schedule.

- **Closing.** Turn off the electronic tuner, and put it back in the gig bag. Indicate to your band mates that you are ready to play. Later, while playing, plan to constantly monitor the tuning, making adjustments as necessary.

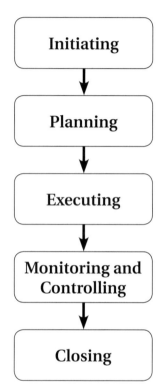

FIG. 1.18. Five Project Lifecycle Phases

For a "micro-project" of simple scope, this would all happen informally. More deliberate project management of a simple action such as this would slow it down unnecessarily, and be inappropriate for the scope of work. Checklists to confirm that each note was in tune would be cumbersome. Meetings to ensure consensus that all strings were in tune would waste everyone's time. Even formally labeling these stages isn't really worth the effort. Still, though, it's the pattern of how the work gets done successfully.

More substantial projects follow the same essential trajectory (with some possible variations that we'll discuss later). There are just more steps along the way to make it turn out right, and more formal mechanisms to keep and to verify that the project is on track. For something like "writing a music method book," the phases might look something like this (greatly simplified):

- **Initiating.** Clarify market and purpose of the book. Choose a working title and teaching objectives, and develop a list of topics. Estimate page length, budget, and publication date. Identify the target reader. Refine book concept based on stakeholder feedback and criteria for acceptance. Sign a contract.

- **Planning.** Itemize the necessary work in detail: content creation, editing, graphic design, indexing, etc. Calculate how much time, money, and other resources will be required to complete the work. Identify points of potential risk and consider strategies for their mitigation. Establish a schedule. Assemble necessary quality control mechanisms. Get approval to move forward with the project. Create a contract between author and publisher that specs exactly what will be written. Determine management strategies. Distribute any helpful templates or models.

- **Executing.** Once the project receives formal approval and the contracts are signed, give the project team their instructions. Then, generate the content: the book gets written, engraved, laid out, and printed. A play-along CD gets recorded and replicated.

- **Monitoring and Controlling.** During execution, the manuscript gets peer-tested, edited, and revised. Exercises are tested by the author's students and reimagined as necessary. Work is continually monitored. Stakeholders are updated on how well the project is meeting its projected deadlines.

- **Closing.** Confirm the proper routing of all invoices, tax forms, copyright forms, and other paperwork. Archive files for future printing or revision. Discard any obsolete paperwork or files. Determine if anything was developed in this project that could be reused in the future, and enter it in a system that will make this possible. Assess completed product and look for errors or necessary revisions for the next edition. Initiate advertising campaign and distribution.

Where the specific activities occur can vary across organizations and types of projects. For example, a project's scope might be finalized in the Initiation, Planning, or Executing phases. Some might sketch out a preliminary scope of work in the Initiating phase, then revisit it after contracts have been negotiated in the Planning phase, or even revisit it periodically during Executing, particularly if user-testing is a crucial dimension of the work. Perhaps the initial plan for the book was twelve chapters but in the actual recording session, a warm-up jam happened to get recorded, and it was so great, we decided to include that in the final book, with an accompanying new lesson. So, the scope could get changed during execution. There might be no reason why you shouldn't let that happen, just because someone says that scope must be set in the Initiation phase.

Again, the point here is more/better music, not project management.

While this name-calling has its limitations, it describes types of activities, and is fairly standard in the world of project management, whether you are playing a gig or sending a rocket to the moon. We'll discuss some permutations, moving forward.

RISKS OF INSUFFICIENT MANAGEMENT

When projects are not managed closely, what generally happens is that creators launch directly into the execution phase and proceed reactively. They create a thing, judge it, and then either continue on, improve it, or chuck it and start over. For experienced workers, this often works out just fine, especially if they have done similar projects many, many times over, and particularly if there is just one person doing the work (or a small, tight group). In fact, the iterative process of creating and refining drafts is often an effective one. An experienced rhythm section might not need massive direction in order to lay down a solid groove. Just give them a few calculated pointers and turn them loose.

However, some deliberate management will improve nearly any endeavor, or at least, reduce the risk that some dimension of it will go wrong. For projects that are not second nature to everyone on the team, insufficient planning becomes more likely to result in negative consequences. Here are three common and fairly brutal types of repercussion to insufficient planning:

1. The backbone vision is unclear. This can result in the need for massive revision. Also, the result will likely become relatively incoherent, which makes it difficult for it to find an audience and market. More often than not, completed projects that are insufficiently defined wind up being relatively unloved (i.e., low sales), as the audience isn't well cared for.

2. The result is over budget, late, and/or of a disappointing level of quality.

3. The project becomes daunting to the creator—seemingly too complicated to complete, and therefore, execution is never actually completed. The project stays undone—a messy stack of paper on a dusty shelf or stuffed in a file cabinet.

That said, overplanning also has consequences. Some project management tools require so much startup time to use that they take time away from the execution phase, so the project isn't completed. Or the system might get half done, creating a confusing workspace where there is a false sense of security, which makes details more likely to get overlooked. And sometimes, while gargantuan planning efforts are being undertaken, something changes in the industry that is a game changer, regarding the project's destiny.

This is particularly common in software development. A current common scenario, caused by shifts in best programming practice between different generations of programmers, is that companies create too much original code in-house. Meanwhile, while they are trudging through, someone releases a free open-source version that does the same thing, and changes the way the project should have been planned. But so much effort has gone into the initial meta-work of the project that it is difficult to change course.

So, project plans need to be nimble and flexible, open to the events on the ground, and not excessively detailed to the point of unwieldiness.

In the following chapters, we will see strategies for completing each of these phases, and they should be used only as they are helpful.

YOUR PATH AS A PROJECT MANAGER

As we begin our journey through some of the tools we can use, let's first pause to consider the likely path of what our progress will look like. The following scale is called a *capability maturity model.* This type of diagram was developed by Carnegie Mellon University to help organizations judge their level of maturity in a given area. It can be helpful to apply it to many different circumstances—both testing the state of individual projects and also assessing our overall knowledge (individual or institutional) of the project management process.

Plenty of successful projects have been completed without particularly efficient processes at work. Better management might have reduced some angst or saved some money, or even prevented a project from failing altogether, but you can find examples of great projects that were made with inefficient processes.

There are five stages of project management "maturity." It doesn't mean you are a good or bad person depending on where you are, with any of these. The scale is just designed to give you a sense of what you should be focusing on next, as you continually improve your skills. You will be at different levels of capability for different types of projects, or different types of activity within your project, and it can be helpful to know what your level of skill is in order to assess what the likely risks will be and where you might start at improving your capabilities, in each circumstance.

5. Optimizing. Finely tuned systems are in place; focus is on incremental improvements in efficiency.
4. Managed. All work is effectively planned and executed.
3. Defined. Work is known and core strategies are in place.
2. Repeatable. Some work is completed strategically.
1. Initial. All work is completed reactively, with no planning.

FIG. 1.19. Project Management Capability Maturity Model

Five Levels of Capability

Let's look at these phases in some more detail.

1. **Initial.** This is where we begin. In an "initial" stage of project management capability, there are no documented systems or procedures. Work is done reactively, in accordance to hunch or whim, and figured out case by case without the benefit of experience. Individual components

of projects are completed without relation to the overall vision. Inter-dependencies of work relationships have not yet been figured out. It's chaotic and inefficient, and good work is done via individual heroics, without the benefit of effective strategy.

> **Risk Level:** High. Because potential costs and time requirements aren't critically analyzed, they can easily wind up constraining dimensions of scope and quality. Logistics are likely to bog down content creation. There's a good chance that the vision won't be realized in its ideal form.

> **Example Failure:** A band goes into a studio to record an album, paying the day rate, which gets them eight hours in which they will record five songs. They all arrive and are ready to play, but the drummer needs an hour to set up. So, they chat, while he's doing that, and thus only have time to record four songs. Common rookie mistake.

If you've identified yourself as being in the "initial" phase of capability for a type of project you are embarking upon, congratulations! Simply entering into this system is a rare sign of self-reflection and an innate desire to systematically improve. Going from "no clue" to "initial" is the biggest step of all.

To advance to the next level, focus on the vision and overall objectives, and also start looking for experienced people to advise you. Don't spend significant money until you are farther along! There is a great danger here of making significant mistakes.

2. **Repeatable.** Major dimensions of the project's work required resources that have been identified, and some rough methodologies have been created. Likely, you've had some experience doing this kind of project, and have an educated sense of how to accomplish the work.

> **Risk Level:** Significant. While there might be expertise evident at some dimensions of the process, there are competency gaps, and the various types of activities are not well coordinated. Much decision-making at this phase is reactive and based on anecdotal experience, which can lead to a false sense of security. There's a likelihood of inefficient practices and redundant work. There are more ways to fail than to succeed, and at this phase, projects are easily derailed by what more experienced managers would consider predictable factors.

Example Failure: A group of musicians get together socially to jam. It becomes more regular and serious, and they decide to call it a "band." They work up a set list of eight songs, and one member finally says, "Great, now let's hire a booking agent to get us some wedding gigs." The drummer says, "I wouldn't play a wedding if my life depended on it." Everyone goes home mad. End of band.

To advance to the next level, focus on a developed articulation of vision, scope statement, and work breakdown structure. Get detailed about your budget and resource allocation. Think methodically about risk factors, and create contingency plans. Continue to observe successful systems at your own level for doing this type of project.

3. **Defined.** The work required to complete the vision has been thoroughly articulated, and it is clear who is responsible for doing what. A general, strategic approach has been identified for how the work will become accomplished.

> **Risk Level:** Moderate. Obvious pitfalls are likely to be avoided at this stage. However, the relative immaturity of the systems makes them vulnerable to the unexpected.

> **Example Failure:** A band gathers at the home recording studio of one of its members. Then, the neighbor decides to mow the lawn, and the lawn mower's sound is audible through the mic. They can't record.

To advance to the next level, focus on developing procedures and checklists to create standardized and efficient processes, and address the unexpected.

4. **Managed.** All of the work is done in accordance with documented systems that will reliably ensure the work's completion.

> **Risk Level:** Present. The work scenario here is robust and can recover from many kinds of problems. However, there are always potential surprises.

> **Example Failure:** A band records an album, and 5,000 CDs are pressed, scheduled to be ready a week before its scheduled release party. They are ready a day earlier than anticipated, and arrive when the recipient isn't home. The delivery truck driver leaves the boxes stacked on his doorstep. Then it rains unexpectedly, and the boxes get soaked, ruining all the CDs.

To advance to the next level, look for more efficient tools or possible refinements to your systems, and ways to manage risk.

5. **Optimizing.** While the work is being done in proven systems, these systems are being carefully monitored and continually optimized for greater efficiency.

> **Risk Level:** Low, but possible. There's always a new way something can go wrong!

> **Example Failure:** You are developing a music education software product, and two months before you are ready to release it, a superior, cheaper product is released by a competitor.

To advance to the next level, when you are working efficiently and productively, leverage your capability, and diversify, so that you are less vulnerable to changes in the marketplace. Start dreaming up new stuff, and help others to become similarly productive. And keep monitoring your processes and researching emerging paths towards greater efficiency.

CLOSING THOUGHTS

A great challenge for project managers is in determining an appropriate balance between planning how to do the work and actually doing it. Many traditional tools and concepts of project management can be helpful for projects of all scopes. However, the literature about these approaches often comes from the perspective of large corporations devoted to manufacturing or software development or the military, and they will be more effective at smaller scales if they are adapted.

We will be looking at many tools and concepts in this book. The important thing to remember is that their purpose is to be useful and make your life easier. In the field, beyond these pages, if they seem to be adding more bureaucracy to your process than making it easier, then take a step back and simplify your approach. What's important is that you are in command of your work, not what specific tools or document formats you use.

PRACTICE

1. **Little.** Choose a small project (up to three hours to complete, like writing a song or playing a gig), and describe a safe path to bring it from end to end, considering the five project management phases: initiating, planning, executing, monitoring and controlling, closing. Write about three bullet points/sentences for each phase, describing your goals, concerns, and criteria for success.

2. **Big.** Choose and introduce a major music project that supports your most important life's work, whether current or intended. Answer the following questions:

   - What is it?
   - What kinds of expertise do you need on your project team?
   - Why do you want to do this project?
   - What does success look like for this project, both from your own perspective and from that of your fans/customers?
   - Describe your goals and concerns regarding the anticipated five phases of this project: initiating, planning, executing, monitoring and controlling, closing.
   - What risks do you imagine might derail this project? Do you have any ideas for mitigating these risks?
   - Consider your own level of expertise at managing projects. What would be an appropriate next step for you, in order to advance your skills? And considering that, what types of project management tips are you on the lookout for?
   - What next step can you take today that will drive your project forward?

CHAPTER 2

Vision and Scope

Among the first tasks in the project's initializing phase is to clarify the project's vision and scope. The *vision* is the dream—your overall grand insight into what the project is and why you are doing it. The *scope* is a specific articulation of our precise aspirations—exactly what it is that you are doing or creating.

The vision is poetry; the scope is prose.

We need both.

OBJECTIVES

By the end of the chapter, you will be able to:

- clarify your project's vision

- assess whether or not a proposed project makes sense for you to undertake

- articulate your project's scope: specifically what you plan to do, and develop a project scope statement

VISION

The vision is the whole point of doing the project. We want our album of songs to express a unique emotional truth about the human condition. We want our community music school to have a profound effect on our students' lives. We want to create an exceptional-quality recording studio that will provide excellent value and a unique, inspiring atmosphere for our customers.

Ideally, everything flows back to the vision. All work done on the project gets generated while keeping an eye on it. Your vision lights your team's pants on fire. The standard of work you demand is spurred to higher depths because everyone genuinely wants the vision to succeed.

Organizations that try to achieve excellent results but sometimes fall short of their intended marks tend to produce better results overall than organizations that aspire to and successfully complete "acceptable" work. The ones that aspire towards more ambitious goals tend to feel more fulfilled in life. So, set your standards high, and try to develop a thick skin.

When we say that we have a vision, we mean that we see in our imagination a successful version of our project concept and glimpse the good that will result from its realization. This connection to our perceived improved reality gives us motivation and inspiration, energizing us to push through the work necessary to turn our dreams into reality. The better we can share our vision and its benefits, the easier it will be to gain accomplices that will help us bring it about.

In this chapter, we look at ways to connect our visions to the work that must be done, by way of a project plan. We arrive at an effective plan of work by precisely articulating what we want our project to be (i.e., our project's "scope"), and then defining the project's required work based on what will support our vision of success. We find our way towards understanding what work will be required through various techniques that we will look at throughout this chapter, and they will all eventually get stored in a planning document called a *project scope statement.*

CHOOSING A PROJECT

Ideas for project visions can come easily. The difficulty is often in determining which project to actually undertake.

So, the first step of the initiating phase of project management is often in deciding what project to do. Doing that requires large-scale existentialist self-reflection, because we are actually talking about visions on three different levels:

1. The biggest picture of the artist organization's overall mission and purpose. Why does the organization exist, or why are you an artist? The answer tends to be stable, and changes to a mission are major upheavals to an individual or an organization.

2. The current strategic needs of the artist or organization. What is the most important type of endeavor for you to be working on right now? This will vary, depending on an organization's maturity. Many

organizations evaluate this annually and then do a longer-term vision-setting exercise every five years. It's not a bad idea for an individual artist to follow suit.

3. The vision at the project level. Does this potential project support the organization's immediate needs and overall mission? These generally get set at the project outset and occasionally refined during execution, but usually, are not profoundly changed.

Whenever a potential project idea comes up, it should be weighed in terms of how well it supports those different levels of vision. How project adoption decisions actually get made will vary a lot. At a mature organization, there could be a fairly predictable way that project ideas get evaluated and selected, such as standing committees and often-used forms for ushering the process through. But an independent artist might simply be drawn to do some sort of project, such as a recording, or major composition, or tour, or new website, or music video, and it is a more emotional than strategic decision (for better or worse). It's easy to get embroiled in projects that might distract from your broader sense of mission or purpose.

Here are some of the motivations that lead us to do projects:

1. Someone invites us to do something. "Let's make a band!" or "Sign me to your label, and release my album!"

2. Financial need: "What can we do to generate cash fast?" Or, a client says, "I want to hire you to mix my CD!"

3. Supporting other projects: "We've released the album. Now, let's go on tour, to promote it."

4. Inspiration: "Let's use this life experience as the theme for a video."

5. Advice: "Suzi's career is going really well because she's playing so many gigs. We should find more gigs too."

It's easy to be reactive and just go with what projects present themselves, particularly early in a career, when possibilities might be sparse or clear career directions are relatively undefined. But being strategic in choosing our projects generally makes life go more smoothly, in the big picture, and it usually results in better quality work.

Let's look at some of the ways to be strategic in selecting projects.

Acceptance Criteria

Begin by considering what criteria are most important to you, regarding how to choose a project. Do you need income? Experience? An artistic challenge? Networking? If you are prioritizing multiple projects, you can start by creating a simple matrix, and then rate the projects in terms of how they fulfill your needs, say on a scale of 1 to 10. This can help depersonalize the process, and it also helps you quickly see projects in relationship to each other, in terms of how they meet your needs. This chart makes it fairly clear that doing the website might not be the best idea, at the moment.

Here, "local gigs" seems the best project to pursue, though other criteria could sway it. It's getting easier to make the decision, now, based on looking at the possible projects on paper, in one place, rather than having the various potentials buzzing around our heads, keeping us up at night. We'll keep drilling down, and make a decision. (And we'll see other techniques for refining studies like this throughout the book, not to mention the project index discussed in chapter 1.)

Criteria:	Income	Experience	Artistic Challenge	Networking	Total
Potential Projects:					
Website	1	1	2	2	6
Album	1	4	5	2	12
Music Video	1	5	5	2	13
Tour	3	5	2	5	15
Local Gigs	4	5	2	5	16

FIG. 2.1. Project Criteria Rating Sheet

Project ideas might get pitched to you or assigned to you. At larger organizations, such as record labels, publishers, schools, or corporations, content visionaries constantly pitch potential project concepts to an acquisitions specialist, department chair, etc., which get reviewed and assessed, and a small percentage of these potential projects get signed.

At, say, a record label, some of the criteria used to make signing decisions typically include:

1. Is it likely to be profitable? (Have similar recordings been profitable?)

2. Does it address a known need? (Have there been requests for something like this from our customers? Did our competitor produce something like this that's selling well? Is our market research indicating that there's a likelihood this will be a hit?)

3. Is it aligned philosophically and strategically with our mission? (Is this artist someone who clearly belongs in our catalog?)

4. Do we have the capacity to do this? (Do we currently have a glut of products in the pipeline, or can we do another?)

5. Does it complement our other products in order to make a more obviously complete whole? (Considered as part of our catalog, does this fill in an obvious gap?)

Let's look at a couple other tools that can help us decide what project to do next.

PICK Charts

One device that can help you make project acquisition decisions is a PICK chart, which is a Six Sigma project management tool that measures an idea's likely benefit versus its difficulty to implement. PICK stands for Possible, Implement, Challenge, Kill. A potential project can be considered in accordance with each PICK chart quadrant, in terms of the ratio between difficulty and benefit. It's a helpful framework for considering potential projects and for weighing other ideas, strategies, or schemes.

EASY	2. Possible	1. Implement
DIFFICULT	4. Kill	3. Challenge
	LOW PAYOFF	**HIGH PAYOFF**

FIG. 2.2. PICK Chart

In order of desirability (reverse 2 and 3 if you like):

1. **Easy/High Payoff:** *Implement* it! An example would be the receipt of a perfectly produced, production-ready recording by an artist whose albums typically result in high sales. This seems like an obvious good fit, so assuming that there are no mitigating factors, the project is a good candidate to be approved.

2. **Easy/Low Payoff:** *Possibly* do it. An example would be receiving a beautifully produced, production-ready master by an unknown artist, who agrees to pay for replication costs. There's a good chance it won't sell, but maybe it will, and the cost might be low enough to include

it in the catalog that accepting could make sense. The decision will be weighed alongside other factors, like general business and need for new products, the context of other releases, and so on.

3. **Difficult/High Payoff:** It will be a *challenge* to make this profitable, but it might be worth it. Say a known artist suggests doing a recording of a live show that has a huge marketing campaign behind it already, but the timelines will be very tight. The label might do this, but careful planning will be required, and they will also be challenged to figure out the right strategy for making it profitable.

4. **Difficult/Low Payoff:** They should probably *kill* this idea. Say an unknown artist shows up with a concept for a recording that is a lot like an album the label released last year that didn't sell very well. A lot of work will be required to create this, and it is unlikely to be a viable product. If the label's goal is to stay in business, they should probably pass.

Rating a project idea or concept might be an easy off-the-cuff assignment, or it could be the result of painstaking analysis that eventually culminates in the PICK chart as the last step.

Keep your vision and highest objectives close, while you do this kind of exercise. The danger is that such methodologies can keep your nose resniffing in the weeds of the details in front of you, rather than looking "up and out," considering your vision and imagining your best path forward. Still, though, it can be a useful filter, and we'll look at some more detailed analysis approaches later in this book.

Portfolio Evaluation

Considering projects in the context of other offerings in a portfolio can also help inform project acceptance decisions. You might maintain a graph of existing products, perhaps organized by genre. If your mission is to create a balance of genres, or a more focused attention to a specific genre, you might consider the new application in the context of that. If you want to be known as a blues label, the chart in figure 2.3 indicates that the blues offerings currently take up a

Products by Genre, 2009 to Present

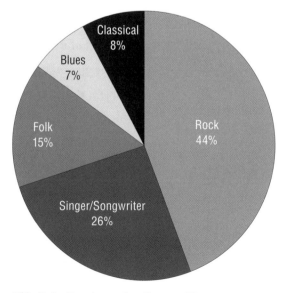

FIG. 2.3. Products by Genre Chart

minority percentage in the product portfolio. If a new blues project possibility comes your way, you might give it preferential treatment.

To get a little more financially focused, you might also compare the titles you've got to how much income those genres are producing. The following bar graph indicates both the percentage of offerings that the different genres comprise and how much income they bring in. One might expect that individual titles across genres would sell equally well—say, that each CD would sell 5,000 a year, whatever the genre. But this label's rock and blues offerings are pulling in greater percentages of sales than other genres. If the record label is cash-strapped, they should probably prioritize signing projects of those more reliably lucrative genres, or even proactively try to recruit some good rock recordings, rather than just reactively publishing whatever walks in the door. If they feel financially flush, they might consider beefing up the classical offerings, perhaps experimenting with new ways to get some traction there. If they want a balanced approach, blues looks like a good way to go, developing a minority share that historically has shown profit potential.

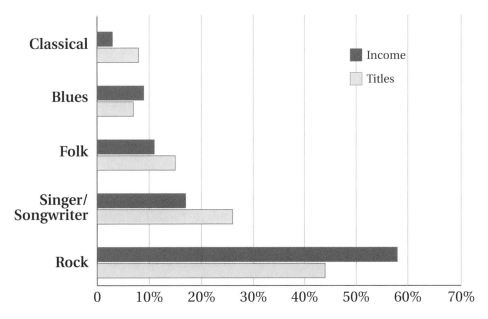

FIG. 2.4. Products by Profitability Chart

CLARIFYING THE VISION

Selecting projects is helped by very clear articulations of what the project will be. In fact, clear articulations of the project's vision and scope help many dimensions of project management.

Someone who is very good at shepherding this type of transition, from concept to actual product, is Gerald ("Jerry") Slavet—an inspiring visionary, who currently spends his time serving as co-CEO/producer of *From the Top.*

From the Top is the fastest-growing NPR radio show of all time. It is a showcase for young classical musicians, and since its inception in the mid-1990s, it has grown into a multi-dimensional organization. These days, they also produce an Emmy®-award winning television series filmed at Carnegie Hall, distribute scholarships to musicians with financial need, conduct educational outreach programs, and train and mentor young musicians as arts leaders. Throughout its evolution and diversification, the overriding vision of *From the Top's* purpose—to support and showcase young classical musicians— has been the great unifier and focusing agent of many successful projects.

The story of *From the Top's* genesis is that one afternoon in the summer of 1995, shortly after New England Conservatory in Boston completed an extensive renovation of historic Jordan Hall, Jennifer Hurley Wales (NEC's special projects director at the time) and NEC board member Jerry Slavet had an epiphany while standing on a street corner. "We should do an old-fashioned radio program!" exclaimed Jennifer.

"Great idea," said Jerry, "but let's focus on kids."

And their first project concept was born: an old-time radio show showcasing kid classical musicians. It's been enormously successful, and Jerry and Jennifer are now co-CEOs/executive producers. A part of the reason why it's been so successful is that they found great clarity in their vision, which is one that they are passionate about, and that they have effectively spread this passion to many others. From the first moment on the street corner, into the months of discussions and meetings that followed, Jerry and Jennifer were always of the same mind about the new experience they wanted to create for the listening audience—in their words, "to make it a fun event with fabulous music, interesting talk, and a little irreverence."

Clarity of vision helps release the motivation required to accomplish the hard work necessary for completing the project. Let's look at some ways to clarify visions.

Definition

A well-articulated project definition helps to focus all the work that comes afterwards. The degree of clarity at this stage has repercussions throughout the entire lifecycle of the project. The clearer the vision, the more closely aligned the work will be in support of it. While excitement, adrenaline, and good vibes are all critical factors, we must be able to communicate the core essentials of the vision to others, to make that fire spread. This will help the project gain traction among those initially determining its destiny, and then later, for motivating people who are executing its required work.

Three elements are helpful in defining a vision. It's worth spending time to get these exactly right.

- Project Title
- Short Description
- Objectives

These form the essential project definition. Their purpose is to clarify your intentions and thus set your potential collaborators on fire. Let's take a look at them one by one.

Title

The project title is the first impression most people will get of your project. It's at the top of every page. When you apply for grants, the first thing the grant reviewer notices is your project title. People who review proposals say "no" far more often than they say "yes," and they can often immediately make a well-founded decision based completely on the title.

For example, at Berklee Press, if someone were to pitch us a book called *Pipe Organ Repair,* I would immediately know what it was about, and could take a pretty good guess at its best market. I might be able to even suggest an appropriate page length and price.

It's a good title that drives right to the heart of the project's content. Different types of projects require different types of titles. Products that are tools (such as books, courses, instruments, and such) generally do well with titles that describe their functionality. *Pipe Organ Repair* is an excellent title for a book. It describes its subject matter perfectly, and the right publisher would do well to use it. If instead, the author titled it, *Fussing with This and That,* nobody would really know what the book is about, and so it would fail to catch on, even though that phrase itself might be catchy and memorable, and to the author, might capture the spirit of the subject matter. But to an outsider, it doesn't speak directly about pipe organs, so it wouldn't be able to cut through the marketplace, show up on Google searches, and so on.

Titles for some types of products can be more metaphorical. *From the Top* is a terrific name for a radio show because it is catchy and memorable, it reveals something essential about the show's content, and serves as a good metaphor. To a musician, the phrase "take it from the top" means "start at the beginning." It also implies a top level of quality, like cream rising to the top. The show's theme music, "You're the Tops," fits naturally with that title. And from a word-smithing perspective, it is short, easy to spell, and easy to remember. An excellent title.

Whether we are describing a tool or a work of creative expression, the title must cut through. It's said, one of the criteria of a good band name is that it must sound good when you scream it into a microphone. That's a pretty good test for many kinds of titles.

It seems trite and obvious, but the title is the most essential distillation of your project's concept. Finding the right one is often surprisingly difficult. If the search for the perfect title is particularly troublesome, it might be a sign that your concept could also stand some clarification and refinement.

Short Definition

Come up with a short sentence to describe your project. Capture the essence, and make sure it clearly articulates what your project is about. Here's one for the radio show *From the Top*.

An old-time radio show showcasing young classical musicians.

This sentence is a companion to your title. When someone asks, "What are you doing?" this is your practiced, stock answer. Whether it's an investor, a fan, or a potential performer's mother, having such a crystal-clear description on the tip of your tongue will serve you well. Keep it as short as possible: say, four to twelve words long.

Related to the short description is the *mission statement*, which is commonly recommended for the same purpose, though on an organizational level, more than a project level. A mission statement is used by an organization to articulate and clarify its grand, overall existentialist purpose and focus. The function is the same as a short description: to provide a guiding light for all decision-making. Generally, though, mission statements aren't particularly conversational. And when purposes get diverse and committees are charged with their articulation, they tend to wander. Too often, mission statements become committee-driven, long-winded affairs that nobody can actually use as an effective tool, let alone remember.

Here's an old *From the Top* mission statement, which they eventually decided was a bit cumbersome and are currently in the process of replacing.

From the Top celebrates the passion, dedication, and personal stories of the nation's outstanding young classical musicians. Through entertaining radio and television broadcasts, online media, and a national tour of live events and outreach programs, these performers inspire the pursuit of excellence, and encourage participation in the arts as an integral part of a vibrant and civil society. From the Top's training and mentorship programs prepare young musicians to connect with new audiences, serve as positive peer role models, and give back to their communities in many ways.

Compare it to the short description generally used in conversation to explain what the organization does:

From the Top *supports and showcases young classical musicians.*

Which description gives a clearer picture? Which is more memorable? To an outsider, a big mission statement might not be all that helpful. However, internally, the process of honing and focusing what the vision is all about is healthy for the organization and for the projects it undertakes—even if the actual result is a bear. A quick vision description is also helpful to have, in everyone's back pocket.

There are a couple perspectives on what/how long a good mission statement should be. Some say it should be about fourteen words, others allow up to twenty-five. In any case, it is a clarifying vision statement. Were someone to suggest featuring the Berlin Philharmonic at the next *From the Top* radio show, the board can turn to the mission statement to see whether it is a good fit. And their question should be, "How does this showcase young musicians?"

Bumper-sticker short is better, for most descriptions.

Objectives

A third way to articulate your vision is by listing a number of key objectives for your project. In three to five short, concise points, answer the question, "What value does this project provide?"

Are you teaching a useful skill? Providing a type of entertainment? Developing a product that will increase your customer's capabilities?

Justify your project's existence. What is the most inspiring thing you can say about your idea? Why would someone pay good money for it? Of what benefit is it to a would-be buyer?

Each *From the Top* radio broadcast offers:

- an entertaining and inspiring radio broadcast, appealing to a wide demographic of radio listeners

- extraordinary performances of some of the best music ever created

- support and advocacy for young musicians dedicated to the pursuit of excellence

In listing objectives, we're trying to capture the project's essential purpose, as well as its features.

Describing objectives is easier for products than it is for art. When describing your purposes with art, you can lean towards spiritual or psychological goals that might be more personal than you want to share. It's okay to keep a private list of some of these. However, it is also important that you share some goals and parameters with your project team.

What is success? Selling tickets? Making a profit? Connecting emotionally? What would success bring you? What would it bring to others? These are the subtext of your objectives, as are the components and features of what you are trying to create.

Keep your motivation close. It will inspire you, and help you maintain the energy to complete the work that lies ahead.

PROJECT SCOPE STATEMENT

The three elements of your project definition can be conveniently stored in a document called a *project scope statement*, which also formally houses some other essential parameters of your project. One of the standard roles of a project manager is to be keeper of the scope statement. Its components often get repurposed into other types of documents, from project charts to legal contracts to marketing materials. The scope statement, though, stores that material's definitive form.

The scope statement is a short document that clarifies to those with an essential stake in the project's existence exactly what the project is and what it isn't. "We are making a CD, not a website." "This is a multi-faceted organization that supports young musicians, not only a radio show." "This is a demo CD we will use to get wedding gigs, not a showcase for our original songs."

The scope statement contains a number of standard types of information that help everyone involved understand our project:

Definition	A title, short description, and objectives, as discussed.
Deliverables	Specifics on what you are creating, based on your "objectives." These include the major components included in your project.
Acceptance Criteria	What are the standards for what you are creating? How will you decide or know if it's good enough?
Exclusions	A clarification of what you are not doing,
Constraints	Known budget, time, and other parameters that must be worked around.
Assumptions	Issues assumed to be true, but if they prove otherwise could affect the project significantly.
Dependencies	Are there circumstances that must occur before this project can proceed? Do we need to consider other projects that depend on this project's progress or successful completion?
Stakeholders	Who has a voice in this project's destiny? And who should always be working from a current copy of this document?

Note that while the above categories are fairly standard, you will find variations in what organizations might include here, as you will with all project management tools.

Parts of the scope statement are often repurposed for use in other purposes. For example, some organizations make certain stakeholders sign an expression of scope called a *project charter*, which is like a scope statement that includes a place for signatures and is used for project approval. Project charters are generally just useful until the project is approved, whereas the scope statement is used persistently throughout all stages of the project. So, the scope statement is the definitive word, and the charter is derived from it. Keeping this core information in a dedicated scope statement makes it easy to track what the current agreed-upon project parameters are.

The project manager is the keeper of the project scope statement, though it might be distributed to others for reference. It is the official documentation that illustrates the currently agreed-upon scope of the project. If the stakeholders agree to a change ("We're doing a website after all"), everyone's sanity will be best preserved by the project manager revising the scope statement and immediately distributing the new one to everyone who needs to be kept up to date. Conveniently, that list of stakeholders is part of the scope statement.

Here are the key characteristics of a good scope statement (strangely, all beginning with the letter C).

- **Clear:** The scope statement is a clear articulation of what your project is and what it is not, designed for ease of comprehensibility by the whole team. It gets shared with everyone integral to the project as a point of clarification.

- **Concrete:** It indicates specific, tangible deliverables to be created and avoids abstract sales talk, grandstanding, and philosophizing. It specifies the work rather than attempts to sell it.

- **Concise:** Useful scope statements tend to be two or three pages long, though they may reference other documents, for larger projects. One-pagers might be okay when the project team has done various similar projects before and much is understood, but it could be a little light. Four pages is getting long and cumbersome, so it's time to start making it more concise.

- **Complete:** The scope statement aims to thoroughly articulate the key features and potential points of confusion regarding the project, with all the critical information likely to be useful in defining its parameters.

- **Current:** When you say you want to "make sure everyone is on the same page," the scope statement is likely the page where you want them to be. While it is the final arbiter of what's to be done, it should also be considered dynamic, changing as the goals of the project change. When a change of course is decided, the scope statement gets updated and redistributed to everyone who needs to have it.

As soon as you can, in the project's lifecycle, start chipping away at your scope statement. There might be some obvious stuff you can fill in right off the bat—particularly constraints (deadlines, budgets, etc.). If your project is to create a choral program chorus that supports a Christmas midnight mass, you will probably have a pretty good idea of the time constraint: the performance will be midnight on Christmas Eve. If it's not, your project's Christmas goose will probably be considered "cooked." So, that deadline will be a great focusing point for your scheduling. Similarly, you might have a known budget, or known repertoire, or known rehearsal space, and so on. When you work on your scope statement, you fill in what you know, and edit it to make the document concise and readable.

Let's elaborate on each of the project scope's elements to help you define yours. As an example, we will use a scope statement for an EP (an album with just three to five songs) being done by Emily Peal, an independent band leader/singer-songwriter, who embarked on this project about a year after graduating from Berklee. We will discuss its particular elements, which are fairly standard, but you should adapt what components a document like this includes to your own needs. We will use Emily's adventures as the basis for a number of examples in this book. Note that I often fictionalize her experience and practices, though, both to protect her privacy and to create more targeted illustrations. For real-life information about Emily Peal, visit her website at www.emilypeal.com, and check out her excellent music. The complete scope statement describing one of her projects can be found in appendix A.

Project Definition

Emily's EP currently has the following information for its definition:

Title: Emily's EP

Description: Three original indie-rock songs, performed by Emily Peal and the Band of Skinny Men

Objectives: We are doing this project to:

- fulfill our artistic desires to continually create and grow
- provide new music to people who appreciate what we do
- create an object to give to prospective record labels, booking agents, and others who might support our work

Deliverables

A *deliverable* is something that gets created as part of the project. Generally, this refers to elements that get delivered to the customer or user, though in some cases, it could refer to anything built for the project, including major administrative components such as the budget, or significant design specifications such as architectural drawings.

The purpose of listing deliverables in the scope statement is to articulate the work that will actually be required by the project, with an eye towards organizing the major dimensions of work to be undertaken. For Emily's EP, the deliverables are:

- three original songs, presented by Emily to the band as lead sheets and rough recordings, to be arranged and developed in collaboration with the band during rehearsals in advance of the recording session
- replication-ready CD pre-master
- original cover art as high-resolution digital file
- 200 sales-ready copies of the completed EP

Now, we know what we are building, and we have an idea of what resources will be necessary to complete the project.

Acceptance Criteria

Beyond describing the project's components, we also indicate in the scope statement the level of quality we are aiming towards. This is specified in a set of acceptance criteria, which should be measurable, assessable parameters. For Emily's EP, her criteria are:

- recorded songs will be artistically fulfilling and at a high standard of sound engineering
- EP replication pre-master will conform to Red Book standard
- EP will be separately mastered to optimize sound quality, loudness relationships, and transitions between tracks
- EP pre-master will have complete, error-free metadata including ISRC codes
- album art will express the spirit of this recording and the band generally
- album art will be a high-resolution CMYK graphics file
- album back cover will have a bar code

We are growing more specific, now, in articulating what the project will look like in its final form. People at the core of bringing this product into existence will gain from this some clear insight into what work lies before them. As you can imagine, this component of the scope statement will inform quality control later on, and also assist in contracting, such as with a mastering engineer.

We are specifying here a level of professionalism, and that will inform the expected costs as well. For example, it is clear from this planning document that she is planning on engaging a mastering engineer, separate from the mix engineer. That isn't always the case, and it is good to clarify that assumption, for planning both the budget and the timeline.

Exclusions

A list of exclusions (sometimes called an "is/is not statement") is an opportunity to clarify what is not going to be included in the project effort. This helps to focus the work and manage the team's expectations and ideas.

When you get creative, competent people to work on a project, there is a natural inclination for them to offer improvements. There is often a pushing of boundaries. "Let's add one more song." "Let's do a website." "Let's sell it in this venue." "Let's do this marketing effort."

These suggestions might be helpful, or they might dilute or derail the primary efforts. This tendency is called "scope creep." It's an expansion of the project, often without first confirming that there are resources available or that the new dimension is in support of the project's essential vision.

One of the great purposes of circulating the scope statement is to nip dangerous, "out of scope" suggestions in the bud. The exclusions list heads off some of the likely suspects. Here are Emily's defined exclusions.

- It does not include sales, marketing, or distribution of the EP.

- It does not include the tour to support the EP.

- It does not include merchandise associated with the EP, beyond the replicated EPs themselves.

The exclusions that she lists could be ideas that are in discussion, but decidedly not part of the current undertaking. The point of listing them here is to clarify that they are not current priority and that the resources for this project are not to be spread out to include these items. Efforts towards completing these excluded items are to be postponed until a new project is set forth that includes them in its scope.

Constraints

You might remember from chapter 1 that project quality is limited by three constraints: time, money, and scope. Remember the triangle? The whole document we're discussing here is about scope, or features, but we also want to give a bit of space to the other two.

Here's how Emily might list her constraints of budget and time. Note the direction to see an accompanying appendix document. This technique helps keep scope statements concise and readable.

BUDGET: See "Appendix A. Budget"

Item	Amount	Funding Source	Comment	Status
EP Creation	$50 (self-packaging) $100 (sticker printing) $600 (artwork) $400 (CD replication) **$1,150 Total**	Emily Peal bank account		Secure
Mastering	$500	Emily Peal bank account	Separate from mixing	Not secure
T-Shirts	$400 (Silk Screening kit already purchased—Cost includes ink and shirts)	Emily Peal bank account	for 100 shirts	Not Secure
Tour Expenses	$3,000	Emily Peal bank account	Transportation, meals, accommodations	Not Secure
Total to Raise	**$5,050**			**Not secure**

MILESTONES:

Item	Date	Status
Songs written		
Song demos (keyboard/voice) distributed to band		
Songs rehearsed and ready for recording		
Songs recorded		
Album rough mixed		
Listener survey		
Album final mix		
Album mastered		
EP cover art approved		
EP replicated		

FIG. 2.5. Constraints in Scope Statement Example

The Status column for the milestones gets filled in as the project progresses. Remember, the scope statement is a living document, to be revised and redistributed throughout the lifecycle of the project. Setting it up to be ready to track progress is a good idea.

Next, consider feature constraints that are external to our resources of time and money. Some parameters of what the project can and cannot be will be evident at the start of the project. This type of constraint has to do with the vision itself. If your project is a composition commissioned for a string quartet, one obvious constraint is that it must be for a string quartet. Commissions and other projects written to spec might list a host of other constraints, such as duration or genre. If you're creating a CD, there are built-in constraints such as that CDs can only physically hold 74 minutes (and still conform to the Red Book standard).

There are also implied constraints based on medium. Songs tend to be 2.5 to 5 minutes long. Albums typically include 8 to 15 songs, or about 45 minutes of music, even though CDs can fit more than that. Concerts generally run about 90 minutes. There can be some variation, and some of these parameters are dictated more by custom than by other features, but many such boundaries can be known before the work begins, and you can store them conveniently in the scope statement. Particularly if there is a written spec for your project, see if you can isolate the boundaries.

The scope statement is ideally a concise document, and so the nitty-gritty of budget and calendar are often provided in accompanying "appendix" documents, where the details can be made available for those interested in them. In the scope statement itself, only essential information is included.

Depending on your case, you might want to indicate funding sources in greater detail, or even just provide a single number without any extra data. The point is to list what the known parameters of the project are.

Be grateful for any constraints you can find. They prevent the project from becoming infinitely complex, or a blank slate that becomes intimidating in its vastness.

Assumptions

We create the future based on assumptions—beliefs we decide to hold as being true, even though we might not have evidence to back them up. If we never acted on assumptions, we'd never get anything done. We build products based on the assumption that people will buy them. We go to sleep assuming that we will wake up in the morning. These are hopefully all good guesses based on previous experience.

Projects often struggle or fail because of critical incorrect assumptions. At one of the *From the Top* off-site performances, they found that the piano in the concert hall was not only out of tune, but it wasn't possible to tune. They made the false assumption that a hall of that caliber would have a decent piano, and it required some last-minute heroics to find a replacement instrument that could be used for the show. They are now more careful about that.

There are endless ways for things to go wrong. As we gain more experience, we are hopefully less vulnerable to being derailed by incorrect assumptions. But the world continues to play its tricks, and we have to work to ferret out potential points of risk.

Part of successful project management is to anticipate and prepare contingencies for potential catastrophes. Sometimes, though, we must proceed while knowing that we are vulnerable to certain assumptions being wrong. If we can identify any of these points of vulnerability, it is helpful to list them in the scope statement, so that they can be tracked. It's a good idea to assign someone to keep an eye on them and then list the contingency plan, given the worst-case scenario.

Here are the assumptions Emily has identified. This project came about because she was given the opportunity to have some free time at an exceptional recording studio. An important assumption for the project's survival is that this offer would still be available when they were ready to record, so that was important to list in the scope statement. Another important clarification to make here, related to the availability of the free recording opportunity, is to articulate that if a Skinny Men regular band member wasn't able to make the (free) recording session, she might try to find a replacement rather than lose the free session. It's good for everyone in the band to understand that this is the course of action decided upon.

Item	To Be Validated by	Status	Mitigation Plan
Free recording studio time will remain available	Emily	Confirmed	Reconsider project
At least $2,000 in funding will be achieved	Emily	Open	Try alternative fundraising sites; postpone duplication but not recording session
Our schedules will coincide to allow us to record for free	Emily, all band members, engineer	Open	If no date can be agreed upon, we will use substitute musicians for the recording

FIG. 2.6. Assumptions

Now, infinite possibilities could go wrong in any project. While we technically are "assuming" that the moon will not fall out of the sky and destroy the city where the recording studio is located, we don't need to list that as an assumption. The reason is that it is very unlikely this will happen. So, not all identified assumptions must be listed. Again, our goal is to make a readable and useful document, and not cloud it with endless inane details.

To make the decision about whether or not to include an assumption on this list, you might use a matrix that weighs likelihood of failure against the impact of that failure. If you discover an assumption, you plot it on the matrix and then only list the ones that seem both likely to occur and will have a serious impact. This matrix is a variation of a PICK chart.

	Low Impact	High Impact
Likely	Probably don't list	List
Unlikely	Don't list	Probably don't list

FIG. 2.7. Likelihood vs. Impact Matrix

Let's test some possible assumptions against this matrix, to see if we should include them:

- Tour van will not break down. Likely, but probably won't impact the project much, so we don't list it.

- Band will stay together and not mutiny or quit. High impact, but not likely because Emily is so awesome, so we don't list it.

- Recording studio will not withdraw offer for free time. High impact, some possibility, so we list it.

In the end, what to list is a subjective call. If you, as the project manager, want to list and track an assumption, go ahead. It's better to consider too many assumptions than too few. If the stakeholders are aware of the project's vulnerabilities, they will be more prepared to help, should events take a turn for the worse.

Dependencies

Projects occur in the context of other work, other projects, and other priorities. Often, events in the world must align in a certain way in order to make the project possible. Your project might depend on other factors happening, and other projects might depend on the successful completion of your current project.

In Emily's case, before her EP project can be recorded, she must have her funding secured in order to pay for it. If there's no money, she can't complete the project.

Similarly, her next project, a tour to promote this new EP, only makes sense to begin after her EP is completed. She wants to use the EP to get gigs on the tour and sell it at her merch table during every concert, so many financial and logistical dimensions of the tour will change if this is not possible.

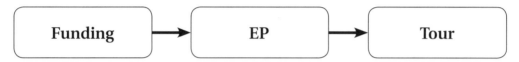

FIG. 2.8. Chain of Three Dependencies

It is often helpful to list these dependencies in the project scope statement. Here is Emily's list of dependencies for this project.

- Secured funding must precede setting the recording date.

- The songwriting must precede the art.

- The art must precede the creation of CD replication and all merchandise.

- This project and all merchandise must precede our planned tour.

Stakeholder List

As we have discussed, the term "stakeholder" is currently used to mean anyone with an interest in the project. This includes people with financial stakes in the project's outcome, such as the owner, people who work on it, vendors who are hired to perform specific tasks or provide gear, creative people who contribute to the content, clients who will buy it, and others. It sometimes seems that everyone in the world could be listed as a stakeholder. Somewhere, a line has to be drawn, for a "stakeholder list" to be useful.

Think of a tent, tied down with stakes. The stakes pull the tent tight in various directions, but in the process, hold it up. The people holding similarly grounding positions in your project are its core stakeholders. Those are the ones who are most useful to list on your scope statement—those who will actively participate in the project's direction, funding, and completion.

A purpose of the scope statement, as well as many other project management tools, is that in an emergency, someone new can come in and replace the project manager, and complete the project by using the tools left behind. A scope statement's list of critical people involved in the project can be a great help, in such cases. Specifying their roles in writing can also help clarify who is responsible for what.

With the stakeholders' names and roles, it is useful to include their primary contact information. This way, everyone in the core team can easily contact everyone else. (We've left that blank on Emily's sample, to protect their privacy, but you should fill it in on yours.)

Additionally, indicate the subgroup of people on this list who should always receive a new copy of the scope statement whenever it is revised. Not everyone needs to be privy to all the information on it. For example, your fans don't need to know how much money you spent on creating the project. Just distribute the scope statement to your core team. Who needs to be updated on this information in order to do their job and be helpful to the project? That's who should be on the distribution list.

Remember that the scope statement serves as the mother of other kinds of documents. If there is discomfort sharing the information in this document with some of the people marked as stakeholders, don't over-share. Consider whether there is some other type of document that will be more appropriate for them that includes only a subset of the information here.

Distribution List	Name	Roles and Responsibilities	Status	Contact	Comment
●	Emily	Artistic director, songwriter, project manager, bandleader. Writes songs, books venues.	Confirmed	[email, cell, etc.]	Approves all project decisions
●	Andrew	Drums	Confirmed	[email, cell, etc.]	
●	Mike	Guitar	Confirmed	[email, cell, etc.]	
●	David	Bass	Confirmed	[email, cell, etc.]	
●	Aaron	Mix engineer	Confirmed	[email, cell, etc.]	
	Alan	Mastering engineer	Pending	[email, cell, etc.]	
	Secret Designs	Illustrator	Confirmed	[email, cell, etc.]	
		Layout designer	Needed	[email, cell, etc.]	
	Tammy	Photographer	Confirmed	[email, cell, etc.]	
	DiscMakers	replication house	Pending	[email, cell, etc.]	
	Sample Audience	Provide feedback on rough mix	Needed	[email, cell, etc.]	

FIG. 2.9. Stakeholder Matrix

Version Control

Whenever the project owner agrees to a change of scope, it is helpful for the project manager to update the scope statement and then provide the revision to all the stakeholders on the distribution list (a subset of all stakeholders).

Versions of this document can be indicated by date and/or by version number. This should be indicated on the first page in the header or next to the project title, easily visible. Each new release of the scope statement should have a unique identifier at the very beginning, to help everyone confirm that they are working from the same one.

An appendix you sometimes see on scope statements is a version history of this document, itemizing major changes in scope decisions. That's generally only necessary with very complex projects that involve great sums of money, generally in larger corporate environments. If you think it could be helpful, use it, but otherwise, don't consider a version history essential. Just update everyone who needs to be informed of scope changes.

MICRO IMPLEMENTATIONS

We hope that our scope will remain reasonably intact, once it is set and the execution phase of the project begins. Reality, though, often informs our plans. For this reason, it is often a good idea to begin certain types of endeavor with a small-scale execution of the plan before we commit significant funds or time. This way, we can learn and then revise the plan as necessary.

There are a few different perspectives on this.

When inspiration strikes and the vision takes hold, we want to begin creating content and setting things in motion right away. Creative artists don't want to plan; we want to *do*. That's how we really get an accurate sense of the reality that lies before us. Organizations and visions frequently falter because too much time was spent planning and not enough time actually doing—sometimes called "analysis paralysis." So, many contemporary styles of project management incorporate execution simultaneous with planning—though they must be closely integrated for this to work well.

The danger of creating significant content before you create a strategic plan is that you run the risk of creating something ill conceived or unusable. I see this in the book publishing industry all the time. An author will spend years in isolation, secretly writing a book—say, a collection of theoretical analyses of famous works by world-renowned artists. Then, when they pitch their completed project to us, they learn that the works they analyzed are all under copyright and that the fees involved in licensing them would be so high that it would be financially unfeasible to clear them all. In other words, all their work to date is effectively unpublishable, for legal reasons. So much for their years of toil.

Or, someone decides to create a product without researching the competition, and then when they are ready to find a publisher or record label, they learn that someone else beat them to it. Something better and cheaper already exists. Oh well.

Without a plan, projects veer off course. People miss critical deadlines (important industry events, the holiday shopping season, etc.) or go over budget. There are endless ways that projects can fail.

The opposing school of thought to the "let's get started" people says, therefore, that you should plan first and then build. "Measure twice, cut once," as the old carpenter's adage goes. Look before you leap.

But again on the other hand, waiting too long can also be a problem. Your inspiration might have come because the timing was just right; something in the air nudged your instinct to understand that there was an opportunity to be had, though you might not be consciously aware of what that could be. "Strike when the iron is hot," says the blacksmith to the carpenter.

One more observation: endless hand-wringing sometimes comes from a place of fear or inappropriate self-doubt. Hesitating and over-planning is an avoidance tactic from actually creating something and thus being vulnerable to failure. People sit on projects forever.

The study of project management is often primarily about strategic planning, but it is important to keep the ball rolling, as well, and to be careful not to let projects languish too long in the planning stages. Plan enough to know how to keep everyone on target, but you should also keep things moving. In this balance, grand schemes can become reality. And, be careful not to spend too much money or time before sufficient planning is underway.

A great type of device that balances the drive towards action with the need for appropriate planning is a *micro implementation* of the end vision: small, cheap, micro versions of your ultimate intentions, designed to teach you how to make your ultimate project better, and to save you money and time by avoiding costly mistakes. These mini versions of your project can take various forms, which we'll discuss next. It's helpful to launch them early. Different types of projects can benefit from different types and strategies of micro-implementation.

References

Referencing existing completed projects that are similar to yours can be an invaluable starting point for discussing your own vision.

Albums can begin with an internal distribution of songs or albums by similar artists, in the same style, for everyone involved in the project to consider, discuss, and sometimes imitate. These references are useful in many different ways, from communicating to band mates ideas about instrumentation, "vibe," lyrical themes, etc., to giving an engineer a sense of different specific sonic elements, such as loudness or transitions between tracks, or providing a graphic designer approaches to album art.

FIG. 2.10. *Music Marketing* Book Cover

For example, author Mike King suggested, as an art concept for his Berklee Press book, *Music Marketing*, that we use the Hatch Show Print style (associated with the Country Music Hall of Fame, circuses, and such) as a reference. So, we circulated a number of old poster designs, and graphic artist Kathy Kikkert came up with this cover, which captures the look and spirit of those great old designs.

Concert concepts (particularly classical music) can start with the preparation and distribution of finished recordings of the same music by other artists. Some musicians avoid these, feeling that it impedes their ability to come up with original interpretations, but others don't mind, and developing unique interpretations isn't always a primary goal (particularly in educational or worship contexts).

Film scores often begin with *temp tracks* in the project's early days, when the director wants to communicate with the composer what music will be needed. A temp track is music in the style of what the final music will be, just to give an idea of mood. For example, *Star Wars* used the music from Holst's *The Planets* as a temp track. John Williams then composed his famous music in the style of that work. (See figure 9.25 for an example format of tracking temp tracks for a film.)

So, references become a point at which discussion can begin and focus.

Mock-Ups

Some projects benefit from rough mock-ups of the intended final version. These evoke the actual project, but they are placeholders, designed to help members or the project team understand and perhaps help develop what the actual product will be by giving them something tangible and "real" to modify, rather than keeping it all within their imaginations.

Recordings can begin with short, simple "demo" versions of songs, with guitar or keyboard and voice, rather than a full band. Even a rough, unproduced recording, with cheesy reverb and some wrong notes, can be a convenient tool for helping you discuss it, determine what it's ultimate form would be, how it related to other songs you are considering, and so on. If you keep the creation effort of these lightweight, you can bang out a bunch of these little scratch recordings very quickly.

Software products can be mocked up with drawings or *wire frames* of the imagined interface. So, get out your crayons, and draw windows with buttons, labels, and so on, to evoke what the final program will look like. It won't do anything; there is no code behind it. But the project visionary can explain what happens, and it is thus more tangible than just wordy descriptions of what you are building. You and your tech team can move pieces of paper around a table, and get a feel for the flow.

Figure 2.11 is an early wireframe of the Berkleemusic online course version of this topic. As you can see, the content is there in the big text box, with two graphics frames, along with dummied up navigation "buttons" (really, just graphic objects) to support the fact that it is an interactive website.

Figure 2.12 is what the actual page eventually looked like. In the end, we decided to include a couple of audio clips as opening examples, in the online course, but the overall structure of it is the same as the wireframe, which took just a few minutes to generate.

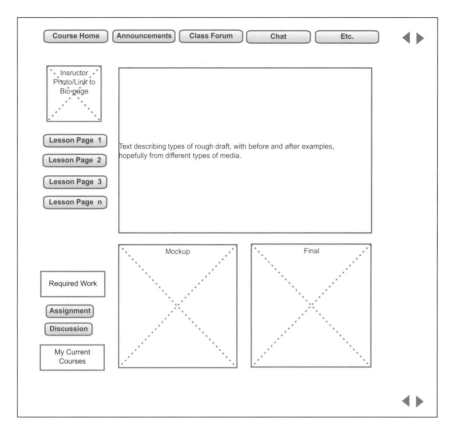

FIG. 2.11. Wireframe of Planned Web Page

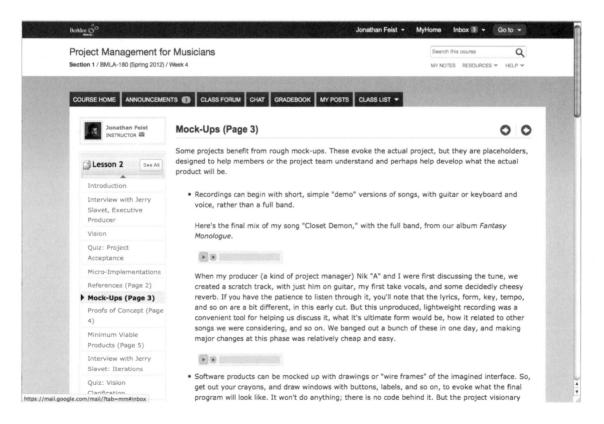

FIG. 2.12. Screen Shot of Actual Web Page

Recording studios or other physical objects can have drawings and small physical models of the final product, built out of plastic, foam core, popsicle sticks, or what have you. These help give a sense of spatial relationships and ergonomics. Architects often do this.

Here are two images from New England architect Frank Shirley (www .frankshirleyarchitects.com, in Cambridge, MA), who specializes in historical renovations and restorations. We will first see his working model and then see the completed house. Models like this make ideas tangible and are a great help towards implementing your vision (and also, checking it against what is actually possible).

FIG. 2.13a. Architect's Preliminary Model of House (Courtesy of Frank Shirley Architects)

FIG. 2.13b. Finished House (Courtesy of Frank Shirley Architects)

Proofs of Concept

Another type of taste is a trial balloon, to serve as a proof of concept. This is a small, test version of a concept with larger aspirations.

A tour might be preceded by a local live gig or free performance, to test out some of the logistical matters (e.g., whether the gear you plan to bring will actually fit into your car, let you run the show, and so on). Isolating the tasks of putting on a show from the demands of travel can teach you a lot about your project.

A full album might be preceded by a home-studio production of a single track or a shorter EP (with just three or four songs). The goal is to recreate just enough of the actual project so that you can test some dimension of it—prove that it is feasible, and prove that it has legs.

Prototyping is a similar concept. In a prototype, you create early models of the project, test some aspect of it, analyze the results, and then make improvements for a new and improved prototype, and then you do it again.

As an example, Wula Drum, a fine manufacturer of African drums based in New York (www.wuladrum.com), wanted to develop a line of djembes using traditional building methods, such as those used before contemporary manufacturing processes made standard a version of the instrument that was cheaper to manufacture but had an inferior sound to the older drums. Wula Drum co-founders Thomas Kondas and Michael Markus coordinated master craftsmen in Guinea to develop a process that combined the best of the old designs with the best of modern materials, for exceptional-sounding but still relatively affordable instruments. During the development process, they experimented with varying different elements of the design, such as changing the original conical shape to more of a bowl, for better tone, and using nylon instead of the traditional goat sinew, for the tuning rope. Figure 2.15 shows a prototype next to an improved instrument.

FIG. 2.14. Djembe Prototype and Final

Minimum Viable Product

The *minimum viable product* (MVP) concept is that bare-bones versions of a product are continually created, scrutinized, and improved, going through many cycles of iterations (as in a prototype), but often actually released for sale early on. This approach is nicely described in the excellent book *Lean Startup*, by Eric Ries.

MVPs are often actual products for sale, tested in the marketplace. Like prototypes, they are especially useful when you are creating or inventing something new, that hasn't been tested, and the exact form it will take is subject to dramatic revision. In this approach, developing significant dimensions of the project vision is concurrent with its execution.

- The process of creating an album or concert set of original songs might begin by completing one song (probably a relatively simple one) as far as you can in the process without spending significant money or time. You'd do a writing session for just that one song, rehearse it, and then record it, perhaps using a laptop and single mic in the rehearsal space, but acting as if it was a formal recording session. This would give the core project team a chance to work through many of the major issues together, learn how to interact with each other, assess timing and work habits, and so on, before proceeding to the more expensive commitment of a commercial recording session. This can then be shared with a few close members of the project community, or shared as an informal "work in progress" with a few fans (maybe on a blog or social media site) to see a small-scale reaction.

- A teaching studio might begin with one teacher and one student. All systems and needs get ironed out for just that tiny iteration before adding a small number of additional students or teachers, and then testing larger dimensions of the project.

- A community music school might begin with a tiny number of course offerings and very few students, to see what is likely to take hold.

- A method book can begin with a single lesson or chapter and then is tested, edited, and otherwise reviewed and improved.

These different flavors of micro-iteration are all means of foreshadowing our projects so that we can see, test, and improve them, before too much investment has been made in building something likely to be inferior or unusable.

Micro-iterations become points at which to start conversations, test assumptions, and clarify ideas. Early in the process, try to find a way to create something minimal, cheap, and easy, but also real.

When you embark on one of these, consider what information you are trying to get out of the experiment. Keep in mind that they are tests, meant to be easily revised and improved, but also, that they are not representing your best work. Because they are sometimes "smoke" versions of what you are actually creating, it is likely you'll get relatively harsh feedback on them. This feedback is more likely than usual to be off the mark, as what your subjects are testing are particularly unpolished. Sharing an unmixed scratch demo track with someone not accustomed to hearing such things might have a strong negative reaction to something that has nothing to do with what you are actually testing. You might be testing lyric development, but they might be listening to the mix and overall soundscape. So, be braced for that, when sharing these early iterations, and try to understand the perspective from which the feedback is coming. Providing clear direction regarding what you are looking for ("Forget how it looks, tell me how it sounds!") will help keep the feedback useful and on target.

CLOSING THOUGHTS

During the project's lifecycle, you begin with the vision, then start defining the scope, and then begin setting the content execution phase in motion. These phases can happen concurrently, as shown in the following graphic. The time spent refining the vision and scope generally decreases as the time spent in execution increases, throughout the project's lifecycle.

The scope statement is a living document, held as the final arbiter of what work should be done, while being a potentially flexible, revisable articulation of the project's highest thinking. By having this articulation of the project's scope in a single place, we reduce clutter and redundancy of the plan. It is all stored in the scope statement.

Periodically, whenever significant decisions are made, the scope statement gets revised to reflect those changes and then shared with everyone who needs to know.

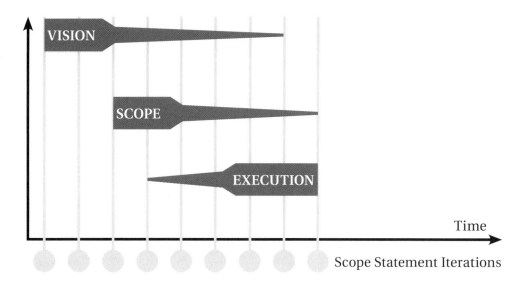

FIG. 2.15. Scope Statement Iterations

We hope that as projects evolve, and particularly, as iterations progress, the focus isn't on simply adding new features. Often, features should actually come out, as the highest vision of what the project can be becomes clear and distractions can be shaved off. Use any iterative process to test specific assumptions and to gain information about how to make your project better, not just bigger. The goal is always to clarify and fulfill the vision.

PRACTICE

1. **Big**. Post a detailed project scope statement for your project. If you don't know some of the information, leave a placeholder, and indicate that this information will follow. Remember that the goal of the scope statement is to be clear and helpful. When you look at one of these, the sun should come out. It shouldn't feel like obnoxious bureaucracy.

   Consider this question: If you had to step into this project as a replacement project manager, do you feel that this document will sufficiently help you to understand what this project is all about?

2. **Little**. What would be a useful micro-iteration of your big project? Create a scope statement for that as well. Will you do just one or many? How cheap, quick, and easy can you make something meaningful? When would it make sense to create it/them?

CHAPTER 3

Understanding the Work

"Don't touch the pretty stars, sweetheart, they're really hot."

In chapter 2, we worked at clarifying our vision and scope. Now, we will explore how to figure out what work will be required to move our visions towards reality.

OBJECTIVES

By the end of the chapter, you will be able to:

- derive detailed deliverables from your project vision

- analyze your project goals and itemize the work necessary to accomplish them

- create a work breakdown structure and accompanying dictionary

WORKING DOCUMENTS

Earlier, we met Jerry Slavet, the visionary co-creator of *From the Top*. Part of his job is to imagine what projects an organization will embark upon. In discussing his successful organization, Jerry always emphasizes how critical it was to bring people on board the organization who have complementary skills: people who are organized, detail-oriented, and adept at making airtight systems that make sure everything comes out right, as a foil to what he describes as his own more impulsive, instinct-based nature. He looks at the skillset of the team, in terms of getting work done effectively.

Elizabeth DeVore is *From the Top*'s production manager, which is essentially a project manager for live performances. Her job is to figure out how to actually make the organization's visions happen. These projects are most frequently some type of broadcasted concert, with several different performing artists, and an audience comprised of thousands of people. Though they often broadcast from their headquarters at Jordan Hall, they also frequently go on the road to other cities or other countries, and do the show from there.

Elizabeth manages every detail of everything going on, and makes sure that it all gets done right.

That is essentially the role of the project manager. Develop good systems, and then run around with a clipboard, confirming that the reality unfolding is in support with what a previously articulated vision says it should be.

What's on Elizabeth's clipboard? A set of documents she has found to be essential for keeping every dimension of a project on track. One day, when we met to talk about her work, I asked what pages she was carrying around, and she had the following documents, which helped her run a live-broadcast radio show at a remote location:

- Production Calendar/Schedule

- Production Budget to Actual Report

- Run Sheet (list of cues and notes for the actual performance)

- Stage Setup Plans

- Parental Consent form for child musicians to perform

- Parental Release form related to travel

- Performer Emergency Contact Info

- Tour Staff Emergency Contact Info

- Travel Guidelines (given to everyone)

- Road Show Checklist

Most of a project manager's working documents, such as these, are checklists that itemize specific components of the work to be done and schedules for coordinating their completion. They are carefully constructed and generated using information gathered from diverse places:

- *templates* from similar projects

- *meetings* with people like Jerry Slavet, who provides specific guidance, but also with the workers who are hanging lights, recording sound, accompanying soloists, and so on, who provide insight into the details required

- *data* based on research, meetings, and on-the-ground analysis of the situation

In this chapter, we will be looking at some of these processes for developing working documents such as these. They are all means of imagining the future, avoiding risk, and figuring out how to make the project result in success.

Managing a project involves planning what work needs to be done, doing that work, and then periodically confirming that it's being done thoroughly and well. The scaffold holding this process together is a set of documents that clarify the project's scope—what you will deliver—and strategies for implementing it. When you're in the thick of the work itself, you want well-crafted tools to help you confirm that the work is on track. And the glue that holds it all together is good communication between the people doing the work.

The end result of this good strategic thinking is a series of checklists and other structures, describing the work and helping you analyze whether it's going well, and getting the project back on track if the work should wander off course. These structures map to your project vision, traveling up through your objectives. They should be well crafted but also dynamic—easy to change, as the need arises.

The essential planning documents for a project manager (called by various names) are:

- Scope Statement, which is now well under way

- Work Breakdown Structure (WBS), which we will discuss this chapter

- Budget (chapter 4)

- Schedule (chapter 5)

- Resource Allocation Sheet (chapter 6)

That's about it. There may be additional checklists, reports, contracts, and other forms derived from the above, but the above are the essential tools. We will cover them all in the next few chapters. As you will see, the first two are used to generate the last three, as well as many others.

This constellation of project management documents are not like the legs of a bar stool, all rigid and leading to the seat, as the focal point. They are more like the tentacles of an octopus, flexible and connected to a giant brain. The brain is the vision; the tentacles are the tools of implementing that vision.

Building useful working documents is a science and an art. They can be back-of-the-envelope simple, or so complex that their sprawl can cover walls, or fill volumes so large that everyone is terrified to look at them.

Unless you're building a spaceship, regular-sized 8.5 x 11 paper is about where you should be aiming. Keep them as simple, clear, and practical as you can. If they shrink while you are developing them, it could be a good sign. Often, early drafts are longer than later drafts, as ideas become refined.

Efficient construction takes added effort, but it leads to tools that actually get used, as opposed to being exiled in a drawer, where they lie feared and despised.

WORK BREAKDOWN STRUCTURES

In our project scope statement, we listed a few key project deliverables. Those reflected a big-picture view of the work to be done, but we also need a more comprehensive itemization of the work required for our project to succeed. To go from a vague vision to usable, 100-percent inclusive working documents like what Elizabeth uses, we need a more detailed analysis of the work before us.

What if, say, singer/songwriter Emily Peal wanted to know exactly what work her EP required, to help her get a more realistic view of her required budget and timeline? What if she wanted to create the equivalent of Elizabeth's lists?

The process to arrive at this begins with imagining the deliverables—the things that you are trying to create. Start by just listing what you know. It's helpful to talk this out with another person, or in a meeting, to drill down and uncover all the different components of your project.

What we're working with here is a comprehensive itemization of 100 percent of the project's anticipated work requirements. The transitional document/step/modeling technique between the vision and the clipboard's checklists (and others) is called a *work breakdown structure.*

For Emily's EP, it might look something like this:

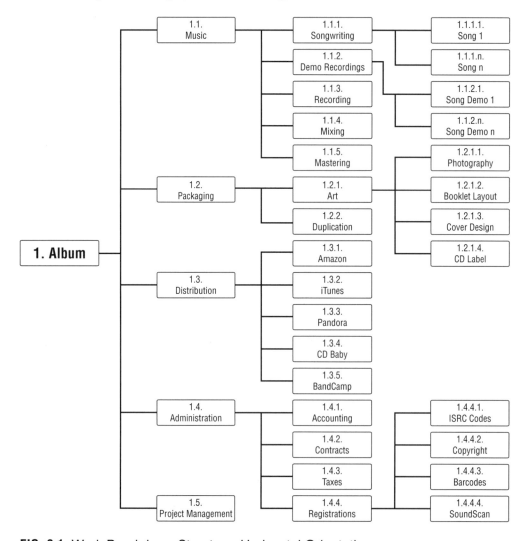

FIG. 3.1. Work Breakdown Structure: Horizontal Orientation

The *work breakdown structure*, or WBS, is one of the classic, most useful tools of project management. It shows what work is required for the vision to be fulfilled, in this case, Emily's EP. It is the precursor to the checklists and other documents that Elizabeth carries around in her clipboard. In building a WBS, we learn a lot about the work before us.

WBS Formats

A WBS might be graphic or textual, oriented vertically or horizontally, and be either relatively simple or fantastically complex and detailed. A minimal version generally gets created early in the planning cycle, and it keeps evolving throughout the project's execution. You might notice little variations between the different WBSs in these examples. That's normal, in the course of a project's evolution, as different work and different priorities become evident.

Here's a vertically oriented version of the previous WBS. You can see, we have the constraint of width now, so the more populous levels need to switch to a vertical orientation, just to fit everything on a page. This makes it a little more difficult, in some ways, to see logical relationships. On the other hand, it is more intuitive to say "higher levels" when certain levels are "above" others. So, it's a tradeoff.

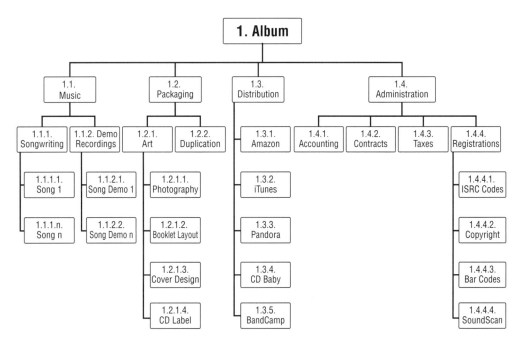

FIG. 3.2. Work Breakdown Structure: Vertical

Here's a text version of the same information. It is a little harder to read these, but they require less technology to create, they are easily edited, and they are easily adapted to various software programs (such as Excel, project management software, etc.).

1. Album
    1.1. Music
        1.1.1. Songwriting
            1.1.1.1. Song 1
            1.1.1.n. Song n
        1.1.2. Demo Recordings
            1.1.2.1. Song Demo 1
            1.1.2.n. Song Demo n
        1.1.3. Recording
        1.1.4. Mixing
        1.1.5. Mastering
    1.2. Packaging
        1.2.1. Art
            1.2.1.1. Photography
            1.2.1.2. Booklet Layout
            1.2.1.3. Cover Design
            1.2.1.4. CD Label
        1.2.2. Duplication
    1.3. Distribution
        1.3.1. Amazon
        1.3.2. iTunes
        1.3.3. Pandora
        1.3.4. CD Baby
        1.3.5. Bandcamp
    1.4. Administration
        1.4.1. Accounting
        1.4.2. Contracts
        1.4.3. Taxes
        1.4.4. Registrations
            1.4.4.1. ISRC Codes
            1.4.4.2. Copyright
            1.4.4.3. Barcodes
            1.4.4.4. Soundscan
    1.5. Project Management

FIG. 3.3. Work Breakdown Structure: Text

Here's a screenshot from within Smartsheet, where we see one of the many uses of the work breakdown structure: inside project management software, creating a framework for managing the completion of tasks.

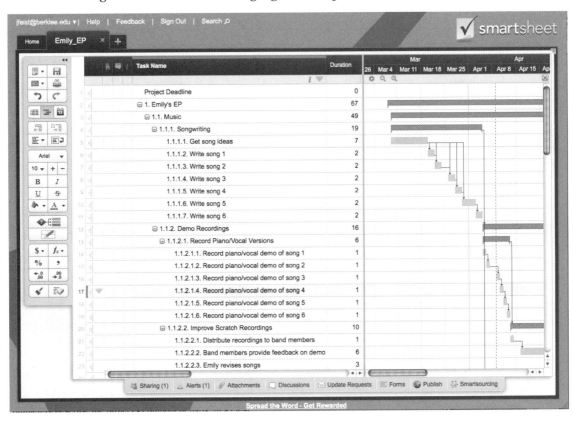

FIG. 3.4. Smartsheet Items: Transferred from Work Breakdown Structure

So, we see, it can be an object for abstract planning and analysis, or it can be adapted to more active uses. In all cases, the goal is to completely describe the project's component parts, in a clear, easily decipherable hierarchical system that gets ever more specific as you drill farther towards the roots—whether reading from left to right, top to bottom, or even other models.

Each level is a logical set of work, and with each generation, the work gets *decomposed* to its components. (Note that as of this chapter, Berklee Press finally has books about both composition and decomposition....)

WBS Code Numbers

A code number, such as the "1.1.2" that accompanies the work packet "Demo Recordings," can accompany the deliverable name, particularly in more formal contexts. This number expands by a decimal point at every level. Levels are named for how many decimal places they take up. So, the 3 level here includes songwriting, art, and so on. The 4 level is a further "elaboration" of the 3 level.

Here's level 2, taken from the vertical orientation. Count the decimal places of the code numbers to reach 2, rather than the physical lines, which logically might not correspond.

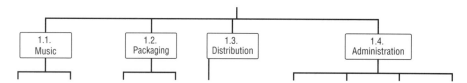

FIG. 3.5. WBS Level 2

These numbers are useful for references to other documents with more information about each item. They can also help distinguish between similar items used in different contexts. For example, you might have photography associated with the album cover design and photography associated with advertising, both coming from different sources and managed independently. The code numbers can uniquely identify what kind of photography you're discussing, in communications or checklists outside the WBS itself.

Each square on the WBS represents a *deliverable*—a unit of work, which you can think of as a sub-project, such as writing a specific song, completing some dimension of the art design (e.g., photography), or registering with a specific distribution channel (e.g., CD Baby). Deliverables can be either *external* (what the client gets, such as the physical EP or its accompanying booklet) or *internal* (created for project administration use, such as a budget balance sheet). The names for these work packets should be nouns, representing the things that are to be created, until the final leg, when you're at the level of the actions to be taken that will result in the work packet getting done.

Here's the node for "Distribution," with its code number 1.3.

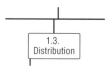

FIG. 3.6. Node

While the code numbers can be helpful in some circumstances, when you're feverishly scribbling down a rough WBS at a cocktail party, quickly showing someone exactly how a dream they dismissed as impossible can actually be accomplished, you can probably dispense with the code numbers.

Figure 3.7 presents a few lines from a simple WBS dictionary, so that you can see the code numbers in action. The scenario is that someone scans the WBS, spots "Distribution," and asks, "What the heck is that?" They then look at the dictionary, and find the "1.3. Distribution" work packet listed in the third row from the bottom, with some more information that wouldn't fit on the chart. We'll discuss dictionaries in more depth later in this chapter.

Level	Number	Name	Description
1	1	Album	3-song EP or original music by Emily Peal
2	1.1.	Music	The recorded songs
2	1.2.	Packaging	The physical presence of the EP: booklet, jewel case
3	1.2.1.	Art	Illustrations and other graphics
4	1.2.1.1.	Photography	Photos of the band
4	1.2.1.2.	Booklet Layout	Design and graphic files for the booklet
4	1.2.1.3.	Cover Design	Art to go on the cover of the booklet
4	1.2.1.4.	CD Label	Art and print-ready files for the CD labels
3	1.2.2.	Duplication	Creation of sales-ready physical copies of the EP
2	1.3.	Distribution	Mechanisms for selling the EP, both physical and online
2	1.4.	Administration	Financial and legal processes
2	1.5.	Project Management	Support documents for planning, managing, and ensuring the quality of the EP creation project

FIG. 3.7. Simple WBS Dictionary

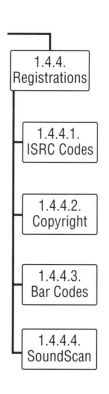

FIG. 3.8. Terminal Work Packets

Where exactly to stop elaborating the WBS is a subjective call that the chart writer makes to suit the required level of usefulness. "One person or team doing one clearly defined task" might be a good ending point." "One invoice point" might be another way to look at it. A common rule of thumb for particularly large projects, such as what might be undertaken by the Department of Defense, is the "8 to 80" rule: the ultimate work packet should require between 8 and 80 hours of work to complete. This strikes a balance between displaying significant units of work and avoiding a WBS that is overly detailed. Smaller projects, such as those likely to be undertaken by the average musician, might drill down a bit farther than an eight-hour packet. Where you choose to draw this logical line depends on your circumstance.

Figure 3.8 is a thread that ends in the individual work packets for "Registrations." These will probably require a couple hours of each to complete, so one could argue that the work packet should have stopped at "Registrations," but this WBS isn't complex enough that this is an issue, so it's fine. Once you've arrived at these different terminal work packets, you can draw up task lists for completing them, which we'll explore later in the chapter.

WBS Evolution

The WBS can be—and probably should be—created in sections, rather than all at once in its entirety. You only need to fully elaborate a thread when it is time to focus on it, rather than exhaustively puzzling out the whole universe of your project only to find later on that major components of it have been cancelled. For example, what if instead of releasing the EP as a physical CD, Emily decides that it will be a purely digital release, with no physical product? That decision would have repercussions throughout the WBS, and any work done on packaging would have been wasted time. On the other hand, elaborating the work for packaging the physical disc can help reveal its costs and thus inform the decision about the destiny of that dimension of the project. Changing the chart might just take a few minutes, so it might be worth it.

You can see that the WBS is a flexible kind of tool, in terms of how it might be rendered and how the process might be approached. Here's a view of the work with just the packaging's art leg elaborated. This time, the WBS is oriented vertically rather than horizontally. You'll see them oriented either way.

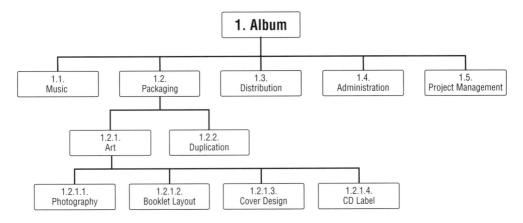

FIG. 3.9. WBS with Packaging Leg Elaborated

This approach of partially completing WBSs is actually a bit controversial.

One camp of project management enthusiasts says, "Remember the 100 percent rule. You have to describe 100 percent of the work required, or else there will be surprises. You'll leave out a critical component that will unexpectedly add time and cost to the project."

The other camp says, "While we execute the project, the exact scope is likely to change, so any planning we do on features that don't make it into the final version will be wasted time."

They are both right. The middle ground is to try to list 100 percent of the work on the project dimension you are consciously trying to figure out, but not 100 percent of the complete WBS.

WBS Best Practices

There are some formal attributes and strategies that the work breakdown structure can include, but the critical aspect of it is that it tells you the truth about the work, so that you can trust it.

Best practice attributes for WBSs include:

- it is written in terms of deliverables, not actions. (Action breakdowns are discussed later.) We want nouns here, not verbs, until the planning stage progresses to the execution stage, where actions take over.

- one hundred percent of the work of its parent element at each level.

- each parent has at least two child elements.

- Project Management at level 2.

- a coding scheme that reflects its hierarchical nature.

- an accompanying dictionary.

And more. A detailed book on the topic is *Work Breakdown Structures* by Norman, Brotherton, and Fried (Wiley, 2008), though most books on project management discuss them.

Even a rough-cut WBS is helpful, though. It is the sort of diagram you could initially scribble on your napkin at dinner, and then start a company based on it the morning after. Elaborate it as the spirit moves you or as the business requires it, and be more formal and complete when you are being more methodical.

WBS Rendered as Text

The graphical WBS version is great for clearly showing the work, at a glance. Use a pencil to create a rough one, and use software to create a pretty version.

As we saw, work breakdown structures can also be rendered as text. While graphical representations are easy to read, they are also relatively technology hungry. You need special software to create a chart, and updating it can be relatively time consuming. If project management tools aren't 100 percent up to date with what we agree to be the project's currently required work, then the tools are hindering efforts rather than supporting them. So, there's also a downside to making a graphical WBS.

Less fiddly, and a bit more flexible for converting into other project management tools, is the text version. Here's the WBS with just Emily's Art leg elaborated, presented as text.

    1. Album

        1.1. Music

        1.2. Packaging

            1.2.1. Art

                1.2.1.1. Photography

                1.2.1.2. Booklet Layout

                1.2.1.3. Cover Design

                1.2.1.4. CD Labels

            1.2.2. Duplication

        1.3. Distribution

        1.4. Administration

        1.5. Project Management

FIG. 3.10. WBS Text Form: Packaging Leg Elaborated

It's the same information. It's a little more difficult to glance at it and see all the component relationships and hierarchies and big picture, but the information is still there. If I tell, say, a member of my project team that she's in charge of Packaging, she'll have to read a bit before she figures out what her duties are. If I tell her she's in charge of 1.2. Packaging, it will be easier, as the code numbers guide her.

Unlike a graphical WBS, a text WBS can be created with any simple text editor. Then, it can be copied and pasted and formatted and tweaked into innumerable different formats and purposes. For example, with a few mouse clicks in Microsoft Word or Excel, she could turn her section into a checklist, to help her track her little piece of the pie.

	1.2. Packaging
❑	1.2.1. Art
❑	1.2.1.1. Photography
❑	1.2.1.2. Booklet Layout
❑	1.2.1.3. Cover Design
❑	1.2.1.4. CD Labels
❑	1.2.2. Duplication

FIG. 3.11. Checklist from WBS

If it is easy for you to maintain a current graphical WBS, that's great, particularly for sharing with others in strategy discussions. If it is difficult, you might want to primarily maintain a text WBS and perhaps make an occasional one-off graphical iteration just for special occasions, such as formal presentations to a project team.

The most important thing is that it be accurate, clear, and easy to maintain.

IMAGINING THE WORK

The work breakdown structure is a foundation document, and many other tools are based on it. The better it reflects reality, the more accurate it will be in helping you later on, when we use it to predict cost, time, risk, and so on.

An individual could figure out much of the WBS by just sitting in a room alone with a pen and paper, just writing down the obvious components, or the ones listed on the scope statement. However, better quality, more complete results can be found with some other approaches. Here are some ideas for how to imagine the work packets to go in a WBS.

1. **Creative Visualization:** Step by Step. Light some incense, close your eyes, and imagine the creation of your project, step by step. What is the next step you need to do, to move the project forward? What would then be the next step after that? And the next? By imagining it step by step, you will try to understand and predict more precisely how you will bring your objective into being, and also uncover items about the required work that you might not understand. Try to see the results of your project clearly, from an end-user's perspective. Where will potential buyers see the EP for sale? How will they get it? Do they open shrink wrap? Is it a jewel case or a digipak? Which do you prefer? What vibe do you want from the cover art?

Or, imagine the project from one of the other worker's perspectives—say, the photographer. If you were the photographer, what would you want the client (i.e., Emily) to bring to a photo shoot, to make it easier and more likely to be successful? In imagining this, you might realize, for example, that bringing sample photos from completed projects would be a big help. This type of deep imagination exercise is helpful for many different dimensions in creating work, from making suitcase-packing checklists to reducing stage fright. It can be very productive. We'll look at an example later this chapter.

2. **Use Case:** Developing use cases is a conceptual modeling technique that winds up being a lot like creative visualization, though more tangible. They are frequently used for software development and the creations of other complex systems, where there are different ways (cases) that the system is accessed or interacted with (used). That's a modeling science in itself, with many books devoted entirely to it, and you might look into that type of modeling if your projects involve complex systems. We'll go through an example on page 92.

3. **Guru Consultation:** Find someone who has done a number of projects like yours, and show him or her your best effort at itemizing the work. Ask what you've omitted.

4. **Model/Reference:** Find a completed version of what you are creating, and analyze it. Imagine recreating it. Have you accounted for every single detail of that product? This can reveal some arcane dimensions of the project that might not be at all obvious, particularly if you haven't done one like it before. For example, on a CD, you might find a barcode on the back. Do you know what that is, whether you need one, how to go about getting it, or how to explain to your graphic designer what must be done with it? To some, the possibility of getting a bar code comes as a great surprise, only uncovered by looking at model projects. (For some info about bar codes, you can look at this link: www.myidentifiers.com/barcode/main.)

5. **Interviews/Team Meeting:** Discussing the project with someone else is likely to uncover false assumptions and missing details. If you can get a description in writing, you can analyze it and derive the work based on that. It would be best to facilitate a conversation with members of the whole team who are going to do the work. This can take the form of a meeting or even a retreat, where everyone discusses the various project

components, as they see them. People who actually do the work generally have the most realistic insight into what is actually required by a vision.

There are many ways to structure a meeting like this. One way to do it is to have a blank wall and give all participants a Post-It pad, in a unique color. They then brainstorm components, and fill in the WBS on the wall, rearranging the hierarchy as inspiration strikes or as the discussion evolves. When it's done, someone creates a physical chart out of it. Digital cameras can be helpful here, but make sure you use dark markers, and confirm that all is visible before you disassemble it.

6. **Micro-Iterations:** As you build and test small versions of your project, you will learn more about the work the final version requires. As you learn, you will update the WBS to reflect any new deliverables or dimensions that become evident. When building a cardboard model of your recording studio, for example, you might realize that you forgot to work out a place to store microphone stands. This component might then be worked into the spec, if everyone agrees. (See chapter 2 for more about micro-iterations.)

One of the reasons why it is helpful to have a separate project manager from the content creator is that it forces multiple minds to consider the upcoming work and create a complete solution. It's sometimes easier to figure out someone else's work than your own, as when you are creating, your priorities and attention might be in a very abstract place, in the land of artistic expression, and possibly encumbered by your emotional attachments to your work, as well as your regular habits. Another perspective might help you take a fresh and perhaps more realistic look.

Deconstructing Text

People sometimes describe the work they need to get done in writing. This testimony can become the basis from which to derive an early iteration of a work breakdown structure.

Here's a paragraph from an email I received from violinist Charys Schuler, of the Frankfurt String Sextet, telling me how her group prepares for concerts.

> *We've found a way of putting on these concerts that works well for us, and everyone pitches in. Ingrid acts as our business head and agent, pitching artistic directors and negotiating fees. Christiana*

> *researches repertoire for us, and coordinates getting the sheet music.*
> *Akemi coordinates rehearsal spaces and schedules. She and I prepare*
> *scores with bowings and plan rehearsals. Maja is a great writer, so she*
> *does our programs, concert introductions, and other written materials.*
> *And Kerstin is in charge of snacks.*

Her sense was that this works pretty well, though there was something just a little haphazard about it. Seeing it organized as a WBS might help to clarify it for them, so that they can consider whether they are missing anything.

The first step in doing this is to hunt for potential deliverables or types of work. These tend to be nouns. Here's the paragraph with the likely nouns highlighted.

> *We've found a way of putting on these* **concerts** *that works well for us,*
> *and* **everyone** *pitches in. Ingrid acts as our* **business head** *and* **agent**,
> **pitch***ing* **artistic directors** *and negotiating* **fees**. *Christiana researches*
> **repertoire** *for us, and coordinates getting the* **sheet music**. *Akemi coor-*
> *dinates* **rehearsal spaces** *and* **schedules**. *She and I prepare* **scores** *with*
> **bowings** *and lead* **rehearsals**. *Maja is a great* **writer**, *so she does our*
> **programs**, **concert introductions**, *and other* **written materials**. *And*
> *Kerstin is in charge of* **snacks**.

These deliverables then get isolated in list form, to clear away the clutter of the descriptive text:

concerts	schedules	writer
everyone	repertoire	programs
business head/agent	sheet music	concert introductions
artistic director pitch	scores	written materials
fees	bowings	snacks
rehearsal spaces	rehearsals	

When you have a list of work like this, you can put the items in a hierarchy, so that you can see them. In writing, there is likely some redundancy, some things that are beside the point, and such, but there might also be some natural organization built in, particularly in this case where the paragraph was describing the roles of specific people.

With some fiddling, some inferring, some wild guesses, and some references back to the paragraph to understand the logic, we arrive at the beginnings of a work breakdown structure.

concerts	music	rehearsals
project management	potential repertoire	rehearsal spaces
resource assignment	final repertoire	snacks
personnel	sheet music	written materials
financial/legal	scores	programs
artistic director pitch	bowings	introductions
fees		
scheduling		

This isn't complete, but it forms a place from which to begin the conversation, and in doing that, we can uncover some details of the undertaking that might slip through the cracks. In translating the paragraph into the WBS hierarchy, I assumed, for example, that the snacks were for the rehearsals and not the concerts. I'd want to confirm this with her and ask whether reception snacks also get coordinated. Will Kerstin do those too? And what about coordinating the concert hall to perform in? That wasn't mentioned in her paragraph. Were we to circulate it to the others in the sextet, we'd likely get much more helpful feedback. Maja might chime in that she writes press releases too. And so on.

The conversation has begun, and we can use the WBS as an easy reference point to see all the work.

Step-by-Step Modeling

Another way to flush out potential work is imagining step-by-step what the user's experience will be. The starting point is the person using the system or product; the end point is that person's goal. Then, describe in a sequence of short and descriptive sentences the actions that are required for the person to achieve their goal. Diagram them, if you like. This can be a solitary meditation exercise, a group brainstorming exercise, or any number of steps in between.

The danger in this type of modeling is that it works at a very low level of detail, which can be distracting at the planning stages of a project, yielding too fine a level of detail for the WBS. The top-down deliverables-oriented model of the WBS is generally considered to be the superior approach to begin with, as a primary means of shaping the work to be done. However, step-by-step modeling can be a useful secondary exercise, particularly for uncovering subtle vulnerabilities. If you don't do it during the planning phases, do it when you are a little farther along, such as during quality control or risk assessment.

This approach is particularly good for fine-tuning requirements for building complex systems, such as administrative bureaucracies or software systems. Particularly for software development, formal "UML Use Cases" are helpful, though beyond the scope of this book, so you might look into them if that is your aim. But these tools can apply to many types of work. In some graphics programs, such as OmniGraffle, icons for doing these step-by-step diagrams are included in a UML category.

Course Placement System Example

To see how this bottoms-up approach might play out, here's a use case model showing what a student's experience might be in signing up for a new course at a music school. In this type of work modeling, the person initiating the activity (i.e., the student) is the "primary actor," those who react to actions initiated by others are "secondary actors," the activity being tested is the "case," and the whole system is the "scenario." In a formal "use case," you are describing a single type of activity within a system: a single "case" of how it is "used."

Here, a student (primary actor) wants to enroll for a new course called "Piano Lab 1." What is required? How must the student interact with the school's bureaucratic system (that we are building, as our project) in order to actually accomplish this?

1. The student desires to sign up for a course and goes to the school's website. We start by drawing the primary actor (student) and their desired outcome (course). We indicate the student with a little stick figure (okay, dress him up if you like), the system as a large box, and the course—our object in the system—as an oval.

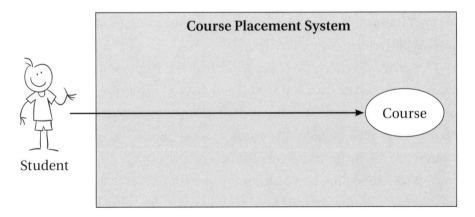

FIG. 3.12. Modeling Step 1: Actor and Result

2. To sign up, the student must first read an online catalog description of *Piano Lab 1*. He will then either have questions or sign up, using the online scheduling tool. If the student has questions, he will contact the academic advisor—a secondary actor. The academic advisor meets with the student, answers questions, and guides the student towards taking a relevant course, perhaps helping him use the scheduling tool. If the student has no questions, he will use the scheduler himself.

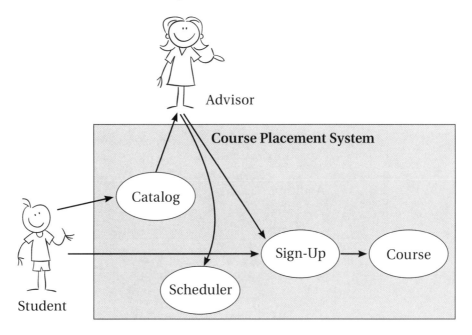

FIG. 3.13. Modeling Step 2

3. The sign-up mechanism launches the online Placement Auditions Scheduler, which in conjunction with the Admissions Committee, coordinates an audition date for the student. As a result of this audition, an Audition Scorecard is generated, which informs the exact section of the course the student can take. The instructor will also use this scorecard to help adjust the curriculum. With each step, the diagram gets more intricate, and new items of necessary work are revealed.

And it continues. Every detail is described, the goal being that you want to uncover every single task necessary to complete this dimension of the project. Nouns and verbs are what you want to pay attention to here: the nouns are the objects in the system (often, product features or necessary resources, and often WBS items) and the verbs are tasks or activities that must take place.

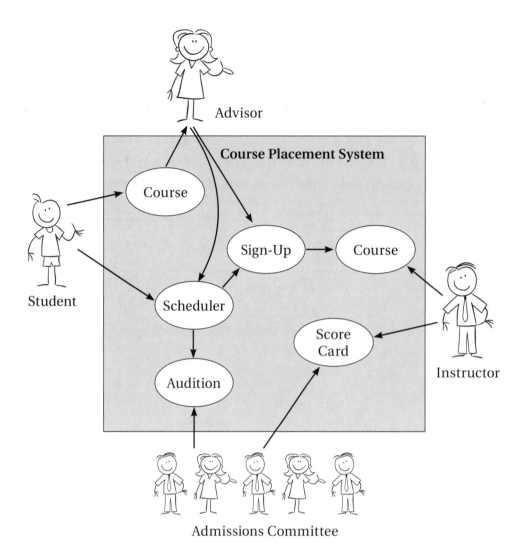

FIG. 3.14. Modeling Step 3

Review all the steps, preferably with someone else or your team, and see if there are any obvious holes. For example, it might say that the admissions committee's involvement in the scenario is triggered by the scheduler, but it isn't clear by what mechanism. A letter? A calender update? Are we certain that the student will be free on that date? That all has to be figured out, at some point, and then integrated into the system.

The narrative path here should be between the client or other system user and their desired objective. In this case, the student's goal is to learn to play piano. What torture must he endure to obtain that? Will he ever get what he wants? This type of exercise can help answer those questions. And it can also reveal to you something that is so awkward and flawed that it needs to be dramatically reimagined.

This step-by-step imagining process is a great help towards understanding the experience that will be had by your potential user/customer/audience member.

Push the boundaries of what you think can be described in these simple terms, to clarify your grasp of how your project is really going to work out.

Here's a broader example of imagining a user's experience step-by-step: a concert set list, very simplified:

Tune 1: Fast, danceable

Tune 2: Sad ballad

Tune 3: Sad blues

Tune 4: Hard rock anthem

Tune 5: Funny story song

Looking at this list, in such grotesquely simplified terms, might inspire you to make some changes, to keep the audience more interested or more energized. Do we really want two sad songs there, back to back? Do we want to end funny?

For Emily's EP, a step-by-step list might be a buyer's experience receiving and playing the EP:

Receive EP in yellow envelope

Open envelope, throw it away

Receive postcard advertisement with $5 coupon off T-shirt on website

Throw away coupon

Receive EP

Open shrink wrap

Throw away shrink wrap

See booklet

Pop EP out of jewel case too hard and break the hinge

Insert EP in player

Tune 1: Rock ballad

Read lyrics in CD case

Tune 2: ....

Love it and want more info, so find band URL on postcard (or did we throw that away?)

Go to website...

It's helpful to go through these exercises with your thought partners, in formal sessions, trying to uncover all the details that need to be addressed. You might discover that you resent the litter you're creating, that you hate jewel cases, and that there are too many pieces of paper to track, here.

Go step by step: what is the work really? Who is the client, and what's the thing of value they are trying to get? Zoom in, zoom out, focusing on details and on over-arching visions.

Generally, in project management, you are always considering two levels of planning: the big picture of the project plan and the smaller plan of the immediate work before you. Those have to be in sync, and you have to consider them more or less simultaneously. So, go through these exercises, and then bring back any significant details you uncover, to revise your WBS and scope statement (after getting appropriate buy-in).

While there is the danger of distraction, when you dip a toe in these waters, anything bringing you closer to your customer's experience seems like a benefit. The detailed step-by-step process of going through the experience of the users or of otherwise addressing the work can help provide a clearer and more realistic picture of the work that lies ahead.

CONTENT AND ACTION BREAKDOWNS

Once our project has been elaborated down to the level of a work packet, we can begin planning the nitty-gritty of what actually gets done. Two ways to approach this are to break down the work by *content* and by *action* (discussed on the next page).

Content Breakdowns

Content breakdowns are creative tools we use for building things. They are the business of individual creators, rather than teams, so this level of detail isn't included in project management documents, but it is a similar process, so I'll include it.

One type of Emily's work packets is the songs. To break down the work required for writing a song, she might organize it like this:

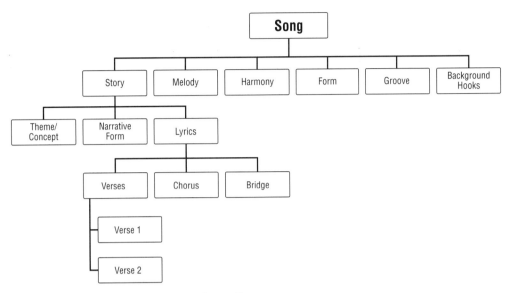

FIG. 3.15. Content Breakdown: Song Structure

Another type of breakdown structure is to analyze equipment needs. Here's a gear breakdown for a home studio. There are two different types of relationships here: "is a" and "has a." They are useful in different contexts, and which way you favor will yield somewhat different results. It's best to be as consistent as you can, just switching at the very last level, if you are employing both within a chart.

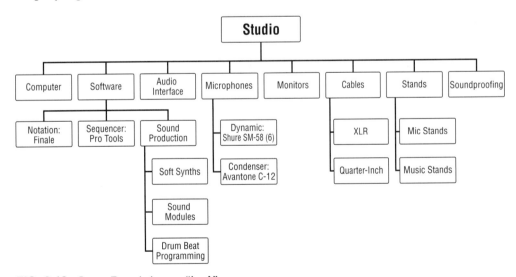

FIG. 3.16. Gear Breakdown: "Is A"

Next, we show the same information favoring "has a" relationships. Here, it is a little easier to see how the system fits together, and you can trace needs systemically. At the last level, it switches to an "is a" relationship. While it might make locating specific items on the chart a little more confusing, there is more logic involved in figuring out what is needed, so it might help you reveal some potentially forgettable object. If you are figuring out equipment needs, you might favor this arrangement. Tracing the system, you might remember that your vocal microphones will require pop filters, for example.

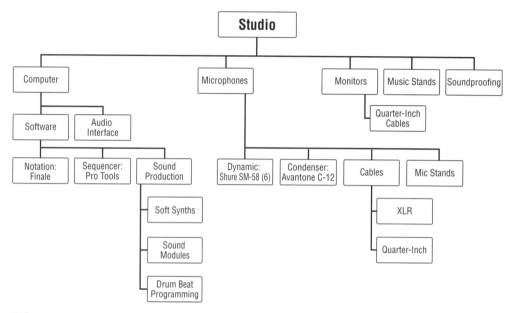

FIG. 3.17. Gear Breakdown: "Has A"

These breakdown charts readily transform into checklists, help predict budgets, and help mitigate risk. We will rely on them throughout the process.

Action Breakdowns/Task Lists

When you get to a terminal end of a WBS thread, arriving at a work packet, it is time to figure out the tasks associated with completing this work packet. This is called an *activity breakdown,* or a *task list.* These itemizations of the work to be done are among the very most important components of your planning. It is at this level of detail that many other specific tools come about: budgeting, scheduling, resource assignment, and so on. It needs to be logical and complete. The better this list is, the more likely your project will be to succeed.

To make a task list for a given deliverable, step by step, answer the question, "What's the next action required to move this forward?"

If you are delegating the work, the flow of the tasks will likely correspond to a general project management flow: Initiating, Planning, Executing, Monitoring and Controlling, Closing.

For example, the task list required to create the CD booklet cover art might unfold like this.

Initiating	Emily writes spec for cover art
Planning	Emily writes letter of agreement with designer
	Emily emails spec and LOA to designer
	Designer signs LOA
	Emily and designer discuss the project in depth
Execution/Monitoring/Controlling	Designer creates samples and emails them to Emily
	Band reviews art samples and gives feedback to Emily
	Emily collates feedback and sends it to designer
	Designer revises art and emails new versions
	Emily chooses final version
Closing	Designer emails invoice
	Designer mails hard copy of final art, plus electronic files
	Emily pays invoice

FIG. 3.18. Emily Task List (Organized by Project Phase)

If Emily is drawing up a task list for something she will do herself, such as writing the songs, it probably won't have all these steps. Still, it might be useful for her to break down the tasks, for purposes of estimating and organizing her time.

Go hiking to get inspiration for songs

Write song 1

Create voice/guitar demo of song 1

Send demo to band for feedback

Revise song 1

Write song 2....

Tasks in Software WBSs

If you are using project management software, the task list might wind up being just another level (or multiple levels) of the work breakdown structure. Here's another example from Smartsheet showing an elaboration of producing the booklet cover.

Here, you can see that "1.2.2.1. Cover Design" is a work packet, and under it, we have a task, which is to write the design spec (1.2.2.1.1). Typically, the required task's level will evolve as the project moves forward, particularly during execution, when new tasks become evident. We're anticipating two rounds of design review (see figure 3.19), but it is likely that there will be more than that, in which case we'd add mockup procedures for rounds C, D, or whatever is required. In the software, each line can be given management functionality, such as triggering emails to the person assigned to the task, attaching files, storing conversations, and many other types of capabilities, depending on the software. Project management execution occurs at the task level.

Task Name	Assigned To
1.2.2. Booklet Cover	
1.2.2.1. Cover Design	
1.2.2.1.1. Write Spec for Designer	Emily
1.2.2.2. Designer LOA	
1.2.2.1.1. Send Designer LOA	Emily
1.2.2.1.2. Send Spec and LOA to designer	Emily
1.2.2.1.3. Get Signed LOA	Emily
1.2.2.3. Cover Design Meeting	
1.2.2.3.1. Circulate Potential Photographs	Designer
1.2.2.3.2. Schedule Meeting	Emily
1.2.2.3.3. Meeting	
1.2.2.4. Cover Mockups A	
1.2.2.4.1. Band Cover Feedback A	Band
1.2.2.4.2. Feedback A Sent to Designer	Emily
1.2.2.5. Art Mockups B	Emily
1.2.2.6. Final Version Selected	Emily
1.2.2.7. Designer Invoice	Emily
1.2.2.7.1. Invoice Requested	Emily
1.2.2.7.2. Invoice Received	Emily
1.2.2.7.3. Invoice Paid	Emily
1.2.2.8. Delivery of Final Art, including electronic files	Designer

FIG. 3.19. Task List in Smartsheet

The grammar might change based on your tools. For example, in Smartsheet, the name of who is completing the task typically gets stored in the "Assigned To" column, so you wouldn't include it in the task description.

We will keep coming back to these task lists throughout the book.

WBS DICTIONARY

A dictionary of components might accompany the work breakdown structure. This is particularly the case for very large projects that involve many different parts. It provides more information on each component of the WBS. Whereas the WBS is intended as an easy way to see the project broadly and observe how the parts interact, the WBS dictionary provides more detailed information about each item.

The exact structure of the dictionary varies. In figure 3.7, we saw a very bare-bones model, just listing each item with code numbers and descriptions. Even this simple format is useful, as it clarifies the difference between administration and project management, which might not be apparent to someone just looking at the table.

A more detailed WBS dictionary would include more information, perhaps a full page for some items. The following details are fairly standard.

- WBS code and label
- description
- owner
- objectives
- schedule milestones
- cost estimates
- other resources required
- functional requirements to be fulfilled
- technical requirements for completing the task
- overall purpose

Figure 3.19 is a more detailed dictionary entry for one of Emily's components: demo recordings.

Item: 1.1.2. Demo Recordings   **Owner:** Emily

Description: Demo recordings are informal keyboard/voice versions of the songs
                                 designed to give the band an idea of what the overall vibe of the song
                                 is.

Schedule: All delivered between 11/15 and 12/19, 2011
Cost Estimates: N/A
Resources Required: Three 2-hour sessions in home studio
Objectives:
- Communicate how the expressive goals of lyrics and music interact
- Provide a starting point at which the band will produce an arrangement together
- Present the song to the band so that they can offer feedback regarding lyrics, melody, and harmony

Functional Requirements:
- Detailed but draft lyrics, melody, harmony, and groove
- Sample arrangement ideas

Technical Requirements:
- MP3 file
- Available in Emily's "EP Songs" Dropbox folder
- Also includes lead sheet with lyrics

Purpose:
- Demos are intended as the first deliverable of each song and the point at which to begin their discussion and development.
- They are designed to communicate basic ideas to the band, and then undergo further iterations and improvements.

FIG. 3.20. Detailed WBS Dictionary Entry

Even for smaller projects, creating a WBS dictionary gives the project manager the opportunity to focus on each component and work out some details. You could add or subtract other types of information as well: dependencies, specific quality requirements, acceptance criteria, contract information, and so on. It can serve as a general place to organize existential information about your project deliverables.

In smaller project contexts, this document might only be used by the project manager, and never shared with anyone else. In larger projects, this document might be indispensable, and referenced as a bible throughout an organization.

Another purpose, in some projects, is to ensure continuity of the work should the role of project manager be replaced. A replacement manager would rely heavily on this document, in the event of a succession. It's good practice to create them with this potentiality in mind, if the project would go on without you.

The WBS dictionary could be a document, a database, or a document that is a printout of a database. It might be arranged alphabetically by deliverable or ordered much like the WBS itself. It is another flexible tool, and again, you should adapt it to be useful and germane to your own situation. Like the WBS, it can evolve as your project evolves. Project scope changes, and this tool can involve a lot of time to create. To avoid creating obsolete entries, it should be elaborated only as the deliverables become confirmed, and as they are required to be discussed or explored.

CLOSING THOUGHTS

Lewis Carroll wrote the story of a king trying to find the ideal scale for his country's official map. At ten miles per inch, it wasn't detailed enough, so they went through multiple finer iterations: five miles per inch, one mile per inch, one mile per foot, and so on, until they arrived at a map that was the same size as the country itself! Alas, the farmers complained that if anyone were to ever unfold it, their crops would fail, so the project was abandoned.

So, how detailed should our plans be? A balanced, common practice is to maintain a general plan for the entire project, and fill in the details as it becomes evident to you exactly what you need to control precisely. Assume that any detailed work on project dimensions beyond your immediate horizon will likely be revised significantly. You can always dream, and plans improve as they are iterated, so it's not necessarily an entirely wasted effort to sketch details of any dimension of your project, but your efforts will be more fruitful if you focus on what's before you currently. Break down the whole project generally, and then fill in the details as the business at hand (cost/time estimating, assigning workers, etc.) requires it.

This ability to imagine work realistically is one of the most important skills a project manager can develop. It's worth practicing. Whenever someone suggests an idea, on any topic, grab whatever scrap of paper is closest, and sketch out what is truly involved. Often, doing this can shut down a crackpot. Better, though, this exercise can bridge vague pipe-dream suggestions of "someone should do something about this" into an actionable plan. It brings seemingly incomprehensibly difficult undertakings into the realm of possibility.

PRACTICE

1. **Big.** Create a WBS for your project, including:

   - elaboration of the project's components to three levels, but with one thread fully decomposed to its ultimate work packets

   - WBS dictionary entries for three work packets

   - a task list for one terminal work packet

   Update your scope statement if this process reveals anything new.

2. **Little.** Create a WBS for a possible micro-iteration of your big project. Elaborate it as far as you like, but at least to three levels.

CHAPTER 4

Finances

In this chapter, we will explore some strategies for understanding and controlling finances of a project. We will examine some essential forms to help estimate and track project expenses, and see how to connect your financial practices to your overall project vision.

OBJECTIVES

By the end of the chapter, you will be able to:

- estimate your project cost and set up a budget
- use essential accounting forms to track income and expenses
- set sales targets to make your products profitable

PROJECT ACCOUNTING OVERVIEW

The goal of financial management is to make sure that you are spending in accordance with your means. Think of it in four stages.

1. Estimate your project's expenses and assets/income.
2. Make sure that you have the money to cover your expenses.
3. Execute your project while tracking every transaction and making sure that you stay within budget.
4. Finish your project and brag to everyone that you didn't go over budget. Take the band out to dinner, just to rub it in their faces.

There is constant pressure for projects to go over budget. It's a universal truth. Undertakings always cost more than anticipated. The consequences for going over budget can be significant: requirement to take on debt, cancellation of parts of the project, loss of reputation, bankruptcy, and so on. If you're working on a simple project with limited consequences for going over budget, use it as practice, so that when you do a larger project next time, the tools and processes will be familiar.

Project financial management happens within the context of your overall business and life. You pay taxes based on the calendar year, rather than your project plan. Projects often span multiple calendar years. So, the details of the project are a *view* of your overall life's financial picture—a way of looking at and organizing a portion of your overall situation. You might work as a real estate mogul during the day and have a blues band at night. If the band's CD loses a few hundred bucks, it's not the end of the world. Parsing these streams can require some effort.

For most of us, there is value in tracking project finances. Beyond being prepared for an IRS audit, understanding the details of how the money actually worked out for the project will inform decisions later on regarding whether and how to do similar projects in the future. So, there's benefit to isolating these expenses from overall business or other life expenses. Some financial planners recommend setting aside different "buckets" of money for specific projects, like $15,000 to produce a CD, perhaps in its own bank account.

Financial management software, such as QuickBooks, makes this much easier, as do good online banking services, such as ING Direct. That said, such programs often have such vast levels of detail and possibilities that it is easy to get lost regarding what information is priority and actionable.

In this lesson, I will focus on the most essential accounting tools. There are essentially three types of financial documents that accountants use to monitor finances:

- registers (or ledgers)

- summaries

- reports

Transaction Registers

Registers record every transaction, and thus, your project register is the most basic and fundamental financial mechanism. They provide the most detail of any financial statement, organized by date. Ideally, they show items and their *accounts*—the type or category of transaction. You will probably have a single register for all financial transactions in your business.

Your checkbook and credit card statements are types of registers. If you do nothing else, keep a register of your transactions—including what you pay using cash, check, credit card, PayPal, and so on.

Registers are sometimes made much more useful by including a column showing a running balance, at the right. You could also start with an opening balance, if you've devoted a nugget of money to your project and want to have a quick look at how that's going. A few lines from a transaction register for Emily's tour might look like this. (Note: The reality of Emily's actual tour finances are entirely different from what I present as examples in this book, both to create simple illustrations and to protect her privacy. But let's pretend, for the sake of the discussion, that this is how it all went down.)

Date	Description	Comment	Account	Amount	Balance
11/1/2011	Opening Balance	raised via IndieGoGo	Donations	5,000	5000
12/22/2011	Loud Enough Studios	recording and mixing CD	CD Production	–2,200	2,800
1/15/2012	Claudia's T-Shirts	200 shirts	Merchandise	–500	2,300
1/17/2012	R. T. Finn Mastering	CD master (deposit)	CD Production	–500	1,800
1/18/2012	Four George Photo	band photos	Ads	–500	1,300
1/25/2012	R. T. Finn Mastering	CD master (balance)	CD Production	–700	600
2/1/2012	Dup House	1,000 CDs	CD Production	–1,000	**–400**
2/8/2012	Merlino Design	graphic design for flyers	Ads	–125	**–525**
2/10/2012	FooFoo Copies	1000 flyers	Ads	–125	**–650**
2/15/2012	Lounge Lillian	fee	Performance	300	**–350**
2/15/2012	Lounge Lillian (cash)	50% door	Performance	106	**–244**
2/15/2012	Lounge Lillian (cash)	sold 4 t-shirts, 2 CDs	Merchandise	80	**–164**

FIG. 4.1. Transaction Register

As you can see in the Balance column, things are looking a little grim, though they get better once the actual tour starts.

There are two points of housekeeping regarding registers I want to mention.

First, they should be reconciled monthly with bank statements and credit cards, to be sure that neither you nor your bank made any errors.

Second, be sure to track all cash transactions, as we do with the door income and merch sales, above (separate from fees paid be venues, which are via check).

Cash easily slips through our fingers, but it is as important to track its whereabouts as it is to track checks. Avoid paying with cash, if you can. Credit cards and checks are also tracked by their banks, which makes record keeping and future research easier.

Summaries

Summaries show us all the transactions organized by *account* (expense categories or types), to help you track what each dimension of that project costs. Financial management software generally lets us view account summaries automatically, if we assigned accounts to each transaction in our register. You can also program Excel to assign account tags, or you could simply do it manually.

Summaries are necessary in part because of the laws of physics—only so much can fit on a page and remain legible. A standard 8.5 x 11–inch piece of paper can legibly show about 55 lines of text, but a project might include hundreds or thousands of transactions. Summaries let us present a higher-level view of the finances and get an overview all on a single page, even for vast projects. Obviously, summaries must correspond to the transaction register with 100 percent accuracy. This is not an issue with software-driven accounting, but if you are managing financial documents manually, without linked documents in financial software, whenever the transaction register changes, all derivative documents become obsolete and need to be updated.

Account Summary for Emily's EP

CD PRODUCTION

12/22/2011	Loud Enough Studios	recording and mixing CD	CD Production	2,200
1/17/2012	R. T. Finn Mastering	CD master (deposit)	CD Production	500
1/25/2012	R. T. Finn Mastering	CD master (balance)	CD Production	700
2/1/2012	Dup House	1,000 CDs	CD Production	1,000
				Total $4,400

MERCHANDISE

1/15/2012	Max T-Shirts	200 Shirts	Merchandise	500
				Total $500

ADS

1/18/2012	Four George Photo	Band photos	Ads	500
2/8/2012	Merlino Design	graphic design for flyers	Ads	125
2/10/2012	FooFoo Copies	1000 flyers	Ads	125
				Total $750

FIG. 4.2. Summary: Subdivided by Account

Alternatively, you might see the register laid out with the accounts in columns. This is a bit more difficult to give a complete picture on standard 8.5 x 11 paper, but it provides a clear way to scan a spreadsheet and see transactions of similar types. Orient the page in landscape mode, to fit more columns, and if you can, print on 11 x 17 paper, if it gets too wide.

An old accounting trick: total each column, and also keep a running total in each row. Then, calculate the overall total in two ways: at the bottom ("foot" in accounting parlance) of the running total column, and then by totaling all your column totals together. This is called *cross-footing*, and it is an opportunity to double-check your math. As an abstract concept, cross-footing many types of calculation, analysis, or other types of activity can help control and confirm the accuracy of many kinds of endeavor—viewing it from multiple angles, and seeing whether you arrive at the same conclusion.

Date	Vendor	Ads	CD Production	Merch	Total
12/22/2011	Loud Enough Studios		2,200		2,200
1/15/2012	Claudia's T-Shirts			500	2,700
1/17/2012	R. T. Finn Mastering		500		3,200
1/18/2012	Four George Photo	500			3,700
1/25/2012	R. T. Finn Mastering		700		4,400
2/1/2012	Dup House		1,000		5,400
2/8/2012	Merlino Design	125			5,525
2/10/2012	FooFoo Copies	125			5,650
2/10/2012	**Total**	**750**	**4,400**	**500**	**5,650**

FIG. 4.3. Summary: Accounts in Columns

Reports

Reports use summaries of the transaction data to help you get an overall view of how the project is going. There are many types of reports. Central to project accounting are *profit/loss statements*. These summarize your assets (what you've got or expect) and liabilities (funds that you pay or expect to pay), and give you the bottom line: whether or not you are financially on track.

Here's a simplified P&L statement for a band tour like what Emily might do. You can see the amount for that account budgeted for the project, how much money was actually spent, and the difference. The total difference is your indication of how the project is going, overall. By keeping this up to date, you can make future decisions on the project that will help bring finances back in line, if necessary. If a tour is losing money (overall, actual expenses are greater than what you had budgeted), for example, you might take austerity measures (pizza instead of sushi; sleep at a friend's house instead of a hotel), or try to rush and do more publicity, or try to find an additional gig on the way. If it's going unusually well, you might start thinking about a celebratory dinner, after the project is done. The point is to be aware of how it's going while there is still time to change course, if necessary. The % Variance column gives you an overall sense of how you're doing—how far off budget you are.

	Budget	Actual	Difference	% Variance
Income				
Donations	5,620	7,270	1,650	29%
Merch Sales	530	600	70	13%
Performance	1,350	1,486	136	10%
Total Income	**7,500**	**9,356**	**1856**	**35%**
Expenses				
CD Production	6,000	5,400	600	10%
Merch	750	668	82	11%
Art	750	700	50	7%
Total Expenses	**7,500**	**6,768**	**732**	**10%**
Total	0	2,588	2,588	

FIG. 4.4. P/L Statement

Notice that the total for the budget is zero. This means the budget is *balanced*: the projected income equals the projected expenses. That's good! But the way we made this balance out is by finding the minimum number we must raise in donations. Overall, we came out 13 percent ahead of where we had anticipated. Perhaps a more useful number, though, is to realize how far off we were regarding what donations we could rake in. Next time around, we can take notice of that, and be secure in estimating a bit higher, there.

BUDGETS

A project's viability depends on our estimating costs accurately and then making sure there are sufficient funds to cover these costs. This begins with a process of trying to reach realistic estimates. The work breakdown structure turns out to be a useful starting tool for estimating what our aspirations will cost. Let's look at a partial WBS for Emily's tour.

1. Emily's EP Tour
   1.1. Project Management
       1.1.1. Scheduling
       1.1.2. Accounting
       1.1.3. Staffing
   1.2. Music
       1.2.1. Programming
       1.2.2. Rehearsals
   1.3. Art
       1.3.1. Promotional Photography
       1.3.2. Ads
   1.4. Merchandise
       1.4.1. CDs
       1.4.2. T-Shirts
       1.4.3. Person at Merch Table
       1.4.4. Merch Table
   1.5. Wardrobe
   1.6. Travel
       1.6.1. Accommodations
       1.6.2. Gas
       1.6.3. Food

FIG. 4.5. Work Breakdown Structure Used in Report

We also set up a WBS dictionary for this project. It's got the various types of information we've discussed, but for purposes of this discussion, we'll only provide the essentials and include estimated cost, with a description (that would be rolled into the general description, not labeled "cost description").

The next step is critical and complex: estimating costs for each item of the WBS. For now, focus on just filling in the terminal ends—the final work packet for each thread. Some WBS objects will have obvious costs (add a dollar amount), some obviously won't cost anything (mark "N/A" for "not applicable"), and some will have costs, but you are not yet ready to make a realistic estimate (mark "?"). Some objects are going to be composites of other fields; those are good candidates for account names, listed in financial transactions. Keeping consistency between the WBS and the financial documents will help keep the whole project organized.

Level	Code	Title	Cost Description	Estimated Cost
1	1.	EP Tour	5 gigs in 7 days	
2	1.1.	Project Management		N/A
3	1.1.1.	Scheduling		N/A
3	1.1.2.	Accounting		N/A
3	1.1.3.	Staffing	Info for 4 musicians (including Emily) and 1 assistant/roadie	N/A
2	1.2.	Music		N/A
3	1.2.1.	Programming		N/A
3	1.2.2.	Rehearsals		N/A
2	1.3.	Art		
3	1.3.1.	Promotional Photography		$500
3	1.3.2.	Ads		$250
2	1.4.	Merchandise		
3	1.4.1.	CDs	Production: $10,325 Replication/500 CDs: $6,480	$16,805
3	1.4.2.	T-Shirts	Replication of 200	$500
3	1.4.3.	Person at Merch Table		N/A
3	1.4.4.	Merch Table	Found at the dump	N/A
2	1.5.	Wardrobe		?
2	1.6.	Travel	5 people, 7 days	
3	1.6.1.	Accommodations	$75 per room in a cheap hotel	$2,100
3	1.6.2.	Gas		$205
3	1.6.3.	Food	$40 per diem each	$1,400

FIG. 4.6. WBS Items Evolving into Financial Report

Many of the final, terminal items of the deliverables will have an associated task list with them, where we can get a finer level of detail regarding what the costs will be.

How to Estimate

Here are some ways to improve your odds towards arriving at realistic estimates.

Reference past experience. If you've ever done something like this before, what did it cost? Perhaps you have already created and sold t-shirts, and know that you can get them for $5 each, plus an initial setup charge.

Get bids. Contact potential vendors, describe the project, and get a detailed estimate from them. Ask them over and over, "Are there any additional costs?"

Ask a guru. Talk to someone else who has done it before, and grill them regarding what hidden expenses you are likely to miss. If they'll share an old invoice with you, that's ideal. Invoices are often an interesting window into how various businesses organize their own financial activities.

The number you arrive at from any of these sources is an assumption. You won't know exactly how much it will cost until you've paid the vendor. Why? Because there are likely to be unexpected or deliberately hidden costs associated with many types of transactions. And modifications to your needs might pop up, like an unexpected need to pay for rush shipment, not to mention instances of scope creep.

Consider t-shirts, for example. You might get a quote for $5 per unit to produce 200 shirts, which comes to $1,000. But here are some questions, on the left, and some likely additional costs should the answer come out against you.

Possible Unexpected Cost	Amount
Does this include shipping? Will the timing be such that you have to pay for overnight shipping, just to make absolutely positive that they arrive in time?	$80
Is the design work included?	$150
Is there a setup fee for the screen-printing?	$50
Are you guaranteed 200 usable shirts, or is there an expectation that a percentage will be damaged in the process? Do they print (and charge you for) a few extras, just to be sure that you'll get at least 200?	$25
Will you have to overnight them a corrected hard copy of an art proof?	$15
Do you have to ship the shirts somewhere after you receive them? If so, will you pay for repackaging and postage?	$80
Is this dimension of the project being managed by a designer who will add a percent of the units purchased to his or her fee? While this is uncommon for t-shirt sales, it is very common for other types of endeavor (engineers renting gear, construction contractors buying supplies, etc.), so humor me.	$200
Is sales tax included?	$70
Total	**$670**

FIG. 4.7. Incidental Expenses

Ouch! Depending on how these answers go, you might end up paying a bit more than you expect. For that reason, when you estimate costs, it is recommended that you add a *contingency* amount to what you think your number will be. This is a pessimistic amount above the price that your research told you to expect. Fifty percent isn't unreasonable, particularly if it is something you've never bought before, or from an untried vendor. When you draw up a budget, note the percentage contingency you are using.

Again, the WBS and associated task list can be helpful in getting a clearer picture. Some tasks will have possible costs, and others won't, but by considering the likely way that the work will unfold, you can uncover some potential additional costs. For example, here, we uncover some previously undetected mailing costs, and also allow for the fact that the artist might use some stock images in her design. A task list for making t-shirts, with associated estimated costs, might look like this:

Task	Estimated Cost
Brainstorm design concepts	
Choose graphic artist	
Choose t-shirt printing company	
Finalize terms with graphic artist	
Finalize terms with t-shirt company	
Describe design concept to graphic artist	
Get three potential art concepts	
Choose one and suggest modifications	
Arrive at final design	
Pay graphic artist	150
Pay any stock art costs	25
Mail final files and hard copy to t-shirt company	12
Pay 50% deposit to t-shirt company	500
T-shirt company sends us proof and sample shirt	
Mark any corrections on proof and mail them back to t-shirt company	12
T-shirt company ships shirts	
Pay balance to t-shirt company	500
Total	**$1,199**

FIG. 4.8. Using Task List to Uncover Hidden Expenses

We're trying to predict what our actual transaction register will look like.

Unfortunately, experience is among the most important factors in how you improve at estimating. Until then, you have to consider and ferret out the subtle ways that prices might work out to be more than you expect. This isn't to say that vendors are trying to rip you off. It's just that the work is nearly always more complicated and more expensive than it appears at first glance.

Income

Funding for your project can have various sources. Before you finish/launch, you might have savings, you might have an annual budget, each member of your band might kick in some cash into a pot, or you might apply for grants. You might get a job to fund it, or a small business loan, or a rich aunt.

Then, hopefully, the project will result in income. Tracking that income might or might not be a part of the project itself, depending on where you draw the line. A concert or a tour will hopefully involve ticket sales during the project execution, and depending on how the income is flowing, you might make changes of scope (e.g., doing some emergency additional advertising, or scaling back of expenses). On the other hand, if the project is to create an object, such as an album or recording studio, you might want to manage sales as "ongoing business as usual."

There are websites that are devoted to raising cash for projects, such as Kickstarter, Indiegogo, and others. The specifics of funding possibilities are vast and personal and beyond the reach of this book. But you need to understand how much you can afford before you start spending.

This might seem an obvious point—to spend within your means—but if everyone heeded this common sense principle, the world would be a profoundly different place, free from credit card debt and a multi-trillion dollar national deficit.

You need to come up with a number to represent the financial resources you can devote to the project. It will be part savings, maybe part loan, and if you are extremely well informed, predicted income from sales of the products that results from your project. Later in this chapter, we will see how to anticipate what to expect, regarding product profitability and how sales relate to income.

Similar to expenses, specify assets/income in your P&L.

Preliminary Budget Report

The preliminary budget is a type of P&L that summarizes your expected income and expenses, and it will eventually be used as the basis for the actual P&L statement, used when the cash starts flowing.

This one includes the dimension of time. In general accounting, a P&L might have columns for each month. In a project, you might instead have columns for specific milestones, such as specific days of a tour.

This budget lists all the objects from Emily's WBS where there are possible dollar amounts, plus a few other items, and then for columns, it lists each day of the tour. You might choose to include a note about where these numbers came from. Here, we indicate that we've already paid the photography expenses, so that's a real number, and we're adding a twenty-five percent contingency to the t-shirt estimate because we've never done that before and are flying by the seats of our pants, with that number.

Title	Pre Tour	3/1	3/2	3/3	3/4	3/5	3/6	3/7	Estimated Total
INCOME									
Contributions	5,000								5,000
Performance									
Fee			300	500	500	300	250		1,850
Door			100	0	200	100	100		500
Merchandise									
CDs			50	70	70	50	50		290
T-Shirts			30	50	50	30	30	50	240
Total Income	**5,000**	**0**	**480**	**620**	**820**	**480**	**430**	**50**	**7,880**
EXPENSES									
Travel									
Accommodations		300	300	300	300	300	300	300	2,100
Gas		40	25	25	25	25	25	40	205
Food		200	200	200	200	200	200	200	1,400
Art									
Photography (already paid)	500								500
Ads	250								250
Merchandise									
CDs	16,805								16,805
T-Shirts (includes 25% contingency over quote)	750								750
Wardrobe	?								?
Total Expenses	**18,305**	**540**	**525**	**525**	**525**	**525**	**525**	**540**	**22,010**
Total	**-13,305**	**-540**	**-45**	**95**	**295**	**-45**	**-95**	**-450**	**-14,130**

FIG. 4.9. Project Budget

We subtract our projected expenses from our projected resources and arrive at a number. If it shows a loss, then we decide if that's a problem or not. Maybe, we have to raise more funds, or change the scope, find a different vendor, or do more precise research on something in order to tell if we are over-estimating costs. If it shows a profit, that's good, but we should still be wary about whether we are being realistic or overly optimistic. And while question marks remain on the page, this document is incomplete and we don't really know what our financial picture will be.

It's looking a little grim! For this project not to become financially problematic, some significant reconsideration of how to accomplish it will be necessary. (Fortunately, Emily did just that!)

Reducing Expenses

Here's a simple expense itemization for the tour. I'll plug in an estimate of $500 for wardrobe, just to avoid the distraction of that open loop for purposes of this discussion, but real life has open loops, and question marks like that help us to track gaping holes of assumptions.

EXPENSES	
Travel	
Accommodations	2,100
Gas	205
Meals	1,400
Art	
Photography (already paid)	500
Ads	250
Merchandise	
CDs	16,805
T-Shirts (includes 25% contingency above quote)	750
Wardrobe	500
Total	**22,510**

FIG. 4.10. Expense Itemization

That's the total anticipated project cost—the amount Emily needs to raise in order to pay for her vision. The venues she's going to play on the tour have committed to paying her a total of $1,850 (plus a percentage of the door), and that's nowhere near enough to cover what she has in mind. She had to find ways to reduce her expenses and/or to increase her available funds, if she doesn't want to accumulate debt to finance this endeavor.

What we have here is a brick wall of one of our three typical constraints: cost. The other two constraints are time and scope, and a way to work around any limiting factor is to consider ways to increase the other two dimensions, to make our old friend the triangle equilateral again.

Here are some ways to improve the current gloomy outlook:

Find angel donors. One of the great current trends in independent music production is that there are a number of organizations available that help artists get funding for projects. Specifically, this is called "crowd sourcing." Websites such as Kickstarter and Indiegogo facilitate people contributing funding to help artists in their work. You set up a page and invite everyone you know to support your efforts, and there's usually some sort of incentive program you can set up: donate $25, and I'll send you a free CD when it comes out. Donate $100, and you get a CD, a t-shirt, and a unique poem I'll write just for you. Donate $5,000 and you can come for free to every concert my band ever performs, forever.

Trade services. Talk to others in the industry whose services you need, and offer to barter favors. Through her connections and a series of interconnected favors too intricate to explain, Emily managed to get free studio time at an excellent recording facility, which greatly reduced her expenses.

Ask for favors. Rather than staying in hotels, she actually planned her tour to perform where she had friends at whose houses the band could crash. This is one of the benefits of being nice to everyone: people are then nice to you in return.

Reduce the project scope. Some dimensions of the project might not directly add value, and can be cut. For example, the wardrobe budget might be cut. Instead of providing a band with new tour outfits, you could simply describe a dress code that everyone will contribute themselves. Similarly, you could reduce props or special effects. Perhaps that fog machine isn't critical to the project, this time around. In really dire scenarios, you might need to reduce your staff, such as doing without a roadie or even a backup musician, but that's beginning to affect project quality, so it's a fairly desperate move.

Shop around. Other vendors might be cheaper, or offer services that ultimately might save money in the long run. Some mix engineers can also do mastering, and it can be less expensive to have the same person do both. That said, mastering is a fine art, and a dedicated mastering house is more likely to ensure a superior result, but it's possible what a given mix engineer could do is appropriate for your needs.

Consider slightly different scope. You might realize that you can achieve your goals in a slightly different way than originally planned. Emily decided to tour the east coast rather than west coast in part because she could more easily hit more major cities within a week. A similar parallel move would be to forego or postpone a physical CD release, in favor of a purely online release. Again, that can be a profound change to a project, but depending on what your ultimate goals are, there might be a cheaper alternative that would actually serve you nearly as well as would your original concept.

Emily was able to record and mix her EP very inexpensively and then find free sleeping accommodations for her band. The tour's financial picture then made a lot more sense.

Breaking Even

Another report to help you predict how your project will work out is the *price/cost report*, or PCR. This form/calculation is particularly helpful for reviewing parameters of individual products to see if and how they can be profitable. Record companies, publishers, and other organizations that sell products routinely "PCR" proposals during the project proposal review phase to help determine whether the product is likely to be worth doing.

Essentially, it is another type of P&L report, but with the specific purpose of determining how many units we need to sell and at what price. Let's take Emily's EP as an example, though I'll again take some poetic license and portray it here as if it were destined for release by a commercial record label.

Ultimately, it shows how many units must be sold to recoup expenses. Given the current estimate, we must sell 2,506 EPs before we start making any money. This number is then compared with historical numbers achieved by similar products. If the ultimate break even number looks easily reachable and almost certainly greatly exceeded, the calculation is a good supporting document for why a proposed project should be approved. If breaking even looks like a long shot, then the proposed project will probably get rejected. Maybe, there will be an invitation to those championing it to sharpen their pencils and try again. Or, it might get rejected outright.

This page is programmed to automatically update the break-even amount, based on tweaks to the numbers. So, you could see how changing the number of songs might affect the project feasibility. For example, you could raise the price.

Sophisticated corporations often have customized software to help produce such things, drawing some information from databases of past sales. For example, adding "indie rock" might access the sales history of the hundred other indie rock titles that the label has released in its history, average their lifetime sales, and pull that number into this form, to compare with the proposed new album. Raising the price might affect the calculation regarding comparable sales, and thus the resulting break-even number.

However, you can build a simple version of this functionality in a spreadsheet (with Excel, or Smartsheet, or Google Docs), or even using your pencil. My father worked as a comptroller for a chain of department stores, and spent much of his career doing all this kind of work with a pencil and an adding machine, before computers became commonplace in the corporate environment. So, don't let lack of technology deter you.

Title	Emily's EP	
Artist	Emily Peal and the Skinny Men	
Genre	Indic Rock	
Format	CD	
# Tracks	5	
Duration	29	
Case	Digi-Pak	
Booklet Pages	4	
Color	4C Cover; 4C interior; 4C CD; shrink wrap	
CD PRODUCTION		
Recording	4,500	
Mixing	3,000	
Mastering	600	
Booklet Layout	300	
Booklet Editing	75	
Cover Art	750	
Photos	1,000	
Misc. (Shipping, etc.)	100	
Total Production	**10,325**	
REPLICATION		
Quantity	3,000	
Unit Cost	2.16	Unit cost is based on quantity.
Total Replication	**6,480**	
DEAL STRUCTURE		
Retail	12.95	What the consumer must pay
Wholesale %	47%	What the retailer pays the label
Artist Royalty %	4.5%	What the label pays the artist (based on retail price)
Gross Profit	$4	Label's profit per unit = Wholesale % of Retail – Artist Royalty % of Retail – Unit Cost
FINAL BREAK EVEN	**2,506**	Quantity needed to sell in order to recoup production costs

FIG. 4.12. Break-Even Projection

FINANCIAL CONTINGENCIES

A *cost contingency* is an extra amount you build into an estimate to cover unexpected expenses associated with that item. When we estimated the cost to print t-shirts, we added a significant contingency because we had no idea what it would cost. Perhaps, our number was based on seeing an ad to print t-shirts. But did that amount include design? Silk-screen setup? Ink? Postage? Perhaps, the advertised unit cost was $4 per shirt, but we added an extra dollar to our early stage estimate (to a total of $5 estimated per shirt) to help protect us from the risk that the actual cost would be greater than anticipated. The less research you've done, the more of a contingency you should allow.

When you're estimating project costs, ideally, your numbers should be exactly accurate. In the big picture, a correct allocation of resources helps keep all the projects happening around you resourced at maximum efficiency. The second best choice is usually that you come in under budget, and so it is common practice to add a bit more to an estimate, to mitigate the risk of an unanticipated expense.

Best practice is often to calculate with pinpoint accuracy your expenses (or time or other required resources), but then to pad estimates for others whom you might encounter, in case they do better with some room. Like, you might have a vendor relationship in which there's a standard haggling game played, where they always present higher prices than what they intend, so you tell them that you have a lower budget than you really do, and thus together you eventually arrive at a compromise price that everyone can live with. Sometimes, that's the culture. Stepping into that dance, you should have a well-researched realistic number in your back pocket of how much you really have, and how much you can really pay.

At certain points in the planning stages of a project, the numbers can be relatively approximate, and significant research to get precise estimates wouldn't really be worth the time. At an early pipe-dream discussion about the feasibility of recording an EP, it might not matter much to the existence of a project whether you are imagining it will cost $8,000 or $12,000. As you get closer to actually spending money, it becomes more important to use numbers with increasing accuracy.

A rule of thumb for contingencies, then, is as follows:

Feasibility Level (early stages)	25%
Schematic Level (advanced planning stages)	10%
Bids to Specification (actual price commitments from vendors)	5%

FIG. 4.12. Recommended Contingency Percentages

So, when you're trying to determine whether a project is feasible, you want your numbers to be within 25% of their accurate amount; your estimates should be up to 25% (hopefully, above) what they will actually cost. When you are creating detailed schemes/plans for getting it done, the numbers should be within 10%. When you are actually getting price quotes from people who will do the work, you want those quotes to be within 5% of the actual costs.

The best-case scenario is that your final estimated amount will be exactly what the project actually costs.

CLOSING THOUGHTS

Let's summarize the big picture of how these financial mechanisms are related.

We started with a project vision. That informed a scope statement, where we specified the boundaries of our goals. We then created a work breakdown structure to fill in details of precisely what work was needed to fulfill the stated scope.

The WBS serves as an estimating tool when developing the budget, as well as helping us clarify the project's scope. Then, during project execution, we incorporate our estimated costs into an operating P&L (profit and loss statement), so we can see how our financial picture is emerging in relation to the budgeted amount. Also feeding the operating P&L is the transaction register (nicely summarized by account), which helps us monitor the way that reality meets our imaginations.

Along the way, as we learn what is truly possible and what is not, we might revise our earlier plans, but essentially, this is the flow.

Thus, the resources we commit become direct descendants of our pie-in-the-sky vision. Our actions align with our dreams, thus giving us the best chances that we can manage for our project's success.

PRACTICE

Create a break-even report for your project. How many units do you need to sell in order to make a profit? How will you determine whether that is realistic?

CHAPTER 5

Time

Time management is one of the very primary tasks of project management. Projects nearly always take longer to complete than anticipated. In this chapter, we'll look at various methods for estimating, organizing, and tracking time.

I just had lunch with producer and Berklee faculty member Mitch Benoff, who owned a recording studio for many years. He recounted how relatively inexperienced bands would come in and book his studio for two days to produce their albums (track, mix, master). They'd find, though, that what they really needed was between fifteen and thirty hours of studio time per song, rather than for the whole album, and this of course would throw their whole endeavor into chaos.

A band of experienced studio musicians might be able to pull off producing an album's worth of songs in two days. They'll arrive completely prepared and do three or four takes per song, and no overdubs. Another band, though, might need to do forty takes per song. If the second band bases their estimate on what the first band recommends, without understanding the big picture of what that means, then they will be in for a surprise.

In this chapter, we'll look at ways to mitigate this kind of circumstance, and to generally get a clear grasp on how long it will take to complete your project.

OBJECTIVES

By the end of the chapter, you will be able to:

- estimate your project's likely duration, using your WBS (Work Breakdown Structure) and estimating tools such as PERT (Program Evaluation Review Technique) and Delphi

- understand the critical path of your project, so you can focus your management attention on the activity that most influences your overall project timeline

- reduce the time necessary to complete your project by increasing concurrency

- understand how dependencies of tasks control your project's timeline

- use Gantt charts and network diagrams to analyze and control your project's time frame

Timing a project's work can require significant strategy, and this is particularly evident in music-related projects. At a point, there will be a concert hall filled with people who bought tickets, and the show must go on—at that exact moment. Many projects have other types of similar necessary completion dates. Marketing campaigns, for example, are most successful if certain components of their efforts are coordinated to mutually support each other. In the music book industry, we've learned not to advertise products too far in advance of their being printed. If we're early, the pattern is that people see advertising, get excited and try to buy it, find out that they can't get it yet, and then their fire goes out. When it becomes available, they have moved on to other interests, or have developed a cynical attitude about communications from the company, and so never wind up buying it. Advertising works better if they can buy it as soon as they learn about it.

The constellation of necessary work can be complicated, and fraught with interdependencies! In this chapter, we will look at some strategies for building an effective schedule.

ESTIMATING DURATION

In our work breakdown structure, we itemized all the deliverables and all the tasks necessary to complete our project. Then, we used this information to estimate project cost. Now, we'll do a similar process for estimating the time required by our project.

The essential process in figuring out how long a project will require involves first taking your WBS, elaborated down to the level of tasks, and then estimating how much time each task will require. If you use project management software, there will be a place for you to add durations (generally, calculated in days). Producing the recordings for Emily's EP might require tasks and durations such as these. (Note that even though the EP will have four or five songs, she writes six so that she can eventually choose the ones she and the band like best.) Then, estimate how much time each task will take—preferably, assisted in the process by the people actually doing the work. Figure 5.1 shows how it might look in Smartsheet, with tasks and durations. (Partial listing.)

Tasks are typically estimated in days, or sometimes hours. These estimates for scheduling purposes are durations, not actual work time. *Duration* includes the time period that we must wait for the task to get accomplished, rather than the amount of time actually spent working on it. Mastering, for example, might take two hours per song, or one workday for a four-song EP. But there generally is an expected lag time between when the mastering house receives the files and when they can actually complete the work. They probably build this into their time estimates. They'll say, "Figure, it's a safe bet to allow for two weeks to master the EP." The work time is eight hours, but the duration we are going to use in our plan is two weeks. They might have a policy that they don't schedule work until the files are received and inspected, and they expect a couple rounds of back and forth with the artist or mix engineer before they can get started. Perhaps certain processes involve computers running overnight while files transfer, and so on. So, work time differs from duration.

Task Name	Duration
⊟ 1. Emily's EP	79
⊟ 1.1. Music	49
⊟ 1.1.1. Songwriting	19
1.1.1.1. Get song ideas	7
1.1.1.2. Write song 1	2
1.1.1.3. Write song 2	2
1.1.1.4. Write song 3	2
1.1.1.5. Write song 4	2
1.1.1.6. Write song 5	2
1.1.1.7. Write song 6	2
⊟ 1.1.2. Demo Recordings	16
⊞ 1.1.2.1. Record Piano/Vocal Versic	6
⊞ 1.1.2.2. Improve Scratch Recordin	10
⊟ 1.1.3. Final Recordings	14
⊞ 1.1.3.1. Rehearsals	3
1.1.3.2. Schedule studio date	1
1.1.3.3. Record songs	2
1.1.3.4. Mix songs	3
1.1.3.5. Master songs	7
1.1.3.m. Final Master	1
⊟ 1.2. Packaging	74
⊟ 1.2.1. Booklet Interior	12
1.2.1.1. Text	7
1.2.1.2. Booklet Layout	5

FIG. 5.1. Tasks and Durations (in Smartsheet)

Similarly, a song might take two hours to write, but the creative spirit can't be rushed, and many songwriters have trouble writing more than one song in a day. Some might want to write a song over two days, in order to sleep on it, and some might have difficulty doing more than one songwriting session in a week. And then, there's writer's block, which can delay a project forever. These factors all make creative projects relatively difficult to time-estimate. While it isn't always possible to control when the muse is being cooperative, from a project management perspective, it is important to know what can be predicted and what cannot. If the creative process is truly an unknowable black hole, with no possible time estimate, then the project really shouldn't be resourced or specifically planned until that creative work is completed. Sometimes, for some people, the muse simply never shows up.

"Never" might well be the most common actual time that creative projects get completed. Forcing an artist to commit to a schedule is a way to turn that into a successful time frame.

If we simply totaled up the number of days required to complete all our tasks, it might look like figure 5.2.

At a glance, it appears that 84 days of work are required to complete this project, between walking in the woods in search of inspiration and having a product we can sell.

You could take that number, 84 days, block them off on a calendar (discounting weekends, holidays, days you know you'll be busy, and so on), and then find a relatively realistic deadline for when to expect to finish the project. Or, start with a known deadline (such as a good day to have a CD release party), and count back that many days, to find out when you should start. Either approach is far better than what many do, in terms of predicting a completion date: arbitrarily choosing a deadline and then being disappointed when it doesn't work out.

We can certainly use some strategies to get a more realistic estimate, and also to compress the timeline to make it more efficient. Project management software makes this much easier.

Let's consider some methods for arriving at accurate estimates for how long the work will actually require.

Activity	Duration (Days)
Get song ideas	7
Write song 1	2
Write song 2	2
Write song 3	2
Write song 4	2
Write song 5	2
Write song 6	2
Record piano/vocal demo of song 1	1
Record piano/vocal demo of song 2	1
Record piano/vocal demo of song 3	1
Record piano/vocal demo of song 4	1
Record piano/vocal demo of song 5	1
Record piano/vocal demo of song 6	1
Write Liner Notes	7
Design Cover Art	8
Distribute recordings to band members	1
Band members provide feedback on demos	6
Revise songs	3
Schedule rehearsal 1	1
Rehearsal 1: Record band demos of 3 songs	1
Schedule rehearsal 2	1
Rehearsal 2: Record band demos of 3 songs	1
Schedule studio date	1
Record songs	2
Mix songs	3
Master songs	7
Lay Out booklet	5
Send to replicator	1
Replicate	10
Release	1
Total	**84**

FIG. 5.2. Sequential Duration Calculation

Refining Time Estimates

You might remember some of the tips from estimating costs. They work for time estimates as well.

- **Reference past experience.** By documenting how much time you spend doing tasks, you'll set yourself up better for success next time you do a similar project.

- **Get bids.** Ask people who do the work how much time (i.e., duration) it will take. Assume they are bragging and it will actually take longer.

- **Ask a guru.** People who have managed similar projects before will have some insight into how much time certain tasks will require.

All of these are likely to yield better results than a WAG (wild-arsed guess). If greater precision is required, here are two other means of refining time estimates (or cost estimates).

PERT: Program Evaluation Review Technique

A PERT (Program Evaluation Review Technique) calculation gives us a deeper concept of the estimated timing. Instead of a single estimate for the required duration, we come up with three: the likeliest duration, an optimistic projection, and a pessimistic projection. We take a weighted average between them, and thus arrive at a more likely scenario than we would if we had just gone with what seemed to be the likeliest estimate.

Here's how it works. We will use a weighted average of our three guesses. Say we are trying to come up with a refined estimate for how long mastering our recording will really require. We call our engineer, ask how long it will take, and he'll say something like, "Oh, about a week. Five business days."

We say, "Is there any way to make it happen sooner?"

He says, "Well, if you deliver the files to me when I don't have anything else in the hopper, and if you can transfer the mixes to me electronically and then pick up the final master instead of relying on snail mail, you might get it back in two days."

You say, "What's the worst-case scenario?"

He says, "The longest it ever took me was three weeks, but that's because there was a problem with the original files, so we had to go back to the mix engineer. Also, I got sick, so we lost a couple days."

We then distill this information into the following chart:

$$T_o = 2 \text{ (optimistic)}$$

$$T_m = 5 \text{ (most likely)}$$

$$T_p = 15 \text{ (pessimistic)}$$

The three numbers can be expressed as $T_o/T_m/T_p$, or 2/5/15.

Now, we take a weighted average. The standard way to weight this is to assume (oh, that word) that it is four times as likely to be on time than it is to be either early or late. We therefore can calculate a weighted average using this formula (a "mean estimate"), yielding an expected time that the task will take: T_e.

$$\frac{(T_o \times 1) + T_m \times 4) + (T_p \times 1)}{6} = T_e \text{ (Better than a WAG)}$$

In this case:

$$\frac{(2 \times 1) + (5 \times 4) + (15 \times 1)}{6} = 37/6 = 6.16 \text{ days}$$

The laws of probabilities thus inform us that this task, of mastering, is inclined to take a little longer than our original estimate. If we call it "about six days" instead of five, our estimate is more likely to be right. And maybe we'll get lucky, and it will take less time.

How likely are we to get lucky? If you like math, you can go deeper into probabilities, though it's not generally necessary. However, since you asked, there are some more advanced principles for using this tool.

First, some more generally accepted likelihoods:

- 5% of all projects take less time than their optimistic estimate (T_o)

- 50% of all projects take less time than their most likely estimate (T_m)

- 5% of all projects take more time than their pessimistic estimate (T_p)

Second, there's the idea that times closest to T_m are likeliest. The graph of the likely time estimate is a bell curve, leading up to T_m. Most projects are within one *standard deviation* (stdev) away from T_m, and the vast majority are within two standard deviations.

stdev = (pessimistic – optimistic) / 6

For our task of mastering:

stdev = (15 – 2)/6 = 13/6 = 2.16

In other words, using our new best estimate (T_e) of 6 days and rounding down to a standard deviation of about 2 days, mastering will probably take 4 to 8 days (a standard deviation of 2 days away from the best estimate of 6 days) and almost certainly take 2 to 10 days (two standard deviations away from 6 is 4, on either side), assuming that our logic is sound regarding those three original estimated scenarios. Communicating 2/6/10 might be more useful than just 6, as you prepare estimated timings for your project, though it will require some explanation. Some people doing the work might appreciate being braced for 10 days, or knowing that if they try really hard, maybe they can get it done in 2 days.

(And since everyone will be confused by looking at an estimated number rendered as 2/6/10, you will probably just use T_e, and say, "Probably about 6 days. Almost certainly between 2 and 10 days." This way, nobody will look at you cross-eyed—at least, not any more than they usually do.)

You can go deeper into PERT (designed by the U.S. Navy for testing missiles), if your tasks are more critical, and we'll see a PERT chart in a minute. But outside of life/death project management applications, the above approach is among the more practical uses for that technique.

Delphi

The Delphi method is an approach to group decision-making and forecasting that is sometimes used in task estimation. (It's also used for estimating cost and other dimensions of work.) The quality of its results vary due to, among other factors, the personality makeup and skill set of the group, but there are situations and cultures within which it has proven remarkably effective.

Here's how it works in task time estimation. There are two roles: *facilitator* and *participant*. It is said to work best with at least five participants.

Participants individually estimate the time a task will take.

The facilitator gathers these estimates, removes the obviously incorrect or misguided ones from the set, and then invites the reasonable outliers, both low and high, to present their arguments regarding how they arrived at their estimates to the rest of the group.

Steps 1 and 2 are repeated for a total of at least three rounds. After the last round, the results of that round are averaged, and that's the resulting estimate used for scheduling.

For example, say two members of the group estimate that mastering is likely to take six days, one says two days, and one says twenty-five days, and one says "Let's not bother with mastering." The "Let's not bother" voter gets omitted from the tally. The two in agreement about six days say nothing, and the other two step forward. If Mrs. Two says "I've done thirty projects like this and they always take two days to master," and Mr. Twenty-Five says, "Actually, I have no idea, it was just a WAG," then Mrs. Two's argument will hopefully be more influential to everyone in the next round. (And we especially hope that Mr. Twenty-Five comes through with a future estimate that is more aligned with the group.) We then explain to "Let's not bother" that we have decided to master the EP, and that the current activity is to estimate the time, not to argue this settled point. Perhaps, by round three, everyone will settle on, say, four to six days.

The group can then move onto another task.

There are many variations. In some scenarios, all communication is anonymous. Some scenarios involve polling more than one group and their resulting answers are compared. Some involve automated systems and no human facilitator. It is a near perfect opposite process than its namesake, the ancient Greek oracles at Delphi, who made predictions as the spirits moved them. In this modern iteration of forecasting, groups are hopefully swayed by high quality evidence and good sense. The fact that it proves to be so effective gives one hope in humanity and the democratic process.

Like PERT, effective use of the Delphi method depends on the estimators being reasonably well informed. The more expert the group, the better the resulting estimate.

When estimating times for project tasks, it's a good idea to be realistic, rather than pad them with expected extra time. We want to get good at accurate forecasting. Also, people have a tendency to push deadlines, so if we give a comfortable or a tight deadline, they'll still likely work up to the last minute. It's better to predict accurately, for your own tracking purposes. However, if you are doing a project for someone else, it might be okay to pad *what you tell them* a little bit, just so that a client isn't disappointed or frustrated by it going later than anticipated. Just make sure that you understand how your time estimate will be used by them. If they are weighing multiple vendors before signing a contract, the estimated timing might factor into whom they choose.

COMPRESSING TIME

One person could execute all of a project's tasks sequentially, not starting a new task until the preceding task is done. This model is a simple timeline. It tends to be the longest route to completing a project, though sometimes, it can make sense. A way to graphically display this is to have a line segment representing each task, with the length of the line segments corresponding proportionally to how much time is required. A timeline such as this is easy to read, as long as there aren't too many elements on it. They get cluttered easily. Even here, I had to move the words "Graphical Layout" out of the way.

FIG. 5.3. Timeline

Gantt Charts

A way to fit more text on a timeline is to have the labels on a Y axis against time on an X axis. This diagram was created using the Gantt chart view from within Smartsheet. Gantt charts are like two-dimensional timelines, and they are very common in project management. We will see some more sophisticated Gantt charts soon.

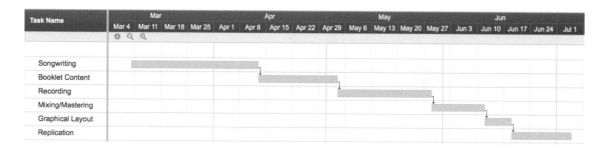

FIG. 5.4. Gantt Chart (in Smartsheet)

Notice in those two above examples that we are simplifying the diagrams by grouping related tasks together, as they are naturally grouped in the WBS. We know that "songwriting" includes many components and tasks, but it is unnecessary to show them in that diagram. Being able to zoom in and out of detail like this helps clarify charts. If the goal of the diagram is to be used by a group, logical tasks for an individual can be combined under a "rollup" (or "summary") label and thus greatly simplify the page. For example, combining the songwriter's tasks of gathering inspiration, writing songs, and creating demo guitar/vocal recordings might be combined into a "songwriting" rollup, for purposes of the whole project team. How the individual arranges her time is her own business. So, the time estimates for this phase get totaled. The rollup can later be re-expanded, if greater detail is necessary.

Here is that same Gantt chart, but showing the songwriting component expanded, to display more detailed sub-steps. Each major component of a work breakdown structure might include many sub items, and being able to roll them up into a summary topic can greatly simplify the chart and let you just focus on what you really need to see. Any project management software that supports Gantt charts should have a similar feature, though perhaps called by a different name.

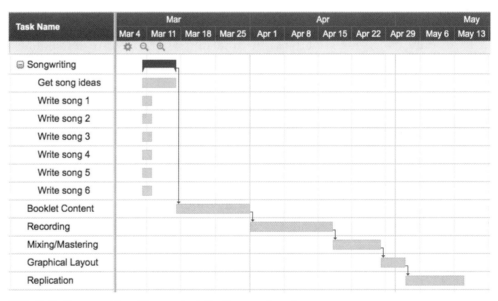

FIG. 5.5. Songwriting Expanded (in Smartsheet)

Simplifying project phases like this can help clarify discussions, and it is common to present diagrams showing just major project components to project management teams, rather than the entire Gantt chart (which newbies often find terrifying). We might also protect some of our workers from the scary code numbers.

In that spirit, for some of the upcoming diagrams, I will be featuring rollups of activities, instead of details. I'll also add a letter code to each activity, to simplify things.

Activity	Duration (Days)
A. Songwriting	25
B. Booklet Content	15
C. Recording	17
D. Mixing/Mastering	10
E. Graphical Layout	5
F. Replication	12
Total	**84**

FIG. 5.6. EP Durations of Higher Level Tasks

Keeping this duality in mind can be helpful: what we do for our own planning versus what we present to others. Simplifying diagrams can help keep our team members from becoming confused.

Concurrency

The total project duration can be compressed by determining which tasks can be done *concurrently* (at the same time) and which ones are dependent on other tasks and thus must be done *sequentially* (one after another). For the sake of this discussion, let's assume that you want to execute the project as quickly and as efficiently as possible. (You might not! But someday, you will likely appreciate having the skill of being able to execute projects with maximum efficiency.)

Tasks are often dependent on other tasks, and understanding these relationships is essential to figuring out a project schedule. In the process shown in figure 5.4, we produced the recording sequentially: songwriting, then booklet layout, then recording, and so on. The little arrows show one task leading to the next. Before you can prepare the booklet content (song names, lyrics, order, etc.), you must write the songs. Before you record, you must lay out the booklet. Or must you?

After some thought, we realize that we can actually produce the recording and develop the booklet concurrently, rather than sequentially. We can shoot band member photos, type song lyrics, gather biographies, and so on, as soon as songwriting is done. No need to wait; it can all happen at once. Here's what that looks like on the Gantt chart. Note that replication now has two dependencies: mastering the recording and designing the booklet.

Task Name		Mar					Apr					May			
	Feb	Mar 4	Mar 11	Mar 18	Mar 25	Apr 1	Apr 8	Apr 15	Apr 22	Apr 29	May 6	May 13	May 20	May 2
1															
2 Songwriting															
3 Recording															
4 Mixing/Mastering															
5 Booklet Content															
6 Graphical Layout															
7 Replication															

FIG. 5.7. Concurrency between Booklet Development and Recording

By developing the booklet concurrently with producing the recording, we can save 20 days from the overall timeline, compared to doing these tasks sequentially. As you can see, maximizing concurrency is a big deal! The key is to figure out what the true dependencies are between tasks: which ones must be predicated on others, and also where there is some flexibility in when they can be undertaken.

To figure out dependencies and potentials for concurrency, grab a task and compare it against the others, one by one. What is the earliest you can begin? Types of controlling factors, regarding what will be executed concurrently vs. simultaneously, include:

- **Logic.** Sometimes, one task must follow another. For example, we can't record the tracks until we have written the songs.

- **Resources.** Our staff/cash flow/facilities don't permit us to do the tasks concurrently. Perhaps, the CD booklet layout artist is also the mastering engineer. If she can't simultaneously master the recording and lay out the booklet, those tasks will have to be done sequentially.

- **Discretion.** While there might not be logical or resource constraints on two tasks, the project manager decides to make them sequential. For example, songwriting and cover art design might happen simultaneously, but a project manager might decide that a better result would involve the art coming from the song lyrics, and so those tasks are instead set up as dependencies.

For just a few tasks, you can list them on a page and figure out the order, if it's obvious. In larger, more complex projects, you might use a large work surface and separate pieces of paper marked with each task. If a group is working this out together, it often works well to write the task names on

Post-it® notes, perhaps color coding them (by task thread, by person in charge of executing them, or whatever makes sense). Then post them and move them around on a large wall or a whiteboard, while you discuss the best sequence. On a whiteboard, you can write lines showing relationships between them, so that's sometimes helpful. When I figure out schemes like this myself, I tend to print the tasks and cut up the paper, as paper is cheaper and always on hand, and I don't have the same concerns about making a big mess when I'm alone. My office includes a long counter, which I use for the same purpose. But Post-it notes are easier to control.

However you do it, the logical process is the same. Take two tasks, and determine whether or not they can be executed concurrently or whether they must be executed sequentially. The goal is to see how early each task can begin. This reveals the maximum flexibility and the shortest possible project completion schedule.

Network Diagrams

A special type of diagram used for this kind of logical thinking is often called a *network* diagram. Our major CD production tasks can be diagrammed like this, for maximum concurrency:

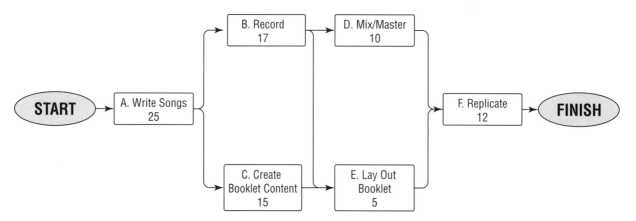

FIG. 5.8. Network Diagram

We can describe these dependency relationships in our chart, as shown in figure 5.9. In this scenario, we find that some activities of CD production can indeed be worked on concurrently. We can make progress on the booklet and the recording at the same time, rather than doing them sequentially.

Activity	Duration (Days)	Dependencies	Note
A. Write Songs	25	None	First, we write songs. Without that, we don't have a project.
B. Record	17	A	Must write songs before recording them.
C. Create Booklet Content	15	A	Once we have a pool of creative work, we can begin working on the packaging (e.g., the booklet). (This is a subjective call; some would prefer to wait until we have a final song selection.)
D. Mix/Master	10	B	Must record songs before mixing/mastering.
E. Lay Out booklet	5	B, C	Booklet layout depends on final song selection.
F. Replicate	12	D, E	Booklet and recording must be done before we can replicate.
Total	**84**		

FIG. 5.9. Dependency Chart

By following the path of dependencies and choosing the longest possible route, and adding up the durations on that path, we can arrive at our shortest-possible project completion time: the *critical path*, which we will discuss in more detail later on. Here, it becomes clear that if we follow the critical path, our project can actually be compressed to take less time. The longest path through here is:

A B D F

The durations of those activities is:

25 + 17 + 10 + 12 = 64 days

This means that if we manage the project carefully, we can cut the CD project duration by 20 days!

This is among the very most powerful concepts in project management. By analyzing the work and maximizing concurrency, we can control how long it takes to get the work done.

You'll find, in examining dependencies, that the relationships between tasks aren't always straightforward. Let's look at this concept in more depth.

Dependencies

Nuances of task dependencies can be diagrammed in network diagrams. These diagrams can be hand drawn, done with special chart software (Lucidchart is a good online free one; Gliffy isn't free but it's also good), or in some cases, done with project management software. Each enclosed area is called a *node*, with arrows indicating which task must come first; arrows point from the starting (predecessor) task to the finishing (successor) task. Inside the node, there is the task name (or a code for the task name that is referenced in an accompanying chart), and sometimes a number indicating duration. Less commonly, there may be an abbreviation on the line, such as SF, used to clarify these relationships as well: S stands for "start," F stands for "finish." So, an FS dependency means that the predecessor task must finish before the successor starts. For example, recording must finish before mixing can start.

Here are the four possible dependencies:

- FS: When A finishes, B can start.

- FF: When A finishes, B can finish.

- SS: When A starts, B can start.

- SF: When A starts, B can finish.

These F and S codes are useful in writing about dependencies, as we are now, but they are redundant with the arrow diagram. So, if you have a code in your node, you might want to blow it! I include them on the following diagrams, just to clarify the concept as I introduce it, but it's not necessary to do so in real life.

We read these diagrams from left to right. Start indications are drawn from the left of the node, and finish indications are drawn from the right.

An FS dependency is a simple sequence of tasks: first you do A, then you do B, and you can't start B until you're done with A. It's the default mode, for most planning software, and sometimes, the only dependency relationship that they support. Two tasks that must be executed sequentially are recording and mixing. You can't start mixing until you've got a recording.

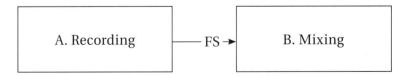

FIG. 5.10. Finish to Start. Recording must finish before mixing can start.

An FF dependency is where one task cannot end until another one does. Booklet layout and the writing of its content might happen relatively concurrently, with dummy text reserving the place for the final copy, but the booklet won't get "finished" until the final version of the text is provided.

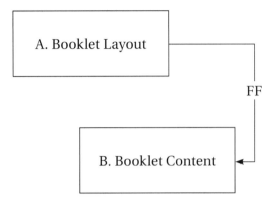

FIG. 5.11. Finish to Finish. Text must be written before booklet layout can finish.

An SS dependency means that one task can start only once another task has started. For example, a songwriter might record scratch guitar/vocal demos as part of the writing process, recording improvisations, or recording various versions of verse/chorus pairs while trying to arrive at the final version. Good progress on the demo recording is made during the songwriting process, though the two tasks are actually also independent.

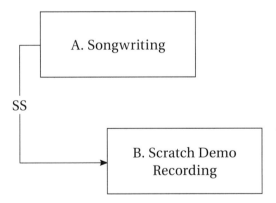

FIG. 5.12. Start to Start. The scratch demos can be recorded as soon as songwriting starts.

Finally, in an SF dependency, once the first task starts, the second one may finish. These are rare, but possible. Perhaps, the full responsibility for the task of scheduling a rehearsal involves both reserving a space at a time when the facility and the band are available, but also making sure that everyone in the band remembers the date and can find the place. You can't really say that the task of scheduling completely ends until the rehearsal begins. If you needed to track a dependency at that specific level of detail, you could draw it like this, though it will rarely be necessary beyond the scenarios of either writing a computer program to monitor it or if there is some contractual rule involving such a dependency. (I'm including this one to be logically complete, rather than to give you something likely to be truly useful in your life.)

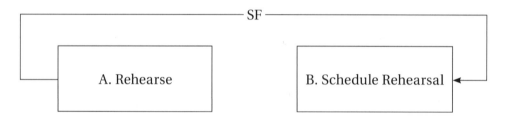

FIG. 5.13. Start to Finish. Once the rehearsal can start, scheduling the rehearsal can finish.

At first glance, tasks often appear to be FS. We assume that we have to do one and then do the other. To crunch total project time, see what FS dependencies can be turned into SS or FF relationships instead, where progress on multiple tasks can happen concurrently.

Using Scheduling Charts

We have two types of time planning charts, then: Gantt charts and networking diagrams. Gantt charts tend to be the most common during a project, with an occasional network diagram generated for special occasions, like early strategic planning sessions.

Unlike simple calendars, these charts let you see large-scale interrelationships between tasks and time. One of the most common and helpful uses for project management software is that it lets you enter tasks, timing, and dependencies, and then plots them in a variety of views, so you can examine them from different perspectives. Smartsheet lets you easily change between Gantt charts and regular calendars, for example.

One thing to keep in mind with these charts is that they can be intimidating at first, and therefore, are most useful among project managers, rather than other project team members. One of my colleagues tells the war story of managing his first team of musicians, after just entering our industry from the world of Wall Street. He opened his first team meeting by showing the gathered musicians a Gantt chart, and immediately alienated them all. They liked him personally, but absolutely detested his management style. They didn't have patience to figure out his charts and such, and therefore, were inclined to distrust many of the practices he was advocating. I've found similar issues, dealing with people who are uncomfortable with technology. They respond better to more familiar calendars and forms of communication, rather than what project management software might spit out.

So, use these tools for your own information, and be prepared to translate the resulting information to others, if necessary. This kind of meticulous planning and organization doesn't automatically win people over! Here's another Gantt chart, this one made in OpenProj. More complex output on small paper can yield a graphic that is pretty hard to figure out. Bigger paper, or using the chart within the software, makes more sense.

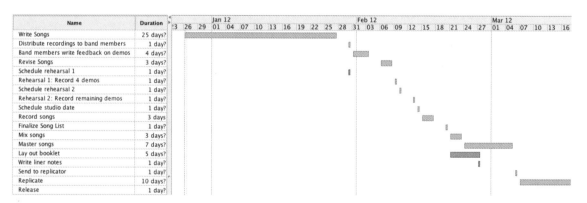

FIG. 5.14. Gantt Chart in OpenProj

Gantt charts have been around for a really long time. They are currently considered most helpful for providing summaries and reports to the project team. Their weaknesses are that they become difficult to read when there are more than about twenty-five tasks, and showing different types of dependencies can be awkward. It is common for project management software to have the capability to create Gantt charts.

Network diagrams are excellent at showing dependencies. Though they can be hand drawn, their electronic construction requires complex software, and they can be difficult to read. Here is an excerpt of a network diagram showing the same tasks (made using OpenProj, a freeware project management program that supports both Gantt charts and network diagrams).

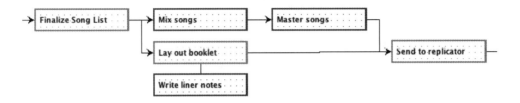

FIG. 5.15. Network Diagram in OpenProj

Network diagrams can reveal points of *convergence* and *bursting*—when multiple tasks compress down to one pivotal point or when multiple tasks emanate from one node. Those are typically good indicators of project milestones, or important potential bottlenecks. In figure 5.15, we can see that once we finalize the song list, we can start mixing and we can start laying out the booklet. (We don't want to mix songs we won't use or include their lyrics in the booklet.) That's a burst. We also see a convergence of tasks: before sending it to the replicator, we need to finish mastering the songs and layout of the booklet.

You'll see variations and hybrids of both types. Some network diagrams set the task name on arrows, some use letters (mapped to accompanying charts) to represent the tasks. Some Gantt charts, such as in Smartsheet, use arrows to show dependencies. Some network diagrams have proportional timelines.

Besides automatically generating these complex diagrams, project management software is good at calculating dates, and updating everything should one of the dates change.

Critical Paths

The timing of some tasks will control how long the project takes to complete. The time spent on songwriting, in our CD project example, controls the rest of the project. If the songwriter takes an extra month, then the project is delayed by a month.

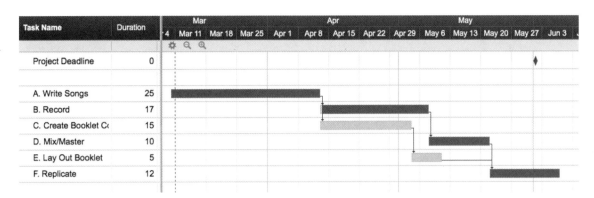

FIG. 5.16. Critical Path

Similarly, the recording session is critical. We can't do anything else until that task is complete. Only after we record are we going to choose the song list, which we know is a critical point in the project. If we take a month recording, the project is delayed.

On the other hand, as we've planned it out now, the timing for creating booklet content isn't that critical. The writer can goof off for a week or two and the project schedule won't be affected. At a point, it will become a problem, but that work is happening independently of the rest of it.

Tasks whose duration directly affects the project timeline are said to form the project's *critical path*, shown with darker shaded bars in figure 5.16. (You can have multiple critical paths.) The critical path is the longest, least flexible possible way through the project. Precisely what tasks are on the critical path might change as the project unfolds. If the booklet content writer is a major slacker, eventually, all other possible tasks will be complete, as everyone waits for the booklet to get written, and so that task becomes on the critical path, holding up the project's completion. A stalled task on the critical path is said to be a *bottleneck*. All future work can be restricted until that bottleneck is alleviated.

Tasks along the critical path require the most urgent management, and doing this kind of analysis and managing using this perspective is called the *Critical Path Method*, or CPM. This orientation helps project managers prioritize tasks.

The available time for tasks off the critical path is called *slack*. One way to look at it is that this is time available for the task doer to goof off. Another way to look at it is that when someone has slack time, they might be available to assist with other tasks and thus help to reduce the time required on the project. We will look at how to calculate slack precisely later this chapter.

Time Reduction Strategies

If a project is projected to take too long, it will be most productive to reduce the timing of tasks along the critical path. Say that writing the liner notes went really long, and that booklet layout therefore moved onto the critical path. It currently takes five days. If we are running two days late and must meet our deadline, it could be worth trying to reduce the timing of the layout activity, and thus the overall critical path.

There are a few standard ways that this is done.

1. **Add resources of money, facilities, or manpower.** It might be worth it to pay the designer more to do it faster, pay for a software upgrade that increases their productivity, or divide that work among multiple designers. Sometimes, a project manager must roll up his or her sleeves and do a task himself or herself, to save time, though that's generally to be avoided. Throwing resources at a task is called *crashing* the task.

2. **Change the scope.** Simplifying the booklet could reduce the time required. Instead of original cover artwork, for example, we could have the cover be a photo that already exists and that we could live with. We could decide not to include lyrics in the booklet at all, which would simplify the design process that is dependent on the lyrics being finalized, which would also allow us to complete the booklet sooner. Changing scope sometimes means reducing aspirations. It is a drastic measure, to sacrifice the quality of a project, like this. But such choices become necessary when budget and timing constraints demand it.

3. **Reconsider discretionary dependencies.** We are currently waiting on starting the booklet until we've settled on the final song list. But if we are reasonably sure of three of the songs, we can start the process much earlier, get everything done except the minor missing parts, and then finish it up when the final decision is made, thus moving much of that task off the critical path. Sometimes, this adds risk to a project, making more happen simultaneously, but it might be worth it.

4. **Reconsider communication mechanisms.** Sometimes, sitting in a room with a worker and having detailed discussions can save time, compared with sending emails back and forth. A face-to-face meeting with a designer to go through art concepts might clarify and simplify the project to come. Having the whole band review and discuss tracks together, in the same room at the same time, can similarly save time. Paying for overnight

shipping and enclosing an overnight-shipping mailer for return of proofs can sometimes save considerable time (and risk). And faxing or emailing scanned PDFs instead of using snail mail can make it even faster/cheaper.

5. **Re-evaluating assumptions can sometimes lead to time savings.** You might determine that a time estimate was too high, or that some resources were not committed after all. For example, you might have assumed that a designer wouldn't do work on weekends, but it turns out that they actually will. Realizing this could cut two days from the critical path.

6. **Ask nicely.** Sometimes, a worker will speed things up if you explain that you're running late, and that it would be great help if they'd rush. Maybe they will figure out a way to make it happen faster. (There's also "cracking the whip," which might accomplish the same thing but doesn't make everyone feel as warm and as fuzzy inside.)

7. **Change the worker bee.** Different people will complete tasks in different time frames. Your designer's required task duration might be long because she's busy with other projects, or simply because she works slowly. A different designer might have more bandwidth and be able to turn it around faster, or works with a team that can set several designers working concurrently. Or, maybe someone in your band knows enough about design to be able to do some of the work, and then you could have the professional do final cleanup work on it. In some circumstances, the best solution is to change who is responsible for completing the task.

There are a couple schools of thought regarding where you should focus on saving time. Some say that cutting time from the start of the project is safest, as fewer things might be set in motion that could get tangled up later on, and more will get resolved sooner, thus freeing resources to work on other tasks later. Others say that simplifying the later tasks is more critical because early tasks running late will require more attention at the end, and thus it makes sense to clear the way nearer to the deadline. The best course will likely depend on your specific situation, so consider both approaches.

There are times when the best decision is to let a project run late. That might be preferable to making everyone crazy or driving up costs. The important thing is to know what your options are.

Calculating Slack

Various additional nuances are associated with activity time, and some are easier to determine once they are all placed in the context of a schedule diagram.

We know that *duration* is the typical amount of time the task will take, and we saw that it might be presented in terms of optimistic, expected, and pessimistic numbers: T_o, T_m, and T_p, which might be used to calculate an expected time via the equation $T_e = (T_o \times 4T_m \times T_p)/6$. That's a PERT estimate. Next, we'll see a PERT chart, which among other things, is used to estimate slack time.

Slack (sometimes called "float") is the amount of wiggle room we have to do an activity—how late it can be before it becomes the bottleneck that delays the project. Activities along the critical path have no slack; any increase in time there increases the time of the whole project. Other activities can be more flexible.

Once you know the critical path, you can determine how much slack is possible, and thus the flexibility of timing some of the other tasks, deriving the earliest and latest dates that these tasks can start or finish. This information helps answer questions such as hiring decisions (choosing workers based on their estimated time frame to complete the work), answering the question, "Is it a problem if this task runs late?," and also, using the same resources on multiple tasks or projects. If a graphic designer has six days of slack time on one project, then they might be able to contribute those six days to another project (or another task within the same project).

If you are tracking these nuances of timing, they are customarily graphed within a node in the following format:

ES	ID	EF
SL	AN	
LS	DR	LF

FIG. 5.17. Node with More Information

ES: Earliest Possible Start   AN: Activity Name
ID: Activity ID Code   LS: Latest Possible Start
EF: Earliest Possible Finish   DR: Duration
SL: Slack   LF: Latest Possible Finish

Here is an expanded network diagram node for the activity "Write Songs." If we don't need all this information, we'll use the diagram on the left: just the activity name and the (expected) duration. If we need more nuanced information, we'll use the diagram at the right. (Customarily, you don't see these labels "Earliest Start," "ID," "Earliest Finish," etc., for each square, but I'll keep them in now for the sake of illustration.)

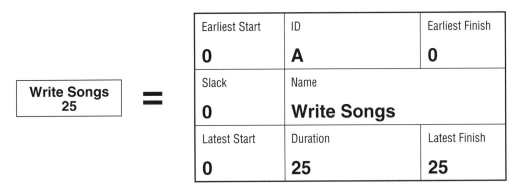

FIG. 5.18. Simple Node and Expanded Node

Let's look at some examples at how this might play out, using a CD project for each example. This technique comes into its own in complex scenarios. We'll start simply, to give you the hang of it.

1. One Task: Write Songs

Activity	Duration (Days)
A. Write songs	25

FIG. 5.19. One Task and Duration

First, we'll look at one task and a deadline. Today is June 30. We want to schedule a recording session for our CD. First, we have to write the songs. We calculate that we can comfortably write the songs or the album in twenty-five days, so that's the duration. We call the studio and they have an opening on July 25, but then are booked until mid September. So, we know that we must start today (the earliest and latest start dates are 0). We must finish this activity in twenty-five days (earliest and latest finish are twenty-five). We have no slack. It must be done by then, or else the project is in trouble.

2. Two Concurrent Tasks

Next, we'll look at a diagram with two activities.

Activity	Duration (Days)
A. Produce CD	27
B. Produce Booklet	21

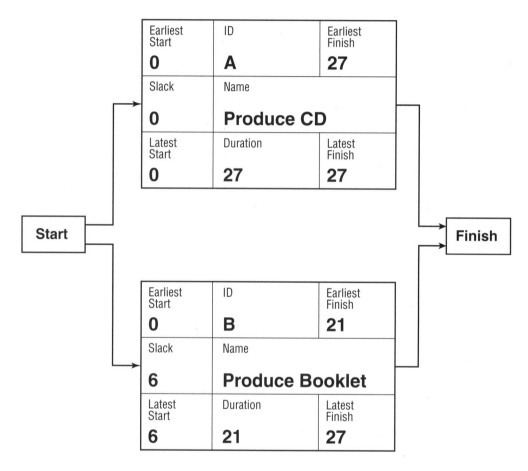

FIG. 5.20. Two Tasks and Durations

In this scenario, we have two activities: producing the CD (recording) and its accompanying booklet. They can progress independently of each other. We can start either one as early as today, day 0. It is fairly intuitive to determine that the project must take as long as the duration of the longer task: in this case, producing the CD. The amount of slack available for the shorter task is determined by a simple calculation: the duration of the longer task minus the duration of the shorter task.

$$D_{Longer} - D_{Shorter} = Slack$$

$$27 - 21 = 6 \text{ Days}$$

So, if the graphic designer assigned to producing the booklet says, "I'm really sorry, but I can't start this as soon as I thought. Could I move my deadline out a couple days later?" You can say, "Yes, that's fine." The designer can take up to 27 days to finish and not delay the project. Of course, cutting it closer to the deadline increases risk, but mathematically speaking, it is fine to give the designer a few more days.

From this chart, we can determine that the latest the designer could start working and keep the project on course would be day 6. The latest she can finish is by day 27. After that, the book production dimension of the project becomes the new critical path, and the project will take as long as the booklet takes to finish.

Note that if the recording engineer requested more time, doing so would increase the overall project timing, so approving that would require more soul searching. It will depend on the repercussions of delaying the whole project.

3. Activities with Dependencies

The first two examples were warm-ups. Now, let's look at a more detailed network diagram, showing the following activities and their dependencies. With more data, we can calculate a more nuanced picture of the earliest and latest possible start and end times for each task, as well as how much slack time (extra time) we have.

We'll start with the familiar diagrams of activities and dependencies, shown first as a simple list (as what would result from a work breakdown structure) and then a network diagram.

The list:

Activity	Duration (Days)	Dependencies	Note
A. Write Songs	25	None	First, we write songs. Without that, we don't have a project.
B. Record	17	A	Must write songs before recording them.
C. Create Booklet Content	15	A	Once we have a pool of creative work, we can begin working on the packaging (e.g., the booklet). (This is a subjective call; some would prefer to wait until we have a final song selection.)
D. Mix/Master	10	B	Must record songs before mixing/mastering.
E. Lay Out Booklet	5	B, C	Booklet layout depends on final song selection.
F. Replicate	12	D, E	Booklet and recording must be done before we can replicate.

FIG. 5.21. Data List

Here is a simple network diagram of the list's information.

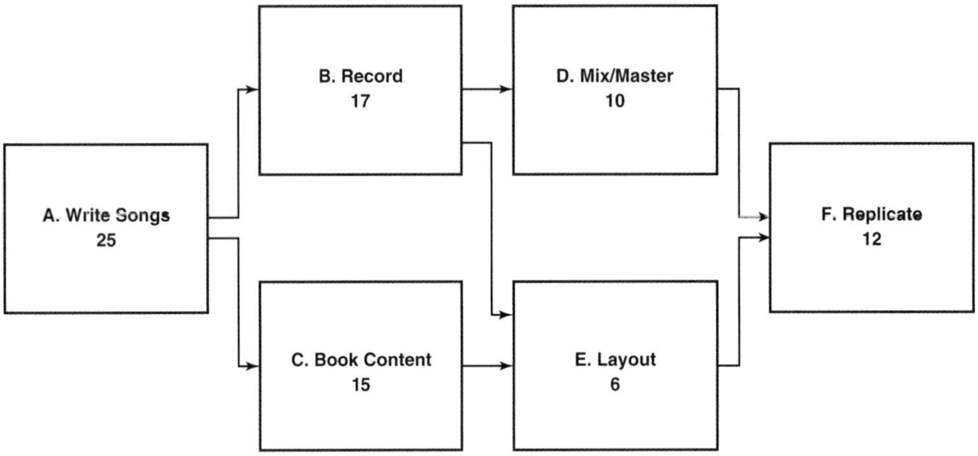

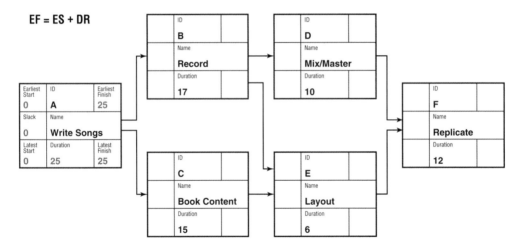

FIG. 5.22. Simple Network Diagram

Now, we can look at the nodes in their more nuanced format, and begin filling in the data. We begin node A (Write Songs) on day 0. It takes twenty-five days to write the songs, so we will finish on day 25. There is no slack; this is all we're doing for the first twenty-five days.

FIG. 5.23. Nuanced Time Data for "Write Songs"

Similarly, we can fill in the other tasks on the critical path, adding the duration to the start dates to arrive at the end dates. For these items on the critical path, there is no slack time or variation in early/late start/end dates, because the length of the task controls the duration of the overall project. Where we have leeway is in the tasks C and E, which are not on the critical path. The finish dates EF are calculated by adding ES and DR.

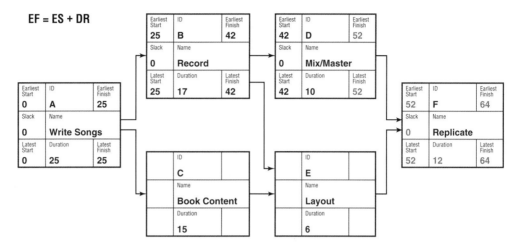

FIG. 5.24. Duration Nuances along the Critical Path

Task C, Book Content, could start at the earliest on day 25, after songwriting is done. By adding the duration, we see that the earliest it could finish is day 40. However, task E, Layout, can't begin until day 42 because it is dependent on task B, Record. In a case of multiple dependencies, you have to choose the greater number. We can't do the booklet layout until recording is done—that is, until we are certain what songs will be on the album. Otherwise, we might waste time doing graphic design on elements that ultimately won't make it in.

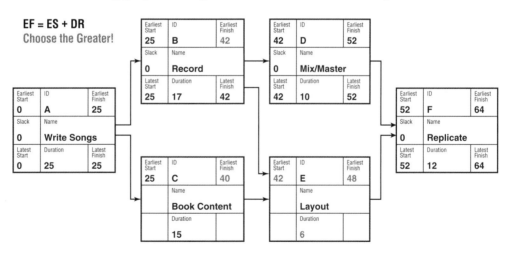

FIG. 5.25. Earliest Start and Finish for the Booklet

At this point, we can begin calculating some of the more flexible times. We know that the latest that the layout phase can finish is day 52, when replication must begin, if the project is to stay on track. We can calculate the latest start date for layout by subtracting the duration from LF, to give us 46. Broad picture, layout can begin at the earliest on day 42 (after recording) or at the latest, day

46, so that we can finish in time for replication to start. If we start later than day 46, layout will affect the overall timing for the project—that is, it will become a critical path task.

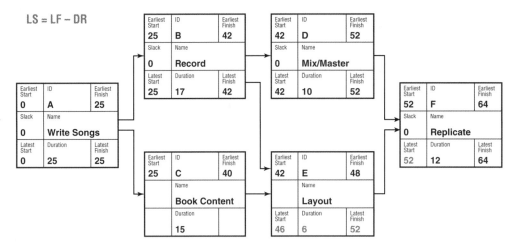

FIG. 5.26. Latest Start and Finish for Layout

When we know the LS date for the layout task, we can calculate the slack time: Slack is the difference between the earliest and latest start times. Here, that's four days. In other words, during mixing/mastering, the layout worker has four days when he or she could be deployed to other projects. Only six of those days must be devoted to layout on our project, for us to meet our deadline. Or, the layout artist could go a maximum of four days longer than anticipated without us suffering negative repercussions in timing, for this project.

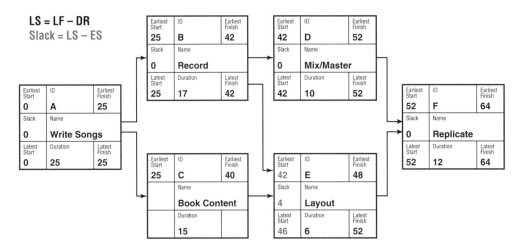

FIG. 5.27. Layout Slack

Here is the finished chart, with the remaining elements filled in for Book Content, which has two days of slack time.

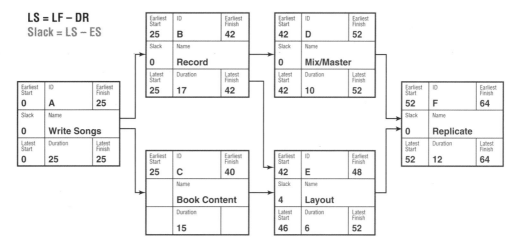

FIG. 5.28. Complete Slack Calculation

To summarize, and to give you a cheat sheet:

$$ES + DR = EF$$

$$LF - DR = LS$$

$$LS - ES = Slack$$

You calculate the earliest start times as you move forward through the diagram (called a *forward pass*); if you encounter multiple dependencies, choose the larger value. You calculate the latest possible finish times as you move backwards through the diagram (called a *backward pass*); choose the smaller value there, if there are multiple dependencies.

This approach will let you identify the nuances of timing and coordinating tasks, should you need this level of detail and control.

EVENTS AND MILESTONES

Events and milestones are two different types of specific dates that occur within the context of a project timeline. They don't have durations; they are markers along the way. They often inform the necessary time structure of a project and its tasks.

An *event* occurs outside the project, but which the project must take into account. They are generally unmovable. Some examples of events that will affect your project's timing:

- **Concert dates**. Your project might be to coordinate the music for a July 4 fireworks display. It *must* be ready on July 4! If you're a week late, that's a problem.

- **Industry events.** In the music products industry, the biggest annual trade show is winter NAMM (National Association of Music Merchants), in California, occurring towards the end of January. Thousands of product manufacturers and gear dealers converge and see what's new. For many kinds of companies, this event controls the development calendar for new products. Berklee Press always tries to release several new books at NAMM. Other events important in the music industry are that of the Audio Engineering Society (AES) and South by Southwest, in the U.S., and in Europe, MIDEM and Musikmesse.

- **The academic year.** Certain types of projects are tied into the school year, such as seasonal concerts, summer theater festivals, and new semester starts. When a book seems particularly destined to be a textbook, we will often try hard to release it before a semester starts. August 1 is much better as a release date than September 15.

- **The holiday season.** This affects certain types of products and ensembles. If you want a New Year's Eve gig or a Mardi Gras float, you'll want to start getting your crew together well in advance.

- **Vendor deadline dates.** Organizations that you deal with might have deadlines you need to follow. If you rent sheet music, there might be a time by which you must place your order to be sure that it arrives for your school year. If your project is bound for a competition, such as the John Lennon Songwriting Competition, the Independent Musician Awards, and so on, those dates will be important for your planning purposes.

- **Contract deadlines.** If your project is under contract, such as for writing a film score, or a commission, or a radio jingle, or a record deal, there will almost certainly be a specified date (which might indirectly be influenced by any of the above).

All these factors might influence your project deadline, and in your planning stages, they should all be listed and considered. Similarly, personal events such as holidays, planned family vacations, visits from relatives, school vacation weeks, and so on might also indicate days of non-productivity (or sometimes, windows of greater availability), and these should also be mapped into your project calendar or timeline.

What are the important, unmovable dates in your project's timeline? Is there an obvious date where your project must end? In the same way that you wrote down every single task and every single expense that you could think of, also write every date that might influence your project's timeline.

Milestones are points within your project that are significant and deserve tracking. They are often listed in the scope statement. Beyond the overall completion date, some important phases to track for the CD project include:

> Rehearsal 1
>
> CD Recorded
>
> Booklet Finalized
>
> CD Master Complete

These are all points of convergence or burst, where tasks come together or disseminate. They have repercussions regarding earlier work that is worthy of note, or are completion points where more types of project progress become possible. For example, the first rehearsal can only happen once a significant number of songs have been written and the band membership is secure. Finalization of the booklet means that all the art and all the writing are also done. Finishing the CD master and completing the booklet layout are necessary milestones to reach before we can go to press (i.e., replicate).

The milestones tracked should be the five or six most important points within the work. Unlike events, milestones might be movable, but it's helpful to predict tentative dates for them. Avoid too many milestones. Minor dates may distract from the ones that truly reveal major project accomplishments (and are disparagingly called "inch stones" instead).

Note: In Smartsheet and many other project management programs, you can make a task read as a milestone by entering a duration of 0. In Smartsheet, milestones show up as diamonds. I like to add the overall project deadline as the first line in a Smartsheet file. You can set the start/ finish dates in columns by those names; for a milestone (duration 0), those two columns will be the same date.

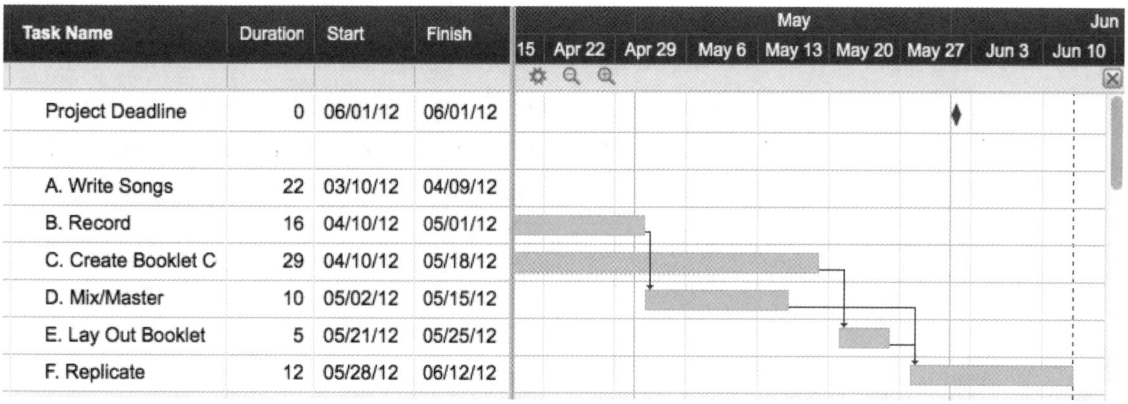

Task Name	Duration	Start	Finish	May							Jun	
				15	Apr 22	Apr 29	May 6	May 13	May 20	May 27	Jun 3	Jun 10
Project Deadline	0	06/01/12	06/01/12									
A. Write Songs	22	03/10/12	04/09/12									
B. Record	16	04/10/12	05/01/12									
C. Create Booklet C	29	04/10/12	05/18/12									
D. Mix/Master	10	05/02/12	05/15/12									
E. Lay Out Booklet	5	05/21/12	05/25/12									
F. Replicate	12	05/28/12	06/12/12									

FIG. 5.29. Milestone

CLOSING THOUGHTS

Estimating and controlling time are among the principal responsibilities and tasks of project management. Most of our time is spent analyzing the schedule and confirming with the team that tasks are getting done according to the allotted time—particularly, critical path tasks. Project management software is a great type of tool for keeping things running on time, and we will continue to explore ways to make that happen, in this book.

PRACTICE

Estimate the required duration for all of your project's activities. Create a Gantt chart using Smartsheet or another tool of your choice. Indicate dependencies and concurrencies, and determine your project's critical path. How long do you expect your project to take? Is that acceptable?

The Project Team

The quality of your project's outcome will depend mostly on the people who are doing the work. If you're leading a rock band, the recorded guitar solos will be as good as your guitarist. If you're a singer, the quality of your own voice may depend on your recording engineer's ability to choose a good microphone and use it well.

Talent, motivation, and availability of your team are constraints, just like money and time. Money and time can help mitigate or expand your team's capabilities. Your team's ultimate effectiveness will be among the most critical manifestations of how those factors affect your project.

Specifics of how people are managed will also play a big part in your project's outcome, and so will the quality of the gear you use, the places where you perform or record, and so on, but the most defining dimension of the project will be the people who work on it: your human resources.

As a project manager, ideally, you are the least expert member of the team. Your aspiration should be to hire the absolutely most gifted, qualified, and motivated experts you can find and afford, and then enable them to practice their craft at the highest level, towards implementing your project's vision. When you hire, you look at the composite skill set of the whole team, note its current deficits, and then use the opportunity to add a new member as a way to make the team's overall capabilities more complete. Everyone should add excellence in a different dimension, while sharing the same overall vision for the project's highest direction. It's a jigsaw puzzle, where every piece is strategically fitted together to form the perfect vision, more so than it is a box of crayons, with many isolated colors that might not have clear relationships or an overall sense of what big picture they are trying to address.

In this chapter, we look at how to assemble effective project teams—how to find the right people to do the work. In chapter 9, we will be looking at ways to manage them productively.

OBJECTIVES

By the end of the chapter, you will be able to:

- match tasks with workers, using a RASCI chart

- improve your budgeting based on your resourcing decisions

- assess the skills you have available and recruit efficiently

- build project teams through needs analysis, hiring, and auditioning

ROLES

Choosing people for a project team should be handled as strategically as possible. The ideal process is first to consider the various dimensions of what the work requires and then determine whether and how the various potential workers will suit those requirements.

So, begin by assessing the needs of the project, and thus, of the project team. Let's recall the various formal roles people will play in your project community, introduced in chapter 1. Some people will be on the team that actively gets the project done. Others will have more passive or indirect involvement. A single person might perform multiple roles. Here are the standard general roles, within a project community.

- **Visionary.** The visionary is the person or group who generates and is often keeper of the project definition. It could be an artist, a company CEO, or a board of directors.

- **Sponsor.** The project sponsor approves a project, makes sure it is funded, and assigns the project manager (and possibly other members of the team). The sponsor might have conceived of the project or might be managing it. In a corporate environment, such as a record label or publishing company, this is likely a fairly high up executive role. Often, in independent music projects, the artist is the sponsor.

- **Project manager.** The project manager develops and implements strategies to get the project done on time, within budget, and at an appropriate level of quality.

- **Other managers.** Some components of a project might be handled by other managers, besides the project manager. A stage manager, for example, might be in charge of overseeing what happens backstage during a concert—curtains, lights, intermission bells, stage setups, props, etc. A graphic production manager might coordinate the physical creation of a concert program booklet, such as page layout, photography, illustrations, etc. Both positions, though, should be coordinated and supervised by someone in charge of managing the whole project.

- **Other executives.** In corporations, schools, houses of worship, and other organizations, the project manager might have higher-ups that have existential oversight for a project, though they might not be much involved in it. A church choir director might serve as the project manager of the Christmas concert, but a priest might also have influence over some details, whether or not the priest is also serving as the project's sponsor.

- **Support team.** Project content and other critical tasks are completed by specialists: musicians, graphic designers, writers, accountants, editors, audio engineers, photographers, and so on, and these people comprise what is generally called the "project team," doing the lion's share of the work. In addition, there might be some general workers, such as administrative assistants or willing friends/community members, who handle various other tasks, such as photocopying, mailing, baking for informal post-concert receptions, and so on.

- **Vendors.** Vendors are contributors who are hired guns, outside the permanent project group. In music projects, typical vendors include venue owners, t-shirt companies, recording studios, and other businesses that get paid for specific services.

- **Consultants/Advisors.** Consultants/advisors lend guidance to the project team or occasional services as needed, but do not have a clearly defined body of work required by the project. They are your gurus.

- **Audience.** The audience/fans might be the most important part of the project community, and they often get utterly ignored until the project is complete (and then we ask, why didn't they buy it?). Sometimes, representatives from the likely/ imagined audience are invited in at various stages, though. They might be queried before a project is undertaken to test sales potential. They might test part of the project before its release as part of quality control. They might do peer reviews—reality checks from people as expert as the author, in the subject matter. Ultimately, they are the ones who decide whether to buy the project or not, which is one of the common measures of success.

- **Competitors for resources.** Also touching your project are those who want the resources you are using. This can include managers of other projects that share your team members, clients who need the same facilities that you do (rehearsal space, etc.), and others in the marketplace who are trying to sell similar projects to your intended market.

- **Angels.** People who provide work, advice, or funding for your project because they like you so much, not because they are on the payroll.

The core team is generally the visionary, the project manager, the sponsor, various content creators, and the support team. They do most of the work.

The extended team includes other executives, vendors, consultants/advisors. They are there to help, but might not have specific clearly defined tasks to complete. Often, though, they need to be kept informed of the project's progress.

The surrounding community includes the audience, competitors, and angels. While their influence is felt, they are not usually formal parts of the team—though they might occasionally swoop in and change everything, for better or for worse.

Some project community members are permanent staff members, so they are in the cubicle next door, purposed with helping you. Some must be hired. Some are friends and relatives, ready to contribute work for free. Some are band mates. Some are a want-ad away, and others are your siblings. And some never materialize at all, so you have to find another way to fulfill their assigned contribution. Anyone who completes a project task is part of the project community.

When you develop your project team, there are essentially four considerations:

1. **Expertise.** You want an appropriately skilled person to complete the job.

2. **Availability.** The person must be available to complete the work in the required time frame.

3. **Cost.** You want the best person you can afford.

4. **Personality.** The person must be a good cultural fit for the project. You should like being around them, and they should have a productive working chemistry with the team. Ideally, completing work like what you need them to do is more or less aligned with what they consider to be the best way they can spend their time, on this earth.

You'd think that the above order is sequenced in order of preference, but it's not always the case, sometimes not an actual possible choice, and frequently a hybrid. Sometimes, you start by choosing a person you want to work with, and then search for a good project that you can do together, so a process begins on embarking to find a vision. A band, for example, will often exist as a group and decide that it's time to put out an album. They come up with a vision, and then determine what skills are necessary to pull it off. Likely, recording engineers will eventually get added to the team, perhaps just for that recording project.

The key for the project manager, though, is gathering together a team and then coordinating that team to do the necessary work—in other words, delegating.

Delegating

Delegating work is one of the most difficult and potentially rewarding activities in life. By having others work for you, if all goes well, you can accomplish much more than you could on your own.

In some organizations, the same cast of characters works on all projects. A sheet music publisher might use the same freelance graphic designer for cover after cover after cover. With independent artists, there is often more variation between projects. A band might choose different producers for different albums, hoping to capture different types of vision. Steely Dan often changed rhythm sections from song to song, even on the same album.

Once you have your work breakdown structure, and particularly its associated task list, you can go through it and determine what tasks can/

must be delegated to others. The goal is to try to get other people to complete tasks so that the project manager can focus on confirming that the project overall is moving according to schedule.

It is very easy for a project manager to get pressured into doing too much of the work, in a project. To counter this natural tendency, try to delegate as many tasks as possible, even if you feel capable of doing them yourself. There might be the sense that it is easier just to do it than it is to explain to someone else how. That is sometimes true, but the more you delegate, the more efficient it becomes. So, try to see delegation as an ongoing skill that must continually be practiced and mastered. Improving at it throughout your career will gradually help you accomplish greater and greater things in life. And there will be plenty of tasks to do on the project that you simply won't be able to find someone else to complete.

Tasks get matched up to people appropriate to do them. To start, the standing team members get as much as they can handle. For example, the Frankfurter Streichsextett (Frankfurt String Sextet) has found a rhythm of divvying up the work necessary for their concert season. This is a part-time chamber group activity that plays about eight concerts annually (plus the occasional recording), while the members have various other gigs with other ensembles. They love playing together, but don't want the administrative overhead of external management.

Consider the following partial task list for putting together one of their concerts, with estimated timings for some major activities.

Task	Hours
Pitch concept to artistic directors	16
Negotiate fees	4
Coordinate rehearsal spaces	1
Schedule rehearsals	3
Prepare scores and plan rehearsals	4
Choose repertoire	4
Prepare scores and plan rehearsals	8
Write program text	6
Prepare concert introductions	2
Bring snacks to rehearsals and coordinate them for post-concert receptions	3
Total	**51**

FIG. 6.1. Task List and Durations

So many groups have a leader who does all the work and inevitably winds up burned out, ultimately leading to the endeavor's end. If one person did all those tasks, preparing for the concert would take her 51 hours. Add some of the other tasks that I didn't list, and we could easily get up to two weeks of full time work per concert, if one person did it all. One person working must complete tasks sequentially, so there's not a lot to do about that two-week time frame.

Fortunately, the sextet realized early on that dividing the work among multiple people allows for simultaneous progress on all fronts and balances the work more evenly among the participants. While some halos may shine more brightly than others, a natural distribution of tasks has formed that works well for them. Different players take the lead for different dimensions of the work necessary to perform each concert.

- Ingrid (viola) acts as their agent, pitching concert ideas to concert series artistic directors and negotiating fees.

- Akemi (violin) coordinates rehearsal spaces and schedules, and sometimes prepares scores and plans rehearsals.

- Christiana (cello) spearheads selecting repertoire.

- Charys (violin) is usually the first violinist and prepares scores with bowings and leads rehearsals.

- Maja (cello) writes program notes and gives introductions before each piece, during the concerts.

- Kerstin (viola) is in charge of snacks.

It's a very chamber-music approach to getting the "other work" done, with each member fulfilling a natural but different role, and it has worked well for them for a long time, achieving an appropriate balance between how productive they are and how much effort the sextet takes. Everyone's work suits how they like to spend their time, and they feel that the load is close enough to being evenly distributed that there are no resentments.

A simple way to begin organizing who will do what is to start with your WBS, listing tasks and timings. Then cluster the related tasks that could/should likely be done by the same person, or by multiple people with the same expertise.

Then, list what people are on hand, and take inventory of their skills and interests. Match up which person would be appropriate for which tasks. Keep a running time total, if you like, just to see how the division of labor goes. (You could all do this together as a group exercise.)

Task	Hours	Who	Total
Pitch concept to artistic directors	16	Ingrid	
Negotiate fees	4	Ingrid	20
Coordinate rehearsal spaces	1	Akemi	
Schedule rehearsals	3	Akemi	
Prepare scores and plan rehearsals	4	Akemi	8
Choose repertoire	4	Christiana	4
Prepare scores and plan rehearsals	8	Charys	8
Write program text	6	Maja	
Prepare concert introductions	2	Maja	8
Bring snacks to rehearsals and coordinate them for post-concert receptions	3	Kerstin	3
Total	51		51

FIG. 6.2. Work Assignment Matrix

Now, before you get mad at the members who do the least amount of work, I'll restate that this is an estimated and partial look at what they do, and in reality, the numbers are more balanced. But charts like this can reveal true imbalances, and you can certainly do them at various points in the life of any organization, not just projects. Generally, in all groups, some people work a lot harder than others and put in dramatically more time. This is frequently not tracked or made explicit, and so nobody calls the slackers out for not pulling their weight, but resentments frequently fester and eventually become major interpersonal issues.

At the planning stage for a project, you might not have any people in place. In that case, the goal is to cluster similar work functions and thus create a series of job descriptions needed for the project team to get a project done.

Some basic information like this will be self-evident when you begin your project. Much of it, though, will need to be strategized more methodically. Let's see how to organize the people and skills in your own project community and map out their roles.

ASSIGNING RESOURCES

Every task needs an advocate. Someone needs to be assigned as the responsible person to get it done. Otherwise, no work will take place. So, once you've created a work breakdown structure and generated the activities required to complete each deliverable, turn it into a chart (or upload it into project management software). Use that to organize how you assign people to complete each work packet, as well as other necessary resources, which can include facilities, gear, and materials. Assigning any type of resources works similarly. We'll use human resources for our discussions, here, but assigning venues, gear, etc. work much the same way.

Who you will decide should do what might be immediately evident/ obvious. If you've got a regular team, such as an ensemble or an office staff or a school faculty/administration, the same people might do project after project, with well defined roles. This is particularly true if you often do projects of the same type. Most role assignments will be easy to figure out. If not, any unknowns will have to be figured out, researched, and potentially, brought aboard. We'll look at ways to do that later in the chapter.

For a more nuanced way of assigning resources to deliverables, we can create a RASCI resource allocation chart. Here, we list the work packets and the team members, and then indicate who is in charge of each and who fulfills various supporting roles. In a RASCI chart (or variations thereof), we indicate who is in the following general roles:

- **Responsible:** The lead person in charge of completing the deliverable (often, the lead content creator, possibly a type of manager)

- **Accountable (or Approver):** Delegates the work to Responsible; approves the final product (such as a project manager)

- **Supporting:** Helps Responsible do the work (general content creators and support staff)

- **Consulting:** Advises as needed (often a subject matter expert)

- **Informed:** Kept apprised of progress, but doesn't contribute any actual work (such as the project sponsor, other executives, and others)

The RASCI chart below shows the work allocation for Emily's EP. There's some grouping of roles, here: the band, the engineers, and the graphics people. You can see, the band will be supporting the recording (actively working on it) and consulted about the photographs, perhaps getting veto authority if there are any photos of themselves that they really hate.

		PM	Guitar	Drums	Bass	Mix	Master	Illustrator	Layout Artist	Photographer	Distributor
ID	**Deliverable**	Emily	Mike	Andrew	David	Aaron	Alan	Needed!	Needed!	Tammy	DiscMakers
1.1.1.	Songs	A/R	C	C	C						
1.1.2.	Demo Recordings	A/R	S	C	C	I					
1.1.3.	Recordings	A	S	S	S	R					
1.1.4.	Mix	A			S	R					
1.1.5.	CD Master	A	C	C	C		R				
1.2.1.1.	Photos	A	C	C	C					R	
1.2.2.	Replication	A									R
1.2.1.2.	Booklet Layout	A	S						R		
1.2.1.3.	Cover Design	A	C	C	C			A			
1.2.1.4.	CD Label	A	C	C	C				R		
1.3.	Distribution Plan	A	R								
1.4.	Administration	A/R									
1.5.	Project Management	A/R									

FIG. 6.3. RASCI Chart

Contingencies

You can also add contingency information to a work assignment chart: alternative workers, if the originally assigned person doesn't work out. (See figure 6.4.) Some projects or roles warrant multiple backups.

In this project, Emily is the ultimate approval authority in all cases, but she also does some of the actual content creation. That is often the case in independent music projects, where the project manager is the same as the artist. It is less common (and less advised) for those roles to be the same in larger projects or corporate environments, though project managers often will generally play a role in quality control.

Software tools commonly let you program in the people who are working on the project, and they will often let you add additional information here, such as contact information, available hours, and so on. Chart form, though, lets you see big-picture what the tasks and resources are, which can help you assign resources more effectively (evenly, fairly, etc.).

	Role:	PM	Guitar	Drums	Bass	Mix	Master	Illustrator	Layout Artist	Photographer	Replicator
	Who:	Emily	Mike	Andrew	David	Aaron	Alan	Needed!	Needed!	Tammy	DiscMakers
ID	Contingency:		Tomo	Larry	Danny	Rob	JW	Kerry	Shawn	Phil	CDVelocity
1.1.1.	Songs	A/R	C	C	C						
1.1.2.	Demo Recordings	A/R	S	C	C	I					
1.1.3.	Recordings	A	S	S	S	R					
1.1.4.	Mix	A			S	R					
1.1.5.	CD Master	A	C	C	C		R				
1.2.1.1.	Photos	A	C	C	C					R	
1.2.2.	Replication	A									R
1.2.1.2.	Booklet Layout	A	S						R		
1.2.1.3.	Cover Design	A	C	C	C			A			
1.2.1.4.	CD Label	A	C	C	C				R		
1.3.	Distribution Plan	A	R								
1.4.	Administration	A/R									
1.5.	Project Management	A/R									

FIG. 6.4. RASCI Chart with Contingencies

As usual, go as deep as makes sense, in terms of what assignments you are tracking. While we might go into more depth in some versions of the work breakdown structure, at a point, reiterating low-level details just adds useless clutter to the chart. For example, the WBS lists figuring out distribution for Amazon, iTunes, Pandora, CD Baby, and Band Camp, as deliverables. But if the same person is going to do all these, probably in the same afternoon, we won't gain much by listing them separately on this chart. Similarly, there will be about six songs written, but all by the same person, so it would be redundant here to itemize them separately. In another case, though, it might be helpful to separate some of these out and assign them to different people.

Some charts indicate position names (e.g., mastering engineer), along with (sometimes instead of) names of individuals who will do the work (e.g., "George"). This way, the document becomes clearer to others regarding what's being done. In relatively small projects, though, with light forces, just names might be enough.

Drilling Down into Tasks

Similarly, each "Responsible" person on a RASCI chart can make a similar drill-down chart of the work required to complete each deliverable, working at the *activity* level of each work packet. You can also add columns for facilities, gear, and materials, as required.

Here's the detailed task list for WBS item 1.2.1.3. "Cover Design" that Emily might make. We're doing a less formal kind of matrix here, but the idea is the same.

Tasks: Cover Design	Personnel
Emily writes cover art spec	Emily
Emily writes letter of agreement (LOA) with designer	Emily
Emily emails spec and LOA to designer	Emily
Emily and designer discuss the project in depth	Emily, Designer
Designer signs LOA	Designer
Designer creates samples and emails them to Emily	Designer
Band reviews art samples and provides feedback	Emily, guitarist, bassist, drummer, band leader
Emily collates feedback and sends it to designer	Emily
Designer revises art and emails new versions	Designer
Emily chooses final version	Emily
Designer emails invoice	Designer
Designer mails hard copy of final art, plus electronic files	Designer
Emily pays cover design invoice	Emily

FIG. 6.5. Task Assignment Chart

Once these assignments are figured out, they can then get fed into a project management program such as Smartsheet or Basecamp and delegated to the people who will execute the task.

Coordinating Groups

You could list groups instead of individuals, in a resource assignment chart, if they were all doing essentially the same thing. If you were the house manager of a concert hall and had a staff of eight ushers, for an overall chart like this, you might just list "Ushers" as a group, and then have an accompanying detail chart that lists each individual and what specific station each one is assigned to. Indicate such accompanying charts in the primary resource assignment.

Something like this:

Project: Concert

	Project Manager	Music Director	Musicians	Stage Manager	Stage Crew	House Manager	Ushers	Reference Charts
Choose Repertoire		R/A	I	I				
Perform Music		A	R					
Stage Setup	A	I	C	R	S			Stage Plan
Program Distribution	I					A	R	Usher Stations
Seat Audience	I	I		I		A	R	Usher Stations
Hall Cleanup	A			S		R	S	Usher Stations, Stage Crew Stations

FIG. 6.6. Group Assignment

This gives an overview of responsibilities. Then, the referenced supplementary charts would indicate more precise information and assignments, for those who need it. Only the ushers and the house manager care about which usher stands at which station, who hands out programs and who walks around with a flashlight (escorting people to their seats), or who is in charge of cleaning up which section of the hall. That information, therefore, can get extracted out into a supplementary chart, "Usher Stations."

This "Usher Station" resource allocation chart has its own unique key, rather than using RASCI codes, which aren't that helpful here. The previous chart showed that the house manager was in charge of the house personnel, and that the ushers supported the tasks indicated. Now, we get more specific.

Usher Stations

Date: January 9, 2013   **House Manager:** Carin

Ushers:	Boriana	Lyric	Lorenzo	Sam	Mike	Craig	Beth	Rob
Stations								
Main Entrance	P	F						
Stairs			P					
L Orchestra				P	F			
R Orchestra						F		
Balcony							P	F
Cleanup								
Orchestra	C	C			C			
Back Hall			C	C		C		
Balcony							C	C

Key: Programs, **F**lashlights, **C**leanup

FIG. 6.7. Usher Station Chart

The event's house manager (Carin) uses this detail chart to make sure that all stations are covered. It then gets distributed or posted where all the ushers can see it, and so usher Mike knows that he has to grab a flashlight and go to the Left Orchestra station, working with usher Sam (who will make sure that there are programs there), and then clean the orchestra section before and after the concert. If Mike is absent, Carin will assign a backup usher to do those exact tasks. At the next concert, the same essential chart of stations can be reused, but perhaps with different people and station assignments.

Network Diagrams for Group Assignments

Network diagrams are sometimes helpful in managing groups that are doing tasks. In the following scenario, we are assigning ushers to perform various tasks for running a concert. While different specific ushers will do a variety of tasks, none requires significant training (besides perhaps a very short explanation, such as "Here's the key to the office. Go there, and get the box of programs.").

Activity	Duration (in minutes)	Ushers Required (Preferred)
A. Get Programs. Carry boxes of programs from office to concert hall	15	1 (2)
B. Distribute Programs. Provide each usher station with programs for audience.	15	1 (2)
C. Prepare Hall. Tidy up hall before the concert, making sure there is no trash, confirming all seats are functional, etc.	30	1 (6)
D. Greet audience. Before concert, attend usher stations, handing out programs and answering questions.	30	5
E. Escort audience. Help audience find their seats (walk around with flashlight).	30	3
F. Attend Stations. During concert, stand at stations to make sure nobody enters during performance, answer questions, point to the restrooms, and stand by in case of audience emergencies.	90	5
G. Clean Hall. After the concert, clean the hall.	30	1 (6)

FIG. 6.8. Usher Time Requirements

Figure 6.8 is an activity list for the ushers running a concert. Our goals here are to confirm that we have enough people working the concert, and also to determine how much it will all cost. We start by charting out the requirements, including the minimum number of people needed. Our hall has five stations, three of which require two people, so we know that we need a minimum of eight people simultaneously to be doing that work. On the other hand, there's always the option of having just one person do the cleanup for the whole hall afterwards, if they put enough time in. So, let's assume that the house manager making this chart has enough technical knowledge to fill in the minimum number of people required for each task.

The next step is to determine the dependencies, and thus, which activities can be done concurrently. In this network diagram, we can include the number of people required, as well as the anticipated duration. The format is:

$$\frac{\text{Activity (required, preferred people)}}{\text{Duration (minutes)}}$$

For example, getting the programs is easier with two people, though one could manage it. It will take fifteen minutes.

$$\frac{\text{Get Programs (1, 2)}}{15}$$

In this variation of a network diagram, where we're mapping activities rather than deliverables, we write the activity name on the arrows, accompanied by the number of ushers required for each task, plus the duration underneath. It is called an *activity-on-arrow* network diagram (AoA). The circles are milestones, labeled with numerals (referencing a key of actions). This diagram is something a house manager might draw up in order to track how many ushers are required for an event.

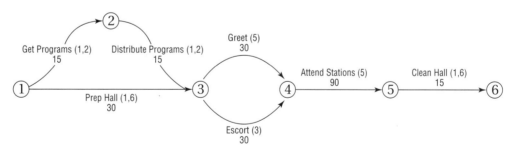

FIG. 6.9. Activity on Node Network Diagram

The milestones here might map to constraints about the evening, or they might just be abstract points of separation between activities. Here, the milestone numerals correspond as follows:

Milestone	Description
1	Building opens; ushers can arrive for work
2	Abstract node, separating sequential activities
3	House opens; audience comes in
4	Concert starts
5	Concert ends
6	Building closes; ushers leave work and go out for cocktails

FIG. 6.10. Milestone Reference List

By diagramming it like this, we can see that the work never requires more than eight ushers at a time, so hopefully, our budget will permit us to hire that many. If we have eight, the process of getting and distributing the programs (steps 1 to 2 to 3) will not interfere with preparing the hall. While the program-related tasks each require two people, they can happen sequentially within the appropriate time frame, and so we never require more than eight people to perform those three activities. Similarly, the sequential activities of greeting and escorting together require a total of eight ushers. Eight is the magic number.

Now, what if the house manager gets a call from the stage manager, who asks whether any ushers would be available for helping the stage crew fold and stack the orchestra's chairs after the concert? The house manager can see (between steps 5 and 6) that he only requires a maximum of six ushers to clean the hall, and there are no concurrent tasks with that. Therefore, he has two ushers available to work backstage, if he has hired eight ushers to work for the whole evening.

Another possible conclusion the house manager could reach from this diagram is that after step 4, he has the option to let two or three ushers go home early. While ideally six ushers would be available for cleanup, the task can be done with only five. Heck, one person slaving away could handle it.

Having a sixth usher stay past step 4 effectively translates into paying him or her for an extra ninety minutes of work when we only need fifteen minutes of work. It might make sense to reduce forces, after step 4, if the pressure to control costs is greater than the pressure to keep the extra workers employed for the full time.

Say, each usher costs $20 per hour. The potential extra usher working from 4 to 6 would get paid for 105 minutes, or $34. To compensate for the loss of the sixth usher in steps 5–6, the remaining five ushers will have to work an extra three minutes each (fifteen minutes missing work from one usher / 5 ushers = 3 minutes) to compensate. That's likely not going to be a noticeable or significant amount of extra time for them, so it probably makes sense (financially) to send usher 6 home early.

From this diagram, we can also see that the building *must* open at least an hour before the concert and remain open at least fifteen minutes after the concert. (More of a buffer than this will probably be required by other activities unrelated to the ushers.)

Time Fragments

Once you start assigning resources to the work, you will likely find the need to revisit timing and cost estimates. Start by estimating actual work-time requirements, using any of the methods already discussed, but with more precision. Back to our CD example, say that you expect the cover art designer to spend four hours actually generating draft cover designs. The next question is to ask what percentage of her time the designer will spend working on your project. A staff designer working in a corporate environment might contribute all their time to your project. However, a freelance designer might spend only 10% of their time working for you. The *duration* of this task for a staff designer (100 percent yours) would be 0.5 days. The duration for the freelance designer (10% yours) would be five days (10% of a 40-hour week).

These different types of reporting relationships will require different types of management. The more closely tied to you and your project each individual is, the more predictable they will tend to be, regarding delivering work on time. The numbers on the chart below show the likely level of natural dedication to your project each relationship will show, with 1 being the most on board and 8 being the least. Higher numbers here will likely require more reminders, more cheerleading, and more micromanaging than lower numbers. Essentially, your direct reports (1 to 4) will be easiest to control. Those whom you share will be more challenging.

	100% Yours		Shared with Other Managers/Clients	
	One Project	Multiple Projects	One Project	Multiple Projects
Completes the job	1	2	5	6
Does a portion of the job	3	4	7	8

Easier to Control 1 2 3 4 5 6 7 8 Harder to Control

FIG. 6.11. Expectations of Reliability

In the case of an independent musician like Emily Peal, everyone involved in the project will probably have multiple projects and taskmasters in their lives. They will all be in the 5 to 8 range. Getting them to deliver will generally require special incentives: financial, inspirational, and emotional (i.e., pay them, make them feel they are part of something great, and/or be their best friend). Their intentions might be to help you, but other factors will control how they spend their time—and thus, your project. If her drummer is in another band in addition to hers, she will have to manage around those competing obligations. The drummer's obligations can become a constraint of Emily's project, and affect its timeline.

For organizations that employ full-time staffers, many of those completing tasks are in quadrants 1 to 4. Managing them will be easier, as the workers' days are framed to filter out competing pulls on their time.

An implication of this is that when you are hiring temporary help, you are more likely to get focused and predictable work if you block out entire days (or weeks) when the contractor is all yours, rather than sharing them with multiple other interests. Each opportunity for them to get interrupted is an opportunity for them to get delayed, distracted, or otherwise derailed. Hiring an engineer for one full day (quadrant 5) will probably yield more predictable results than hiring the engineer for two half days (quadrant 6, but risking moving into quadrants 7 or 8). This isn't always possible or even the best choice, but it is generally a good idea to reduce fragmentation of your team's attentions, as you can.

Criteria for Assigning Tasks

Task assignments are made primarily based on skills, cost, availability, proximity, and personal compatibility or cultural fit.

- **Skills.** The task must be matched with who is capable of doing the work. Obviously, a bass player needs to understand how to play bass. Less obviously, an ideal usher might be required to lift boxes of programs or help fold and stack chairs. We'll look at some tools for tracking skills later in this section.

- **Cost.** Different levels of workers require different pay rates, which affects the project budget. Do you require a senior graphic designer to do all the work, such as design a cover and lay out the text, or can you get by with a senior designer to do the actual design work and then a more junior/less expensive designer to pour the text into a template created by the senior designer?

- **Availability.** If the required task is on the critical path, the precise availability of the resource becomes more urgent. You might be able to wait for the ideal guitarist's schedule to free up, but your completion date target might require you to go with someone else.

- **Proximity.** A local worker will have advantages over a distant one, in some cases, but it doesn't always matter. Increasingly, recordings are done remotely; a soloist with a home studio can download files and overdub their part over a rhythm section, then send it back to the engineer for mixing. The result might be absent the same magic that happens when musicians play in the same room together, but it might not matter much. Choosing a CD replication house based on distance might affect project timing. Shipping between countries takes time and includes some additional expenses. The overall cost savings might be worth it, though, and the added time requirements might not be a problem.

- **Personal Compatibility/Cultural Fit.** Whether a team enjoys working together can be among the most critical reasons to place someone in a role. If the essential skill set checks out, the next most important factor might well be personal compatibility or cultural fit. The danger of this is in bringing aboard people who have redundant skill sets or outlooks, which can ultimately lead to creative stagnation (plus other diversity issues). So, a balance needs to be reached between hiring people that bring new qualities but also fit in comfortably with the rest of the team. In cases where vendors get hired to do specific technical tasks, this might not matter at all. If you like the Red Sox and your CD replicator likes the Yankees, assuming all other factors check out, you can probably compromise on this seemingly insurmountable cultural divide.

On the other hand, if you are forming a non-profit organization designed to introduce classical music to inner-city youth, one of the challenges will be crossing the cultural divide between the staff and the community. The project's personnel must be able to cross that line, culturally, between the blue-haired, aristocratic little old ladies who sit on the board and the community they hope will start downloading MP3s of Mozart string quartets. Bringing effective people into the project who can cross this line might be challenging, but it will also likely be among the most critical determining factors regarding the project's success.

Most of these factors are fairly obvious to determine, when matching people to tasks. Managing skill lists can be relatively complex, and there are a few different tools to help clarify this dimension.

We have already seen resource allocation charts. There are two precursors to these: the WBS (or its activity list) and a skills inventory.

A *skills/resources inventory* is a chart itemizing the capabilities possessed by your team—the primary skills they are hired for and also secondary abilities that might be helpful at some point. Variations of skills/resources inventories can be used to match people with tasks and also to see what skills are necessary when we add people to the team.

Depending on how big your project is, you might want to make these more or less formal. Here's an informal list showing possible skills and gear for Emily's band.

Name	Role	Other Skills	Gear/Other
Mike	guitar	sound design Web design multi-instrumentalist speaks Japanese	home studio trombone, trumpet, clarinet
David	bass	good connections to other musicians music teacher arranging	Zoom mic/recorder
Andrew	drums	producer/engineer excellent cook	tour van amp collection PA system

FIG. 6.12. Team Skills/Resources Inventory Example

It's a good idea to periodically ask your core team to remind you of what skills/gear they have and are willing to contribute to the effort. Get their current résumés. It's possible that a skill you need is already on hand.

Analyzing Work for Required Skills

When you are building a team, it's important to analyze the work that needs to be done and use that to help you decide who to hire. It will translate into job postings and candidate review checklists, as well as help you match people to tasks.

This more robust type of skills inventory generally includes more items, which you can organize into four groups: technical, administrative, leadership/interpersonal, and business/strategic. The same inventory of skills can be used for multiple similar roles, which can make comparing the documents much easier. For example, we need to add some different types of graphics workers to help with our booklet: people to do illustration, graphic design, and text layout. This might be a single person, but depending on the skills, availability, cost, etc. of the potential people we find, we might divide this work among several different people.

We have to start by isolating the different skills we need for the work at hand. We'll start with cover design. To create a skills summary, start with the actions, but frame them as more generic skills, in concise language. Let's see what we can derive from the "Cover Design" task list.

Tasks: Cover Design
Emily writes cover art spec
Emily writes letter of agreement (LOA) with designer
Emily emails spec and LOA to designer
Emily and designer discuss the project in depth
Designer signs LOA
Designer creates samples and emails them to Emily
Band reviews art samples and provides feedback
Emily collates feedback and sends it to designer
Designer revises art and emails new versions
Emily chooses final version
Emily emails invoice
Designer mails hard copy of final art, plus electronic files
Emily pays cover design invoice

FIG. 6.13. Required Skills: Cover Design Task List

We scan the list of tasks, and then extrapolate the following necessary skills from it, into the skills inventory. Here, we have a row for each skill, with columns showing how critical each skill is to a given task and then columns for candidates, indicating how competent the worker or candidate currently associated with that role is. We'll fill in the criticality here for the role of cover illustrator, using a scale of 1 (not important) to 4 (most important). For the illustrator, we primarily care about their ability to create usable art. The administrative necessities would be helpful, but for a brilliant artist, we are willing to roll with someone who might need some prodding, regarding paperwork. As long as the project manager can handle the leadership skills, those deficits won't matter here.

Role: Cover Illustrator

Skill	Criticality	Competency Candidate A	Competency Candidate B	Competency Candidate C
Technical				
Graphic design, for creating both evocative art and commercial products	4			
Illustration: can create evocative art that expresses articulated spec	4			
Graphically creative, able to create multiple concepts	4			
Conversant with computer-generated graphics and producing to printer-ready technical specs	4			
Administrative				
Generate work agreements	3			
Route paperwork	2			
Collate multiple opinions into clear directives	3			
Stick to budget	3			
Leadership/Interpersonal				
Achieves group consensus	1			
Accepts feedback	4			
Business/Strategic				
Direct graphics generation to support overall product vision	2			
Negotiate contracts	1			

FIG. 6.14. Candidate Competency Tracking Matrix

Then, for each candidate we consider for the illustrator position, we track how well they suit each task. We can compare them side by side, and thus make an informed decision based on how well they suit the work we need to get done.

HIRING

Choosing who will be on your project team is among the most important things you do, and it will have a huge impact on your project's outcome. A bad manager can achieve good results if the people doing the work are experts. A good manager with an ineffective team will struggle.

There are three dimensions to hiring: skills, vision alignment, and chemistry.

1. **Skills** are the specific capabilities of the person you hire, mapped to the specific technical needs of the project. The charts we just made will help confirm that.

2. **Vision alignment** means whether the person is passionate about your work. The more inspired and committed the team is to the project's over-arching purpose, the better job they will do.

3. **Chemistry** is whether the person will be a mutually inspiring and positive presence on your team, making the community more pleasant and vibrant. Meeting with people in person helps anticipate how this dimension will work out.

Consider the case of hiring ushers. Being an usher often doesn't require many specific technical skills: be able to show up on time, learn the floor plan of the concert hall, follow some basic directions, look reasonably tidy, and so on. If your staff of ushers has these basic qualities, they will probably do an adequate job. People in the audience will be able to find their seats and the restrooms. However, if you hire ushers who adore music, find it fun to be part of a performance, and genuinely like assisting people, the hall will have a different vibe. If the ushers find it a little exciting whenever a pre-concert warning bell sounds, that excitement will carry over to the audience experience. If the ushers truly believe that the event will be better served if the ushers are polite and tidy and cheerful, they will embody those values without being nagged into doing so by the house manager. The concert experience will be better if the ushers have more emotional buy-in with the event, and genuinely want the concert to be a certain way. And the experience will be a lot better if every single person hired to participate in putting on the concert, similarly shares excitement for the vision, from the ticket sales person, to the stage manager, to the conductor, to the customer support staff. Conversely, a grouchy, cynical usher who tends to hate the music being performed will detract from the concert experience, no matter how well he can hand out a program or use a flashlight.

It all comes down to making good hiring decisions, and hiring at all levels (including choosing vendors, such as CD replicators, engineers, shipping companies, and so on) should be done carefully, to ensure both a match of competencies and to make sure that new hires share enthusiasm for your project vision. Take these decisions seriously. You are who you hire.

You want to be able to delegate the work to people you can absolutely trust to get it done to your standards.

Delegating a task to someone who has a special gift for accomplishing such things is a rare pleasure. Give a master guitarist a solo to play, and you are setting magic in motion. On the other hand, giving someone a critical task that is beyond their means is a singularly painful experience, particularly when there is a lot at stake for them getting it right. And firing people sucks. Most people get fired because they shouldn't have been hired in the first place. Obviously, the loss of a job is a horrendous, often life-defining event, and it is often a pain that could have been avoided if the hiring practice was more careful.

Hiring must be methodical. It's tempting to go with the personality that you like best—just the best cultural fit. And you should hire for chemistry. However, before you get to the level of chemistry, you must confirm that the prospective team member has the requisite skills, or at least innate talents, to knock the gig out of the ballpark. Hopefully, you will dig up enough of a pool of well qualified candidates that you can make a good-conscience decision to hire the person you like being around the best.

Stages of the Hiring Process

There are essentially five stages, in reviewing candidates.

1. **Quick screening.** Review résumés and demo tapes to weed out everyone obviously inappropriate and to confirm that the requisite skills are present.

2. **Quick communication.** Use email or a quick phone call to confirm that basic parameters, such as availability, are adequate.

3. **Test.** Give them a task to do that will give you the chance to work together. This might be a mini project, or a set of detailed questions to answer. This is the most useful step towards providing insight into their competency.

4. **Substantial interviews.** Grill them in depth, trying to determine their potential level of commitment and their work history. Give everyone they will work with closely the chance to interview new team members. At this point, you are trying to determine chemistry, more than skills.

5. **Reference checks.** Find people who have worked with them previously, and try to understand their actual experience, rather than their canned speech. Like the test, it is a reality check.

The first step is to generate a checklist of all the skills you require, starting with referencing your RASCI chart, but adding space to make notations about mission buy in, time availability, test score, cultural fit, and financial parameters.

You'll use this checklist as a job candidate filter. If someone doesn't have any critical item on this list, then they are disqualified, even if they are your best friend. Even if they are your relative. Firing your relatives is just awful. So is including an inappropriate team member in your project—particularly a recording, where a sub-par player brings down the whole effect, and often the morale of other members on the team.

Don't hire relatives because they are available or cheap. Hire them because they can contribute as much or more in their role than anyone else on the team.

HIRING FAMILY AND FRIENDS

Your relationships with friends and relatives are always more important than the outcome of any stupid project. If people close to you are involved, prioritize their having a positive life experience over the good of the project. Dig deep into your own bank account and work into the wee hours of the night to make their experience working on your project positive, if you have to. Don't be mad if they aren't up to the task. It's your own fault for bringing them on board, rather than making a business decision that would have been better for the project's outcome. Edge them out gracefully, if you must, and make sure that they maintain face. Apologize and pay whatever is necessary to whomever to make it come out right. Note: Everyone will probably end up mad at you anyway. Generally, work is much cleaner when there are no relatives or close friends involved.

Job Descriptions/Want Ads

When your checklist is set, create a job description. This document will get distributed among people whom you trust (to ask whether they know anyone appropriate), or posted as an ad, featuring all or most of the most critical criteria and a few of the others. In some settings, getting too specific with a want ad can turn people away needlessly, but at some point, they need to see a comprehensive job description in writing. You can also fill in the details when you talk to the person.

Post it on LinkedIn, Craigslist, the Berklee network, Monster.com, and other places that people look for work. The job description might also be incorporated into a contract or letter of agreement, so be sure that it is complete.

Then sit back and wait for the résumés to start pouring in.

If you can afford it, it's helpful to have a third party do an initial screening. This saves time, weeding out obviously inappropriate candidates. Also, it allows someone else to be the "bad guy," by depersonalizing the process, which might be helpful if there are relationships that need to get preserved.

A short ad might look like this:

Wanted: Live sound engineer with at least five years experience for hard rock band, just out of college, going on tour of southwestern U.S. and Mexico 6/4/2012 to 7/1/2012. Must have experience wiring multiple kinds of venues. Ideally, have your own high quality PA system and vehicle. Contact George at George@velvetsunshine.com. Please provide us with a recording of your hard rock work.

That's just a teaser, though. A longer ad that really describes the position in detail will likely give you better quality responses. Figure a page or two, based on the checklist we produced earlier.

Generally, you will get a lot of responses to any advertised job, and nearly all respondents will be completely inappropriate for the position. Beyond the fact that so many people take a shotgun approach to job hunting (which is generally ineffective), a reason why ads generate so many unqualified queries is that current requirements for out-of-work people seeking jobless benefits, in some places, require that the recipient prove that they send a job application every day or every week. It is common practice for people to send résumés to any posted ad, even if they aren't really serious about the position. That creates extra work for the job screener.

As soon as you can disqualify someone, do so, but be kind and realize that the person looking for work could well be at a low point in his or her life and could use some compassion. They might not be right for this position, but maybe in two years, they will be exactly right for something else. So keep all interactions positive, including rejections.

> Dear [applicant name],
>
> Thanks so much for your interest in [your project/band/company/etc.]. We're really looking for someone with [some qualification that they don't have, though you can leave this out, if you like], so this isn't a good fit, but you seem great, and we wish you the very best of luck with your search.
>
> Sincerely,
>
> [your name, role, and organization]

Use the checklist of criteria. Anything that goes against your must-haves is a disqualification, even if you like the person's personality a lot. If there is rare, magical chemistry, you might consider them for another role, if you can afford it, but keep focused on finding exactly the right person for the job. You will always regret bad hiring decisions, and they can sink a project.

In the name of saving time, try to screen first via email. Reviewing résumés and cover letters might also help you screen out obviously unqualified people.

If those check out, get a sample of the person's work, and review it, before talking to them on the phone. Remember, you're just looking for one person. Disqualify anyone inappropriate as soon as you can. They will be on their very best behavior at this point in the process, and so anything weird or inappropriate should be a red flag to take seriously.

Always ask for a résumé, not only to see a candidate's history, but to see how they execute their résumé as a project. Notice every typo and every inconsistent formatting choice. This should be the best-quality document they ever create, except perhaps their wedding invitation, so it makes sense to judge it carefully and unforgivingly. This is particularly the case for anyone doing work intended for publication. (It might be okay to hire a roadie who doesn't understand the difference between an en-dash and an em-dash, but not a graphic designer or a writer.)

A résumé can be misleading, though. People sometimes have other people (or professional companies) do their résumés. That's not bad, as it's such an important document to get right, but it can be confusing to a job screener. It's important to get spontaneously generated materials as well, to see what they are capable of themselves.

If their email seems good and their sample work looks great, then call them for an interview (or a phone screening). Keep first interviews short—just fifteen minutes. You might give them a task. Assign a bit of work to see how they do, and to test your interactions. Put them on the spot. Ask them to offer advice. Ask them to record a thirty-second bass groove in F♯ minor that includes some slap articulations. See how you like working with them. If you never hear from them again, then that's an excellent indication that they won't have sufficient interest to commit to you enough.

Meanwhile, throughout all these interactions, fill in the checklist, adding columns as you decide to include additional criteria.

Ultimately, you'll get similar information for everyone you interview. You might want to score them, if you need to compare them easily against each other. The goal is to make an objective decision, based on who is most likely to do a great job completing the work needed. Making a friend in the process would be terrific, but put the work first, and hope that like-minded people will show up.

Tests

Serious candidates should get a chance to show their stuff. Résumés and interviews reveal some basic characteristics, but actually working with someone reveals so much more. You will learn about their specific skill set and about how you can communicate with them. The more significant the job and the pay scale, the more hoops it's appropriate to have them jump through.

When I hire editorial assistants at Berklee Press, I make them proofread some writing about music theory (designed with various traps to test their attention to detail and knowledge of rules of grammar), and also ask them for a Finale file, so that I can see their technical skills and general attention to detail. If you're hiring performing musicians, you need to hear them play live; demo tapes can be as misleading as résumés. (We'll discuss auditions later in the chapter.) While it is probably not fair to ask an artist or engineer to actually produce art or engineer tracks for you, you can discuss specific work together. For illustrators, in addition to seeing their portfolios, you can send them some illustrations you like and some you hate, and get them to discuss their reactions. This can reveal how they think about their work, and also give you more insight into what their capabilities are.

How well they perform on this gets marked on their scorecard. It is helpful to have a consistent scale you use in assessing test results, to make it relatively easy to compare candidates against each other.

Interviews

Interviewing a candidate reveals a lot. Beyond what they say, it is revealing to see how they dress, how they move, and generally, how you get along with them. Beyond the pragmatic answering of questions and determining of how well qualified they are, you should be trying to gauge their overall enthusiasm for your project's purpose, and also generally how competent they are in dealing with the world.

In interviewing someone, you want to learn how they approach work. A common mistake is to talk too much, when you are interviewing someone. It's more effective to get them to talk, most of the time. Let them explain to you what they think are their strengths and weaknesses. Get them to tell the story of why they left their previous job. Were they fired? Did they get along with their boss?

You can often tell immediately that someone won't work out, just by meeting with them—even if you meet with them remotely, such as via Skype.

Does the candidate have an accurate image of themselves, with their strengths and weaknesses? Do they speak well of past colleagues? Do they harbor deep resentments? Are they perpetual victims? Are they committed to quality? What are their big picture goals in their careers? Do they seem excited about your project?

Keep them talking, and pay careful attention to anything that strikes you as negative.

I've found that when I've hired people despite seeing red flags, those issues have generally turned out to be revealing of deeper issues. One candidate absolutely reeked of cigarette smoke when I interviewed him. I thought that was a little odd, but hired him, figuring that he was just nervous before the interview and needed a smoke beforehand to calm down. It turned out that he was frequently overcome by a kind of paralyzing nervousness that translated into poor quality work whenever deadlines were looming.

Another administrative assistant candidate had a kind of tick in his answers, saying "I can probably manage that," whenever a skill set question came up. That should have struck me as meaning, "I am capable of doing this, but I don't much want to." He did exceptionally well on my proofreading test, though, so I hired him. But his attention to detail was uneven, when he was working. While he was capable of good work, he wasn't compelled to produce it all of the time. I remember, I once had him photocopy a large 11x17 proof that we had to send to an author on a very tight timeline. He "managed to do it," but he didn't excel at that simple task. He didn't straighten the pages, so the pile was disorderly. Some were upside down. I had him straighten it out before shipping them, but when the author received the proof, he reported that twenty pages were missing. I reported this to the (former) assistant, who said, "Oh, that's no problem, I'll copy them now." It was a problem, though, and his tenure as my assistant was short.

But hiring him was my fault, as I noticed the signs in the interview that his attitude wasn't right. In terms of skill, he was the best candidate, but in terms of having a vision for excellence, he wasn't there. I should have kept looking, though, rather than making a bad hire. It is estimated that a bad hire costs fifteen times as much as their salary, factoring in both costs for lost time, lost potential revenue, and ancillary expenses. It's worth trying to avoid that.

Auditions

Hiring performing musicians is like hiring other types of workers. There's generally an initial screening, and then an in-person audition phase or phases involved, such as this:

1. Applicant sends résumés and/or recordings.

2. Applicant performs audition. Usually, this is about five to ten minutes long, possibly in multiple rounds.

3. Applicant plays alongside the rest of the ensemble. This might last an entire rehearsal, or it might involve an extended trial period.

A formal scoring process makes this much easier. This can include a detailed chart of qualities being sought, or a simpler overall rating system.

Rating Auditions

Some auditions might have hundreds of auditionees to listen to in a day, in hopes of filling a single position. There's the cliché line, "Thank you, next!" that heartless jurists say when someone has barely started their prepared routine. But do the math. If you give each auditionee ten minutes to show their stuff and there are a hundred people auditioning, and there are two minutes of bustling around between each, that's 1200 minutes, or twenty hours spent auditioning applicants. The novelty wears off, after a couple days of this. Also, when you've been at it for a while, you can actually make a pretty good assessment in about five seconds regarding whether the person is among the best so far for the available position. When someone begs to do two songs instead of the single song specified by the advertised parameters, do the math. Multiplying the extra three minutes times one hundred applicants gives your jury an additional five hours of work.

It's often helpful for each jurist to fill out an individual form for each candidate. Then, all the jurists should take a moment to discuss the audition they just witnessed. Someone might have missed something. An audition scorecard might look like the one in figure 6.15, and you could rate each dimension on different scales, if you want to give additional weight to some dimensions over others. Then add the scores together to get a final score for the applicant.

Bass Auditions November 10, 2012
Candidate Name/Contact Info: **Jurist Name:**

	Score	Comment
Technique	1–20	
Improvisation	1–5	
Stage Presence	1–5	
Melodic Memory	1–5	
Reading	1–10	
Sense of Timing	1–25	
Sound	1–30	
Total	**Out of 100**	

FIG. 6.15. Audition Rating Sheet

After each audition, take a minute or two to discuss the candidate with the group, and then mark an overall score on a log sheet that looks like this:

Name	Score	Yes	No	Maybe	Comment

FIG. 6.16. Audition Summary Matrix

The goal here is to capture the gist of the audition while it is still fresh in everyone's minds. The columns for yes and no can help you overrule the average score; sometimes, you have to allow for breaking the rules. But this can help you compress a tremendous amount of data into something you see at a glance.

When it's done, see what the data reveals. If you feel like you've got a lot of qualified candidates, the break point of where to invite people for further audition rounds could become evident. Essentially, you want to determine how much time you want to give phase 2, decide what you need to test for, and accept the most qualified candidates to go through another round.

Not everyone does as detailed a scoring approach. Here's how the process works at one of the major orchestras in Europe (which asked me to keep their name anonymous, as elements of the process are secret!). Appointments at this level might last an entire career (forty years!), so they are handled very carefully and methodically, with participation from a great number of people in the orchestra. They have found that because so many people weigh in, they have to keep their scoring process simpler. Here's how it works.

1. **Initial Screening.** First, applicants send résumés, which always include photos. All members of the relevant instrument section will rate each resume Yes, No, Maybe. For an opening in the first violin section, they recently received 415 résumés, so all eighteen members of the first violins reviewed all résumés. Then, they get collated, and each candidate gets a point for each "yes." The top scoring thirty to forty candidates from this screening round are invited to audition. About twenty to thirty of them typically decide to continue in the process.

2. **Audition day.** There are generally three rounds of auditions, all done on the same day.

   The first round of the auditions is set up with the instrument section on one side of a screen, the candidate on the other, and two thirds of the full orchestra in the audience, observing. The candidate is asked to play a section of a classical-era concerto, such as Mozart, accompanied by a piano. If three or more section members show interest, the candidate is asked to play a cadenza to this concerto. They also play an orchestral excerpt. They each play for about four minutes, total. Then, the section votes about whether they advance to the next round or not. If they vote no, the rest of the orchestra can then vote to push the candidate to the next round anyway, by a two-thirds vote. Between two and eight candidates will advance.

   In the second round, each candidate is asked to play a Romantic-era concerto, such as Brahms, again accompanied by a piano. They get about eight minutes, and the candidate is no longer hidden by a screen. The section then votes on whether to advance the candidate to the third round, or whether to stop the process and re-advertise the position, if nobody adequate is present. The top two or three candidates will advance to the next round. Again, if the section votes no, the orchestra can advance a candidate to the third round by a two-thirds vote.

After round 3, a final decision is usually made. Candidates play orchestral excerpts, unaccompanied. The orchestra members can communicate with them, asking for different tempos or other modifications. At the end of the round, the orchestra meets together, and the section recommends who they want to hire. The orchestra or the conductor can veto this recommendation, but they cannot force a different "yes" decision.

3. **Trial Period.** New orchestral members get a one-year contract, which includes an eight-month trial period. After five months, they are informed whether the position is likely to be permanent, and at eight months, a final decision is made.

This is a careful, deep process designed to ensure that the new member of the orchestra will be a good long-term fit. The series of processes in place gives the orchestra the opportunity to head off disaster at multiple points. Everyone in the orchestra is included in the process, and that helps ensure a good cultural fit, and ultimately, the cohesiveness of the ensemble.

It seems a big investment of human capital. Audition day can involve fifty members of the orchestra for at least four or five hours; that's 250 person-hours of investment, and at the end, they might not wind up hiring anyone. The orchestra's success speaks for itself, though. It is among the world's best, and there is no arguing with success.

In the end, it comes down to the belief that the results are primarily dependent on the people involved.

Auditions are among the very most stressful events in a musician's life, so in the name of basic human compassion, be kind to the person in the hot seat. Everyone auditioning is trying to change their life circumstance. They might have been out of work for a long time, or they might have had a tragic life event that is throwing them off their game, and they might actually be a much better performer than how they are playing that day.

It is usually not necessary to give feedback to everyone who auditions, and doing so can add tremendous time and emotional energy to the process.

References

Always check at least two or three references. Ideally, these are people you research, rather than people your candidate suggests. If you are hiring a mastering engineer, find a recording that they mastered, and then contact someone involved in the project. Listen to that random recording, if you can (though, understand that the end result might not be entirely under the engineer's control).

Pay close attention to what recommenders are saying. They might be hoping you'll read in between the lines, but are avoiding telling you too much truth out of fear of legal or personal repercussions. They should gush. If they are being slightly aloof, then they might be holding back. Be creative in the questions you ask, to get to the bottom of it.

> You: How would you describe this dude as an engineer?
>
> Him: He's great. Consummate professional, nice guy, and he really got an amazing sound for us. He also knows a lot of people in the industry and connected us with some people that helped us out a lot.

[*Translation*: This reference sincerely thinks well of the guy. There are more positive details than requested.]

Or:

> You: How would you describe this dude as an engineer?
>
> Him: Uh... Fine.

[*Translation*: They had a problematic relationship, and this reference resents being stuck in this position of having to talk to you.]

If the candidate can't get a couple of gushing references, there's a problem, and you should move on.

One technique is to ask the reviewer to rate the candidate on a scale of 1 to 10, on various criteria: technical ability, promptness, ability to come in on time/within budget, and so on. Again, though, the reference should gush: 9 or 10 on all critical dimensions. There's an expression in the human resources industry, "A 6 is a 2." People will tend to rate their colleagues high. Consider anything less than a rating of 8 indicative of a problem.

Figure it takes a couple months to hire someone for a long-term position. Once you give them the green light, they might need a couple weeks or more to extricate themselves from their current job or other life circumstance, so be sure to build a buffer into your timeline. If they are leaving another job, it's possible that they haven't had a vacation in a while, so you might want to give them a break before they start.

Throughout the hiring process, you are keeping a scorecard, quantifying all the skills you can. You could total them all up and compare them, though some criteria are easier to quantify than others. Availability dates, for example, probably need to be considered separately, as does commitment to vision.

STAKEHOLDERS IN SCOPE STATEMENT

As you bring people aboard, keep your project scope statement up to date regarding who is working on the team and performing significant roles. Update your stakeholder chart, and as an attachment to the scope statement, include your resource allocation charts.

This, then, completes the scope statement. In doing so, the major planning tools for the project have been created. Conditions will change, as the project progresses, and these documents will evolve, but once you've got them fleshed out, the rest is just details.

CLOSING THOUGHTS

While writing this book, one of the people I interviewed was Peter Jackson, a retired and highly distinguished project manager who worked for the Army Corps of Engineers for over twenty years, before he went freelance. I wanted to talk shop about project management with someone who was experienced with running very large projects (~$200 million, such as the mid 1990s cleanup of Boston Harbor, which Pete managed), so we sat down for a couple hours, discussing network diagrams, how to calculate float time, critical paths, and such.

Finally, he sat back and said, "You know, while these tools are all helpful, mostly, project management is personality management."

For projects big and small, it all still comes down to people, and therefore, communication. It's a cliché and perhaps a disappointingly mundane reduction, but there it is.

When you hire people, you're building a team, and developing a team that has a healthy communication dynamic is critical on so many levels. Careful hiring is key to achieving great results.

PRACTICE

Complete a RASCI resource allocation chart for your project.

CHAPTER 7

Risk Management

What music-related disasters have you witnessed? What were their repercussions? Could they have been avoided?

There is constant pressure on every undertaking for it to take an unintended direction. Consequences might be minor delays that don't have much effect, or they can be complete fiascos that end the project in failure. Sometimes, these new directions are actually potentially positive developments, such as the risk of too much demand for your music. In any case, they are called "risks," and their occurrences are ideally considered and accounted for before it is too late to accommodate them.

In this chapter, we discuss risk planning.

OBJECTIVES

By the end of the chapter, you will be able to:

- anticipate many of the risks likely in your project

- prioritize which risks are most important to plan around

- develop contingency plans for dealing with those risks

RISKS AND ISSUES

A *risk* is a possibility that something unexpected will happen (more often bad than good!). Similarly, an *issue* is a certainty of something that has happened or will happen. The primary difference is that risks are always present, but hopefully considered and mitigated in the planning process. Issues are realities that come about during execution.

A risk has two parts: the condition and the impact. "If the piano is out of tune, then the recording will be unusable." That is a risk. To mitigate it, we schedule a piano tuning before the recording session. If on the recording day, we arrive at the recording studio and find that the piano is out of tune, we have an issue. While the project hasn't necessarily suffered yet, it is an urgent matter that must be addressed immediately, or else the recording will certainly be compromised. So, well in advance of the session, we arrange for a piano tuner to be there right before the session begins. Scheduling a piano tuner to come out a few weeks in the future is generally less expensive than calling a piano tuner to drop everything and come right away. You can see that risk planning is important to a project's overall success.

While we're defining terms, let's remember our earlier discussion of *assumptions*—things that we choose to believe are true. But if they turn out not to be true, the project could suffer. We assume that the recording engineer will keep his studio piano in tune. If we are incorrect in this assumption, the recording session might not result in a usable product. Assumptions are inherently risky, to one degree or another.

Risk planning, then, becomes a methodical process of checking our assumptions and imagining possibilities for how things might go wrong. For some dimensions of the work, we are confident that they are under control. Others, we know are risky, and we can plan for issues to surface. The most dangerous parts of the project are the risky dimensions that we haven't imagined. So, we drill down as far as we can in our risk analysis, and hope to unearth the most likely possibilities for disaster. Or opportunity.

Risks come in all shapes and sizes, affecting matters big and small. Every single dimension of your work has risks. Some risks could threaten the existence of the project. The out-of-tune piano is such an example. Other risks affect lesser dimensions of the project, such as the usual constraints: time, money, and quality. Perhaps delays in schedule are the most common risks to a project. While these could conceivably compromise the project completely, they are more likely to simply raise tension and stress, or require that you find a bit more funding. If you delay the recording, rather than record the bad piano, the project might be saved.

Deliberate attention to identifying risk pays off. It is an ongoing consideration, throughout all project phases. It probably warrants at least one substantial team meeting, where everyone on the core project team considers all the project details and imagines what could possibly go wrong. In some cases, for large, complex projects that involve a great deal of funding, it makes sense to hire someone to do a *risk audit*—a methodical evaluation of an endeavor's overall risk profile. Some organizations turn this role into a full-time staff position, where someone examines all systems for potential risks and develops ongoing risk management plans to address them.

IS RISK PLANNING WORTH IT?

Does this seem like overkill? It's just music, after all. It's not a matter of life and death, like what project managers in the aerospace industry or in hospitals or in disaster relief have to deal with. Or is it?

In 2003, the Station nightclub in West Warwick, Rhode Island, had a fire. The band Great White had a pyrotechnic display as part of their show, and it set some sound insulation alight. The fire killed 100 people and injured another 236.

Berklee is within gigging distance of that club, and I remember how spooked many of my colleagues were about this incident. Some had played there. There was a sense that this could have happened to any of us. Our industry has a relatively laid back culture, regarding certain dimensions of what we do. Dive bar? No problem, sounds fun! But this comes with inherent risks, and in the case of that fire, the convergence of inattention to detail on many levels (lack of sprinkler system, use of flammable soundproofing materials, insufficient care with the pyrotechnics, no emergency plan, etc.) came together and had dire consequences.

Another famous story is that of Van Halen's contract rider requiring a bowl of M&Ms in the backstage area, with all the brown ones removed. Otherwise, the band would refuse to play the concert but still be due their full compensation.

That sounds like over-the-top rock 'n' roll outrageousness, but there's a serious story behind it. They were concerned that the safety requirements for the show were so complex that there was a high risk of danger if the technical stipulations were not followed explicitly. They therefore inserted the M&M rider into the contract as well, as a test to see whether the details were being followed. Brown M&Ms would indicate that details were being overlooked, and thus, that the venue couldn't be trusted to keep everyone safe.

Things go wrong in our industry—sometimes, in live performance in front of thousands of people. Stages collapse. Spotlights fall. Wardrobes malfunction. Microphones don't get switched on. Instruments get stolen, houses burn down, trumpet players forget to show up for the gig, and clients don't pay. So yes, it makes sense to plan for risks, as we can.

REASONS FOR RISKS

Gear failures, then, are one category of risk. These might be related to human error, or they might just be bad luck. Aging ribbon microphones will fail, and cables will wear out. On the other hand, engineers will spill their coffee on their recording consoles, or neglect to regularly confirm that their studio monitors are still providing equal signals (which results in a panning imbalance). So, it's not always the object's fault.

There are many other types of human error that increase risk. For example:

- **Planning errors.** Incorrect estimates of time, finances, or other resources, increase risk. Sometimes, estimates made during planning stages turn out to be invalid by the time execution begins because world circumstances change. Oil prices might go up, which can have a trickle-down effect to many industries, from shipping to construction. Housing prices could change, which could change the availability and rates of local builders whom you want to build your studio. Or, certain expected partners become unavailable, which would force you to use someone else more expensive.

- **Communication errors.** Work delegation might be misstated or misunderstood. You hire someone to record a bass line, but instead of the funk sound you were after, they give you something with a strong acoustic jazz feel.

- **Hiring errors.** People sometimes misrepresent themselves when they look for work, and if this isn't caught in time, the project can become compromised. You might have hired someone to do a website, for example, believing that they are knowledgeable about setting up payment mechanisms so that you can sell your CDs and other merchandise directly. But it turns out that the person you hired is really just a graphic designer with only rudimentary technical skills, and you don't find this out until after you've blown your budget on an unusable result.

  You might also engage someone who turns out to be less of a supporter than you had anticipated. A student composer once wrote a string quartet for his master's thesis. His girlfriend played cello in a string quartet, and she convinced them to play her boyfriend's piece for free. The day before the concert, the first violinist told the composer that he was just offered a paying gig for that night, and he'd only play the composer's concert if the composer compensated him at the same rate: $200. This was a stretch for the composer, and he also was forced to make the uncomfortable choice of either not paying the violinist and cancelling his thesis performance, or paying him (a financial stretch) while not paying the other three members of the quartet. One lesson to be learned here is that the worse you compensate people, the riskier their participation becomes.

- **Under-reporting.** Under-reporting is another type of communication error. Besides misunderstanding the work, workers left unchecked for too long might stray from the path. Someone who schedules too much time to do a body of work, such as a year to write an article, might fill the slack time with other tasks that become distracting and eventually derail the work on your project. Slack time isn't goof-off time! It might be a luxurious possible buffer to use if the work takes less time to do than anticipated, but ideally, it is then devoted to doing other productive work on other projects or other tasks. In any case, people should be working towards getting work done at the beginning of their allotted time, rather than at the end.

  In my work, we include manuscript delivery dates in author contracts. If we sign a contract in March, the delivery might be in November. That doesn't mean that the author starts writing in March. They likely start in June, after the school year ends. So, March to June is *lead time* (time before the work starts), not slack time, and it doesn't usually make sense to ask for weekly status reports early on, as there is no expectation that any work will be done then. The real start date of their participation is June, and that's when the reporting makes sense.

Life Happens

Dis-aster: "against the stars."

—A particularly appropriate term, for our industry

Beyond these controllable dimensions of project work, there are other less predictable measures we need to account for.

Stage fright can ruin a performance. Particularly when working with inexperienced performers, this can become an issue. There are various ways to mitigate it, such as yoga and other practices. Frequent public performance, starting in small and informal settings, is another way.

Alien performing environments can also compromise performances. Similar to stage fright is when a concert happens at a totally different time of day than when its rehearsals had been occurring, or in a different performance space. This can be a problem for some performers. As an example, an orchestra might decide to include a children's choir in one of their performances. Perhaps, it makes sense to rehearse children on Saturday mornings. If the performance of that piece begins at 9:15 P.M., some of the kids will be entirely unaccustomed to being awake at that time, let alone singing in top form—let alone being in the spotlight in front of a thousand people in the audience. You don't want kids freaked out under hot lights. Their performance is almost guaranteed to be far from their best.

It is important, then, to rehearse at least once at the exact time of the performance, preferably in the exact hall, and in the same costume and lighting conditions. If that is impossible, try to have a partial run-through the night of the concert, an hour before, even if it is just for fifteen minutes. Rehearse some easy parts first, to get them comfortable with the hall, and then some difficult parts, just to break the curse of the unfamiliar circumstance. End that with something within easy technical reach, so that everyone will anticipate a successful performance.

Major family events. People get sick or become otherwise unavailable, often unexpectedly. I currently have two pregnant authors writing books, and one is scheduled to deliver her complete manuscript on the same date that she's scheduled to deliver her baby. As a father of two children who were born prematurely, I'm not counting on her ability to make this deadline.

Something else I've noticed, over the years, is that with surprising regularity, one of our contracted Berklee Press authors experiences the death of a parent. I usually manage about forty projects, and the majority of my authors are forty to sixty years old, so a lot of them have aging parents.

Perhaps this is the law of averages, but it is a periodic cause of project delay, as they deal not only with the initial emotional shock, but then often matters related to disposition of their parent's estate, and then a period of depression. It is all both heartbreaking and also, sadly, predictable, given the demographics of our portfolio.

While we're on this dark note, I'll tell the story of a film orchestrator who hired three of his former students as copyists to help him render his sketches into legible parts in a very tight deadline. He had five days to prepare the parts before the recording session, and he gave them three days to complete their drafts, which he'd then review and send to the orchestra librarian. On day 2, the copyists all reported that their work was nearly done. On the morning of day 3, two delivered, and the third one (sounding a little tired) said he was almost done but needed a couple more hours. Five, six, seven hours passed with no delivery. The exasperated orchestrator finally called him that night, but there was no answer. He called again the next day. The copyist's distraught mother answered the phone and reported that her son had suffered a brain aneurism the day before and suddenly died. Rather than ask if he could come over to get the Finale files from the deceased's computer, the orchestrator offered his sincere condolences, and then he and the other two copyists recreated the missing parts themselves, working into the wee hours of the night, while they mourned the loss of their friend.

I'm not making this up. Life happens, and we have to deal with it.

RISK MANAGEMENT PLAN

Dwelling on all of the ways a project might fail is likely to cause anxiety. To prepare for the worst, we add a new component of our project plan: the *risk management plan*, the essential document of which is the *risk register*.

A risk register lists the most critical possibilities that we need to track. It indicates:

- **Cause.** The condition that will exist for the circumstance to come into being. "Piano is out of tune."

- **Impact.** What dire result will happen if the risk isn't somehow alleviated? "The recording quality will be compromised."

- **Contingency.** How we will alleviate this risk: "We will schedule a touch-up tuning for the morning of the session."

- **Owner.** The project team member who is assigned to be responsible for tracking this risk. "The recording engineer."

Risk Register			
Condition	**Impact**	**Contingency**	**Owner**
Piano is out of tune	Bad recording	Schedule touch-up tuning for the morning of the session	Recording engineer

FIG. 7.1. Risk Register

Now, we have a plan. The project manager has delegated the oversight of this potential risk to the recording engineer. The engineer is responsible for getting that piano tuned. Not only is the risk mitigated, but the responsibility for it is now shared, which will hopefully both reduce our anxiety and make it more likely that the situation will be addressed. (If the engineer and piano tuner are competent!)

IDENTIFYING AND QUANTIFYING RISKS

The process of identifying risks is ideally done with members of the core project team, preferably representing different dimensions of the endeavor so that you can get a wide swath of perspectives. This should be a formal meeting. Larger projects might devote a full day of retreat to risk management, and then follow up with an employee devoted to monitoring the ongoing effort.

There are a number of tools to help with this. Again, we have a one hundred percent rule: examining one hundred percent of the work for potential risks.

This can yield a very large number of identified risks! For example, if we take the band on tour, someone might suggest that not enough tickets will be sold to recoup the costs. Someone else might suggest the possibility that the tour van will explode.

We don't necessarily want to spend time planning contingencies for every single potential risk that could conceivably happen. That would take forever. So, as we work to uncover the risks worthy of planning time, we can calculate a *risk factor* to prioritize all our potential risks.

For each given risk, rate it in terms of *potential impact* and *potential likelihood*, on a scale of 1 to 10. Then multiply the two numbers to get the risk factor:

Impact x Likelihood = Risk Factor

Then, take your long list of risks and risk factors, and choose the top twenty percent or so to address. (The *Pareto principle*, or "80/20 rule," states that in any list, eighty percent of the value comes from the twenty percent of top-prioritized items. It's a widely used rule of thumb in risk assessment and other types of statistical analysis.)

Let's try it.

Insufficient Ticket Sales:

> *Impact:* If we don't sell enough tickets, the tour will be a bust, so we rate it a 9.

> *Likelihood:* There's a possibility, though probably tending towards the unlikely side, so we'll rate that a 4.

> 9 x 4 = 36

Another risk:

Bus Exploding:

> *Impact:* Fairly devastating, worst case scenario, if there were injuries, though if nobody gets hurt, the tour could go on. Rate it an 8.

> *Likelihood:* Not likely, it's a new vehicle, and was recently inspected. Rate it 2.

> 8 x 2 = 16

Once we have our list, we can prioritize all the different risks by their risk factors, and develop our plan of how to mitigate them. A rule of thumb regarding how deep to go: For your project, try to identify at least thirty to fifty risks, and then prioritize the top ten, or so. Or, group them low, medium, and high risk, and see how many fall there. (If your project is a circus, don't stop tracking at ten risks!)

Keeping this in mind, let's look at some ways to identify potential risks.

Risk Breakdown Structure

A *risk breakdown structure* (RBS), such as the one on the next page based on that in the *PMBOK Guide*, shows common general categories of risk. We informally discussed a few of these earlier, but this is a more comprehensive itemization. All these dimensions are types of risk that we can potentially incur. Consider them one by one, in terms of your project.

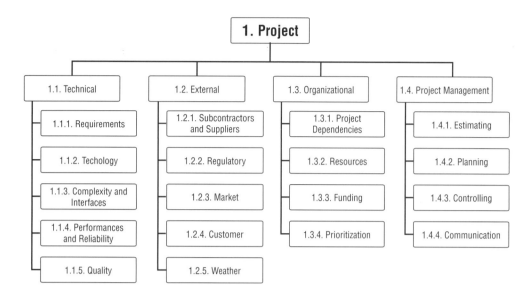

FIG. 7.2. Risk Breakdown Structure.*

Take it square by square, and consider how it relates to your project. Use the RBS as an outline to categorize the risks you see as possible. For example, 1.2.2. Regulatory. How might regulations affect our project? We might have issues related to copyrights, or noise control, or the need to get permits for an outside concert. A parade license, perhaps? Not all of these will apply to every project, but it is helpful to consider them all, one by one, methodically, to see if they help you recognize any potential risks. Add or change dimensions of this, as you see fit. For example, a "Venues" thread might be helpful for music projects, to help you consider issues related to concert halls, recording studios, practice spaces, and so on.

A *risk analysis chart* is a similar structure as the RBS that similarly helps facilitate the consideration of risks, but here, directing your attention towards focusing on internal and external issues. Use it the same way, and fill in each square. "People/Internal," for example, could include your band, your engineer, your assistant, and others on your project team. "People/External" could include fans, vendors, your niece who is getting married on the same day as your concert, and so on. Adapt the rows as is helpful for your project.

* A form of this chart originally appeared in the Project Management Institute's excellent publication, *A Guide to the Project Management Body of Knowledge, Fourth Edition*, Project Management Institute, Inc., 2008. Copyright and all rights reserved. Material from this publication has been reproduced with the permission of PMI.

	Internal	External
People		
Gear/Facilities		
Content		
Context		
Systems		
Communication		
Resources		

FIG. 7.3. Risk Analysis Chart

Referencing the RBS is a good first step because it will get you (and your team) thinking about many dimensions of a potential problem.

Other documents that itemize your work are also helpful in identifying risks. Your work breakdown structure is an obvious choice. Look at it item by item, and imagine what could go wrong. (If you were a computer, you would run every single RBS item by every single WBS item, looking for potential risks. That could take a while, but we should nod to best practice.) Your resource allocation chart is another one, reviewing all the team members, and considering their life circumstances. Who is likely to get busy, or have a baby, or drop everything to go on tour with the band that's their primary gig? Is anybody planning a trip? Or a wedding? Or in poor health?

These documents we have been creating are done methodically, and they are often useful in multiple circumstances, such as risk management.

Information Gathering

Information gathering includes a variety of approaches to getting information that can help with risk identification. These techniques can complement any others we are discussing here, and form the framework for meetings devoted to risk management.

1. **Brainstorming.** A brainstorming session with your project team and any other smart/experienced people can help identify risks. Using the preceding charts is a great help in uncovering risks by methodically looking at different dimensions, but ideas might occur to you in a free-form thinking session that won't be uncovered by more prescribed approaches. We will discuss brainstorming in the next chapter.

2. **Delphi.** We used the Delphi method earlier, to estimate cost and duration, but it can also be used to identify and quantify risk. To review, get a

group of people together, and have them discuss potential risks, their impact, and their possible mitigations. For each item, see who agrees that it should be a priority, and then let the outliers explain why their opinions should be considered. Repeat two more times.

3. **Interviews/Research.** Discussions with project team members, fans/ customers, and others in the project community might uncover some risks that you might not have considered via other means.

   As an example of a way to get customer feedback (beyond just talking to customer support), for Berklee Press, I will often review Amazon reader reviews of our products. We have a music theory book that is very successful and often reviewed. A common thread in many Amazon reviews, and also feedback to customer support, was that readers really wished there was an answer key in the book for the ear training exercises. We actually deliberately omitted including that, originally, because we thought teachers who used the book for testing would prefer that students not have access to the answers. We never got the feedback, though, that this is how the book was being used. In fact, teachers were requesting the answer key! So, we eventually published a second edition of the book that included such a key.

   To reduce the risk of this happening again, we are now more inclined to include answers to any questions posed in our books, rather than operating under the assumption that the questions will be actually used by teachers for assessment purposes.

4. **Analysis Diagrams.** In the same way that the WBS can help us identify potential risks, so too can network diagrams, or others that we are creating. When examining a network diagram, note points of extreme concurrency that might be increasing risk. If someone is producing a CD booklet while the songs are still being recorded, something dire could happen in the recording session that would render all work on the booklet unusable. The band might break up halfway through and cancel the project, but if the writer of the booklet was already contracted, that would be an expense required for something that turned out not to be necessary. Examining diagrams while considering potential risks can uncover some points of vulnerability.

   Other diagrams and planning materials could similarly reveal risks. For example, a cause and effect (aka "Fishbone" or "Ishikawa") diagram used in quality control can also reveal known points of likely failure. (We will discuss those in chapter 10.) While Q/A diagrams are often used after the content has been created and there are issues to be discovered, they can also be used in risk planning to spark our imaginations regarding risk mitigation, and then hopefully prevent those issues from ever becoming manifest. For example, if we know that not having enough microphone cables is a likely circumstance, we can take measures well in advance of the event to make sure that they are in sufficient supply—much better than confirming this circumstance at a point when heroics will be necessary to save the event.

5. **Checklist Analysis.** Like diagrams, checklists are commonly used to assist in quality control, and we will look at these throughout this book. If your organization has checklists, they can be a helpful source for uncovering risks. At Berklee Press, we use this "Transmittal Checklist" when shipping a book off to graphic design, after editing has been completed, to make sure that everything is in place for the project's next phase of development. By analyzing this checklist at other times, such as during a risk planning process, we might uncover potential problems down the road. For example, there is the item "Marketing endorsements," which are quotes used on the back cover, website, and so on. The process of getting these has to be timed carefully so that waiting for them doesn't hold up the ultimate printing process. They have to be scheduled relatively early in the process, if the schedule is to be as hoped, so noticing that and confirming that they are in the works can help mitigate a risk that could delay the project's publication.

BP Book Transmittal Checklist

❏ Hard copy of manuscript
❏ Data CD of all files for book
❏ Audio master
❏ Cover art files
❏ Back cover copy
❏ Marketing endorsements

FIG. 7.4. Transmittal Checklist

Checklists can be an encapsulation of an institution's historical memory. Each item might reflect a disaster that actually happened! They are therefore helpful in anticipating future risks. Similarly, after disasters happen, updating checklists can help mitigate repeat occurrences.

6. **Assumptions.** Assumptions contain risk. An assumption is something that we choose to believe is true, for purposes of moving forward with our project. We assume that our music is good and will find an audience. If it wasn't for this assumption, many of us wouldn't get out of bed in the morning! That assumption is necessary for us to move our project forward. To reduce the inherent risk in our assumptions, we need to be aware of these items that we are taking on faith, and consider what will happen if we are wrong. Not an easy task. All of these discussions and examination techniques will help us uncover our assumptions and reduce the risks associated with them.

7. **SWOT Analysis.** SWOT analysis is a method of analyzing potential activities to see whether they are worth undertaking, developed by Albert Humphrey. SWOT stands for "Strengths, Weaknesses, Opportunities, and Threats." Like a PICK chart ("Possible, Implement, Consider, Kill;" see chapter 2), SWOT is a framework for comparing internal considerations (strengths and weaknesses), which we can control, with external (opportunities and threats) considerations, which we might not be able to control, for any part of the project, big or small. It's another planning tool, sometimes helpful in considering project acquisition or scope, but also in risk assessment.

   It starts by considering and weighing the various internal factors for the endeavor under consideration. Then, that analysis is considered in terms of the following matrix, in hopes of arriving at a decision in which the risks are revealed, so that we can go in with our eyes wide open.

	Helpful	**Harmful**
Internal	Strengths	Weaknesses
External	Opportunities	Threats

FIG. 7.5. SWOT Matrix

Say a band is considering going on tour. They might do a SWOT analysis of the various four dimensions, and plot them in this matrix. The "Harmful" column indicates the likely risks that you want to plan for, but also consider the Opportunities quadrant. Are you ready to be interviewed on TV, if the opportunity comes up? Do you have a means of replicating more CDs in a hurry if demand is surprisingly high?

	Helpful	Harmful
Internal	Strengths: • Great music • Great stage presence • Love to tour • Love doing projects together	Weaknesses: • Scheduling is tight • No available funds
External	Opportunities: • More fans • More exposure • More fun • More income	Threats: • Could be financial disaster if we don't sell enough tickets • Not enough fans

FIG. 7.6. SWOT Analysis for a Tour

To actually use this diagram to help make a decision, consider the weight of the potentially helpful to harmful items. For example, the weakness "no available funds" might be satisfactorily mitigated by the opportunity "more income." The strength "great music" could overcome the threat "not enough fans." Then again, we have a weakness "scheduling is tight" and no counter "helpful" item regarding flexibility of schedule, so this is an issue that will need to be discussed further and addressed, before the decision to actually move forward with the tour, should it be undertaken.

This process will generally leave you leaning towards one of the strategic quadrants. If the points of risk seem to be surmountable, then the decision to move forward becomes easier.

8. **Subject Matter Experts.** Talking to subject matter experts—people who have done this work before—is a good way to uncover potential risks, similar to how we used these conversations to uncover the necessary points of work earlier. Buy them a beer and ask what catastrophes they've witnessed. Individuals represent biased perspectives, so talking to multiple people is a good idea.

COMMUNICATING ABOUT RISK

When risks are discovered and deemed to be high priority, the appropriate stakeholders need to know about it. Uncovering serious risks, or actual issues, might have repercussions throughout the project. Anyone who has the authority or power to affect the risk's outcome, or who might be affected by it, should be informed.

The music community in Boston recently witnessed a potentially dangerous episode of insufficient risk reporting. At a music school, it was discovered that a convicted pedophile was hired as the videographer for a children's orchestra, and the conductor who hired him was well acquainted with the videographer's past and chose not to report the circumstance to the school's administration.

The repercussions? When the situation came to light, the videographer and the conductor were immediately fired, and the parents of the orchestra's participants were furious: some at the risk that the school had exposed to their children and others because they thought the administration was overreacting in firing their beloved conductor. It was a lose-lose situation. The bottom line is that the school's brand became tarnished and a popular program that brought in significant income was damaged.

There are a number of ways to read this story, but one I'll focus on is communication: lack of sufficient reporting. The conductor apparently didn't feel obligated to provide a complete report of the situation, regarding the hiring decision he had made, perhaps out of concern that a decision about it would be made with which he would disagree. Therefore, the board members were kept in the dark about a risky situation, and so, it festered. Fortunately, the information came to light and the situation was addressed before anyone was hurt.

However, the perception of risk became a new issue, even though the risk of danger to children did not actually result in the feared damage. Instead, the result was that the music school suffered a lack of trust due to a rogue employee's behavior (i.e., the conductor)—a consequence actually only tangentially related to the pedophilic videographer. Whether the legacy of this matter will be the administration's quick correction or their checkered hiring history is yet to be seen.

Had something gone wrong, the administration would have been among those taken to task for it. Consider what happened to Penn State with an analogous situation in its football program. The president of the institution was among those forced to step down, due to the under-reporting of crimes being committed by staff members.

Developing a culture of open communication is best. Your project team and particularly the project sponsor are there to help. If it is a healthy organization worthy of your participation, the team will rise to the occasion to set matters right.

During execution, the project sponsor should receive a report regularly, regarding the progress done on the project, any significant variance between what is planned (i.e., estimated) and what is happening, and any noteworthy risks that become evident.

Should significant issues surface that could threaten the project's overall success or the safety of anyone involved, they should be reported right away.

Ways to Mitigate Risk

Once potential risks are recognized, here are some specific ways to reduce likelihood that they will actually become issues.

1. **Project management**. All the techniques we have learned so far will help reduce risk, particularly risks of going over budget or missing deadlines. Be thorough in planning the work, the budget, and the schedule. Communicate often. These are the best ways to avoid most risks.

2. **Written agreements.** Having written communication greatly reduces the risks of misunderstanding. Contracts, letters of agreement, and general formality in business interactions are all ways of mitigating risk. We discuss these in detail later in the book.

3. **Checklists**. Checklists help you remember important details: procedures, gear items, points for conversations, people who need certain information, and more. Checklists are among the most effective tools used to reduce risk.

4. **Cross-footing.** Whenever you can, and particularly when you are doing complex calculations or analyses, calculate the data in more than one direction to confirm that it is correct. For example, if you are leading a children's chorus on an international tour and need to make sure that you have all their passports, keep a checklist of passports received, but also, count the number of passports in your stack, confirming that this number matches the number of children.

5. **Empowering competent people.** If multiple competent people are empowered to make decisions on the ground, they can react more dynamically to complex situations and recover from the unexpected more easily. As long as clarity in communication is maintained, having deputies with decision-making authority can help the overall process go better. This often comes down to careful hiring, particularly in high-risk situations. If a recording must be produced within a tight timeline, you will be more likely to succeed if you hire a recording engineer who is very experienced and whom you trust to make decisions in your absence. The higher the risk, the more you want to make sure that you can delegate tasks to rock-solid reliable people on your team, and then have them run with it. Save opportunities for training less experienced people for when the stakes and risks are lower.

   Hiring people who are smarter and more competent than you are can reduce risk. They can help you avoid or recover from mistakes that you might not have imagined, and your aspirations will be less constrained by your own limitations. As a project manager, the last thing you want is to be the smartest person in the room.

6. **Emergency plans.** Developing and maintaining protocols for emergency situations can help address difficult situations, when they arise. The production manager at *From the Top* tracks emergency contact information for everyone involved in a show, and she keeps this form handy, in order to get it.

FROM THE TOP – TOUR STAFF EMERGENCY CONTACT FORM

Date _____

Name:_____

Physical Address:_____

City: _____ST _____ Zip:_____

Local Phone: _____ Cell Phone: _____

In Case of an Emergency, Please Contact:

Name:_____ Relationship _____

Work Phone:_____ Home Phone: _____

Address:_____

City:_____ State_____ Zip:_____

Medical Information / Emergency:

Primary Care Physician:_____

Address: _____

City: _____ State: _____ Zip: _____

Work Phone: _____ Home Phone:_____

Allergies: _____
_____
_____
_____

Medications: _____
_____
_____
_____

Previous Health Conditions (ie: Diabetic, Epileptic, Etc.)_____
_____
_____
_____

This Information Is To Be Filed With the Production Manager and Used Only For Emergencies While On Tour

FIG. 7.7. Emergency Contact Information Form (From the Top)

7. Written instructions. Distributing detailed instructions of policies, procedures, and best practices can help avoid difficult situations. Much of this information might seem like common sense, but distributing it in writing helps clarify what expectations are, and can make people more inclined to use what common sense they might have.

Here is a set of travel guidelines from *From the Top*. They help reduce the risk that delays will occur due to travel issues.

FROM THE TOP
TRAVEL GUIDELINES

Once your flight is booked...

1. Check with your airline prior to your flight to ensure that your instrument meets the size requirements for the aircraft. Cellos may need seatbelt extensions if flying as carry-on baggage. For more information, see: http://www.tsa.gov/travelers/airtravel/assistant/editorial_1235.shtm
2. Make sure you have proper picture identification, (if over age 18) as required by the Transportation Security Administration, along with your flight confirmation number. The confirmation number can be found in the flight itinerary email from Orbitz or your airline.
3. If your instrument is on loan, check with the lender to ensure their policy on instrument travel. Some lenders may have specific travel requirements.
4. Make arrangements for ground transportation to and from the airport. From the Top does not provide ground transportation to and from the airport.
5. If you have a medical condition or disability that may affect your ability to fly, or think you may require additional assistance, please notify From the Top as soon as possible.

24 hours before your flight...

6. Check your flight's status before departure. Your flight may have been rescheduled or cancelled.
7. If possible, print out your boarding pass at home and prepay for any checked baggage. This will save you time and money at the airport.
8. Re-confirm your ground transportation to and from the airport.
9. Before packing, check the Transportation Security Administration (TSA) website (http://www.tsa.gov/index.shtm) for prohibited items and liquid rules for carry-on baggage.
10. Prepare your instrument for flight travel (for example, for string players, loosen your bow and strings).
11. TSA has issued an official letter allowing one musical instrument per passenger through security screening checkpoints in addition to other carry-on baggage. If you are planning on carrying your instrument onboard the aircraft, we recommend you print this letter and bring it with you. (Letter attached).

The day of your flight...

12. Check your flight's status once more before you leave for the airport to check for flight delays.
13. Always arrive at the airport at least 2 hours before the scheduled flight departure.
14. Call FTT's Production Manager, Elizabeth DeVore on her cell phone at (   ), if you encounter any unexpected travel issues, flight changes, or cancellations.
15. Be flexible and go with the flow. Delays, seat changes, and flight cancellations are always a possibility!

Helpful links:
Tips for flying with an instrument:
1. http://www.parttimemusician.com/2009/07/10/flying-with-musical-instrument/
2. http://www.americanorchestras.org/advocacy_and_government/traveling_musicians.html

String instrument care:
1. http://www.hobgoblin-usa.com/info/stricare.htm
2. http://www.sharmusic.com/Pages/How-To/Instrument-Care-and-Maintenance/

Woodwind and Brass instrument care:
1. http://www.musiccenters.com/care.html

FIG. 7.8. Travel Guidelines (Courtesy of From the Top, Inc.)

Similarly, here's an excerpt from a cover letter I send to people who are writing quotes for the back covers of our books. These directions, and other info that we send them such as examples of good quotes, make it less likely that they will write something unusable.

> *The purpose of endorsements is to show that successful, knowledge-able people in the field feel that this product opens doors to career success. We are positioning this book as [book description].... Your quote should be short—three to five sentences.... Please relate the book's content to your personal experience and perspective, and try to articulate what you see as its strengths.*

These guidelines seem simply like helpful communications, and they are. But they are also risk management devices.

RISK RESPONSES

Once you've identified and prioritized your project's risks, it's time to systematize how to address them. Remember, some risks result in disaster, and others could result in opportunity. How to deal with each type is different. Once you decide how to plan for these risks, include the strategy in your risk mitigation plan.

- Risks of Problems: Avoid, Transfer, Mitigate, Accept
- Risks of Opportunities: Exploit, Share, Enhance, Accept

Risks of Problems

Avoid. Avoiding a risk means changing course, away from that risky circumstance, to make sure that it doesn't manifest as an actual issue. If you have identified that the lighting designer you have hired is a drunk, you might decide that rather than risk him ruining a concert, you will avoid that possibility by replacing him with someone sober.

Transfer. Transferring a risk means sharing the risk with another person or organization. Insurance is a way to transfer the risk. Instead of being vulnerable financially, if someone outside your theater slips on the ice, you take out insurance, and thus transfer that risk to the insurance company.

Mitigate. Mitigating risk means taking action to reduce its likelihood. Flight delays are a risk. To mitigate that, you can have a policy that you arrive in the city where you will perform a concert on the day before.

Accept. Accepting a risk means that you will do nothing and just live with the possibility. There is a risk that everyone will hate your music and storm out of the concert. But you decide to just live with that.

Risks of Opportunities

Exploit. Exploiting a potential opportunity means being ready to make the most of it. You are launching a new website, and feel that there is a possibility that it will get a very large number of hits in a short time, because you're about to go on *Saturday Night Live!* So, you make sure that your CD and other merch are available there well in advance of the anticipated surge.

Share. You can share the risk of a surge with your hosting service, making sure that they are ready for the incoming traffic and that their server won't crash. You might try trading them a banner ad for an upgrade in your service to accommodate this circumstance.

Enhance. Given an extraordinary performance opportunity, you can increase the possibility of success by both preparing extra hard technically and by bringing in additional experts, such as a choreographer, that will provide dimensions to what you are doing that might be different than what you've done before.

Accept. You can simply accept the possibility that a great opportunity could come, but decide not to do anything specific to prepare, besides just bracing yourself.

Some Music-Specific Techniques

Let's discuss how to reduce some of the risks associated with music projects, after you've identified them.

1. **Performance quality.** We have already discussed how dress rehearsals can help alleviate the risk of bad performances. Being hyper-prepared technically is also important. Music should be rehearsed faster than it will be performed, preferably to a metronome. Rehearsing mistakes and recovery is also an important part of practice. Once the music is basically in control, technically, introduce train-wreck recovery into your rehearsals. As the bandleader, during a guitarist's solo, break his attention at a random moment, and let him practice recovering.

   Practice smiling calmly during disasters. There's the story of the new dentist who was treating a patient while being supervised by an experienced dentist. The new dentist made a minor slip, and said, "Damn!" The experienced dentist took him into the hallway, and said, "You need to train yourself not to say 'damn' in front of a patient. Say instead, 'There!'"

Even dentistry is partially a performance art! And physicians who have good results prescribing placebos certainly understand this lesson.

If they can do it, so can musicians. By training yourself to look pleased with your performance no matter how it's actually going, you will reduce the risk that the audience will perceive a mistake for what it is.

The mindset for a performance should be that everything you do is gold, and your responsibility to the audience is that they believe they are getting a good quality product. Self-flagellation should be private, done when you are practicing and trying to solve actual issues, never onstage.

2. **Performers.** A rule of thumb is to have two potential backups for every critical member of the project team, and that can include performers. The more unreliable they are, the closer you need to manage them and the more you need to be ready to find an alternative.

An organist was recently doing a solo tour of large Texas churches. He timed it very tightly, and one day, was scheduled to give a morning concert in one city, hop on a plane, and then play another concert in another city. Unfortunately, he got confused in the airport and wound up missing his afternoon flight, which made appearing at his concert impossible.

Fortunately, the event's organizer had a backup plan—a local performer, waiting in the wings, scheduled to be on hand for such circumstances. The audience got an analogous concert, though different than what they'd hoped for, and also the option of getting their money back. That's better than having them show up (after driving for an hour and paying for a babysitter) and finding that the concert was simply cancelled.

If you are forced to have a team member participate who is not competent enough, you have to deliberately work around that. If it's a musician (say, a relative), minimize the negative impact they will have. Create parts that are simple, and/or mic them low in a mix. Give them extra coaching, and reduce their capacity to cause significant damage, including to the morale of the rest of the team. If possible, create a circumstance in which they are not critically important. For example, you might have the person record in an overdub session, rather than live with the complete rhythm section, so that their (awful) part doesn't leak into other mics and therefore become uneditable. They might also perform better with less pressure.

Another dimension to this is to manage the expectations of others. If you must have your nephew (the terrible conga player) record with you, discuss the circumstance with the band and the engineer. Clarify that you really want to make it happen, but that you won't let it derail the project and embarrass anyone. Use an isolation booth, and get ready for some audio quantization....

3. **Gear/Facilities.** Any critical equipment should have a backup close at hand: guitars, microphones, computer, etc., particularly when it is to be used in performance or a recording session or other time-critical event. Computer hard drives should be backed up, preferably offsite, using a service such as CrashPlan™, Carbonite™, Gobbler, etc. Gobbler is optimized for audio applications, and can be a helpful risk mitigation tool.

Also have a backup for facilities, such as a concert hall or recording studio. If you are booking a concert, the project will be safer if there is a potential backup venue available, just in case of disaster. Concert halls sometimes have a network with each other that will include such a contingency, so ask the hall manager about that.

4. **Contracts.** Contracts reduce risks. They specify all the details, responsibilities, and business parameters of a relationship, and therefore settle some questions.

5. **Smaller iterations.** Work is less risky when it is monitored closely, and when smaller chunks of work are reviewed in short bursts, rather than allowing massive amounts of work to be done in huge, tremendous efforts. Work goes into black holes. Delays might come because two people are each waiting for each other to do something, but neither is getting around to actually asking the other for an update. Weekly or daily check-in meetings are often appropriate. Comprehensive monthly meetings might be okay, as long as there are quick check-in meetings more regularly than that. If you're not talking to a team member at least once a month, that component of the project is likely at risk.

Something the software industry is really learning these days is how important it is to release products in iterations, rather than waiting too long to release massive amounts of work that turns out to be unusable. By releasing simpler, more manageable versions, asking users how they like it, and what new features they really think are most important, software developers can more easily encourage the evolution of their products so they match what the marketplace actually desires.

In this "build/measure/learn" approach, there is less risk of creating a failed product. It is a risk reduction technique.

6. **Checklists.** Again, checklists help you remember critical details, and they are important dimensions of quality control. As you become experienced at projects of the type you are doing, you will find that certain issues recur, and checklists will help you control them.

Figure 7.9 is a checklist I've developed for when I receive CD masters to accompany Berklee Press books. The mastering engineer will have his own checklist, and the replicating house will have theirs. But these are some issues that I've found over the years that might not be obvious. Every CD master we receive gets checked for these items before the master gets sent to replication.

CD Master Checklist

CDs should conform to Red Book standard.

Among the things to confirm:

CD:

- ❏ 74 minutes maximum; less is better
- ❏ 99 tracks maximum
- ❏ 1 to 4 seconds between tracks
- ❏ files are WAV or AIFF and *not* MP3 (iTunes likes to sneak in MP3s)
- ❏ Works in audio-only CD player; don't test it only on a computer
- ❏ CD label has project name and date of CD, what type of CD it is (audio, data, CD-plus, etc.), and whether it is intended as the actual master or a draft

Content:

- ❏ Recorded notes match notation in book
- ❏ Examples are repeated in accordance with book's notation
- ❏ Tracks are in the correct order, matching "CD Tracks" page in the book
- ❏ Track names are correctly spelled, and rendered just like "CD Tracks" page
- ❏ Track numbers match "CD Tracks" page and icons in the book
- ❏ Countoffs/clicks are used consistently
- ❏ No distortion
- ❏ No pops
- ❏ No random talking or other extraneous noise, particularly at beginning and end
- ❏ No long spaces of silence at beginning or end of tracks (more than 4 seconds)
- ❏ Volume levels are consistent from track to track

FIG. 7.9. Berklee Press CD Master Checklist

Checklists should be as simple and as clear as possible. They should have actual places where the reviewer makes a check mark and then initials it when they are done. Otherwise, they are likely to just glance at the list without actually performing every single check. Also, without the boxes, people might be tempted to cross out the items instead, which makes them illegible and, therefore, inconvenient to reference later.

7. **Auditioning and hiring.** As we saw in chapter 6, careful, painstaking attention to hiring, including checking references, is a way of avoiding risk. Include only the best people you can find on your team! Don't settle. That increases risk.

CLOSING THOUGHTS

Anticipating risks requires imagination. With experience, we witness more and more disasters, and will hopefully become better at anticipating the common risks to certain types of projects. Unfortunately, though, the universe will always be more creative than we are, and new possibilities for how things fail will continually present themselves. Talking to more experienced people about their work and trading war stories should be ongoing activities for any professional. Listen to what went wrong, and imagine similar circumstances in your own work. How might you prepare for such occurrences, if they seem likely?

PRACTICE

Consider the potential risks that your project could suffer, and create a risk management plan, showing at least ten potential risks and your mitigation strategy for each.

CHAPTER 8

Contracts, Copyrights, Tax Forms, Insurance, and Other Existential Delights

Contracts, insurance riders, copyright forms, tax documents, and other ruminations are among the most mysterious dimensions of a project, but they can also be among the most important to get exactly right. Their typically tedious language makes them seem perhaps the polar opposite to our project vision statements, but with the proper spirit of imagination, their purpose is equally as soaring, fascinating, and fulfilling, giving us a chance to pause and consider the grandiose, existential dimensions to what we do.

When we manage projects, we engage others to join us in conforming the world to our vision. Contributions of time, compensation, and creative collaboration are clarified, protected, and held to their highest standard by carefully crafting articulations of precisely what we agree to do. Similarly, society has codified various dimensions of how property—even our most personal and spiritual of insights—is owned, and careful navigation of these boundaries helps to ensure that everyone is fairly compensated for their contributions.

These subjects are deep, and this chapter could easily be expanded into four full-length books. Here, it is only designed to present an overview of some of the major topics, to spark your imagination regarding work to be done and potential risks to be managed, in an effort to help you keep them organized. This material should be either the beginning or a review, regarding your education about these critical matters, and it is not intended to be used as comprehensive or complete legal advice. Any significant commercial endeavor/project will almost certainly need the services of a lawyer, tax accountant/financial planner, and/or insurance agent involved somewhere in the chain of events to navigate all of these matters properly.

Some of the advice here is specific to American law and business practices. If you live outside the United States, make sure that you understand the analogous mechanisms for where you work.

OBJECTIVES

By the end of the chapter, you will be able to:

- obtain, understand, and organize various types of contracts and payment mechanisms used in music projects, such as royalties, advances, works for hire, and different ownership arrangements

- register with performance rights organizations

- get necessary permissions in place so that you can use copyrighted materials, such as for covering songs by other artists, or using artwork in commercial publications

- navigate issues of intellectual property law, including copyrights, patents, and trademarks

- identify and organize some of the types of insurance and tax documentation required in music-related projects

- create an effective invoice

CONTRACTS AND LETTERS OF AGREEMENT

A good contract should make everyone involved feel safe and valued. It should protect everyone's best interests, like a big brother, always looking out for you. Contracts lean on the full power and grandeur of the legal system, which is intended to protect us with the full strength of our government. In that way, they tie your endeavors to the greater context of society. A legally binding contract is a moment to pause and smell the roses—to consider fundamentally, in grand terms, exactly what you are trying to do.

While the language can seem tedious, the aspirations are soaring.

Legally binding contracts might be either verbal or written, but it is much safer and more useful to have them written. There are essentially two purposes for contracts: clarification and saber rattling. From the optimistic perspective, which I'm trying so hard to deliver here, the contract articulates the exact scope of what the participants in the relationship promise to do for each other. "I will do this specific scope of work, and you will pay me exactly this much money, according to this schedule." A written contract permits everyone to reference the specifics, later in the relationship, and remind ourselves of exactly what is expected of us, so that we can be sure to fulfill what is needed.

To consider the darker dimensions, ever so briefly, contracts also specify the horrors that result, should the promise be broken: legal recourse, mechanisms for addressing conflict, financial penalties, criminal prosecution, and so on. Hopefully, such repercussions will never be made manifest, in your dealings.

Broadly speaking, there are four essential elements in a good contract.

1. the promised work to be done

2. the consideration: what benefits will be enjoyed by the participants

3. the agreement, which confirms that all sides came to the agreement voluntarily

4. an invocation of law, specifying that it is intended as a legally binding document, and that all parties agree that the promise is ultimately answerable in accordance with your society's legal system

Similar to how project managers try to figure 100 percent of various dimensions of their work (100 percent of the work in a WBS, 100 percent of the potential risks, 100 percent of your work systematized, and so on), lawyers have the "four corners" rule. This is the goal that 100 percent of all dimensions of the agreement are articulated within the four corners of the contract's pages. In other words, disputes will be resolved in accordance with the contract terms, and not rely on rules or procedures that exist outside of it, such as general practices in the industry or general law. This compulsion to have contracts be 100 percent comprehensive and inclusive leads to what might be perceived as their excessive length and rambling. However, if something awful happens in the relationship, you might be grateful for seemingly obscure nuances tucked in there.

Contracts must promise exchanges of value, or *considerations*. "For a fistful of daisies, my heart." That is a proper contract. Each side promises consideration for the other. Cross that, and the angels will weep.

A *unilateral* contract is signed by just one side. A *bilateral* or *multilateral* contract is signed by both sides. Either way, for it to be considered legally valid, there needs to be an exchange of value between the two parties. Contracts are not just confessions or official statements. They are articulations of mutual benefit. Should the worst-case scenario present itself, and a dispute be settled in a court of law, a grotesquely unfair contract might be considered an act of coercion, rather than a well intentioned agreement, and declared invalid and non-applicable.

Contractual language is to be cherished and savored, with every word pored over and its implications digested, as you would examine an impassioned declaration from your beloved. Read through the lines for hidden meanings. Consider the possible dimensions and repercussions of every word. Test them with a trusted accomplice, using an attorney to decipher the essence of its meaning.

Let's consider some of the types of contracts.

Some Types of Music-Related Contracts

Financial Terms

The most common reasons for a contract are to specify the agreed-upon financial terms of a relationship. There are many ways to get paid:

1. **Lump sum.** You play accordion for two hours at my wedding, and I'll give you $500.

2. **Royalties.** I'll fund your record production and give you 10 percent of the retail price of every album sold. If we price it at $12.50, you will get $1.25 for each one. Royalties are generally paid at regular intervals during the year, such as every six months or every quarter. There are often minimal payments, such as they won't write a check for under $50, and instead roll the low amounts into the next pay period.

3. **Advance.** We will pay you royalties, as discussed above, but we're going to give you some money upfront as a gesture of good faith, and to help you survive while you're working on the project. So, we'll pay you $2,500 before we even sell a single copy. In this example, the advance amount is based on selling 2,000 albums at $12.50 each, and you will start receiving additional royalties when more than 2,000 are sold.

Ownership Terms

Contracts are drafted to clarify who owns certain dimensions of work. A school will generally own the curriculum developed by its faculty on faculty time. While the faculty member created the work, the school is paying for them to have the time and other resources to create it, and so the school might own the copyright. This means that technically, if a music theory teacher wants to write an article for a magazine, they might have restrictions on what materials they can include in it. While the college can't control what topics someone writes about, they can control the dissemination of certain documents or graphics, so it's important to be clear on this before going to press.

This is periodically a source of confusion between songwriters and sheet music publishers. Often, the sheet music publisher will own the rights to the specific notation used in the product, but the songwriter owns the publishing rights to the song. So, a songwriter can't scan the notation in the published sheet music and resell that in a self-published edition. However, they might be able to create a new arrangement or recording of that music. It's a subtle difference, and contracts will help clarify exactly what the tricky technical terms are for slippery issues such as this.

Collaborative songwriters should have ownership agreements with each other. When bands write songs together, they really should work this out in advance. Songwriters commonly either split ownership evenly or one person takes all. If someone writes the music and someone writes the lyrics, they frequently will split it 50/50, even if one person contributed one hundred hours and the other contributed three minutes. If songwriter A is stuck on something and then shows it to songwriter B, and songwriter B provides even one word that makes it into the final song, there is a traditional dance that happens: Songwriter A offers songwriter B an even writer's share of the copyright. That's the moral obligation. Songwriter B then says, "No no no, dude, it's all yours. You just help me out next time."

That's the nice way it works, particularly among friends. But songwriter B might also simply accept the offer, with the vague intention of repaying the favor in the future. Even best friends should do the dance, though. Clarity is often the important thing, not the actual terms.

Information Control

A *non-disclosure agreement* is often used to clarify what information must be kept secret by the participants in the business. If you hire someone to help develop a new product, you might have them promise not to go blabbing everywhere what your business model is, to limit the possibility that they will then provide this information to a competitor.

Similarly, *non-compete agreements* clarify that someone who works at your company can't jump ship and join a competitor, sharing with them all your strategies and vulnerabilities. These can be difficult to enforce, and many people won't sign them, but it could be worth a try.

Releases

Releases are forms that give permission to use someone's image, artwork, performance, etc. in a commercial project. The person who signs the release gives permission that their image, work, art, or whatever can be used, edited, modified, sold, and made public. Everyone who appears in a music video needs to sign a release. If you use a photograph, the photographer owns its copyright, and you should have a signed release before you feature it.

Ideally, get releases signed before any real work has been done, to make sure that you have permission before spending the effort and resources that could potentially be unusable.

Releases are also used to "release" an organization from liability in case of disaster, to help keep from getting sued.

P.S. I LOA MOU

If a contract is a full-bore treatise on love, a letter of agreement is more like a sweet note. These are more intimate than contracts, and often warmed by a greater sense of trust between the parties. Either way, mutual benefit is declared (that is, a reciprocal agreement). But the abbreviated form is done when the stakes are smaller and less formal, or as addendums to contracts. They are often used when finances are simpler, such as for lump-sum payments, rather than ongoing royalties, or with extended payment plans. If you engage a few players to play a gig, you might just use a letter of agreement. If you want them to permanently join your band and play paying gigs, you'll likely be better off with a more comprehensive contract.

These documents might be called letters of agreement (LOA), memos of understanding (MOU), letters of understanding (LOU), memos of agreement (MOA), or statements of work (SOW). LOA, MOU, LOU, MOA, SOW—they all seem like diminutive French romantic sobriquets (well, maybe not SOW). Though often used interchangeably, there are technical subtleties. An "understanding" or "statement" is a clarification, often used to supplement a contract and refine some nuance. An "agreement" is a starting point for further action, and often more like a mini contract, but without all the formal components and sweeping legal scope of a contract. One or two pages, not ten or fifty.

Often, lawyers are bypassed in their creation. Three is a crowd, and the function here is to be relatively simple, light, and cheap. That said, these documents are actually still types of contracts. They are generally legally binding. They are just not as long-winded and thorough, and therefore, not as tough or complete. In other words, if a lawyer isn't involved, it is probably riskier. It might be just fine, though, for many purposes, particularly when the terms are simple and the money is short.

Do You Need a Lawyer? Or an Accountant?

Most small business owners need the services of a lawyer and a tax accountant, at some point. Also, an insurance agent. If they are any good, these professionals will be fully dedicated to mitigating your risk exposure. They can sometimes also provide general strategic business advice. They meditate on disaster scenarios and all the myriad ways that people can be awful to each other, and so when they craft agreements or do your taxes, they are trying to find 100 percent of the possible ways to protect you that they can. Lawyers can wield words to become a noose around someone's neck, strike terror into the hearts of your adversaries, and create little prisons in which to keep your slaves. You want one on your side as your ready champion against the onslaught of evils that lie in wait. While some amateurs might muddle through these arenas unassisted, the very best way to mitigate risk is by having a professional or two be your guide and protector. You can get periodic advice, deep audits, ongoing counseling, or task-specific services.

Lawyers can be horrendously expensive. Good ones tend to cost at least $150 an hour, often twice that, and you could certainly spend ten times that much, if you try. In addition to hourly fees, because they are so thorough, they will often charge you for every single little thing they can dream up. If you call them to ask a question, they might charge you for every minute they spend on the phone with you. If you ask them for an extra copy of your contract, they might charge you a dollar a page for their photocopying services. They think of everything! Which is their job. Just clarify your budget with them in advance, to keep legal costs from getting out of hand. For certain kinds of predictable tasks, such as a simple contract in the realm of their expertise, they might have flat-fee rates available. Like, a standard co-songwriting contract might be $500, from someone who has done a lot of these. If a lawyer needs to step out of his comfort zone and start from scratch, rather than use *boilerplate* (standard, portable language, reusable between contracts), they might need to charge an hourly rate. So, asking your real estate lawyer to set up a music contract might not be the most cost-efficient route. On the other hand, if you have an ongoing relationship with someone, they might give you a price break, so it might make sense to start with someone you know and trust, as your plan A.

When Do You Need a Contract?

The most common points of music projects where you need contracts or other written agreements are when you:

- hire someone to do something (contracts for musicians, managers, employees)

- collaborate creatively on a writing project (contracts for authors, co-songwriters, as well as copyright paperwork)

- rent something or join a service (rental agreements for concert hall, gear, or membership agreements for unions or performance rights organizations)

- use someone else's creative work in your own project (releases for sound files, photos)

Those are really common types of transactions in our industry and predictable points where formal paperwork is necessary. They are so common that mature businesses that engage in these activities will have standard, boilerplate contracts that cover them, and they might not need to be generated from scratch. For some, you might be able to find a free sample on the Internet that serves your needs adequately. Today, I Googled "wedding band contract" and got 25,800 hits. Odds are, one of those will be good enough to cover most betrothed's needs, so that they won't have to hire a lawyer to write a unique one.

There might be other points of legal vulnerability for you, though. To determine when and where you need contracts or LOAs, and in preparation for asking a lawyer to help figure this out, you might want to begin by assessing your project for points of vulnerability, similar to (or as part of) your risk assessment process.

Review your work breakdown structure, and for each node, ask three questions:

1. Is there an exchange of *value*? Most commonly, someone creates something for money: records a track, provides a service, shares an idea, sells a product, appears in a photograph, etc.

2. Is someone's *wellbeing* potentially at risk? Consider their safety, health, and state of mind. Is that singer being coerced into over-singing? Is the tour bus roadworthy? Is there an emergency evacuation procedure? Also consider the well-being of inanimate objects. Is that Stradivarius insured? Is the hall's sprinkler system operative? Will the engineer carefully archive your recording after the project is done?

3. Do any *laws* or other regulations touch this? Such as, are you hoping to build your studio in a historical district? Do you need to clear any copyrights? Does your school have a policy about performing songs that include swearing, or religious themes, or ensuring diversity?

Answering "yes" to any of these questions is a red flag that there should be a document, somewhere, clarifying the promise and the considerations, and also, the responsibilities.

Value, Wellbeing, Laws. Remember these with the admittedly annoying mnemonic VoWeL: "Buy a VoWeL before you throw in the towel!"

So, crack out the work breakdown structure, and consider the VoWeLs. Look for red flags. If there is the potential for an issue, consider whether it is currently addressed in a contract or an insurance policy. If it is, you might be all set and won't have to worry about further mitigation. If there is no mechanism in place, consider talking to a lawyer about what is necessary and appropriate.

Let's try it. Say we rent a hall and put on a concert. Here's a WBS.

1. Concert
    1.1. Music
        1.1.1. Music Selection
        1.1.2. Rehearsals
    1.2. Program
    1.3. Facility
        1.3.1. Stage
        1.3.2. House
        1.3.3. Sound
        1.3.4. Lighting
    1.4. Personnel
        1.4.1. Musicians
        1.4.2. Concert Hall Staff
    1.5. Publicity
    1.6. Project Management
        1.6.1. Planning Documents
            1.6.1.1. Budget
            1.6.1.2. Schedule
        1.6.2. Execution Documents
            1.6.2.1. Stage Setup
            1.6.2.2. Lighting Schematic
            1.6.2.3. Sound Schematic
            1.6.2.4. Run Sheet
            1.6.2.5. Gear Checklist

We go through it methodically, as usual, and set the most paranoid part of our imaginations at work: VoWeL. Let's try a couple of examples.

1.1.1. Music Selection

- **Value:** There are several types of value being exchanged here: the sheet music itself, the performance rights for the music, and the selection of the music. We bought the sheet music from a store, so that is settled. The performance rights get taken care of by the venue, which regularly submits reports to performance rights organizations. The duty to select the music should be clarified in the concert's artistic director's contract.

- **Wellbeing:** The matchup between the music and the participants must be such that nobody will be harmed by it. So, if the music contains mature themes, we warn the audience who might bring minors to come hear it.

- **Law:** We should confirm that we have the rights to perform the music.

Then, consider the next item: **1.1.2. Rehearsals**

- **Value:** Are musicians being compensated fairly for their time? How much they get paid and how much rehearsal time will be required should be clarified on a document, somewhere. Are we sure that the hall will be available for as long as we need it to be? Do we have an exact hard stop, regarding rehearsal times (when we absolutely must leave), or can we have the hall for as late into the night as we need it?

- **Wellness:** If it snows before our rehearsal, who will make sure that the sidewalk gets shoveled and de-iced? Does the rehearsal space have a sufficient insurance policy?

- **Law:** How long do union rules permit me to rehearse musicians without a break? Are there local noise control regulations regarding when we have to stop rehearsing? How late are we allowed to use this room? Can we use the coffeemaker?

All these possibilities need to be clarified, somewhere. Maybe it's in a contract, maybe it's in an email, but there needs to be clarity. Contracts might specify that insurance is covered, or that workers are licensed, and so on, so the precise articulations can involve chains of documents, referencing each other. It just needs to be covered, somehow.

The more comprehensively you address these issues, the less risk you are taking on, and the clearer your relationships will be. And if you do a full-blown legal contract for every single one, you will spend all of your time and money annoying people, and so these issues need to be prioritized and considered, in terms of what kind of mitigation is truly necessary, as well as your budget.

COPYRIGHTS, ROYALTIES, AND REGISTRATIONS

Copyright law often touches music projects, both from consumer and creator perspectives. Let's trace the cycle of work and compensation.

1. Content is created, generally by a team of people and organizations. This includes songwriters, performing musicians, audio production people, publishing companies, and even investors. The form can be a sound recording, video, or sheet music. While a dozen or a hundred different entities might be involved, generally, between one and five (or so) own the music rights, in the end, and the rest get paid one-time lump sums for their participation.

2. Media outlets make the content available. This can include concert halls, radio stations, websites, film, television, cafés, street buskers, or anywhere else that music gets played.

3. Administration organizations receive reports from the media outlets, get paid, and then make sure that the content owners receive their due.

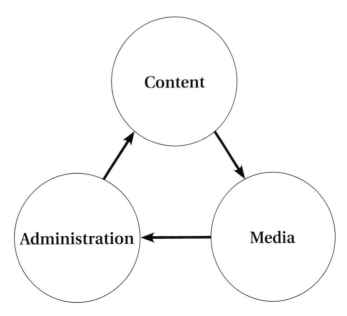

FIG. 8.1. Administrative Flow of Copyrights

For this system to work, content creators need to register with the adminis-tration organizations. This should happen early in every commercially minded musician's career and then updated and maintained as new works are created. So, there are copyright maintenance chores that are commonly part of the general project administration. Specifically, new creative works need to be registered with the organizations that administer rights, as well as with the government's copyright control agency.

Depending on what kind of work you are doing, this can include various categories of organization:

- performance rights organizations: ASCAP, BMI, or SESAC

- digital rights organizations: Sound Exchange

- recording rights. If you want to cover another artist's song on your own album, you need to get the rights. Those are administered by the Harry Fox Agency, which powers various other tools such as Soundfiles.com.

- synchronization rights: Rights to use music in film and TV are generally negotiated directly with whoever controls the publishing rights.

As a songwriter, for the rights organizations to know about you, and thus, send you checks now and then, you have to register with them: both for the writ-er's share and the publisher's share of the rights ownership. When you create new works that you want them to track, you have to register the works with them. Doing so is one of the standard dimensions of music project manage-ment. It's tedious but not too bad, once you've done it, and the tools online for taking care of all this bureaucracy continue to improve.

Establishments that play music, such as TV and radio stations, bars, concert halls, restaurants, department stores, and so on, pay annual licensing fees to the PROs. The PROs then pass some of the money they collect to some of the songwriters they represent. (ASCAP typically takes about nine months to pay.) It's kind of a black box, and it certainly isn't one hundred percent fair, but that's how it works. One hopes that this will eventually become more equitable, as digital files and digital music systems do a better job of tracking actual usage. The technology is certainly there; now, we just have to wait for the will of all the middlemen to catch up.

For what it's worth, I was trying to find some "wisdom from the trenches" about these mechanisms, and contacted a number of people I know who work in the various industries where music is provided to the public: a retail

store owner, a concert organizer, a social event organizer, a performing/
recording artist, and even an ASCAP licensing agent. All of them said that
they didn't understand the process as thoroughly as they felt they should,
and all but the ASCAP rep confessed that they were probably doing something illegal. So, we all muddle through....

Intellectual Property Protection

Similar to the organizations that administer royalties, there are a number
of different organizations that you will deal with that help you declare and
track what you create. These include protecting intellectual property, and as
we will see in the next page, various codes to make buying and selling easier.

Here are the three most common stops for establishing ownership of
intellectual property:

1. **Copyrights.** In the U.S., to formally register a copyright, use the U.S.
   Copyright Office (www.copyright.gov). While you technically own
   the copyright to whatever you create, paying $35 to the government
   officially documents it, which offers much greater protection. As part
   of this process, you will send the Library of Congress a copy of your
   final published project. That's actually a small thrill, for me, as it
   really feels like a formal contribution to all that human civilization
   has produced. It's like achieving a tiny bit of immortality.

2. **Patents.** Like a copyright, a patent establishes ownership of
   intellectual property. If your project is inventing something, including
   certain types of software and procedures, you might need to get a
   patent, to make sure that you get paid. This is a much more complex
   process than getting a copyright, and generally requires the services
   of a lawyer. It might be a necessary procedural step for you, though,
   so you should track it. They are administered by the U.S. Patent and
   Trademark Office.

   Speaking of immortality, here's an excerpt from a patent my
   grandfather, Sidney E. Feist, procured in 1921, for his invention of a
   mechanical ballroom dancing practice partner. He owned a dance
   studio in Brooklyn and patented a number of similar inventions.
   While none realized the vast fortune he likely hoped would come of
   them, they did delight and crack up his great-grandchildren fifty years
   after his passing.

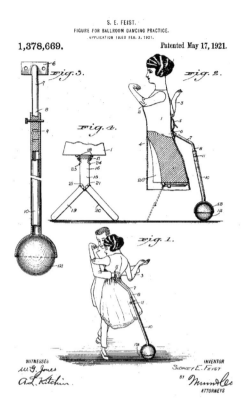

FIG. 8.2. Patent Diagram for Mechanical Ballroom Dancing Partner

3. **Trademarks.** A trademark is like a copyrightable name of a product (or service, which is more properly called a "service mark"). Like patents, these generally require the services of a specialized lawyer. The purpose, though, is that if you invent a product (such as a new guitar, or effects pedal, or app), you want to confirm that you have the ultimate rights to its name. You can't invent a guitar and call it a "Les Paul" because that name is already trademarked. It's better to find this out relatively early in the process, before you create a few thousand of them with an illegal product name engraved on them.

The U.S. Patent and Trademark Office administers these as well, as you might have guessed. Their site includes an excellent searchable database, so that you can do some homework before engaging a lawyer, and disqualify some obvious problems. For example, a search for "Les Paul" generated a list of instances in which those words are used in a trademark: guitars, basses, picks, various other instruments, and so on. Gibson has it covered. Clearly, a luthier would have a hard time naming a new guitar that. A sidewalk café might be possible, but not a guitar.

More information is available at the U.S. Patent and Trademark Office's excellent website at www.uspto.gov/trademarks/basics/.

Product Codes

Besides protecting intellectual property, another administrative step involves getting appropriate code numbers required for packaging. This is important for selling CDs, books, sheet music, digital downloads, and other products you might try. What you will need depends a bit on where you plan to sell them.

1. **Barcodes.** Barcodes are used on any physical commercial object to make them scannable by optical inventory management systems. A UPC barcode is used in the United States, and an EAN is used internationally. Some other more niche barcodes are popping up as well, such as QR codes, but they are currently less universal.

   Barcodes make products easier to sell, and many stores (including Amazon.com) require that all their wares have them. They don't have any other benefit to the creator, besides making the product easier for some establishments to sell. If you are targeting a specific sales outlet with a physical product, find out their barcode requirements before you begin your graphic design of the packaging. Barcodes often have specific requirements for where they are placed.

   Buying a barcode can be a pain in the neck, because the companies that administer them are optimized to sell great numbers of them to large corporations, rather than just one to an independent rock band. There are enumerable websites that will overcharge you for these. However, you might be able to get a barcode for a relatively nominal fee (say, $25 to $100) from a replication company. For books, you can get them from the U.S. ISBN Agency at Bowker. When you buy one, you get an electronic file, which you then integrate into your graphic design, based on precise layout parameters.

2. **ISBN numbers** are assigned to books and sheet music, and many vendors require an ISBN number on all products that they sell. They get administered by the U.S. ISBN Agency at Bowker, which also sells barcodes for books.

   Many services exist that will take care of these registrations for you, generally at a significant markup. It's not difficult to get them on your own, though, once you know where to look, which is here: www.myidentifiers.com.

3. **ISRC codes** are an international standard for providing unique text identifiers for digital music files, necessary for digital royalties to be tracked and paid. To sell a song on iTunes, the file needs an embedded

ISRC code. Currently, ISRC codes are generally assigned for free by mastering engineers and by digital music sales outlets (such as iTunes, etc.). They are necessary for tracking the sales of download files. ISRC code format is: CC-XXX-YY-NNNNN, which are placeholders for Country: AssigningOrganization:YearAssigned:UniqueNumber. In this way, a lot can be determined about a sound file from its ISRC code.

Clearance and Permissions

In addition to these considerations for protecting what you create, part of your project might entail using work created by others. This can include:

- samples of music by other artists (sound or notation)
- photos of people or products
- artwork by other people

These are generally handled by a formal *license* or release, which itemizes what the image or body of work is, and the parameters surrounding its usage. There might be a financial transaction, or there might be a clause regarding how the credit should read. The license should clarify the *term*—how long it is in effect. Ideally, the term is in perpetuity, if you are using some work as part of some other work, like using a drawing as your album cover.

For clearing songs that have received significant traction in the industry, services such as RightsFlow.com help clear copyrights for these usages. Getting the permission for works by creators on a less national stage might instead involve contacting them and negotiating with them or their estate.

Similar to these are permissions for special types of work. These vary a lot, and the list could grow nearly infinitely long, but here are a few types, just to prompt your imagination regarding necessary dimensions of what you intend. Getting any of these permissions might take a long time, and so if there is a need, an early task should be to ascertain what the timeframe is for getting them.

Note: Laws about these permissions will vary on locale, and some are being debated as we speak, so double-check your local laws before making any assumptions.

1. **Building permits.** And as part of building permits, there might be other interconnected permits, such as in navigating historical districts, conservation districts, school zones, and so on.

2. **Liquor licenses.** If you are hosting an event, getting a liquor license might be your responsibility. You might be surprised to learn that not only do

you need the license, but you need to hire a dedicated bartender, or you won't be able to serve alcohol.

3. **Work permits.** Make sure that everyone you hire can work legally! Assuming, of course, that you value such things.

4. **Outdoor performance permits.** Outdoor public performances and gatherings could require parade permits, busking licenses, vending licenses, or other similar permissions. Some of these requirements are periodically reexamined and sometimes even discontinued as unconstitutional, protected by first amendment rights, but laws remain in effect, in many places.

Type	Contact	Notes
Contracts		
Employees		
Contractors		
Service Providers		
Facilities/Venues		
Vendors		
Rights Management		
Performance Rights Organization (Join One)	ASCAP	Register once, and then update them with new content
	BMI	
	SESAC	
Digital Downloads	Sound Exchange	
Intellectual Property		
Copyright	U.S. Copyright Office	Register once the product is in print
Patents	U.S. Patent and Trademark Office	
Trademarks	U.S. Patent and Trademark Office	
Registrations		
Barcodes	U.S. ISBN Agency at Bowker	
ISBN	U.S. ISBN Agency at Bowker	
ISRC	Your mastering engineer	
Licenses		
Mechanical Rights	Rightsflow	
Synchronization Rights	The copyright owner	
Outdoor Performance	Your local town hall	
Liquor License	Your local town hall	
Building Permit	Your local town hall	

FIG. 8.3. Bureaucracy Checklist

Tracking all these details can be daunting. Maintaining a checklist of them all helps keep them organized, so that you can jog your memory when you're working on a new project. Figure 8.3 is the start of one, which you might use to help build a template for all your projects. When you have a new project, figure out what subset or extension makes sense for what you are doing, and make sure that this rather tedious dimension of project management gets addressed. If your specific type of work requires other permissions, contracts, licenses, and so on, then add them to your master list.

Remember, you are not necessarily responsible for all or any of these. In some cases, someone else will likely take care of it. As a project manager, you just want to make sure that somehow, it gets done.

INSURANCE

Insurance is another means of mitigating risk, generally to protect against theft or disasters such as fire or flood. The idea is that you pay a small amount of money to an insurance company, and if there is a major disaster, they pay for it, rather than you. It's a kind of betting. In their advertisements, they try to raise your level of fear and convince you that their rates are low. In their contracts, disreputable ones might insert tricky language that will actually exclude them from paying. So, there are many scams. But if tragedy strikes, proper insurance can have permanent repercussions on your life and career.

Annual fees for insurance are offset by deductibles—the amount you are willing to pay before insurance kicks in. If you insure a guitar for $10,000, you might pay, say, $250 a year for it to be insured. If the deductible is $500, they will pay you $9,500. You might be able to raise your deductible, say to $2,000, and get a lower rate, such as $125 per year. That way, if it gets lost, they will pay only $8,000. The higher the risk, the less of a deductible you might tolerate, but it is generally considered a good idea to live with the highest deductible that you can manage. If losing $2,000 won't dramatically impact your life, then definitely have a deductible that high, to lower your annual costs. Probably, your guitar will be fine, and you will never have to file a claim.

As a project manager, you might be in position to get group insurance rates for your project, rather than for insuring specific people or items. It might also make sense to set up a group rate with an insurance company and then have your team optionally participate, even paying all or a portion of the costs themselves. A touring band, for example, might collectively own a lot of sound equipment, which gets insured. Individual musicians might elect to join this program to insure their own instruments or other gear.

There are probably hundreds of types of insurance you can buy, from life insurance to kidnap/ransom insurance. Some that are relatively likely to touch music projects are the following.

1. **Instrument insurance**, for loss or theft of a particularly valuable instrument. I once passed a violinist friend on the street in what was then a relatively rough neighborhood of Boston. She was carrying two instrument cases. She said, "Do you know what this is?" I said, "Uh, no, what?" She said, "It's a million dollar Strad!" I gasped. She held out the other one. "Do you know what this is?" I said, "Hmm, no, what?" She said, "It's a *$2* million dollar Strad! I have to choose which one I'm gonna borrow for the next year." I gasped again, and she giggled, and said, "Don't worry, they're insured!" I tried to convince her to take a cab rather than the subway....

   Your instrument or other gear might be covered under an existing insurance policy, or you might need to take out a specific policy for a particularly valuable item. Some people use $5,000 value as the point at which they will start considering having specialized instrument insurance, which will cover some hazards particular to instruments, such as damage during travel. You will need to submit a formal appraisal of your instrument, which you can get from a good repair shop.

   While you might not have a single item that's worth more than a couple thousand dollars, all your gear collectively might be worth a considerable amount, and you can get policies that will cover collections, as well as individual items.

   Homeowners' policies might cover personal property loss, such as instruments, up to $2,000 or so, but that might not be nearly enough to cover a significant item or collection of items, so this is something to look into.

   Boston-based classical guitarist Aaron Larget-Caplan suffered a house fire in 2007 that resulted not only in significant injury to his wife but in the loss of seven instruments, about $30,000 worth of scores, his CD collection, and many electronics (amps, effects pedals, sound gear, etc.). He learned the hard way that homeowner's insurance won't cover business property loss, and because his income came from music, that included a lot of stuff that he didn't anticipate, such as his Twisted Sister CDs. Six years later, he's still embroiled in law suits over this catastrophe, which resulted from shoddy construction work. Now, Aaron has a business schedule in his homeowner's policy that covers all of his music related assets, as well as additional liability coverage for the students who come to his house for lessons. He also has specific instrument insurance to cover his guitars. Before the fire, a small percentage of his gear was covered by Clarion Associates, Inc., which specializes in instrument insurance, and they sent him a check ten days after the catastrophe, which was a rare bright spot during that dark time.

Here is a photo of Aaron's office, after the fire.

FIG. 8.4. Office of Aaron Larget-Caplan After the Fire

Here is one of the guitars he lost, which was unfortunately uninsured.

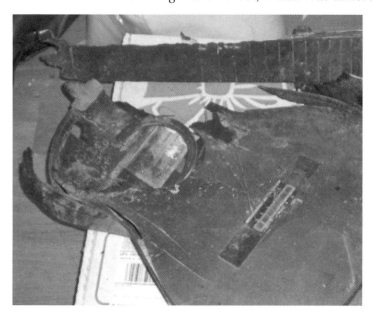

FIG. 8.5. Uninsured Guitar Destroyed by Fire

Aaron recommends paying careful attention to your insurance coverage....

2. **Travel insurance.** Travel insurance can cover a host of calamities that might occur while traveling, from lost luggage to emergency medical costs to cascading financial effects due to canceled flights. Say that you schedule an overseas concert tour and buy $30,000 worth of non-refundable plane tickets for your band. If the tour needs to get canceled for some reason, like the whole band suddenly contracts malaria, then travel insurance will let you recoup that $30,000.

3. **Liability insurance** covers other people, if they get damaged due to some act of negligence on your part. If you have a jazz club and the Steinway rolls off the stage and onto an audience member's lap, liability insurance pays any claims awarded. There will be a cutoff point, though, for how much they will pay, so it is not a one hundred percent guarantee that you or your business will not be profoundly affected. You can get special "Event Insurance," for a one-time occasion, such as hosting a one-off rock festival in a cornfield. Clarion will also help with that type of insurance, and you can try their interactive worksheet on their website: www.clarionins.com.

4. **Employment-related insurance.** If you are hiring actual employees for your project, there are various types of insurance you might need to provide: disability, unemployment, health, and so on.

These are just some common insurance types related to music projects.

As always, specific projects might have specific insurance needs, so talk to an insurance agent (or two, or three), and get a sense of what makes sense.

This is terrifying stuff. That said, also be careful not to overbuy insurance. Its general purpose is to protect you from financial ruin, in the case of extraordinary circumstance. If the worst-case scenario is really a fairly recoverable situation for you, you might do better not to buy instrument insurance, or some other types. If your guitar is worth $1,000, you don't want to spend $250 a year to insure it. Just get a good case, and be careful not to leave it in a taxi. But also be realistic about how much money you've got tied up in your music-related assets. We can accumulate a lot of stuff over the years, and its collective value might be more significant than we realize.

TAXES

Taxes for musicians can be relatively complex affairs because we can draw income from so many kinds of places. We might have a salaried position, do freelance gigs, and get various kinds of royalties.

My frank advice is that you hire someone to help you with your taxes. Professional tax preparers often pay for themselves, through their advice and by helping you avoid mistakes that result in fees. There is no shame in having someone help you do your taxes. My father, an accountant, first does his taxes by himself and then pays a professional to do them a second time. Then, the two of them bicker into the wee hours about the details. But he's seen enough costly mistakes over the years to feel that this approach is important for risk mitigation. There's something about having an outsider look at your finances fresh that gives you a more objective and thorough perspective.

Way back in the mid 1990s, I took a career digression for a couple years and worked for a software company that developed massive database management systems. One of our largest clients was the IRS, and I spent a week advising them, deep in the inner sanctums of their data processing center in Washington, D.C. One lesson I learned is that you must make everything completely crystal clear for the IRS, or else they will bury you in a vast and baffling mountain of red tape. And they will always win by exhausting you. They will lose your address, send you a bogus fine when you don't respond to their queries, and then seize your grandmother's assets, to make her pay for your bogus fine. Not an exaggeration.

So, you need to pay exactly what you owe before it is due, without any complications, and in a way that robots with no imagination or compassion can understand instantly. Tax professionals can speak their language and lower the IRS's suspicions. I can't recommend them highly enough.

As a project manager, your task of focus is in organizing the paperwork for when the tax return gets done, which I recommend you try to do early, rather than late (in the U.S., February, not April). If you are a business owner, you will probably be concerned with providing your employees and contractors with four forms, though this can increase awfully fast. As a project manager, probably, your finance or HR team will handle these forms, but there might be some overlap that spills into your work, so I'll mention them.

- **Form 1040** is an individual's central tax form, where you list summaries of all the information about the year's finances. It currently has 11 or so "schedules," which are attachments potentially used to calculate specialized dimensions of the 1040, such as for itemized deductions (business expenses), investments, farming income, and so on.

- **W-2 forms** are generated for employees by their employers. An employee's annual W-2 must be received by the employee before January 31.

- **1099-MISC** is a catchall form for miscellaneous income. It is required for contractors paid over $600 in a year—very common for paying audio engineers. It is also required for royalties in excess of $10. Recipients need a separate one for each source of non-employee income, so musicians might (hopefully!) amass quite a few of them.

- **W-9** is a request for a taxpayer identification number. When you hire an employee or a contractor (paid over $600 per year), you will need this number in order to fill out their W2 or 1099. Give them this form as soon as you engage them, in order to avoid a mad scramble in January, when the deadline approaches. In practice, this is the only one that I find necessary to track, as a project manager. The financial reporting forms are handled by the finance team. But at the start of the relationship, the project manager is the primary interface with the team, and so it often makes sense for the project manager to be charged with procuring the W-9. It's important to make sure this is handled smoothly because without a W-9, your business department might not want to release their payment. But a service provider might not deliver a final deliverable until they get paid. This dance, of waiting for the W-9 to be sent, signed, and received back, can introduce unexpected delays and tensions into the project, and those delays are often close to major deadlines, when there isn't any wiggle room. Also, this little dance of inconvenience can result in fractured relationships with providers, who dislike the red tape you're throwing at them, and who really need the money right now, please. So, getting the W-9 is a good checklist item.

All these forms are available on the IRS website: www.irs.gov. The IRS website is actually a wonderful information trove—an amazing accomplishment, in many ways. It is deeply complex but also informative and helpful, with a clarity of language and layout that one might not expect.

The other dimension of what you have to track are your expenses and income, saving every receipt, and itemizing any cash you receive, such as for t-shirt sales at gigs. Receipts related to your project need to be kept, organized by year. This includes all business costs, from rental fees to celebratory lunches. Also track mileage and gas, particularly for touring. These all can be deducted on Schedule A of Form 1040.

INVOICES

Invoices serve two purposes. First, they help us get paid. Second, they provide a permanent record of the transaction. You can turn an invoice into a receipt by marking it "paid."

When a billable task is completed and approved, the service provider should immediately give the client an invoice. The invoice should clearly state the client's name, what the project is, what the work being invoiced is, and what the terms of the invoice are, such as "Payable within 30 days." If there are code numbers to help identify clients, projects, or transactions, those can be helpful as well. Include contact information for both sides.

As a project manager, you might give invoices for your own services, or you might receive them from others. It's a two-part process: giving the invoice and then tracking whether the payment has happened or not.

Cash flow is among the most difficult strains for any small business, so it's helpful to be vigilant about making sure invoices get paid promptly, whichever side of the equation you fall on. Manage the expectations of your vendors. Find out how long it takes your organization to pay invoices, and let them know. Some people might be used to getting paid in cash immediately, and it drives them crazy to have to wait a month for a corporation to write a check. They should know what to expect as early in the process as possible, so that their frustration doesn't fester. As a project manager, review their invoice for completion before forwarding it to the accounting department. Try to spot and rectify anything amiss about your vendors' invoices, to avoid delays in the processing. This stage of a relationship is where strains are introduced.

Relationships easily sour due to misunderstandings about money. Be a champion for everyone on your team, and take responsibility for the finances working out smoothly. You might find it best to generate an invoice for someone on your team, and then submit or route it where it needs to go on their behalf. It doesn't have to be anything fancy. It just needs the right information. And remember, if it is over $600, they might also need to submit a W-9.

Invoice

To:	Berklee Press
From:	Maria Walker
Date Submitted:	March 22, 2012

Project:	*Songwriting for Film* DVD
Author:	Maria Walker

Description	Amount
Guitar for recording session	$250

Payable upon receipt. Please mail to:

Maria Walker
123 Sarah Circle
Boston, MA 02215

FIG. 8.6. Invoice

CLOSING THOUGHTS

All these types of documents and administrative procedures help to ensure your project's success by reducing risk and clarifying communication. It's important to confirm that all these administrative steps are handled as well as they can be, and I recommend getting a professional to help you sort this out: a financial planner, a lawyer, an accountant, and/or someone else who has expertise in small business administration. The potential risks are too high not to take this seriously.

PRACTICE

Create a matrix of all the bureaucracy associated with your project: legal forms, agreements, invoices, insurance, copyright forms, tax forms, or whatever else it needs. Include due dates of when everything should ideally be completed.

CHAPTER 9

Execution

At a point, you have to stop monkeying around and actually do the work!

In this chapter, we circumvent any possible "analysis paralysis" and look at how to get the project's work done right.

At this point, we've seen how to get the key work strategies figured out. We dwelled on it a bit, but it's good to do so. Planning is relatively cheap and easily modified, compared with execution. In planning, you can change a program in ten seconds, with no cost. In execution, changing a program can require thousands of dollars and weeks of work. So, we end planning and start execution with a wary eye.

One of the primary goals during execution is to make sure that we don't lose sight of our good planning work. In the heat of battle, such as during a recording session or rehearsal, or pounding the pavement to raise funding, or being crushed by whatever load of work you're under, it's easy to make reactive, short-sighted decisions, rather than doing what's best for the big picture. We want to make sure that the work being done conforms to that good cool-headed analysis of the situation we did before execution started.

In execution, some work is done, which then gets monitored and either approved or revised. In monitoring it, it is checked against the plan (i.e., scope statement, WBS, etc.). Hopefully, it fulfills what was spec'd. If not, either the work gets redone or the plan gets revised.

In this chapter, we will review some techniques to support the execution phase of the project.

OBJECTIVES

By the end of the chapter, you will be able to:

- use your project plan to make sure that the work is done appropriately

- launch your project, disseminating the work to your team in a way that will encourage its success

- communicate well with your project team and your stakeholders

- lead productive meetings that lead to effective action

- monitor progress on your project so that you can keep it on track

- correct the course of the project execution, should it veer off track

WHAT HAPPENS DURING EXECUTION

Mentsch tracht, Gott lacht.
[Translation: Man plans, God laughs.]
—Proverb

In project execution, work that was specified in the project plan gets completed. Content gets created. You told someone to record a bass line, and now, they record it. It becomes real. Hopefully, it is fun!

The process involves communicating what needs to be done to whoever will do it, and then them doing it. To give the created content the best possible chance of being actually usable, while the work progresses, progress is monitored—and, if necessary, redirected. Problems are figured out. Stakeholders receive reports regarding how the project is going, and make existential decisions as necessary.

Various ways of controlling the work are undertaken to ensure that everything goes according to plan. Here's the big picture: planning and execution are intertwined.

FIG. 9.1. Planning and Execution

In this diagram, you can see that there isn't a clear division of the project stages of planning and execution, with planning ending and then execution beginning. Success is more likely if the plan is flexible and can be refined based on what is learned as execution unfolds. Surprises unfold. For example:

- On the third day of your weeklong recording session, you might get a call from a long-lost college friend who became a world-renowned electric violinist. You realize that the project would be better with him playing a solo on your album, so you have to rejigger some decided issues of timing, budget, and schedule.

- A political election result goes down in Oklahoma that you just can't live with. In deciding to boycott all things having to do with that state, you want to cancel part of your upcoming tour.

- While trying to rent a building for your community music school, you come to the realization that it makes more sense to buy a building instead. You re-evaluate and update the scope, budget, risk register, and so on.

- You create a vocal effects app, and test it out on some potential users. They give you the feedback that there's a major feature they all really want.

Your plan needs to evolve in order to suit such needed changes that are revealed during execution, whether because of something you created or because of some change in the world.

Transitioning from Planning to Execution

As pure planning moves into the execution phase, there's something of a transitional period. Here is how one evolves into the other.

- **The plan settles**. Documents get printed and distributed. Some issues get finalized, such as the selection of an appropriate project management approach for the execution phase (i.e., choosing the right lifecycle model, as discussed in chapter 1). The plan itself comes together as a coherent whole. (We'll look at the components and function of the plan next.)

- **Approvals are finalized**. The work becomes officially authorized by all necessary stakeholders. Contracts get signed.

- **Money might move**. Advance payments might be necessary to kick off certain kinds of work, such as publishing contracts, or deposits on gear or facilities. Similarly, funds might travel between bank accounts in order to become more easily accessible.

- **Project management software gets loaded**. Information from the work breakdown structure, budget, personnel matrix, and so on get entered into Smartsheet, or whatever software you are using. This leads to the production of an operating schedule.

- **Work gets delegated**. This can be a simple directive ("Please play this bass line!"), a detailed conversation about the work, or a team kickoff meeting that is as much to do with building team spirit as it is to clarify the details of what the work will be.

Content Creation in Context

Let's look at delegation in the broader context of project management. Shaded, we see the content being created. Numbered items are what the project manager is doing to make sure that the work comes out right.

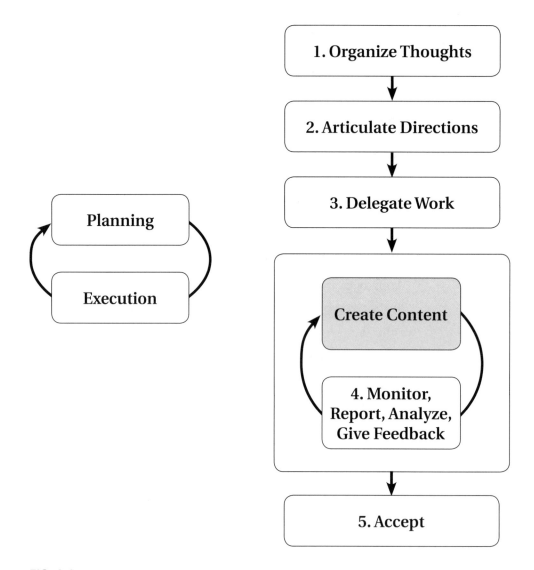

FIG. 9.2. Task Delegation Process

1. **Organize Thoughts.** In preparing to delegate a task, we first consider our project plan and over-arching goals.

2. **Articulate Directions.** We develop a detailed description of what we want, which we will give to whoever is doing the work. It's helpful to have this in writing. It will serve as a reference point for the worker. It should describe what success looks like, in detail, and also include relevant deadlines, budget information, and any other known constraints for the work.

3. **Delegate.** Give the directions to whoever will do the work, and tell them to start.

4. **Action/Monitoring.** While the content is being created, it is regularly monitored and considered, and feedback is provided at regular enough intervals to ensure that all work is being done in accordance with the plan.

5. **Acceptance.** The work is complete and confirmed to be right.

Assemble Your Project Plan

Projects often get out of hand during the work phase, and the reason is commonly due to insufficient monitoring and too little feedback. People simply do inappropriate work because they didn't understand what was required. For example, you ask someone to record a bass line, but it is too busy or in the wrong style.

Small variances can be nudged back into the fold. A great help towards keeping the project generally on track is by keeping the project plan close, and using it as a constant reference for all work. Look at your stated purpose, content outline, vision statement, and other elements. Make sure every new person brought on board understands the essentials of what you are doing, both at the detail level of their part, but also at the macro level of the project's overall purpose.

All the planning documents remain useful and active during execution. Some of them might evolve continually, such as nuances of the work breakdown structure, or the Budget to Actual worksheet. Others will tend to remain static, but get used for reference, and to create working documents, such as quality control checklists (to be discussed later in the book).

Think of your project plan as a set of reference points regarding the decisions that have been made. Work gets checked against what the plan specifies in order to confirm that it fulfills the requirements.

The plan should reflect high quality decisions, made strategically in accordance with the constraints of budget and time, and reflective of the input by all the stakeholders.

One of the dangers during the execution phase is that the work done isn't actually usable in the project. This often happens when individual workers aren't given clear enough direction and feel that they have more latitude to make decisions in isolation than they actually do.

For example, a mix engineer is given rough tracks, and the recording that emerges has too much of a pop feel, rather than the acoustic feel that was desired, and so it has to be redone: argued about, waited for, and perhaps paid for a second time. Closer management of its execution could have prevented that kind of setback.

The following set of documents comprises your project plan. You might include other supplementary documents as well. Keep them all together and convenient in a folder.

- Scope Statement

- Work Breakdown Structure and Dictionary

- Budget

- Schedule

- Stakeholder Register

- Resource Allocation Chart(s), with contact info for your whole team

- Risk Register

- Bureaucracy Checklist

- Project Lifecycle Diagram

Some of these may be primarily electronic in implementation, particularly the schedule. Hard-copy backups of these are important, though. If you are relying on cloud-based project management software such as Smartsheet, an extended power outage could wreak havoc with your ability to manage the project, if you don't have a backup.

Whenever you complete a major work effort, and at least once per week, print out a backup of all relevant documents that have changed—particularly your schedule and your contact information for your project team, if they have changed. You want to be able to keep your project more or less running using just your backup hard copies and a telephone, if necessary.

DELEGATING THE WORK

The *launch* phase of execution is the formal beginning of the work. This is the point when the project team members are given the official go-ahead to begin, as well as detailed instructions on what they are to do.

The first step is to review the tasks specified in the work breakdown structure, and determine what can be handed off. Some of these will be simple (have an administrative assistant photocopy a stack of paper) and others will more substantial (tell a composer to write an opera). There are similarities between them, though, no matter what the scale. The project manager needs to provide clear direction, and have a system to help track progress—such as a column on the task list indicating the status, or a list of delegated tasks that the manager is waiting for others to complete.

Clear management will help keep people on course and avoid disaster. And what are the common disasters that happen when you delegate?

1. **Not doing the work.** For whatever reason, signals get crossed. Emails get missed. People zone out during conversations. Managers dream that they delegated tasks, but they actually did not.

2. **Doing the wrong work.** Your team spends time and energy completing tasks that aren't actually useful. This is usually a communication problem. (Most problems are communication problems.)

3. **Doing the work poorly.** The responsible person is unqualified for the assigned task. This is usually a hiring mistake.

4. **Blowing the budget or timeline.** The work is more expensive or time consuming than anticipated. Or, the worker is busier than anticipated, so they aren't as productive as promised. This is again often a communication problem regarding the scope.

5. **A worker becomes unexpectedly unavailable.** Life intervenes. This is a constant pressure with all projects. If there aren't sufficient contingencies in place, this can completely derail a project.

To minimize the risk of these, the project manager needs to create detailed directions describing exactly what work needs to get done—whether a short email or a formal contract. These directions might be prepared during planning, too, depending on when you engage your team members.

The project manager gives the worker authorization and direction, essentially handing the "Responsible" role to the delegate, and assuming the "Approver" role, though the project manager remains ultimately responsible for all tasks. The delegate (now "Responsible") in turn gives the project manager a commitment that he or she will do the work according to plan and, hopefully, will follow through. Delegates in the big picture role of Supporting, Consulting, or Informed will still be in the Responsible role for fulfilling specific tasks, at the lower level. No matter what their overall role in the project, everyone needs to be clear on the scope, price, timeline, and quality level of what they will deliver, when given a task.

Written directions are best, as they can be referenced afterwards. There might be an in-person meeting or phone call first. Sometimes, it makes sense to ask delegates to sign something, such as a work directive, to confirm that they received it. That adds gravitas to the process.

At Berklee Press, for our book projects, here's what different types of team members receive, to kick things off:

- Authors get an extended formal contract, itemizing general terms of their compensation (such as royalty rates, non-compete agreements, clarifications on how many free copies of their book they get, etc.), as well as specifics, such as the book's proposed length, focus, and table of contents. The contract gets signed by people at Berklee and by the author.

- Vendors generally get a "Letter of Agreement" (LOA) specifying the precise details of what they are to deliver. These documents are shorter than contracts, usually just a page, but specify what the exact deliverables, cost, timeline, and quality parameters will be. Arrangers who help prepare songbooks, for example, get LOAs. These transactions are lump-sum payments, rather than royalty structures, so they are simpler. They also get signed.

- Some contractors get a simpler work directive, if we have an ongoing relationship and the financial details have been established elsewhere. For example, my regular cover designer gets a "Cover Art Direction Sheet." Because we've done this exact transaction previously and have already signed a letter of agreement about our working relationship, this document is simpler, and much more directly related to the content, without any language about the business relationships, other than the fee.

- Office mates get direction in an email. It's relatively informal, has no business language, and doesn't usually require a signature, though they might "initial" certain documents to show that they have read them.

Providing instructions in writing is important. The more specific you can be, the more likely it will be that they will produce what you need from them.

Assigning Tasks

Assigning someone any task should be a two-dimensional process. You tell a delegate what to do, but you also set the task in some kind of tracking system, so that you will regularly monitor its progress, and make sure that it doesn't get lost in a black hole somewhere.

At a minimum, a project manager needs to track:

1. the task name
2. who is doing it
3. when it is needed (possibly, in several installments)
4. the current status, including how much is left to do (percent completed)
5. when it makes sense to ask for the next status update

The person being charged with completing the task needs to know:

1. why they are doing the task and how it fits into the larger vision of the project
2. the task name
3. the task deadline
4. how much time they are expected to devote to the task
5. exactly what needs to be done
6. the method they should use to complete the task
7. what resources they can devote to it
8. what constraints they should remain within, including time, money, personnel, legalities or procedures, equipment usage, and so on
9. what supporting materials (documents, recordings, models, checklists, templates, etc.) they should use or reference
10. when and how they should report their progress, and who needs to know what about what they are doing
11. how to deliver their work

These items might be tracked using various reports, charts, lists, calendars, and so on. Good project management software helps keep all of this information organized. Here is a view of Smartsheet, showing columns for most of these items. Each row has an "Assigned To" field, and filling that out sends the person assigned that task a communication with the task name, deadline, link to an extended description, and other critical information. Additional built-in communication and reminder tools further facilitate the process of delegating work, allowing you to add more descriptive text, as well as email all the information to the person charged with completing the task. This kind of comprehensive support for delegating and tracking tasks is one of the very most useful dimensions of project management software.

	Task Name	Assigned To	% Complete	Status	May 20
					F S S M T W T F S
	1.1. Venue		85%		
	1.1.1. Book concert hall	Ingrid	100%	Complete	Ingrid
	1.1.2. Negotiate fees	Ingrid	100%	Complete	Ingrid
	1.1.3. Draft contract	Ingrid	25%	In Progress	Ingrid
	1.2. Repertoire			In Progress	
	1.3. Rehearsals		13%	In Progress	
	1.3.1. Schedule rehearsals	Akemi	25%	In Progress	
	1.3.2. Rehearsal 1				
	1.3.2.1. Coordinate space	Akemi		In Progress	Akemi
	1.3.2.2. Bring snacks	Kerstin		Not Started	Kerstin
	1.3.3.3. Lead rehearsal	Charys		Not Started	Charys
	1.3.3. Rehearsal 2			Not Started	
	1.3.4. Rehearsal 3			Not Started	
	1.3.5. Rehearsal 4			Not Started	
	1.4. Program Booklet		13%		
	1.4.1. Design Graphics	Maja	50%	In Progress	Maja
	1.4.2. Write program text	Maja		Not Started	
	1.5. Promos			Not Started	
	1.6. Concert			Not Started	

FIG. 9.3. Task Tracking in Smartsheet

Alternatively, you could send a written work request, with the description and deadline (or series of deadlines) to the person who will complete it, and then maintain reminders to yourself on a calendar or other list to prompt you to ask them for updates at appropriate points.

The purpose is to confirm that the work being delegated is being done according to plan, so that something usable will be received on time. If you find that workers consistently miss deadlines, try reminding them at more frequent intervals, breaking down their task into smaller deliverables that they report to you. Deadlines get missed because:

1. Time estimates are unrealistic

2. The worker is underperforming

If you know that the worker is competent and well intentioned (and if the hiring process went well, they probably are), try to determine why the time estimates are off. There might be a communication issue, a process issue, or simply a misunderstanding of what is required to complete the work properly.

Formal Task Acceptance

More substantial tasks follow a similar trajectory to simpler tasks, though the resource commitment will be higher. You still need to describe the required work and then track it. However, there might be more formal documentation and discussions surrounding the work, if the stakes are more significant.

For substantial contributions, having people sign documents is a powerful psychological tool for getting them to commit to their work. It's not just about being legally binding, or so that you can wave their signature in their face when they claim they never agreed to what you're saying. It's integrating a step into their process that is inclined to make them take the task before them more seriously.

Some projects should begin with an extended team meeting or retreat, in which the project team holds intense work sessions to kick off the project launch. There might be brainstorming sessions, facilitated discussions, jam sessions, generic team-building activities, dinner/dancing, and so on. There might be sessions devoted to clarifying the mission or to discussing how upcoming conflicts will be resolved. The goals are to clarify the work, build enthusiasm, and transform the assembly of individuals into a coherent team.

Pete Jackson of the Army Corps of Engineers recommends concluding such kickoff retreats with everyone on the team signing a formal document stating their devotion to working together to create the best outcome possible. That signed document gets framed and displayed in the project office, where the most project participants are likely to see it. If the project turns out well, it might be displayed publicly and permanently on site of the project itself. He finds it to be a powerful tool for getting project participants to buy into what they are doing, and try hard to make it come out right. The project is acknowledged as an element of their life's work, and their participation is publicly recognized.

Everyone who works on the project signs that: senior executives, truck drivers, administrative assistants, engineers, consultants, graphic designers... everybody.

Kickoff Meeting

When you delegate any work, an in-person meeting to start things off is important, if you can get it. Face to face, we get deeper commitments and make human connections. It's easier to read emotions and concerns, and to communicate enthusiasm for the overall vision. The relationship becomes real.

Virtual relationships are increasingly common, and work is delegated to people whom we will never meet. Work might get outsourced to companies overseas. While this global orientation towards work often reduces cost and increases the likelihood of finding a perfect "fit" for needed skills, it also creates detachment from the work. Some real-time, in-person interaction will deepen the relationship. A phone call creates a deeper relationship than an email, and a video teleconference (such as via AIM or Skype) is deeper than a phone call. Even those of us with big noses and grizzled dispositions get the benefit from this.

In person is best.

There are multiple dimensions to the kickoff meeting:

- solidifying the team relationship and commitment to the work

- inspiring the worker about the project vision, hopefully aligning the work they will do with what they see as their most important life's work

- clarifying what work they will do, regarding work quality, schedule, budget, and compensation details

- answering questions about copyright ownership or other details of the contract

- hammering out any lingering housekeeping details, such as their mailing address, and so on

Many of these details can be described in email, but a real-time meeting can be an efficient way of getting many of these issues sorted out. And you want them to leave the meeting all fired up, ready for action.

The meeting paves the way for the written agreement to follow. By talking things through, you can save time, energy, and other back-and-forth that might result from someone just reading a contract sent via email.

The other side of this meeting is listening to what the worker has to say, often reading between the lines. Do they seem to have any concerns about the task before them? Are they hesitating to tell you anything? Is anything happening in their life that might add risk to the schedule? Like, are they planning to move? Or have a baby? Or change jobs? Or change book topics? Personal details like this are more likely to emerge face to face.

Additionally, the people actually doing the work will often have the best insight into how events will actually unfold. In hammering out details at this stage, they might help you uncover a risk or planning flaw that would best be addressed earlier, rather than later.

Having a person explain details humanizes the experience, and positive relationships make the project go more smoothly overall. It also provides an opportunity to ask any random question that comes to mind. Someone might hesitate to ask something relevant, if they have to write it in an email. But if there's a guy sitting next to them, they might bring it up after all, clarify some confusion, and save everyone some work and heartache down the line.

MONITORING AND CONTROLLING PROGRESS

While the team is executing the work, the project manager needs to monitor their progress. Through various reporting mechanisms, we need to continually track the following, beyond the basics already mentioned, and maintain a large-scale view of how well the project is progressing. You want to confirm that:

1. **The rate of progress will result in milestones being met.** As a simple example, if we estimated a task is to take 10 days, at 5 days, we might hope that the task be 50% complete. Now, duration isn't the same as working time, so this isn't always accurate. It might take two weeks to do the task because the person only works on Fridays and can only work 5 hours per day. On the first Thursday (day 4), there's no need to panic if he's not 40 percent done with the work, as he wasn't really expected to do anything until Friday. However, by Monday (day 6), if he hasn't started yet, then the project will be in jeopardy.

Project management software often shows the amount of progress, as well as the estimated amount of time for a task. (In Smartsheet, the column where this is entered is labeled "% Complete.") In the example below, we have a project deadline coming up in ten days for a project with one task: compose an overture. The allotted amount of time is ten days for this task, and if the composer keeps to that schedule, we will meet the deadline (indicated with a diamond shape). On the first Thursday, four days in, our composer reports that he's 60% done. This means that he seems likely to finish before the deadline, if that level of productivity keeps up. In Smartsheet, the percent complete is shown as a darker line within the lighter Gantt chart line.

Task Name	Duration	Start	Finish	% Complete	Mar 18							Mar 25					
					S	M	T	W	T	F	S	S	M	T	W	T	F	S
Project Deadline	0	03/30/12	03/30/12														◆
Task: Compose Overture	10	03/19/12	03/30/12	60%													

FIG. 9.4. Percent Complete in Smartsheet

2. **Actual costs don't exceed budgeted costs.** There are two dimensions to tracking financial expenditures. First, we need to check the actual money being spent (receipts) against the budgeted expenses, to make sure that our budget was reasonable. Second, we need to check the timing of these expenditures. An overall cash surplus might not actually indicate that we're in good financial shape. It might instead indicate that some of the work isn't getting done on time, or someone is making unauthorized decisions to reduce quality.

Here's a snapshot of a production budget-to-actual sheet, based on one from From the Top. For each concert/broadcast of the season, this report shows how the actual expenditures they incurred (for flights, ground transportation, and equipment expenditures, and others too, on their real one) map to the budgeted amounts for these categories. One of production manager Elizabeth DeVore's ongoing tasks is to keep spreadsheets like this up to date, so that any problems can be addressed before they get out of hand. They were doing pretty well, over there! Just one concert went a little over (Boston, #240) while the others were under, so overall, it's on track. Going into the next Boston show (#243), there is a little buffer that has accrued, in case that or later shows go over budget. Elizabeth always tries to accumulate such a buffer earlier in the season because the possibility to make up lost ground becomes increasingly difficult.

Name Show #:	Chicago, IL #238	Ocean City, NJ #239	Boston #240	Washington, DC #241	Santa Fe #242	Boston #243
FLIGHTS						
Staff 1	286.4	228.75		173.40	351.30	
Staff 2		99.40			500.80	
Staff 3	354.4	99.40	313.00	159.40	436.30	
…						
Talent 1	1,463.6	1850.40	854.00			
Talent 2	566.4	1289.40				
Talent 3	623.7	344.80				
…						
Actual Spent	$7,354.90	$7,151.12	$1,864.40	$5,333.30	$8,953.60	
Budgeted	$7,400.00	$7,400.00	$7,400.00	$7,400.00	$7,400.00	$7,400.00
GROUND TRAVEL						
Staff 1						
Staff 2						
Staff 3	350.00	179.47		89.27	155.27	
…						
Talent 1						
Talent 2						
Talent 3						
…						
Actual Spent	$350.00	$768.42	$0.00	$445.72	$856.78	
Budgeted	$1,500.00	$2,000.00	$500.00	$2,500.00	$2,000.00	$500.00
EQUIPMENT TRANSPORT						
Actual Spent	4,100.00	2,612.00	350.00			
Budgeted	4,200.00	3,500.00	500.00	4,800.00	5,000.00	500.00
ACTUAL SPENT TOTAL	$12,373.23	$11,201.15	$6,012.95	$7,432.32	$9,770.76	
BUDGETED TOTAL	$13,929.90	$12,201.54	$5,869.05	$7,969.02	$9,810.38	$5,869.05
TOTAL VARIANCE (CUMULATIVE)	$1,556.67	$2,556.06	$2,413.16	$2,949.86	$2,989.48	

FIG. 9.5. Budget-to-Actual Sheet Excerpt (Courtesy of From the Top, Inc.)

3. **The quality is as it should be.** If you can glimpse into the work being executed before it's too far along, you can confirm that the quality is what it is supposed to be. For example, if you've coordinated a choir

to sing a New Year's Eve concert, you can observe a rehearsal to get a sense for how things are going. Or, you might listen to the mix on one of twelve tracks that you've had recorded, just to hear the sound. Some tasks, though, such as getting CDs replicated, don't offer obvious windows into how the quality is coming along, but it's always best to try to get proofs to review, if possible.

4. **Scope remains in accordance with the current project scope statement.** During execution, it is very common to discover that the anticipated scope of the project requires some adjustment. Estimates might be off, or testing of micro-iterations could reveal design flaws, and so the project will require more resources, or different features. Such changes need to be appropriately communicated and approved. This might come via an official form called a "Change Request," or it might simply be requested and approved via email, but it is important that anyone with a stake in the change be notified before it is too late. Changes to scope should be articulated in the scope statement, and a revised version should be distributed to everyone on that distribution list.

Reporting

The goal of monitoring progress is to take corrective action before minor variances become catastrophic and threaten the project's outcome. This is easier when the reports given to us have the appropriate level of detail in them, rendered clearly. It's not helpful to be given a lengthy report, and spend a long time reading through discursive text (not to mention ebullient rants) only to learn that everything is fine and no action is required.

Week to week, here's what each type of participant generally needs to know:

- **Team Member:** What new tasks need to be done, by what deadline, and with what instructions regarding quality or procedure?

- **Project Manager:** Is every task on time, within budget, and of the appropriate level of quality?

- **Project Sponsor:** Is the project on track to meet its target deadline (yes or no)? What obstacles can I alleviate for the project manager? Are there requested changes of scope that need to be evaluated, possibly approved, or communicated to others in the organization?

- **Other Stakeholders:** Probably nothing, week to week. Only existential changes and significant resourcing issues related to the project need to be communicated.

How often you should check in with each team member is a subjective call. When a task is on the critical path, you should be checking in *at least* every couple weeks with everyone who is actively engaged, though sometimes, daily or even hourly check-ins are warranted.

People working on tasks with slack time might not need as regular monitoring, at first, but it's important to be able to track whether that slack time still exists or not. If their task takes sixty days, and they have one hundred days to do it, if they haven't started by day fifty, then they are now on the critical path and do not have any more slack. They must then be monitored more closely.

Progress is reported in various ways.

1. Most simply and informally, the project manager contacts the worker and gets a verbal status update, either by a phone call or asking them in person. For frequent, informal updates, this might be fine. The downside is just that there is no record for either party unless someone is unusually proactive about documentation. Sometimes, it is helpful to go back to written reports, to see if or when something was done.

2. Tasks are checked off in project management software. Simple "percent complete" updates are easy to get, and more detailed information can be attached in documents.

3. The team member submits a regular report, in a consistent format, itemizing the work that's been done. This form includes clear places to present information on a single project. This can be set up as a simple memo but with standardized headings to make it easy for the sponsor to get at the critical information at a glance, rather than a wordier communication in paragraph form.

The goal in reporting is clarity. Headers, bulleted lists, or charts can help the reader access the critical information. Long, discursive paragraphs of description, such as typical email communication, are less efficient.

To: Producer (Project Manager)

From: Composer

Date: May 15, 2013

Re: Status Update for *Overture* First Draft

Estimated Delivery Date

June 20, 2013 (On time)

Status

First draft about 50 percent complete. We are still waiting
to see how many tympani we can get.

Progress This Week

- Orchestration is done for the first third.
- Essential concepts are now sketched
  through the end.

Goals for Next Week

- Solidify structure of the middle section.
- Determine how many tympani we can get.
- Schedule copyists.

Questions

Could we get more help preparing parts? About 20
additional hours of copying time would be enough.
We'll be ready to begin copying by May 28.

FIG. 9.6. Composer's Status Report to Producer

When managing or reporting on multiple projects, a chart can be helpful, particularly if all the projects share basic lifecycle stages. In the following example, a club's booking agent reports on the various artists scheduled for the room. The number-coded checkboxes make it easy to see their status, at a glance. (Color codes are effective, too, though not in a black and white book!) Also, the Priority column helps clarify between a manager and a team member what should be considered most urgent. A "date due" or other milestone-related column(s) is key and should be easy to find.

This format can be helpful in our own life project index, as well as for reporting purposes.

Project Status   March 9, 2012   Bob the Booker

Priority	Project (Artist)	Progress This Week	Status	R	S	CS	D	P	F	Date
1	Stevie and the Nishikis	Received query, will follow up.	Scheduling info call		N					7/1?
2	Naomio	Concert scheduled 5/14 at 8:00 PM. Drafted/sent contract.	Awaiting signed contract.	5	5	4				5/14
2	The Bud Beagle Project	Finished pre-concert meeting. Ready to go for 3/21.	Perform 3/21	5	5	5	5	5		3/21
3	Jessica Josh	Called again. Still not returning my calls. Will give them one more week, then give up.	Contract sent, but no communication since December. No reply regarding request for references. They wanted April 18, but I might let it go.	4	5	1				4/18
3	Lily and Cricket	Concert was great! Got the key back. All done.	Done	5	5	5	5	5	5	2/14

KEY:
Columns:
R: References Checked • S: Scheduled • C: Contract • D: Deposit Received • P: Pre-Concert Meeting • F: Finalized
Status Codes:
None: Not started • 5: Done • 4: Almost Done • 3: Going OK • 2: Needs attention • 1: Stalled • N: Not necessary

FIG. 9.7. Club Booking: Multi-Project Status Report

Data Gathering

In addition to assessing how your project team is progressing, execution sometimes also includes paying careful attention to outside forces that might influence the activities being undertaken by your team. There are many approaches to this type of monitoring and market analysis, and the specific tools get a bit industry specific. What's important, though, is ongoing research about what you're building and its surrounding market context, such as having users beta test software, give feedback about certain songs, try out prototypes of new products, analyzing competitors' catalogs and

blogs, and so on. The data might be gathered in person or by surveying potential customers to see what they want, using a tool such as Survey Monkey®,
SurveyGizmo, etc. You might monitor clicks on Web pages using a tool such
as Google Analytics. Or, you might use a more industry specific tool, such as
Topspin®, to monitor activity surrounding digital files.

Updating the Schedule: Jogging Line and BCF Analysis

Whichever way this information is communicated, the project manager must
then take this information and analyze it for variance from projected estimates,
in order to determine whether corrective action is required or not. There are a
number of techniques for doing this.

Jogging Line

One way to see the big picture is by using a hard copy of a Gantt chart, and
drawing a *jogging line*. To do this, go deliverable by deliverable, and determine
whether it is progressing on schedule, early, or late. This is a common "project
war room" exercise, when a group of people are gathered to discuss a project's
status and come up with a realistic schedule, during execution.

In this example, we are looking at the process for scheduling a concert. We
start with a Gantt chart, exported from Smartsheet.

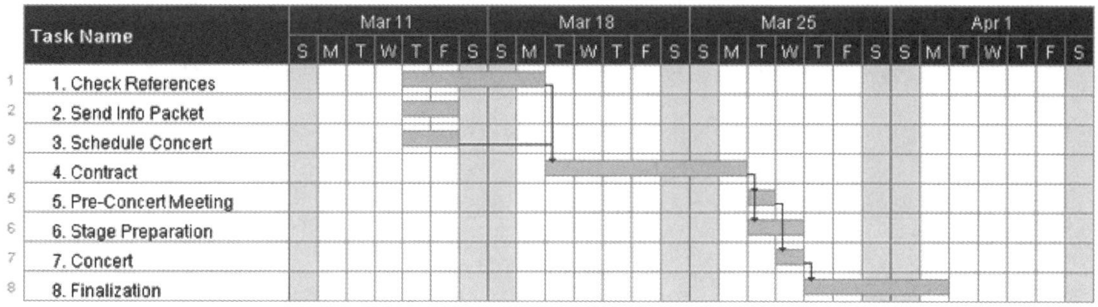

FIG. 9.8. Gantt Chart

As workers report in, the project manager/meeting facilitator draws a
vertical line at each point, showing the current anticipated completion date.
This reveals at a glance how things are going. Then, the verticals are connected,
to form the "jogging line," shown in figure 9.9 as in a darker line. We can see
that "Check References" finished early. But "Contract" is a day late.

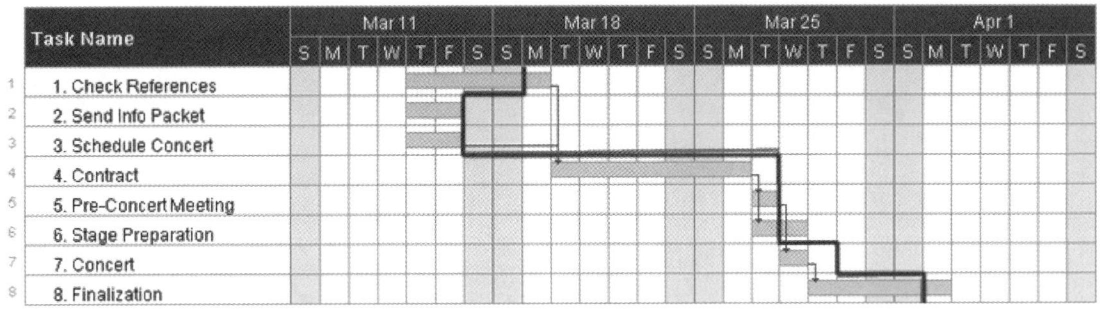

FIG. 9.9. Jogging Line

Then, the impact of this status update is considered. Deliverables arriving early don't always impact other tasks, but sometimes, they do, even if indirectly. Perhaps, the early-bird tasks will free up resources that can then be applied somewhere else. But the most useful information in the jogging line will probably be critical path tasks that are running late, such as "4. Contract" and "7. Concert" above. Those delays might be alarming. Perhaps the person assigned to "1. Check References" can be moved to those late tasks, to speed things along, or you can use some other strategy to crunch the timeline. The jogging line exercise gives you an overall view of the work, which can help inform such resource allocations. It is also a starting point for other forms of detailed analysis.

BCF Analysis

The next step after doing a jogging line exercise is to revise the Gantt chart. A result of this study might be a BCF analysis: Baseline, Current, Future. In a BCF analysis, you take the original **baseline** Gantt chart (originally projected), the **current** state of affairs (resulting from the jogging line), and then project a **future** schedule, based on lessons learned from the prior steps. If we realize that the contract is running late because of a reason that might similarly result in, say, the Finalization stages running late, we might factor that into the "Future" projection, which is something of a worst-case scenario forecast. This kind of analysis can be a healthy reality check. The Future projection is informed by whatever insights and data you have available, but inspired by the jogging line.

It might look like the following diagram. Then, the Future iteration gets circulated and considered to determine whether it is acceptable or whether some more strategic rethinking needs to happen.

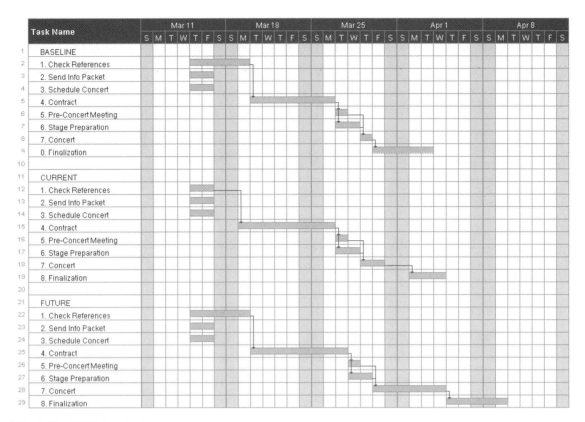

FIG. 9.10. BCF Analysis

Trend Analysis

Tracking trends in the progress of a team member or subgroup can be revealing. To do this, create a graph showing the trajectory of their assigned tasks and due dates, and then another line showing the actual performance. This is sometimes called a "milestone progress chart." It plots completed tasks against time.

Say we have a notation engraver who has 120 pages to render in 12 days. She completes it on time. We want to track her progress over time, so we create this kind of diagram. First, we had estimated that this job would take about 10 days to complete, so we drew a line (lighter gray in figure 9.11), from day 1 to day 10, and a straight line going from 0 pages complete to 120 pages complete. Then, we plot (in black) how many pages she completes every day. This could be done at any point during the project execution, not at the end. It might look like this.

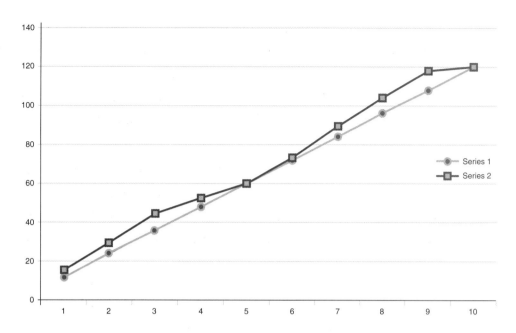

FIG. 9.11. Trend Analysis

We can see that she was fairly consistent in accomplishing more than twelve in a day. What does that mean? There are two rules of thumb that are commonly used to help analyze the results in a chart like this:

1. **Four or more points on one side of the equation indicate a trend.** If it's low, it might be indicative of an estimating mistake, a resourcing problem, a skill deficit, or a morale deficit. If it's high, as it is in this case, it could still reflect an estimating mistake. While her exceeding of the goals appears to be completely positive, maybe the job is easier than we anticipated. The correction at day 5 might actually be a day when the engraver decided to slack off because it was going so fast. Or perhaps, she is doing it so quickly because she is inappropriately simplifying the task—leaving out dynamics, or only doing the full score and not copying parts. Or maybe, she's just a wonderfully fast copyist, who tends to work eighteen hours a day because she is so dedicated, and then drops from exhaustion on day 5. We don't really know anything except that there is a trend that might be worth looking into. The variance might be a team member's fault, or it might be a strategist's fault. In any case, it reveals a likelihood that reality is not going to conform to what was planned, for better or for worse. In this case, we hope it's a pleasant surprise.

   Being early is often "good," but not always. If she finishes early and thus drops off the hard copies outside the composer's doorstep late Friday afternoon, after he has gone home, instead of early Monday morning, the parts might sit outside in the snow over the weekend, rather than being brought inside right away. So, not to be cynical about what might be a wonderful copyist, here, but the data suggests that we need to pay close attention to what's happening. Our estimated schedule isn't exactly right.

2. **A jump of more than two standard deviations from the norm indicates some anomaly** in what's happening, and whether it is to the benefit or the detriment of the overall timeline isn't necessarily obvious. Are there individual heroics going on, for some reason? Did something really bad happen that is causing a sudden derailment? Was a problem resolved? Did someone disruptive go on vacation? Or were/are you getting bad reporting data at some point in this project? In this example, the copyist was generally three or four pages ahead of schedule. Here's a graph showing the pages per day, and how many that varies from the estimate of twelve per day.

Day	Pages Done	Variance from 12
1	15	3
2	14	2
3	15	3
4	8	4
5	7	5
6	14	2
7	16	4
8	15	3
9	14	2
10	2	10

FIG. 9.12. Tracking Variances

That's an average of 3.8 per day. Call it 4. But on day 10, she does ten pages fewer than average—2.5 standard deviations. Are the last two pages much more difficult? Did she realize upon finishing up the last two that she had to go back and make a bunch of revisions to the others? Did she finish the two remaining pages in half an hour, go to the beach, and charge us for a full day? Or did she simply make a reporting error? It would be nice to know the answer to this significant deviation, which looks fairly subtle on the trend analysis graph. The reason might be acceptable or not, but in any case, knowing the truth will help us estimate future work.

Burndown Charts

Burndown charts are similar to milestone charts in that they show a project's ongoing progress, mapping work done against time. Here, though, you typically quantify the tasks in terms of how many there are still to be done, and then progress towards zero, as they are completed. So, you have a list of tasks. The total number of outstanding tasks is graphed against a timeline. Then, you plot two lines. One shows the ideal schedule, showing the required "burn" of completed tasks at regular intervals (or at completion points), reaching towards the deadline of zero. The other line shows how many tasks are actually completed. (No credit is given for partial work done on a task! It's either done or it isn't.) Periodically, the project manager graphs the number of tasks that remain, and thus can predict how well the team is advancing towards their desired deadline.

I recently found it useful to have a burndown chart on an instructional drum video shoot. The production crew and one of the artists featured on the shoot all came from out of town, and the shoot was filmed at Berklee. We scheduled a few hours to set up on the evening before the shoot, and then a full day of filming. It seemed awfully tight, but possible, so long as we were organized.

On the setup day, the production crew arrived fairly road weary, after a six-hour flight. But they were troopers, and put in a few hours, getting the room looking right, figuring out set backgrounds, meeting the artists who appeared, discussing the order of shooting, and so on. They arrived at 6:00 P.M. and left at about 10:30 P.M.

The next morning, they planned to arrive at 9:00 A.M., set up for an hour, and then shoot. Unfortunately, they got lost between their hotel and Berklee, and so they started at about 10:00 A.M. instead. Right off the bat, they ran into a technical problem; an adapter that they were counting on had gotten damaged, and so they needed to figure out a workaround. They weren't overly concerned, but for a reality check, I decided it was time to create a burndown chart, large on a whiteboard, where everyone could get a realistic glimpse of the day and how we projected the timing of the shoot to unfurl.

I started with a chart showing our original plan. There were eleven cues/ scenes to shoot. The ideal was to finish by 5:00 P.M., so that we could have a nice, relaxing dinner. That pipedream of a time frame (which nobody really believed would happen) looked like this:

Video Burndown Chart: Initial Plan

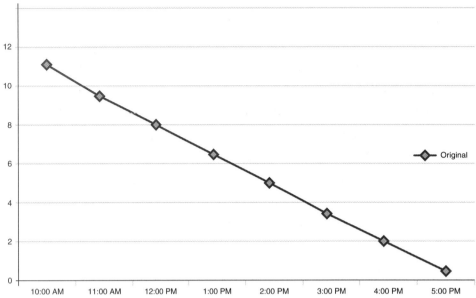

FIG. 9.13. Burndown Chart: Initial Plan

We started actually filming at 11:00 A.M., and worked very consistently. Every time we'd finish a cue, I'd plot a new dot on the "Actual" line, shown in light gray. By 2:00 P.M., when we broke for a late lunch, we were looking at the following rate of progress.

Video Shoot Burndown Chart: At 2:00

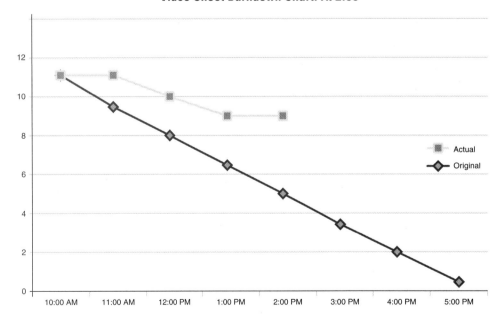

FIG. 9.14. Progress at 2:00 P.M.

To be realistic in projecting how much time the shoot would actually take, you need to extend the gray line out, through the actual rate of completion, to see where it would eventually land. We had to take a sobering look at the day, at this point. There was no way we'd finish by 5:00 P.M. Continuing at that rate, we'd be working straight through to 8:00 A.M. the next morning! Which, let's face it, isn't realistic. The projected rate is shown in medium gray, here.

Video Burndown Chart: 2:00 Projection

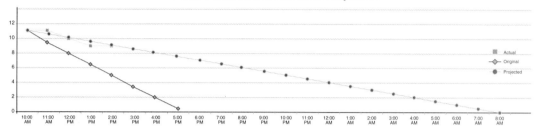

FIG. 9.15. Projected Completion

The chart helped underscore the case that it was time to buckle down and get some scenes filmed. We took a short lunch, and then burned through the rest of the scenes. There were no breaks longer than five minutes, and we sent an assistant out to bring us snacks, so that we wouldn't starve, during this locked-door session. We postponed some decisions about how to handle certain graphics for another day, when we weren't shooting. We simplified one of the intended lessons. There was no monkeying around. (Okay, there was only quick, focused monkeying around that wasn't time consuming; I mean, these guys were drummers, after all....) In the end, we finished at about 11:00 P.M.—somewhat bleary-eyed, but still cheery, and without the need to dip into our emergency time we had reserved for the next day.

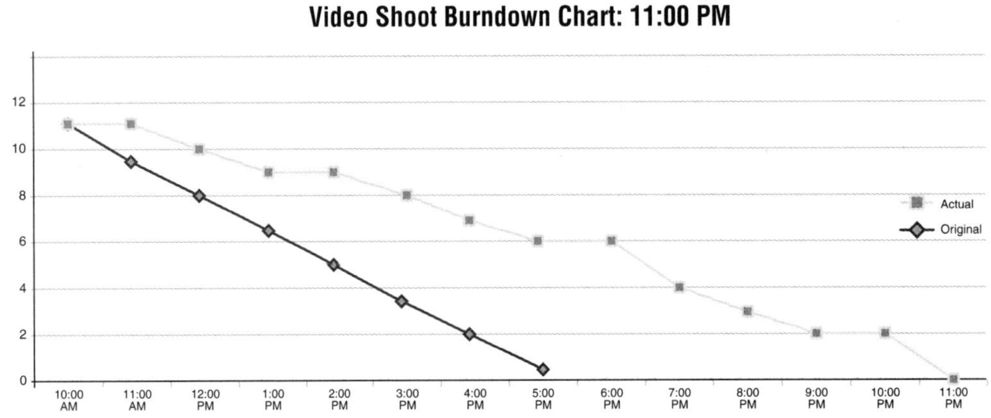

Video Shoot Burndown Chart: 11:00 PM

FIG. 9.16. Final Chart

Every time I plotted a new dot on the chart, there was a little (slightly sarcastic) cheer from the crew. The burndown chart clarified exactly where we were and how much longer we had to go. It was a clear, objective view of the progress, and simply plotting out a line that illustrated reality as we all knew it to be true was a lot nicer than me simply nagging everybody all the time to keep things moving. The need was illustrated clearly, for all to see.

This is an example of a burndown chart being used in an intense, single-day session, but they are often updated daily, weekly, or at whatever interval is useful. This one was organized in terms of filming scenes, but you could instead total the number of generic tasks, and keep counting how many tasks are left, at regular intervals. The math isn't always perfect; some tasks are more complicated or time consuming or risky than others. Still, though, it is a helpful clarifying and motivating tool.

You can also use burndown charts to monitor financial resources. Instead of tasks, show a budget and plot how much money remains. They are commonly used in the Scrum project management style (popular in software development), featured at daily Scrum standup meetings. Everyone quickly reports in on their progress, and the chart gets updated.

The goal is to understand the trend of what's happening while there is still time to save the project, somehow.

Control

There are a number of ways to bring projects back on track, when they veer off course. The right way will vary according to priorities, available resources, and so on.

Let's say that our project is to commission an original arrangement for a jazz orchestra. The composer is old school, and he insists on writing out his score and all the parts by hand, rather than using Finale, which would be much faster. It's day 12, and we learn that he is only forty percent done copying parts. This is a critical path task, so if it goes longer than the allocated twenty days, the parts won't be ready in time for rehearsal, which must begin eight days from now (20 days – 12 days = 8 days). On day 60, we have our concert.

So, we take a detailed look at the timing of that task and the current obligations of other people in this project community who are capable of copying parts: the orchestra librarian and the conductor.

Activity	Duration (Days)	Owner
A. Copy Parts	20	Composer
B. Organize Music	12	Orchestra Librarian
C. Write Program Notes	5	Conductor
D. Rehearse	40	Conductor

FIG. 9.17. Tasks, Durations, Resources Chart

The critical path here is that the composer is copying parts, and then the conductor will start leading rehearsals once the composer has finished. During the Copy Parts activity of the critical path, the orchestra librarian is organizing other music, and the conductor is writing program notes. They've got some slack with those tasks, though, as we can see in this network diagram:

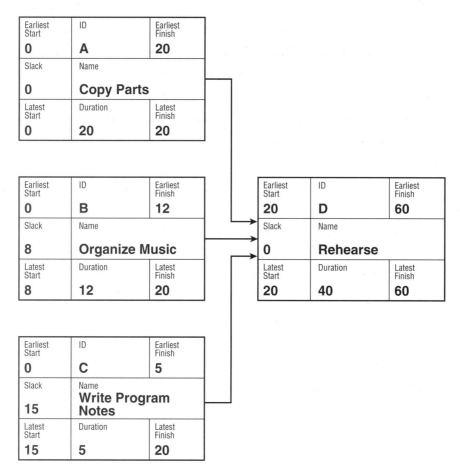

FIG. 9.18. Network Diagram for Controlling Schedule

So, what are our options, for making sure that we are ready for the concert on day 60?

1. **Crashing.** Crashing means adding resources. This can be money, time, or personnel. We could crash this task by adding another copyist or paying for a copying service to do the parts instead. You could also work to improve the capabilities of the team, either by training the composer to do it faster (perhaps, to use Finale as a copying tool, rather than doing it by hand) or by replacing him with someone else who can do it faster. Generally speaking, crashing a task means trading one type of resource for another, generally reducing time by adding money or people.

2. **Use Slack.** Slack time is said to be the only truly free resource at a project manager's disposal. By analyzing the existing slack time of other tasks, it might be possible to pick up time or other resources. For example, we can see that while the Copy Parts task is happening, there was slack available in the two other tasks shown. We can therefore try pressuring the orchestra librarian and the conductor to finish their tasks early and then help the composer copy the parts, rather than simply sitting on their chaise longues, eating bonbons, while they await rehearsal day.

3. **Fast-Tracking.** Fast-tracking is the process of forcing concurrency when it is not logically ideal. For example, the ideal sequence here is to first complete copying parts and then start rehearsals. However, there might be some work to do during rehearsals that does not involve these specific parts, such as rehearsing other music, or rehearsing the first part of this piece, which is already copied. Or, some players could lay out or read similar instrument parts, while they wait for their own parts to become complete. None of these solutions are necessarily ideal, but one of the options might still allow us to achieve our overall project deadline, at day 60. Possibly, for one rehearsal, it won't matter much.

4. **Mainline/Offline Scheduling.** Another way to buy time within a project is by reassessing the critical path tasks and seeing whether some of them could be done outside of the critical path. The Copy Parts activity might involve some subtasks that could be done outside the regular timeline. For example, part of that activity might involve creating a style template to be used for all new music commissioned by the ensemble. That task would require various approvals, which takes time. However, it might not be necessary for that task to be completed for the current project. Therefore, by removing that dimension of the work from the immediate deliverables (moving it from "mainline" to "offline"), the overall project timeline can be shortened.

5. **Change a Constraint.** The last thing to try is to change the requirements for quality, time, features, or budget. In this example, decreasing quality could mean that rather than copying new parts for each instrument by hand, we instead photocopy the conductor's score, and use scissors, glue stick, and Scotch tape to hack together serviceable parts. They'll be ugly but functional. By increasing funding, we might get the copyist to work nights and weekends in

order to make the deadline. Perhaps the least attractive option along these lines would be decreasing rehearsal time, in favor of increasing music copying time. That's almost certainly a bad idea, but it remains a possible option.

MEETINGS

Meetings are useful ways to gather and share information, and also strategize on how to move a project forward. They can be productive, transformative, and inspiring, or they can be complete wastes of time!

To get the most out of a meeting:

- Before the meeting, plan what you need to get out of it. Prepare an agenda or checklist.

- During the meeting, take notes of all decisions that get made and any work delegations that occur.

- After the meeting, follow up in writing with all attendees regarding what they agreed to do. Implement/systematize all the decisions and work assignments that resulted from the meeting.

How formally you do this will depend on the nature of the meeting and the work at hand, but the three levels of organization are helpful for all business meetings.

Meetings tend to either be *standing meetings*, where a regular influx of work gets processed, or *ad hoc meetings*, which are called when the need arises.

Standing meetings take place regularly: daily, monthly, weekly, etc. These shape the workflow of the project group. Their benefit is that everyone works their schedules around them, as they are at regular times. A common pitfall of standing meetings is that they might take place even when there is no productive reason for them. Business sometimes gets brought to them that could have been dealt with more simply. It's often better to cancel them. However, there is sometimes benefit in regularly getting certain people in a room together to talk about the work happening.

Ad hoc meetings occur as necessary. They can be more difficult to schedule, as their occurrence isn't predictable. However, they have a clear purpose and tend to be strategic and useful.

Meetings are most effective when the person running it has a clear idea of the meeting's purpose and keeps the meeting focused on exactly that. Have a deliverable in mind that you will get from the meeting—a set of decisions, strategies, or a completed body of work. Here are some possible reasons to have meetings and the deliverables to work towards.

Strategy meetings involve determining how to proceed with a project. You might have a meeting to figure out the solution to a problem, to decide which vendor to work with, to determine whether to fund or authorize a significant body of work or expenditure, or to discuss some other aspect of how to do the work. You might meet with a stage manager in advance of a concert to walk through stage setup diagrams, needs for special equipment, and other issues. In a corporate environment, a project manager might meet with a project sponsor to determine whether to sign a new project or not. For example, a record label's project manager might discuss with a vice president a number of potential artists to sign.

Deliverable: Decisions, action steps, directives. Possibly, signed documents.

Work delegation meetings are for assigning work to others. Someone gives clear instructions to someone else. The work is explained and the criteria for acceptance are clarified. If compensation or other matters of resourcing aren't obvious, that too gets clarified. Monitoring and reporting systems are also set in motion. The kickoff meeting is a type of work delegation meeting. If you are commissioning a composition, you might meet with the composer first to discuss the parameters of what you want. Similarly, if you are hiring a carpenter to soundproof your studio, there should be an initial meeting to discuss details of how the project will unfold.

Deliverable: Action steps for how the work will get done.

Status update meetings are to quickly give stakeholders a snapshot of the work that's happening and to discuss any problems that can be resolved by the stakeholder.

In the Scrum approach to project execution, there's a regularly scheduled "standup" meeting every day, where the project team meets, standing up (so people don't linger) for up to fifteen minutes. The idea is to maximize efficiency and communication. Everyone on the team takes turns answering three questions:

1. What did I do yesterday?

2. What will I do today?

3. What's currently obstructing my progress?

Each member is expected to give this information in about one minute. The team confirms that they understand the implications of what was done, that it makes sense to do today's work in the way that you plan, and then tries to help you find a solution to your stated potential obstacles. The "Scrum master" (a project manager) conducts the meeting. In addition to making sure everyone gives their update, the master crosses completed items off the list of outstanding tasks and updates the burndown chart.

This exact format works well when there is a team of workers performing similar tasks, such as in software design, when a project team is doing similar and interconnected types of work, but potentially in individual isolation. The general approach works well in targeted communication usually, though: regular communication and updates.

Deliverable: Information is shared, strategies for overcoming obstacles are developed, and overall progress is updated.

Content creation meetings occur when people gather together to do work collaboratively. An ensemble rehearsal is a kind of content creation meeting, as is a co-songwriting session.

Deliverables: The work is moved forward.

Special Types of Meetings

The following different strategic focuses might feature nuances because they are also of the following meeting types:

Public meetings are necessary when an organization funded by taxes is in charge of its expenditure, and they have some legal requirements that you might need to know about. For example, if you are developing a program that might get adopted by a school system, the school committee (or charter school board) might need to discuss this in *open session,* meaning that anyone from the public might attend (not necessarily participate). There are various rules regarding posting the meeting's agenda in advance, taking minutes, and so forth, and those rules might affect how you need to plan your participation. While it is likely a standing meeting, there might be a timeframe by which you must communicate your need to discuss this issue. There might be a legal requirement that the school committee's agenda be publicly posted at least forty-eight hours in advance of the meeting. In addition, they always finalize the draft agenda two weeks in advance of that, and certain board members must agree to put every item on the agenda before going public. In this case, you would need to time your request for meeting time with sufficient warning, or else the board might not legally be able to make a decision (or even discuss the issue).

Retreats are group getaway meetings where a task group, project team, or even a wider project community all goes away together (generally offsite, if they have a regular meeting place) and perform various activities designed to enhance relationships, communication, and the pool and flow of ideas. There might be a clear business focus, such as a band renting a farmhouse/barn in Vermont for a week, where they can collaborate on creating new material. There might be team-building exercises, generally facilitated by a consultant, such as various games or craft activities, which theoretically provide transferrable skills to the actual work environment. Or, they might be purely social affairs, like a skiing trip, where the project team simply spends time together and develops relationships.

In their best form, retreats are a way for the project team to become reinvigorated by the project's mission, work more collaboratively, and encourage good ideas that were stuck in the shadows to come to light. At their worst, they can be extraordinary unnecessary expenditures of resources that have no business benefit and disrupt everyone's lives, decreasing morale rather than increasing it.

Social meetings are an opportunity to hang out with a colleague whom you like. While they might be dressed up as a business meeting, their true purpose is to brighten your day. There might be side effects of moving business forward, such as brainstorming ideas, networking, talking with subject matter experts, team building, and so on, but let's call a spade a spade and say that some meetings are called primarily because people are social creatures and we like to visit. And that's fine! It's fun to hang out with people. The danger is only when these meetings are couched as other types of meetings and, therefore, prioritized inappropriately. There should be consensus that this is the purpose of the meeting. If one person is lonely and the other person is really frantically busy, trying to get real work done, the first person shouldn't force the meeting.

On a more cynical note, some entire endeavors are established under the pretext of doing work, but they are actually social mechanisms, foremost. Volunteer boards, or hobby non-profit organizations are examples. An outsider being brought into such a scenario might have difficulty navigating this kind of structure, with its web of personal relationships, and potentially non-business-oriented approach towards timing, budgeting, quality control, and so forth. For example, a sound engineer might record an amateur band in which one person is dramatically worse as a musician than everyone else, but that musician never gets taken to task because he's a relative. For the engineer, deciphering how to navigate that might be confusing. ("No, we're not going to replace the bongo player, even though he can't keep a steady beat. Set it low in the mix, and edit it as much as you need to in order to make it sound good—whatever it costs.")

There's nothing necessarily wrong with this type of structure. It's just important for everyone to understand what the overarching goals are (social vs. business), and what parameters are necessary for making it work.

Making Meetings Better

The following practices will make your meetings more effective.

First, consider your meeting's ideal duration. Meetings should be the right length to get the essential work done, and not any longer. Ten minutes is a great length for a meeting to discuss logistics. It's considered unhealthy to sit for more than half an hour at a stretch. An hour and a half is about the maximum that any group can stand to be in the same room together. If you truly have more work to do than this time will allow, take a break. For a critical, complicated, multi-faceted meeting, you might have to go up to two hours, but consider breaking it into multiple meetings, if it must be longer than that.

Also, consider the time of day for your meeting. This will depend on your group, but most people think the most clearly in the morning. There is generally a lull in energy after lunch. Some people can work at night, and in some circles of musician, it is the traditional and preferred time for collaboration, but others will have great difficulty staying productive after the sun goes down.

While we're at it, let's consider the days of the week, and how they relate to people's schedules. This varies across cultures and types of work, so consider analogous circumstances for those with whom you work.

Mondays, people are getting back into a work mindset after the weekend. Many people devote Monday morning to planning their week. If you have project team members who are working on your project part time, they might use the weekends to do the bulk of their work, and so it is common for materials to be delivered/received Monday. This means that Mondays tend to be hectic, particularly in the morning, and thus potentially relatively difficult for impromptu meetings.

Tuesdays, people are getting down to business, getting work done. It's often our most productive day, and still early in the week, so people tend to be optimistic about what they can accomplish. It's a good day for meetings, delegating, and setting new things in motion. Sales professionals often prioritize Tuesday as the day to hawk their wares, as people are most inclined to say yes.

Wednesdays are good days for getting things together and mailing them to others, as they are easily received by Friday. This means that the recipient can work on it during the weekend, or still have time to do some light work and resend it to someone else, for receipt early in the following week. There is often an energy lull on Wednesdays, but they are good days for meeting and delegating, as there is still time in the week to get significant work accomplished. Wednesdays are almost as good as Tuesdays. Then, the potential for "getting to yes" starts to decline.

Thursdays give you a view about what will realistically be accomplished that week. Any materials to be mailed and received by Friday must now be sent by overnight mail. It tends to be a full, buckle-down work day, but it's still good for meetings.

Fridays, people are either frantic with deadlines or they have reconciled themselves regarding what they will accomplish. People commonly try to arbitrarily finish things "by the end of the week," so that means Friday. By Friday afternoon, people are either stressed because they are trying to finish something by the weekend, or they are mentally on vacation already. So don't start anything new on Friday.

Saturdays are a life catch-up day. People might intend to get good business work done (that is beyond their responsibility during the week), but they often find that they need a break from work, so they aren't as productive as they'd hoped. It is the preferred day for making progress on projects outside the normal scope of one's regular job.

Sundays are often reserved for not working, but depending on how Saturday goes, it might be a catch-up day. People tend to resent business meetings on Sundays.

Meeting Checklist

Before going into any meetings, prepare a list of the critical points you need to communicate, and also any specific information you need to get out of it. We saw an example of this in figure 9.4.

Here's a checklist I have for Berklee Press pre-signing meetings, where we discuss some details before authors receive their draft contracts. They are generally excited at these meetings because they recently got the good news that their book will be published. They want to talk about the fun stuff: the content, illustrations, how much their students like the materials they are going to write about, and so on. This checklist helps me remember to discuss the important business points: their mailing address, explaining contract terms, and nailing down a realistic delivery schedule for their materials. Some of this information is necessary for us to actually complete the contract (e.g., delivery date). Some is just technical information about how our work will unfold (e.g., we need separate notation files for each example). By using this checklist, I'm unlikely to forget anything critical.

Berklee Press
Pre-Signing Meeting Checklist

Project Name: **Date:**

	Author Contact Info	
	(mailing address, phone number, email)	
	Contract Terms	
	Advance Amount	$X
	Royalty Rate	X%
	• 50% on BP's receipt of complete draft	
	• 50% on author's acceptance of final edited manuscript and our receipt of two copies of CD master	
	Audio CD Budget and Parameters	
	Budget	$?
	• 79 minutes, allow time between tracks (1 to 4 seconds)	
	• Maximum: 99 tracks	
	• Invoices get sent to Hal Leonard Corp.	
	Schedule	
	• Allow 8 months for production, after manuscript/CD are finalized	
	First Draft Manuscript	
	CD Master	
	Technology	
	• Separate files for each notation example	
	• Reference examples by file name within text file	
	• CD track references within text file	
	• Template files	
	• Feedback: Track Changes in Word	
	Other	
	• Marketing Blurbs	
	• Author Guidelines	
	• Copyright	

FIG. 9.19. Contract Pre-Signing Meeting Checklist

Agendas

Agendas are schedules showing the meeting's topics and how much time will be devoted to them. Agendas are particularly helpful for long, complicated, and/or important meetings. In a meeting of a public body (such as a school board), they might be legally required. (See your state's open meeting law for details.)

Agendas help everyone stay on track and provide an overall sense for what work needs to get done. After the meeting, they provide a record of what topics were discussed, and can therefore serve as a helpful reference.

Everyone present at the meeting receives a copy of the agenda. Ideally, a draft agenda is distributed in advance of the meeting, to help them prepare and give them the opportunity to suggest additional matters that require group discussion.

A good agenda includes:

1. a header that includes the date, location, purpose, and time of the meeting

2. major topical heading for each item to be discussed

3. an estimated amount of time that each discussion will require

4. a list of any distributed documents

5. an indication regarding what decisions or votes will be taken

Here's an agenda for a meeting that Emily might have had with her band, regarding critical logistics for her upcoming tour.

Emily Peal and The Band of Skinny Men
Agenda: Tour Logistics Meeting
February 2, 2012 • 8:00 PM • At Emily's House

Topic	Duration	Decision	Attachments
1. State of the Band	10 min		
2. Confirmed Venues	20 min		Tour Stop Chart
3. Accommodations: • What do you want to pay for hotels? • Any friends nearby where we can stay for free?	25 min	x	Potential Hotels List
4. Van Repairs	10 min	x	Mechanic Assessment
5. Committee Reports	20 min		
6. What's on your mind?	20 min		
7. Goals for next month	5 min		

FIG. 9.20. Agenda

Advance Packets, Minutes, Work Assignments, and Follow-Ups

Advance materials, also called "advance packets," are sets of documents for the meeting participants to read before the meeting, so that the meeting will take less time. It can include reports, schedules, proposals, suggested reading, and so on. Also include a draft agenda, so that if anyone wants to add an item to the actual agenda, they can let you know.

Send advance packets well enough in advance of the meeting so that people can review the materials and ask any questions.

Minutes are summaries of topics, discussions, and decisions. They are helpful particularly for long, complicated meetings where new things were set into motion and decisions were made. They are not transcripts of the meeting. Instead, they summarize the critical work and serve as a reference to what happened, and can help settle disagreements long after the meeting, as they record decisions. In some formal settings, meetings begin (or end) with an official approval of the minutes from the previous meeting. They are legally required for any public organization, so if you are pitching a project to a public school committee, their minutes from the meeting will be publicly available.

Minutes generally follow the order of the agenda. They include a list of the meeting's attendees and end with the name of whoever took the minutes—ideally, someone other than the person running the meeting, or playing a critical role in it.

Figure 9.21 is a sample of what minutes look like.

Work assignments often result from meetings, and at the meeting, you should document who agrees to do what tasks. These might be included in the minutes, or they might be separate (or replacement) documents.

As you discuss issues with someone, you can create a document that spells out exactly what they agree to do. It's essentially a to-do list, which you will then systematize after the meeting. Getting specific about the work during the meeting is best, if you can, while the work is still fresh in everyone's minds. You can then follow up with a refinement afterwards, if necessary, if what's required seems to change after you've reflected on it for a while.

Emily Peal and The Band of Skinny Men
Minutes: Tour Logistics Meeting
February 2, 2012 • 8:00 PM • At Emily's House

Present: Emily, Mike, David, Andrew

Absent/Late: Mike arrived right before the Accommodations discussion

Guest: Aaron the mix engineer

1. State of the Band

Emily updated us on timing of upcoming rehearsals and recording session (2/18).

2. Confirmed Venues

We reviewed the different stops on the upcoming tour.

3. Accommodations

We agreed to each pay up to $80 per night for our own separate rooms.

Mike will see if his friends outside Memphis will put us up. We will all send feelers out to people we know in New Orleans, or decide to pay for hotels, by March 1.

4. Van Repairs

We agree to pay for the new brakes out of band funds but will hold off on getting the van detailed until after the tour.

5. Committee Reports

T-shirts will arrive by 2/21.

Aaron the engineer says that we can have the studio at a 25% discount during month of August, but we have to decide by March 15.

6. What's on your mind?

Mike thinks the website is due for an overhaul and will present a plan next month.

7. Goals for next month

Decide if we will be ready to do more recording by August.

Minutes by,

David

FIG. 9.21. Minutes

Follow-ups after the meeting are to summarize what transpired and who agreed to do what. They might consist of the minutes being emailed, or they might be conversations to clarify what was decided.

All these devices help harness the potential power of meetings. It keeps them organized and focused, and encourages active follow-through after the fact. Meetings are potentially when some of the best decision-making occurs during your project, so being strategic in their execution will help you get the most out of them.

PRODUCTION DOCUMENTS

Similar to meetings are content production events, such as recording sessions, concerts, and film spotting sessions. Content is organized with various sheets that log what transpires. Like agendas and pre-meeting checklists, their creation can sometimes begin in advance of the event. Like minutes, their details get filled in while the event is in progress, documenting the details that unfold. Production documents exist for many facets of music production (and related endeavors): input matrixes, take sheets, cue sheets, spotting notes, stage layout diagrams, wiring diagrams, audio schematics, lighting diagrams, and others. The formats vary, and there are many variations and derivations of each.

An *input matrix* is used to log what equipment was used in a recording session. This can be helpful if you have to go back and overdub part of a song or recreate a track at a later date. Additional columns can be used to track pre-amps, effects, or other special information that affected the sound. Similarly, you can create a chart to track outboard gear used in mixing.

Instrument	Song	Track	Mic	Modifier	Note
Voice	"Here"	1	AKG C-12	UA 610 Mic Pre	No pop/he ate the mic; isolation booth
	All others	1	Neumann 67	UA 610 Mic Pre, pop filter	Isolation booth
Guitar	All	2	U47	Guitarist has list of pedals used	
Bass	"Here"	3	Shure SM81	Amp, Big Muff	Notes are backwards, no attack
	All others	3	Direct		
Drums:					
Snare	All	4	Shure SM57		
Hi Tom	All	5	ATM-25		
Low Tom	All	6	ATM-25		
Bass Drum	All	7	AKG D-12		
Overheads	All	8	Neumann U67 (2)		No individual mics on cymbals

FIG. 9.22. Input Matrix

A *take sheet* is used during recording sessions to keep track of each recorded pass. In the old days of tape, take sheets were absolutely critical for organizing information. Today, with digital audio workstations, much of the information can be stored within the tracks, but take sheets are still useful, and old-time engineers often lament their falling out of fashion. Typically, a take sheet has the track name, take number, description, comments, and overall quality rating. The best take gets circled.

Name	Take	Description	Comments	Quality
"You and Only You"	1	Full Band	Complete but rough	OK
	2	Full Band	False start	Bad
	③	Full Band	Very strong; must overdub vocal in verse 2	Best
"You…" guitar solo	1	Vocal overdub to "You…"	Good enough. Do another if time permits	Great
"Immortality"	1	Rhythm section only	Too slow	Bad
…				

FIG. 9.23. Take Sheet

Ideally, each recorded pass begins with a *slate*—a recorded spoken identifier for the take, to match the take sheet. For the first line of the take sheet in figure 9.23, the engineer might begin the take by recording himself saying, "'You and Only You' full band, take 1." That will help the mix engineer organize the tracks. Audio software facilitates the naming of takes, which makes slating less of an issue, but it is still a helpful practice.

A type of take sheet designed for vocal tracks is a *lyric sheet* (or "vocal take sheet"), which includes lyrics, line by line, organized in a chart. In figure 9.24, the columns indicate take numbers. For each line, the artist or engineer marks whether the take was good (+), bad (–), or somewhere in between (?). Later, the engineer can use this to cut up the audio tracks and create a composite take of the best elements of each. Numbering each verse and indenting each section of lyrics helps clarify the form. In figure 9.24, there have been three takes recorded. The composite track will primarily use take 2, with a few lines from take 3, which was a partial recording just to get those lines that were known to be bad. If time permits, there remain columns to support two additional takes.

	1	2	3	4	5
1. What made you shave your head in Amsterdam?	+	+			
When you turned off the moon and walked out of the room?	+	+			
Did you find the crooked smile that you'd been waiting for?	-	+			
The skeleton key to your world away from me?	-	+			
For a while I would wonder if I broke it	+	+	(+)		
Now I know that I couldn't if I tried	-	+	(+)		
I don't have your special knack for self-destruction	-	-	(+)		
That's your gift and it's why I say	-	-	(+)		
You and only you could make Paris a dry town	-	+			
Without the faintest hint of romance in the air	+	+			
You and only you could dissipate its sweet perfume	+	+			
You and only you wouldn't care	-	+			
2. Life's been up and down these twenty-seven years	-	+			
Since you left me in Spain to run off with what's her name	-	+			
…					

FIG. 9.24. Lyric Sheet for "You and Only You" by Jonathan Feist

In the film industry, *spotting notes* are used to track what music is required for the different scenes. Typically, a director, composer, music supervisor, and possibly others involved in creating the audio tracks will meet, go over a storyboard or rough cut of the film, and talk about what music or other sounds are required. Spotting notes must be very precise regarding timing, giving starting and stopping points using SMPTE code to identify precisely where they begin and end. They might include a cue from the dialogue, general descriptive text regarding what's needed, and possibly a reference to the temp track (a dummied up soundtrack of music close to what's to be created).

Here's an excerpt from the preliminary spotting notes for the upcoming film *The Repatriation of Henry Chin*, by author/screenwriter Isaac Ho. He included references to the temp track to help clarify the style of the original music to be developed. Also included are notes regarding sound effects (SFX).

	Video	Audio
Scene 21:	The shuttle bus slowly snakes down a cordoned off street lined with protesters.	SFX: The rumble of the bus's engine transitions into the low, steady drumbeat of: MUSIC CUE: MILITARY MARCH BEGIN 00:12:35;16 (Temp: TRY, 06 The Greek Army and Its Defeat 0:00)
Scene 22:	The first view of the Rose Bowl surrounded by armed soldiers. Reaction shots of Henry and Elizabeth.	MUSIC CUE: ADD SOMBER HORN SECTION TO MILITARY MARCH. (Temp: TRY, 02 Troy 0:30) BEGIN 00:13:07;03 MUSIC CUE: Duck under dialogue until:
Scene 23:	A CLERK inspects Elizabeth's luggage.	<u>CLERK:</u> You can't take all three suitcases. MUSIC CUE: Ends. END 00:13:45;42
Scene 23A:	A burst of ORANGE, BLUE and GREEN FLAMES shoot up from the trash can. Henry kicks over the trash can and grabs Elizabeth.	<u>HENRY:</u> Follow me! MUSIC CUE: BEGIN SUSPENSEFUL CHASE MUSIC. BEGIN 00:15:55;10 (Temp: MI3, 04 Helluvacopter Chase 0:48)
Scene 24:	Henry and Elizabeth race toward the fence, evading soldiers.	MUSIC CUE: SUSPENSEFUL CHASE MUSIC CONTINUES UNTIL:
Scene 24:	Henry and Elizabeth's path is blocked by a chain link fence.	MUSIC CUE: CHASE MUSIC TRAPPED TONE. BEGIN: 00:17:01;14 (Temp: DVC, 02 L'esprit Des Gabriel 1:00) <u>ELIZABETH:</u> Now what? SFX: Henry lets out THREE QUICK WHISTLES.
Scene 24:	Clyde appears and snips the chain link fence with bolt cutters.	MUSIC CUE: SUSPENSEFUL CHASE MUSIC RESUMES AND CONTINUES. BEGIN 00:17:20;19
Scene 24:	Clyde leads the way for Henry and Elizabeth to a waiting cargo van. Armed guards search nearby.	MUSIC CUE: SUSPENSEFUL CHASE MUSIC RESUMES UNTIL:

FIG. 9.25. Spotting Notes for *The Repatriation of Henry Chin* (Courtesy of Isaac Ho)

A *cue sheet* (or "run sheet") is used to track musical pieces or scenes in a concert, theater, film, or television production. They contain all essential information required by the stage manager, such as directions for lighting, camera directions, sound, props, curtains, or other information. Figure 9.26 is a run sheet from a *From the Top* live-concert taping of the radio show.

FROM THE TOP RUN SHEET
SANTA FE SHOW #242 • LENSIC PAC • OCTOBER 25, 2011

Piece/Visual	Cue	Move	Notes
TOS Preset			Video Screen In / Piano w/E-stand / No music desk Black Podium set SL
House to 1/2			SLAVET, BANKER & ROBINSON standing by
House Out	Video play on DeVore cue	Banker & Forbes hide DeVore under podium	SLAVET, BANKER & ROBINSON standing by
End of Film	Video Ends / Screen goes to black	CREW Strike / Kill Video / Slavet Enter to Mic #5	O'RILEY, ROBINSON & HUGO KITANO standing by
Warm-Up	Joanne Enters w/ suitcase	DeVore Exits with podium SL	HUGO KITANO standing by
Chris to Piano	*You're the Top*		HUGO KITANO standing by
Chris Leave Piano		Move E-stand / Change out piano bench	HUGO KITANO standing by
PIANO PIECE	HUGO to Mic #5		AUDRA VIGIL standing by
HUGO Interview	HUGO to Mic #3	Set bench & foot rest to spike	AUDRA VIGIL standing by
GUITAR PIECE	AUDRA VIGIL to Mic #5		MICAELA ALDRIDGE standing by
AUDRA Interview	AUDRA to Mic #3	Strike bench & foot rest	MICAELA ALDRIDGE standing by
VOCAL PIECE	MICAELA to Mic #5		
MICAELA Interview	MICAELA to Mic #3		RUSSELL HOUSTON standing by
BREAK PIECE	*O'RILEY PIANO PIECE*		RUSSELL HOUSTON standing by
Audience Shout Out	Wireless Mic to TBD in Audience	Tim with hand held mic in audience	RUSSELL HOUSTON standing by
CELLO PIECE	RUSSELL to Mic #5	Set cello chair to spike / **Needs page at mic #3**	AMELIA SIE standing by
RUSSELL Interview	RUSSELL to Mic #3 AMELIA to Mic #2	Strike cello chair	AMELIA SIE standing by
AMELIA Interview	RUSSELL to Mic #3 AMELIA to Mic #2		ALL TALENT standing by
VIOLIN PIECE			ALL TALENT standing by
Curtain call		All onstage for bows	

FIG. 9.25. Run Sheet for *From the Top* Radio Broadcast: Santa Fe, 2011

Stage layout diagrams indicate what needs to be onstage for a music setup. These are often hand-drawn in pencil, to make them easily updatable on the spot. Typically, this type of diagram includes chairs, music stands, monitors, risers, platforms, podiums, and non-portable instruments, such as a drum set, piano, marimba, timpani, harp, and so on. Lighting and sound gear might be included or there might be separate, analogous diagrams for those dimensions of the setup.

A few standard symbols are frequently used. Often, an x is used to indicate a chair, – is for music stands. Other less standard symbols also commonly appear, such as • for stools, M for monitors, arrows for microphones (and their directions), and circles for timpani, so a key of explanation is useful once you get away from x and –.

Figure 9.26 is an orchestra's stage setup plan for a piano concerto. In the key at the bottom right, the total number of each object is listed, as a way for the stagehands to double-check their math. Instrument section names help make double-checking it easier.

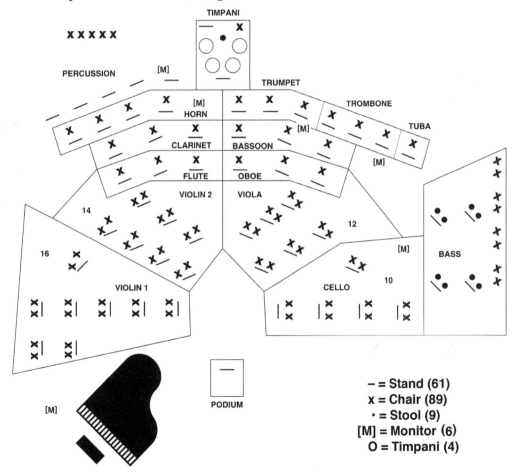

FIG. 9.26. Stage Plan

Production documents, like meeting documents, are among the most critically useful tools that will be created during a project's lifecycle. They often stand on the shoulders of giants, though. The work breakdown structure, scope statement, Gantt chart, and other planning documents help inform the creation of production documents. Though they generally won't be substantially realized until during execution, it's helpful to begin developing production documents early, if possible. The process of creating and studying these tools often helps clarify what is truly needed for the project to run. Creating them can also cause the planning documents to evolve (e.g., "Uh oh, we need to get a podium for the conductor...."), along with everyone's expectation of what is truly possible.

CLOSING THOUGHTS

The execution phase is when a project manager most needs to apply pressure to the project team, making sure that all the work is getting done correctly and on time. Besides simply assigning work, the work must be continually monitored and evaluated, and communication has to be constant, to confirm that all is going as it should be. The project plan must be in constant use.

PRACTICE

Determine the tasks you will be assigning to your team, and then launch the execution phase of your project. Delegate and track work assignments as appropriate.

CHAPTER 10

Managing Workflow

In this chapter, we look at the flow of information, ideas, and objects in our lives as project managers, and how to be efficient in processing what comes our way. We will consider our workspaces and how to optimize them.

OBJECTIVES

By the end of the chapter, you will be able to:

- organize your project office (and the rest of your world)

- capture and systematize the paperwork, objects, and obligations that come your way

- focus more clearly on the business at hand, and avoid some of the factors that are likely to fragment your attention

THE COST OF INTERRUPTIONS

To set the stage of some upcoming preaching about why we should organize our surroundings and become passionate about simplifying our environment and reducing clutter, I am pleased to present the following neuroscientific demonstration.

How much efficiency do you think you gain or lose through multitasking—doing more than one activity concurrently? Make a note of your estimate.

Now, we will test it. In the following exercise, you will time yourself doing the same exact work twice, but using a different approach each time. Then, we will compare the difference in timing. So, get a timer. I'll wait....

Ready?

Once you start your timer, you will write three lines:

1. The sentence, "How much do interruptions cost?"

2. Under that sentence, write the numerals from 1 to 26, with a one-to-one correspondence between these numerals and the letters in the sentence above.

H	o	w	m	u	c	h	d	o	i	n	t	e	r	r	u	p	t	i	o	n	s	c	o	s	t
1	2	3	4	5	6	7	8	9	10	11	12	13	14	15	16	17	18	19	20	21	22	23	24	25	26

FIG. 10.1. Interruptions Exercise: Sentence, Numbers

3. Then under that, write your name, over and over, until you fill up the 26 positions of lines (1) and (2). (By chance, my name worked out exactly, but yours might end in a fragment.)

H	o	w	m	u	c	h	d	o	i	n	t	e	r	r	u	p	t	i	o	n	s	c	o	s	t
1	2	3	4	5	6	7	8	9	10	11	12	13	14	15	16	17	18	19	20	21	22	23	24	25	26
J	o	n	a	t	h	a	n	F	e	i	s	t	J	o	n	a	t	h	a	n	F	e	i	s	t

FIG. 10.2. Interruptions Exercise: Your Name

Then stop the timer, and record how long that took you.

Ready? Do that now....

How long did that take? I've found that most adults take thirty to eighty seconds. Kids take a bit more time. How do you feel? Relaxed? Bored? Cheerful? Stressed? Game for whatever? Annoyed? Bemused? Tired? Gung-ho?

Next, time yourself writing the same three lines, but instead of going across, do it vertically, column by column. You'll write: H 1 J o 2 o w 3 n m.... So, partway through, it might look like figure 10.3, with the ? where the next character (4) would go.

H	o	w	m																						
1	2	3	?																						
J	o	n																							

FIG. 10.3. Interruptions Exercise: Vertical

Record your time. How do you feel now? Stressed? Tired? Annoyed? Flabbergasted? Cheery?

Compare the two times. Is the percentage difference similar to what you predicted earlier, when I asked what you thought your efficiency change was during multitasking? Also, consider how much effort the second approach felt, compared to the first way.

You will probably find here that the first approach went faster, was less stressful, and was more accurate. You might have felt slightly stressed or pressured, doing it the second way. Even angry!

The reasons for these reactions, from the amount of efficiency to the emotional response to stress and distraction, has to do with how we are hard-wired. Our magnificent brains are brilliant at finding patterns, and this leads to efficiency. We don't have to think about every letter, when we write, or every numeral in a sequence of numbers. We can do the work in chunks, all at once, if we are focused.

Musicians know this well. When we read music, we are constantly looking for patterns, such as scanning written melodies for scale sequences and chord tones, rather than looking note by note. The better we are at spotting patterns, the easier reading music gets. It's a reason why studying music theory improves the ability to sightread, and to perform. Deeper understanding helps us to spot more patterns, which then frees us from continually concentrating on the printed page and permits us to focus instead on creative expression and communication.

And in this exercise, we saw all that quantified. Commonly, I find that the second attempt takes people twice as long as the first attempt, to produce the exact same work result.

The difference in time is due to the amount of time it requires your brain to change gears, a change of brain function that is also called *transiting* or *switching*. When we write the lines horizontally, we gain efficiency because our brains organize the words and numbers into patterns. But in going column by column, continually changing focus from completing the composite thought in our mind's eye to reassessing the situation to figure out the required next character, this patterning capability is disrupted, and our efficiency suffers dramatically.

Consider the repercussions of this. I first saw the principle at work in a demonstration to make the point that multitasking doesn't work—that people's professed abilities to do several things at once is a fiction, and that our work quality is much better when we focus on tasks sequentially.

Now, consider our potential interruptions during a workday. We get a constant bombardment of emails, texts, phone calls, and real-live humans knocking on our doors. As I typed that very sentence, one of my sons (age 9) burst into my office to show me a secret code he had just developed. (I therefore made him take the test. He scored 1:57 and 4:21, and misspelled his own name during the second attempt.)

Consider texting while driving, or doing homework while watching television, or performing a quality control check on your nuclear reactor while someone is talking to you about his weekend. A co-worker knocks on our door every single time he has something to say. A cell phone lights up and vibrates whenever a social media site wants to tell us that one of our long-lost acquaintances posted yet another photo of his adorable puppy, or an angry political tirade directed at our own preferred candidate. Should we take the bait and respond, or should we go back to proofreading that boring index? All of these are common circumstances, but we have just seen how dramatically our competency decreases when we are constantly switching between one thing and another—constantly interrupted, and that doesn't factor in the time spent in the digression ("Yes, your puppy is awfully cute; let me quickly take a photo of my cat and show it to you…."). The question is, how much do these interruptions cost? Answer: A LOT!

A principle of organization, then, is to simplify, in order to reduce these attention switches. Ruthlessly. It's war out there, and we are besieged by a constant bombardment of attacks designed to complicate our lives and derail our focus. Constant. You might have even been interrupted while reading this topic. Was it worth it? Could it have been avoided?

"Simplify" isn't just a trendy bumper sticker, or something Zen masters say so that they can get more enjoyment out of their tea. By simplifying, we are trying to shape our world in such a way that we can think more clearly and be more effective.

"Simplify" is our mantra, in this chapter, as we look at ways to organize the flow of work that surrounds us.

THE FLOW OF STUFF

Throughout our projects, as in the rest of our lives, stuff will come at us. Every item on the work breakdown structure and every supporting task will result in incoming communications, documents, objects, and obligations. I typically get about two thousand pieces of paper for every book project I do, plus several cartons of finished books, a few CDs, and other objects. Multiply that by about forty simultaneous projects currently in development, at one stage or another, and it's a lot of stuff!

This stuff is in one of three states.

1. Chaos. It is just out there, disorganized, requiring attention.

2. Systematized. It is in a system that will result in its completion.

3. Resolved. It is in its ideal, permanent place, and doesn't require further attention.

FIG. 10.4. Chaos to Systemization to Resolution

The goal of processing stuff is to bring it from a state of chaos to a state of resolution as efficiently as possible. We don't want any chaos. We want things to be either resolved or in a system that will result in them getting resolved.

Yesterday, one of my authors emailed me a solo guitar transcription, which is to be included in his book. The system for getting it done, in this case, was to send it to an editorial assistant who would check it against the recording, note for note. Once I assigned her that task, the transcription was no longer in a state of chaos. While it was not in its permanent home, it was on its way, and I therefore do not currently need to give it any more of my attention.

Now, when I first received the transcription by email, I was quickly reviewing a number of emails that had come in. I looked at it and then moved on to the next thing, without addressing it. What did that transcription do then? It festered! It remained in my inbox, in a state of chaos. But worse than unknown chaos, it was chaos that joined all the other bits of known chaos in my imagination—that massive cloud of things I knew I should be doing but hadn't addressed yet.

Until it was systematized, it was like a little tiny vampire, sucking just a little drop of life force out of me.

Such unresolved issues are sometimes called "open loops." Taking control of the work before us involves rooting out these little slivers of chaos and either resolving them or systematizing them.

In the interruptions exercise, we saw the efficiency cost in switching between thinking about various different things. All of our open loops play in the background of our consciousness, similarly competing for our attention and focus. We switch between focusing on what we are doing and what we feel that we should be doing.

A file that arrives by email has the advantage that it is physically tidy. We can turn off our computers and not have them in front of us as visible distractions.

Physical items, though, compete more intensely for our focus. An unresolved stack of paper on our desk is an open loop. It requires attention but is not yet in a system, so it joins that dark cloud that surrounds us of things that we should be doing but are not.

Clutter, then, serves to remind us of our limitations. It is stressful. And it is a constraint, reducing our efficiency.

The solution to this is to develop systems that will result in the reduction of chaos, in our lives, and the reduction of time it takes for chaos to enter into the system. This means developing good habits but also useful tools. And all tools are only useful if they are efficient and easy. There are not universal right and wrong answers for how to deal with stuff, because people have different tolerances. Whether you use a paper calendar or an electronic calendar isn't as important a consideration as whether you have a calendar at all. While I might argue that electronic calendars are better, if you find them so confusing that you don't keep them up to date, then it's obviously not an effective system for you. Effective specific approaches can be subjective. The principle is the important thing.

Let's consider each of these three states of stuff. Then, we will look at specific practices for addressing it.

Chaos

There are many forms of stuff that arrive on our doorsteps, and there are also many different places where stuff accumulates. The more fragmented this is, the more chaotic and out of control life will seem.

Adults generally spend their time at home, in an office, or in their cars. Each of these can include multiple traps for chaos, where things fester.

Home. Every room has its own system and quality of chaos. Bedrooms will tend to have dirty clothes, kitchens will have dirty dishes, bathrooms will have jumbles of personal care products, but you can also find each category of chaos in any room. Every single room of my house has seen its share of stray Legos and used coffee mugs. Mail starts in the mailbox, but then can accumulate any number of places: the kitchen, the staircases, the bedroom. A basement, garage, toy closet, barn, trash shed, and attic will each trap a wide variety of chaos.

Office. Offices tend to accumulate stacks of paper and obsolete electronic equipment. Office supplies and gadgets abound, including dried up pens, staplers, label printers, telephones, and more. Because many of us spend so much time in offices, we might bring some decorative objects into our offices, and these easily multiply to become vast hoards. Every work surface of an office can act as a clutter accumulation point: desks, file cabinets, extra chairs, the floor, unused machinery, bookshelves, music stands, and so on.

Car. Cars are chaos traps. Trunks can hold items for years without us noticing them. Receipts from parking garages can accumulate in the door pockets, together with maps and printed out directions from journeys long completed. We also find more stray coffee mugs, kids' toys, and simply dirt.

What other chaos traps can you think of? Any other locations or types?

Ideal Locations

> "'Tis gift to be simple, 'tis gift to be free,
> 'Tis gift to come down where you ought to be.
> And when you find yourself in the place just right,
> It will be in the valley of love and delight."
>
> —From the Shaker Hymn "Simple Gifts,"
> by Elder Joseph Brackett

The opposite of chaos is the ideal locations where items find their ultimate destiny.

Very little belongs in our cars, permanently. Perhaps something to brush the snow off, some quarters for parking, a couple maps, a GPS, sunglasses, the registration, and maybe cleaning supplies, in case the dog gets sick. That's about it.

Paper usually belongs in file cabinets. Supplies should go in storage closets or cupboards. Books go on bookshelves.

Work that someone else should be doing belongs in their space, not yours.

Decorations belong either displayed or in deep storage, awaiting periodic consideration to see if they might cycle out into the world, for a spin.

Dirty dishes belong in the dishwasher; if you don't have a dishwasher, you have to clean them right away and put them back in the cabinet. Trash belongs at the dump. Anything you don't want belongs outside of your life completely.

Most things that you won't use within the next couple days belong stored away somewhere, out of sight.

Otherwise, the derailing cacophony will intensify.

Systems

How to fit the chaos into a system that will result in its fulfillment is the least obvious part of this process. There are many ways to do it, and different procedures required for different objects.

Consider the guitar transcription I mentioned earlier. If I simply saved the file to my hard drive and then went about my regular business, I would have tidied up my email inbox, but there is a good chance that I would forget all about it and never give it the attention that it deserves. To make sure that its destiny gets fulfilled, I need to add more value to it. I need to alert the person who is responsible for checking it, and then build in a monitoring system to confirm that it actually gets completed.

What is missing is a reminder mechanism that will force us to track progress on the required work. Some ways to do this:

- I could email it to the assistant with instructions and a deadline, and then track this (and all delegated tasks) on a list that I regularly review.

- Project management software often includes functionality for delegating and tracking tasks, automating the process mentioned above.

- Calendars are a great help in systematizing work, entering items on their due dates and programming email reminders.

- Systems of processing work, such as Getting Things Done, offer systemic ways to process work.

Somehow, you need an index into the work that must be completed, which must account for every last detail. Without reliable systems, it is too easy to lose track of things.

What I find most helpful is the life project index, as discussed in chapter 1. This set of charts lists all active projects, indicating the next thing to do to move them forward.

Priority	Project	Next Action (Due Date)	Completion Date
1	Article for magazine	brainstorm topics (5/15)	6/1
2	July 4 concert	decide on final program (6/4)	7/4
w	Pub gig	pub owner will send contract	September 1

FIG. 10.5. Project Index

Keeping this list current will help us track what we need to do. Simple projects, of just a couple tasks, can be maintained here completely. More complex projects, such as substantial music projects, will have more comprehensive information regarding what is due, perhaps maintained in project management software.

Living out of an index like this makes it useful. Visit it multiple times daily, whenever you finish a task, or need to check on what is urgent. As new obligations come your way, add them to the index and then prioritize them, so that you can see them in context of your other work.

OFFICE ORGANIZATION

Office organization is something that most people are never taught, but it can make a very profound difference in how effective and efficient we are in our work. You might struggle with this, or it might come easily to you. I will discuss these ideas in terms of a project office, but they will also work for your recording studio, classroom, kitchen, barn, and basement too.

The project office is where the chaos gets systematized and ultimately resolved. Sometimes, you get to create chaos, too, and then send it off to someone else. In an efficient office, all components work towards this pattern of resolution. By minimizing the potentially fragmentary nature of where the chaos emerges and resides, the overall workload comes under control, and hopefully, our stress levels do as well.

An office is like a funnel. Chaos enters, gets transformed, and then exits as a systematized deliverable. The office needs to be completely organized. Otherwise, the risk increases that details will be overlooked, which generally increases the risk towards project failure.

Let's consider the components of an office, with their highest functions.

Workspaces

In your life, you need a dedicated work area, devoted to organizing the endless stream of stuff that comes in and must be processed. Ideally, this is a room dedicated as an office. If you don't have a room to devote to this, you'll have to use part of a room, which is a precarious situation because the sprawl is more difficult to control, but maybe that's your architectural reality. You'll just have to be extra protective of boundaries, if this is the case. You definitely need an office space at home, to run your personal life. You might also have an office space out of the home for your work.

If you live in a single room, if it's not as organized as a submarine, you're never going to get relief from your work and from the tedious business of life. It will always be in your face, with clutter constantly weighing on you. Carve out areas for different functions. Don't let your mail (bills, bank statements, etc.) touch your night table. You need to be able to escape your work, relax, and get some sleep.

Ideally, you'll have a dedicated room where you can close the door, either to keep out the disruptive hoards outside it, or to lock up the demons that lurk within, so that you can take a break.

Possibly, you'll have multiple offices: one at home and one at a place of business. Similar organizational principles will apply to each. Overall, though, you'll need to develop some strict systems for the ideal, permanent locale for where all objects live and how they get there—not to mention, portable tools for keeping stuff organized when you are in between.

The office is your engine for processing stuff and getting things done. Minimize anything there that disrupts your focus.

Within the workspace are three critical points: the inbox, the file cabinet, and the desk. Let's call this the "office triangle," not unlike the kitchen triangle of sink, refrigerator, and oven. The office triangle's components correspond to the three states of work, discussed earlier.

- The *inbox* is the single point of allowable chaos in an environment. It is the one place where stuff can be deposited, where its status is unsettled. When an object pops up that you can't deal with immediately, it goes in the inbox: not in a pile on a table, not on the desk, not on the piano, not on the floor. Then, at least once per week, the inbox is completely organized and emptied, with all objects that find their way into it becoming systematized, and finding their ideal location.

- The *file cabinet* is the permanent home for documents (and perhaps, other media). While the file cabinet is likely the most active storage area, as paper is generally the most common type of item that comes into an office, there are other storage places too, such as bookshelves, closets, display structures, and places to store large trash/ recycling/stuff to give away. This is where stuff lives, long term, when you're not going to use it again within a couple hours. Storage units within reach contain essential stuff, potentially useful multiple times per year. If something is not useful once per year but must be kept, it goes into long-term storage, far away from the work environment. And if it's not needed at all, it goes to the place where things live that are on the way out of your life.

- The *desk* is where stuff gets systematized. These systems are maintained in your project plan, calendar, project index, and such, which all help keep you informed about what current work you have to do. With effective systems, nothing gets lost in the file cabinet, because there are live documents that keep you completely informed regarding what needs to get done. Likely, the most active documents reside on a computer, or perhaps divided between a computer and a clipboard.

By militantly, painstakingly adhering to this work triangle concept, you can keep completely organized, and avoid wasting time searching for critical documents and objects.

Inbox

The inbox should be the single source of chaos in your office. Periodically, during the day, put things that are not systematized and that you can't deal with right away in your inbox. If you are cleaning up a place that got out of hand, put it all in your inbox, and if it doesn't fit, expand the "box" temporarily so that it holds what you want. In a serious intervention, maybe a table becomes an inbox, during your cleaning frenzy. Maybe, even a whole room. Or, if you've got a pathological hoarding tendency, you might need to call your whole living space a giant, chaos of an inbox.

Hopefully, though, it's just a basket, say eighteen inches square. Unorganized stuff goes in. When you have the bandwidth, and certainly no less often than once a week, you process every single thing in your inbox and empty it completely.

Take each thing and deal with it. Avoid putting things back in, after you've looked at them. Don't store things in your inbox. Throw it out, execute it, put it into a system that will ensure its completion, or settle it in its permanent home.

On the following page is the best inbox I ever had. Its predecessor was a cheap plastic thing that I hated every time I used it, for years and years. This one is both bigger and more attractive.

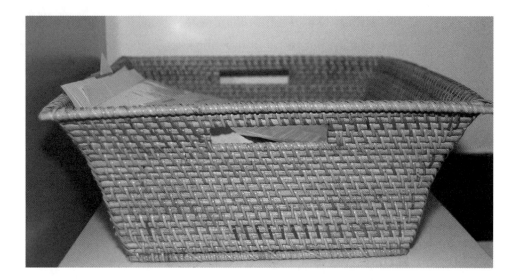

FIG. 10.6. Inbox

File Cabinet

Most people need one four-drawer file cabinet for all their paperwork. Some work might require multiple file cabinets to hold all the relevant stuff that comes your way. Nearly everyone who works or runs a household requires at least one four-drawer file cabinet. All paper should reside here. My strong recommendation is that folders in the file cabinet be organized simply, A to Z, with no sub-categories. This makes for simplest retrieval. So, rather than having all financial documents going under "F," put the Bank of America stuff under "B" and the Fidelity stuff under "F." This greatly simplifies the process of finding things.

Don't label hanging files. Only label the manila folders. Hanging file labels needlessly create awkward extra work and slow down organization. Some file cabinets require that you use them. If you must, use them to hold other folders, but don't label them. They are good at holding more paper than what might fit in a single folder. But those little plastic label sleeves add unnecessary work.

Keep blank folders and extra labels within arm's reach from your desk chair so that you can file things easily. For many people, this means dramatically more folders than they are accustomed to using. Folders are cheap, though—say, a nickel apiece. A box of file folders might make a great difference in your life.

If you have a category (such as a project) that takes up more than half a file drawer, it might warrant its own complete drawer, or even its own dedicated file cabinet. For a while, when I chaired a town board, I was tracking so much stuff that I kept a separate file cabinet for all that work. When I stopped my involvement there, I moved those papers out of my office: some to Town Hall, and some to my long-term storage cabinet in a dark and creepy corner of my basement, where documents go that can't be thrown out but aren't likely ever to be referenced either.

You can file other stuff besides paper in a file cabinet too, even temporarily, so that it isn't cluttering up your work area. If you are straightening up and have a new box of ukulele strings that you don't know what to do with, stick it in your file cabinet under "Strings," until you find a better place. Maybe move them to a storage cabinet of instrument-related stuff, if you decide that's a better place, but at least in the file, you'll be able to find it easily. The only likely deficit is that they might take up a bit too much room, depending on the packaging. Then again, it might be the best place for them, even if it seems a little unorthodox.

Rejoice whenever you can file something. Eventually, you start creating fewer new folders, day to day. Folders are cheap and helpful, so use them liberally.

Some efficiency gurus advocate using a label maker for file folders. Printed labels do look nice. Try this, but you might find that it slows you down too much, making you less likely to file things. If so, just omit that step from your process.

There are a couple of dangers with file cabinets. One is that things get filed there without being systematized, and so that dimension of the work can become lost. Another is that documents eventually become obsolete. To keep file drawers from becoming bloated, periodically grab a fat folder in the cabinet and see if you can get rid of any of its contents. Whenever you close a project, purge its folders of all obsolete drafts and documents as part of your standard project closing procedures.

In addition to the primary file cabinet in your office, you will probably benefit by having remote files as well, for archival storage. I've mentioned that my work involves about 20,000 to 30,000 pieces of paper per year, and I've been at it since 1998, so I have touched a lot of paper. I store my usual business work in two lateral four-drawer files. In addition to these active files, I maintain another four filing cabinets for archives—files that I don't expect to need for a very long time, if ever, but that I need to keep. These cabinets are stored outside my office, as they are only accessed every few months.

Similarly, in my basement at home, I keep two more file cabinets that include old tax information and other rarely accessed personal documents. It is almost never visited—essentially, an archive, just like those cabinets in my campus office.

The job of these remote archives is to relieve the pressure from the more active file cabinet in an office.

Desk

Your desk is where you think and act—where you make organizational and strategic progress on much of your work. It is a clear surface for you to create content, and also to examine and systematize the stuff that comes into your life. Additionally, it is your communication hub: email, chat, Skype, maybe a phone, and even (gasp) physical mail.

Likely, your computer takes center stage on your desk. Depending on your work and your furniture, this might preclude your desk from similarly serving as a place where you can work on physical documents. If this is the case, you might need a separate area where you can spread out papers.

If your work involves computer audio tools, you might have essential gear (MIDI keyboards, patch bays, mixing boards, outboard gear, etc.) that shares your desk with your computer. The desk therefore becomes awkward for working with paper, and you'll need another clear surface in your office for doing that—or ideally, a second desk. In my own paper-intensive work, I make frequent use of a long countertop in my office. On this, I can fit twenty pages, which is a great help when I am trying to look at entire chapters or extended musical scores at a glance. Before I had this office, I would spread papers all over the floor, for such tasks, which required a lot more crawling around.

These active work surfaces easily become clutter traps, but they are also the most imperative places to keep absolutely clutter free—particularly the working surface. Only keep objects there that you use multiple times per week. This is likely to include:

- Computer

- Cup of hot coffee

- Telephone

- Clipboard with documents that help manage your day

- Pen/pencil/eraser (if you are old school)

- Possibly, specialized gear that you use multiple times a day (MIDI keyboard, headphones, metronome, scanner, printer, etc.), though minimizing this on the work surface is best

- Blank folders and labels, for easy filing

The purpose of the desk is to display to you the current critical documents of your work and help you systematize your chaos. Anything else is in the way. Within arm's length, you should strive to omit everything that you haven't needed to touch within the past week.

Is there a modem or router on your desk? It can probably go farther away, because it is seldom necessary to interact with these devices physically. Are there speakers or obsolete electronics that you don't use? Get rid of them, if you can. That cool plastic dinosaur? Ask yourself every time you see it whether you would both be happier if it lived a bit farther away.

What about your stapler? When did you last staple something? Is your stapler on your desk because it seems standard to have a stapler on your desk—maybe because your father keeps a stapler on his desk? Or is it because you actually use it every day or two? If you only actually staple once every few months, maybe it makes more sense to keep it in a supply cupboard or a drawer.

Desktops are not for storage. They are for active work, where you can move stuff around so you can see it. Be ruthless in keeping this sacred space completely free of clutter. You need it for your active work, and making progress on the business at hand becomes easier without the distractions of clutter.

OTHER OFFICE ELEMENTS

Storage Cabinets and Containers

Good storage areas help you keep your active work area clutter free. Like file cabinets, storage closets, cupboards, bins, and boxes are permanent homes where chaos should ultimately reside.

Besides the usual Post-it notes, extra pens, paper, and so on, it's helpful to be able to store items that are seldom used: outboard audio gear, instruments, microphones, specialized printers or scanners, and so on.

Certain objects are best stored out of sight but in easy access. For example, I use my camera every few days, but it is an unwieldy object. I found a couple of wooden storage containers that serve double duty as art objects and storage areas. The Shaker oval box on the left (see figure 10.7) stores three sets of headphones, which I use frequently. The firken, on the right, holds four cameras. Well, three, at the moment, as one is out being used to take this photo!

FIG. 10.7. Storage Containers

Items inside storage cabinets likely need to be stored in small containers or bags within it, rather than shoved in haphazardly as they are. Clear plastic makes it easier to find things: pens, binder clips, stationary, etc. Extra USB, telephone, and Ethernet cables seem to spontaneously generate like maggots, and they become unmanageable if they are not isolated from each other. To get that snake tangle under control, you can sort them by type, and use wire ties, Ziploc® bags, various commercial devices for the purpose, and so on, to keep them organized, rather than tangled together.

For cables in active use, it's helpful to label the plugs, to help you trace what gadget they lead to. Snakes, patch bays, tubes, and various boards help keep more complex wiring schemes (such as for wiring recording gear) in order.

Trash/Recycling

You must have adequate trash receptacles in your office, so that you can chuck stuff that deserves it *right away*. It is a joy to remove things from your inbox or desktop and then throw them out or recycle them.

Here's my office recycle bin. Isn't it lovely? It improves my life, empty or full, but because it is a nice object, I get extra joy after it is emptied, with the recycling moved to the trash shed outside my house, ready to go to the dump. (That trash shed is also a lovely object.)

FIG. 10.8. Recycle Bin

Here's my home office wastepaper basket. True, plastic is easier to clean, but it has no soul. I searched the world high and low for a trashcan that I actively liked, until this one finally showed up at my town dump. I think it originally stored nails at a hardware store. How cool is that?!

FIG. 10.9. Wastepaper Basket

Do you see a pattern here? The point isn't to convince you to decorate with old handmade wooden things. It is a recommendation that you consider every component of your office, and try to find items that you actively like, as opposed to just settling for what the big-box stores have to sell. For me, this creates more of a sense of investment in my workspace and thus my professional activities, and an orientation towards constantly improving it, which I find helpful, in the big picture. Recall the capability maturity model, from chapter 1, where the ultimate aspiration is to optimize systems that are already functioning reasonably well. That's what we're doing, here. It's a process. While there may continue to be elements in your office that you dislike, even though they are functional, try to look forward to upgrading them someday. Over time, things will improve.

There are other models for choosing office objects and outfitting workspaces than this. One current trend is to completely depersonalize workspaces in hopes of helping people utterly omit all clutter, to help workers focus. Some companies adopt the model where workers don't even have regular desks; they plug in their laptops at whatever station is open and don't have the same neighbors two days in a row. The counter-argument to that is that this makes people have a sense that their positions are ephemeral and that their relationship to the company they work for is transitory.

Different people and organizations will gravitate towards the different cultures. Finding this balance between efficiency and humanity is one of the great themes of the human condition.

Chair

Your desk chair should be considered among the top most important objects in your life, along with your mattress and your shoes. Those three are your primary physical interfaces with the world.

Invest in as comfortable/ergonomic a desk chair as you can afford. You will be spending a lot of time sitting on it. A bad chair can cause you a lot of pain and lead to decreased productivity.

No matter how comfy it is, don't sit for more than half an hour at a time. Get up and stretch.

You might keep an extra chair in your office for visitors, and a third close by, for the rarer occasions when you have two visitors. More than two, and you will probably prefer to meet in a larger room than your office instead.

Briefcase/Bag

If you work at multiple locations, you will likely have a briefcase, laptop bag, or some other type of luggage that you use to carry stuff between locations. These can be clutter traps. Upon arrival at a work area, it's a good idea to dump its entire contents into your inbox. Only immediately relevant objects belong in your briefcase: essential project organization documents, laptop, pen, blank pad, lunch, letters to drop in the mail, checks to bring to the bank, and other documents you will use within a day, or that you absolutely must remember to bring to an upcoming meeting. Most other stuff is likely just junk you're hauling around out of habit. Lighten your load. Empty your bag completely at least once a week, if not every day, and start fresh.

Also, consider your wallet, purse, gig bag, gear duffle, car, or other items you always take with you. Do you know whatever every single key on your key ring is for? If you carry an Epi-pen, is it expired? Is every item in your wallet, etc., truly important for you to carry around always? Do you need to keep all of those guitar picks with you all of the time? Or can you get rid of some of that stuff? Maybe, put them in your gear closet or file cabinet?

Notebook/Clipboard

A notebook/clipboard is useful for capturing ideas, information, and tasks that you agree to do. Some people like to use a notebook or journal, so as to keep all their notes in one place. I prefer clipboards, as I can then file the pages, or write multiple pages and look at them simultaneously. I also like being able to combine music manuscript paper with blank white paper. A clipboard can also be a convenient way to keep the most critical documents such as schedules, checklists, and so on, that you need all the time. They can become clutter traps, though, and require frequent weeding.

Bookshelves

Bookshelves are the neatest way to store books in a way that provides easy access to them. Some books, though, are appropriately in closer reach than others—maybe a style guide, dictionary, and references for your immediate work that are in active, immediate use. If you have the luxury of space, you might want to keep some books relatively accessible and others more out of the way. Bookshelves take up a lot of space. In my office at home, I have just a few reference books, on one shelf. Most of my books are in the central room of my attic. At Berklee, I keep two bookshelves in my office, but only because I want to have many books close at hand, for showing my authors examples of how they might render certain types of information in their own books. At home, this isn't necessary, as I rarely meet with authors here.

There was a time when I believed it was practically a sin to get rid of books, but I came around, and now will only keep books that I actually expect to read someday. During a massive office purge a few years ago, I decided to get rid of twenty linear feet of music books and scores I had been collecting for several decades. I donated them to my alma mater's library, at New England Conservatory. It was a somewhat difficult and traumatic decision for me at the time, as I somehow thought of myself as the sort of person who would have books and scores like that on my shelves. But after they were gone, I never regretted it, not for a single second. I much prefer to have the clutter-free space.

Outbox

An outbox is used for stuff that belongs out of your office: mail, reference material belonging to others, supporting documents of tasks that you are delegating, dirty dishes, and things to donate. This is very much like a wastepaper basket, in many ways, except that it may have critically valuable things in it. It's important to continually empty it, even several times a day, so that nothing important gets lost in there. The stuff might not be your responsibility, but it might be very important to someone else. At the end of the day, it should be empty.

Desklike Objects

Besides the usual desk for housing the computer and active papers, people in the music business often have large, expensive, critical objects that often take on desklike qualities, but they don't function well in that capacity: most commonly, pianos and mixing consoles. Somehow, these easily become repositories for humongous stacks of paper, and other miscellaneous objects. How many Steinways have I witnessed, worth tens of thousands of dollars, whose beautiful lacquered finish and world class acoustic properties were compromised by a six-inch thick layer of manuscript paper, ungraded student assignments, CDs, exercise books, copies of *Keyboard* magazine, and various extra-curricular objects? Or mixing consoles, where huge swaths of panpots and faders are hidden under ancient copies of *Mix*, random (broken) effects units, and mic cables, not to mention X-men® action figures and empty coffee cups.

Might I humbly suggest that these critical surfaces be kept completely free of their imprisoning clutter?

PROCESSING STUFF

If our offices are to be efficient engines for getting work done, we have to process all the stuff that comes into them. And to start, that often means a significant effort in getting it in shape.

Let's discuss some specific strategies for how to process our stuff, moving it from a state of chaos to a state of resolution.

The operating principle is that clutter—disorganized stuff—is a source of interruptions. It disrupts our focus, increases the time required to get work done, and takes up psychic space. Ideally, every object should be in its ideal, permanent location, or else integrated into a reliable system that will result in its arriving there.

In an efficient office, everything unprocessed—all the chaos—resides only in the inbox, and besides that, every single last little thing not currently being worked on resides in its ideal permanent location. No clutter is in sight. There isn't a sheet of paper visible on any work surface. Dirty dishes are not on our desks; they are in the dishwasher, or on their way there. Books are on shelves. Just one or two pens are on your desk, and the rest are in storage.

Every possible thing that can be thrown away or recycled is so dispatched as quickly as you possibly can.

Within your reach, while you're at your desk, should only be things that are used at least once per week. If it isn't, find a new place for it to live, farther out of the line of fire. Don't treat your tape dispenser as a decorative object. If you don't use tape much, put it in a storage closet or drawer.

There might be a few decorations in your workspace, but you'll have better luck keeping the place organized if you only display objects you love dearly. If you don't cherish seeing it every single day, then put it somewhere else. Send it to its ideal permanent location. A gift to a friend? A thrift shop? A box in the basement? The trash bin?

Aspire to have a 100 percent tidy and orderly working/living environment. I certainly haven't managed that yet, but I'm improving, and as I do, I'm becoming generally more effective in everything I undertake.

LIFECYCLE OF A THING

So, the chaos is gathered into your inbox, and then you periodically (daily, or no less often than weekly) go through it, item by item, processing it. The rules are that you can't put things back in the inbox. You have to dispose of it, no matter how much you don't want to.

Grab the thing on the top of the heap, and take a good, hard look at it. Then, the choices are essentially to throw it away, store it, or systematize its journey towards its final destiny.

If it can be thrown out, chuck it immediately.

If no action is required on it but you want to keep it, then file it or otherwise put it in its "forever home," as they say in the animal rescue business.

If it requires work to fulfill its destiny, determine whether you can move it along in under two minutes. If you can, just do it. If not, file it, but first put it into a system to ensure that it will move along. This could mean adding a task in a software program (project management, etc.), making a note on a calendar, or some other index into your work life that will prompt you to revisit the item.

Some Examples

Let's consider a few examples. You get the mail, recycle the obvious junk before it ever even gets to your office, address the urgent stuff, and then toss the rest of it in the inbox, along with a few other things you've accumulated. Then, when you are able to focus on processing the stuff in your inbox, here's what you do with several of the items you find there.

CD Master to Review

This will take more than two minutes, and you are currently in a cleaning frenzy, so block off an hour in your calendar when you will focus on reviewing it, and put the CD in its project folder, in your filing cabinet.

A Book

Someone gave you a book to read. You can't chuck it. You want to read it, but not right now. If you must read it by a certain deadline, write a note in your calendar or your operating work structure saying "read x book." Then, the book can go on a bookshelf, out of the way until you are ready. If you don't have a deadline, you might instead maintain a list of "To Read" items, and enter it there. That way, when you are looking for something to read, you can scan the list and be reminded that the book exists.

Then, the book is no longer cluttering your workspace, but there is a mechanism in place that will result in your reading it.

A Note to Call Someone

You find a post-it on your door saying "Call Jonathan at Berklee, 1-866-BERKLEE." You knew it wasn't urgent, so you toss it in your inbox until you have a minute.

If the call can/should be done in two minutes, make it, and then recycle the Post-it note. You might want to enter the phone number in your contact management system.

If you can't do it immediately, enter the info into your "To Call" list or your calendar, and then chuck the Post-it.

Fragment of Lyric Idea

You're giving a student a lesson, and during it, a metaphor comes to mind that you think could evolve nicely into a song. You write it down quickly on a page of your clipboard, then toss that page into the inbox. When you process it later, you decide that you're not going to use it anytime soon, but want to keep it for a rainy day when you want to write a song but no ideas are forthcoming. So, you create a Songwriting Ideas folder, and file it.

A Cactus

You receive a cactus as a gift. Send them a thank you note immediately, or if you must, add doing that as a task to your list. If you love the cactus, put it in a sunny spot. If you are neutral or negative about it, get it out of your life as soon as you can. Give it to someone else, or dispatch of it via Craigslist, Freecycle™, etc. Even compost it. But don't let it take up room and psychic space in your life any longer than it has to. If your friend asks you about it, say it caught a fungus and died.

Data Files, Email, Voicemail

Organizing your computer is similar to organizing your physical office. Systematize and empty your email and voicemail inboxes at least once per week, if not every day.

The analog to the file cabinet is your Documents folder, and in that, you should develop a system of folders that will help you easily find and retrieve your work.

Often, people complicate their lives by mixing data files in with their applications or leaving them on their desktop. These are inefficient practices, slowing down the process of finding files and complicating making backups.

Speaking of backups, is your computer kept archived? If the hard drive failed, would it be a catastrophic loss for you? Note that hard drives tend to last for about five years, and then they die. There are several ways to protect your data. Safest is an online service, such as Carbonite, CrashPlan, Gobbler, or Mozy®, which will back it up automatically. Having a remote location like that protects your data against fire and theft.

The other approach is to have a dedicated hard drive (or two) on site.

Computer files should have names that make them easy to identify, no matter who is looking at them. People send me documents related to their projects with file names such as "book.doc" or "forjonathan.doc." Not so helpful, from my perspective! I'd prefer a title like "2_MajorTonality.doc," indicating a chapter number and content descriptor. Using the underline instead of spaces makes describing the file in email more obvious. Just use one period, only before the file extension, to avoid issues of file portability.

Email

An email inbox is analogous to a physical inbox. It's not for storage, it's for collecting chaos. After you read an email and resolve it, store it in a folder, called something like "archive" or "resources," rather than having individual folders for every category. The search function of contemporary email reading software lets you organize and find files as you need to, and too many nested folders become cumbersome, especially if you ever need to change email software.

You can also set up active folders for storing communications that are still in play. Adding an _ or a @ symbol before a folder name will make it first, alphabetically, so naming a folder something like _ToDo or +_Action can help separate important, actionable communications from the general chaos of your email inbox. Empty your email inbox at least once a week, if not every day.

A great help in processing emails is to set up email rules to automatically file certain types of mass communications that you don't want to interrupt you during the day, such as promo items from vendors. A rule is a condition followed by an action. For example, if the sender's name is "clothes.com," automatically file that email in a "Sales" folder, rather than keeping it in the inbox, where you would have to click, read, and then file/delete it yourself. You might set up folders called Ads, Newsletters, and/or whatever other types of categories of communication you are certain you can skip reading but might eventually want to reference on your own terms. Let the rules file those communications automatically. Then, if you ever actually want to buy or read something, you can go into those folders and see what's current.

Email rules can save you dozens of distractions per day. Here's how rules look in the OSX Mail program. They are common in email programs.

FIG. 10.10. Email Rules in Mac OSX Mail

Voicemail

Voicemail messages are inconvenient because they force you to listen to them in real time, and retrieving them from the voicemail system can require several minutes. As you listen, write down the message details or type them into a computer file (such as your project index, or an email to yourself, or as an item in your favorite task organization program). When you hang up, transfer that information into a system: a "calls" list, or a calendar entry, or your WBS, or whatever. Ideally, you will only need to listen to a voicemail message once. If you don't have time to put it in a better system, write the details on a piece of paper, and chuck it in your inbox.

It is helpful to have as few voicemail and email accounts as possible, as the need to check each one further fragments your attention. An email program can collect mail from multiple accounts, so if you maintain an account through Gmail or Yahoo to use as a spam trap (say, for purchasing things or for social media, to avoid inevitable marketing efforts going to your business or primary personal account), you can still have the mail appear in your email software. This is more efficient than using both an email program and a Web browser to access different accounts.

For consolidating voicemail, there are services that let you forward calls and voicemail between phone accounts, or transfer voicemail messages to email (including text transcription services). These offerings continually evolve. If multiple voicemail accounts are complicating your life, consider how to reduce their number. For example, you can give a preferred voicemail phone number on the message of a phone number where you don't check the messages every day, and inform callers that you don't check it. Or, encourage people to communicate with you via email, which is far easier to manage.

Processing Objects and Vanquishing Vampires

Paper is relatively easy to organize because it fits so nicely into file cabinets and recycle bins. Larger objects, from headphones to unwanted sofas, can be more challenging to dispatch.

Obsolete gear, rarely used tools, mediocre decorations, and anything non-work-related will get in your way and reduce efficiency. That said, while I'm down on extraneous décor, personalizing your workspace creates a lens through which you can continually improve it and reconsider your processes. Keeping decorative objects that also support your work can help you build an efficient, continually improving work environment where you love to be. Ideally, your office also becomes inviting and reassuring to clients and colleagues who happen by.

Personally, I like to have instruments kicking around my office. Not only do I just like them, as objects, I like how they set the tone of the work—both for me and for the musicians/authors/music industry professionals who visit. I reached a point, a few years ago, though, when my collection got a bit out of hand. There were about forty instruments in my office, in plain sight! They completely covered my long work counter, rendering it unusable for work. That was before my Great Enlightenment, when I transformed into a much more organized person. In an extreme two-week effort, I removed everything from my office, painted it, and only moved back the best décor items—a small fraction of what had been here. The rest is stored in a few trunks, somewhere. When I feel the need to redecorate, I'll switch some things out. (It's been several years, now, and the whim has yet to strike....) When possible, decorative objects do double-duty as work support objects, like my antique Chinese bucket that also serves as my recycle bin.

The result is a much more pleasant and functional space. Objects on display are now easier to see. The effect of my office is more like a thoughtfully designed space than like a tag sale.

Decorative objects can be rotated. You don't need to display every trinket you've ever brought home from a vacation, all the time, or every framed photo. Periodically, scan the decorative items around you and ask yourself, "Do I love this?" If not, either chuck it, give it away (i.e., remove it from its current location and move it somewhere where it will make progress on its journey), or put it in storage. Whenever you get the urge, go through a box of stored items and ask yourself whether you love one of those things so much that it should come out and be with you again.

Also ask every item in your path, "Are you in my way?" If it is, relocate it.

Certain objects find their way into permanent positions even when their value doesn't warrant their presence. I call these *vampire objects*. They suck energy, but have been there for so long that they are no longer consciously perceived as a problem. Old computers, for example, are common vampire objects. They are difficult to dispose of, not only because they often can't be simply thrown away, legally, but because they might require a bit of energy before they will be ready to dispose of. What if there are still useful files on it? Or private data?

(You'd think that our stakeholders would be of more use in battling vampires, but I digress.)

Objects similarly might have sentimental value. When my grandparents sold their upholstery shop and moved out of their house, I inherited their upholstery tools (not that I will ever reupholster anything…). For a couple years after he died, I displayed my grandfather's accumulation of eighteen tack hammers in my office. Not particularly strategic, from a music project management perspective, but those hammers were a little difficult for me to eventually put away in a box. (Once I did, I never thought about them again until just now.)

Over the years, such objects accumulate. Regular purges are necessary to rid our environments of extraneous stuff, like this. Keep only the best of it. For example, I also have a peculiar button-making machine from the upholstery shop (see figure 10.11). It only takes up a small amount of room, and it is much more successful as an art object than were the eighteen hammers, so that one stays.

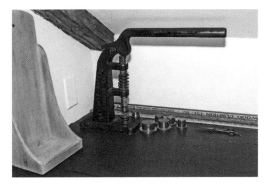

FIG. 10.11. Button Machine

Disposal Strategies

Here are some excuses for why we let certain types of objects linger, paired with strategies to help break their spell. Systematizing these things and moving them into storage can help you see things as the obtrusive junk that it is, rather than as an inevitable component of your life.

Excuse	Disposal Strategy
It has financial value.	Sell it on eBay®, Craigslist, etc. Write today's date on it, and move it out of your living space. In six months, if you haven't sold it, consider giving it away instead.
It is inconvenient to get rid of it.	On your calendar, block off the time you need to figure it out.
You might use it someday.	Write today's date on it, and put it in storage. When you happen upon it, notice how much time has passed, and then reconsider whether you are really going to ever use it again or are ready to get rid of it now.
It is part of you.	Store it away neatly. You don't have to get rid of it. Just minimize the impact that it has.

FIG. 10.12. Excuses and Strategies

Figure 10.12 is a diagram to help manage objects, particularly those that have a degree of sentimental value. If you love it and it has design or functional value, you can keep it around. If not, move it out of your immediate stomping grounds.

For each object, the big question is, why must you keep it? If you don't have a rock-solid compelling answer, send it on its way.

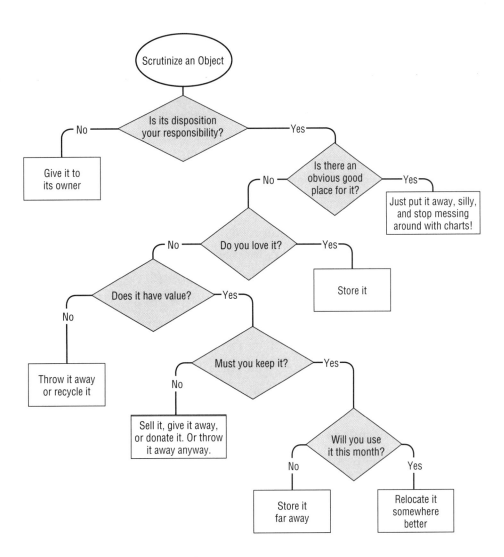

FIG. 10.13. Object Disposal Chart

Huge Messes

Sometimes, we are overcome with huge, colossal messes. They can evolve naturally, if you have certain tendencies towards chaos (as... ahem... this author will profess to suffering from). They can also happen when you move, do a major renovation, or under emergency circumstances, such as a sudden foreclosure or the passing of a relative. These situations can be overwhelming, both emotionally and physically.

While you can use many of the methods discussed above, some additional strategies can be helpful, when the scale of the situation is a bit greater than your standard messy office.

This is a scalable approach. It's presented in terms of organizing a project office, but you can use it for a completely out-of-control house or for just a chaotic closet or shelf.

Here are some tips for cleaning up a huge mess.

1. **List what belongs in your office, and only allow that in.** Begin by planning. Consider the room's function, and itemize what should be there to fulfill your work. Only put those objects in the room that functionally facilitate your work, at least to start out. The rest needs someplace else to go, particularly if you have hoarding tendencies. Save adding purely decorative items for a later effort.

2. **Get the right infrastructure.** Consider whether you have the right supporting furniture for your needs: all the essential office items discussed, plus any furniture for more specialized work (outboard gear cabinet, music stands, dog bed, piano, etc.). Examine your list of the stuff that needs to reside in your office, and consider where it will go, in order to be out of your way. Instead of your electric bass living on a stand on the floor, can you store/display it on the wall with a bracket? Maintain a list of what infrastructure items you need to improve your office's functionality.

   Also consider what you need to facilitate long-term storage and the cleanup effort itself. For long-term storage, big plastic bins are helpful, as are additional file cabinets and storage cupboards. (Yes, I bring home interesting old trunks from the dump too....) For the cleanup effort, contractor bags are sturdier than usual garbage bags, and they are a big help in major cleanouts.

   A five-bin approach can be helpful. Get five large boxes (or other large containers), and label them Trash, Storage, Donate, Sell, Keep. Then one at a time, put each object in the appropriate bin. When the bin is full, move it to its best location. Trash goes with your other trash. Donate goes to your car, or some interim place where it will wait for you to go on a donation run. Sell goes where you can store it until you have the time to figure out how to sell it. Storage goes to your attic/basement/barn/etc. Keep also goes where you put Storage, until you clear out enough space where you can put it back.

   Consider renting a dumpster for a very major cleanup effort where there is a lot of trash. That might let you accomplish more by cutting down travel time, or by avoiding the constraint of your usual trash storage area's capacity.

3. **Start with a blank slate.** Begin by emptying the space that you are trying to transform. This lets you dissociate the mess from the space

and get to a point of order as quickly as possible. First, move the mess out, then organize the infrastructure, then add only the appropriate contents. Dimensions of the mess you are not ready to address can get boxed up and moved to the basement, for a while. By emptying the space, you disrupt the patterns and habits of the old regime, and overcome the sense that there is an inevitability to the current catastrophe.

Get to the underlying effective infrastructure (walls, critical furniture), and then have an early vision of what success looks like. The dysfunctional system needs a shock, so shake it up. Paint it! Get to a clean, ordered, pristine place, and then address disposing of the contents as a separate effort.

4. **Plan to devote significant time to major cleanup efforts.** It might take a weekend to completely reorganize a room or an office—more, if painting/construction is involved. Picking away at it for half an hour here or there might not work, because you won't be accomplishing something significant enough to change your habits and make you want to protect it.

5. **Break it down.** Consider how much time you can truly devote to the cleanup effort, and don't give yourself an impossible amount of work to do, during it. Cleanups are projects, and project management approaches will help you complete them successfully. As a micro-iteration, you might start small, and time yourself organizing just a few cubic feet. Then, you will be better able to estimate the duration of the whole task.

6. **Do one room at a time, not the whole house.** If your whole house is a disaster, designate one room to make perfectly orderly, so that you can escape the chaos. Then do another room. Then another. Perhaps, start with your bedroom, so that you can retreat to an orderly place. Then do your office, where you spend most of your awake time. Then the bathroom, then the kitchen.

It might help to temporarily designate one room as the house's inbox. Gather all the chaos just there, removing it from other rooms, and get those rooms in shape. Then, address just that one fiasco point.

7. **Start by doing a quick sweep where you get rid of just large trash, rather than starting with the closest object.** If you spot an empty pizza box or a broken chair, just grab it and chuck it. Get rid of obvious trash as quickly as you can. This will help you maneuver around the smaller stuff, which will require more careful consideration. If, in your cleanup effort, you spot any food that is even slightly questionable, throw it away immediately. Food poisoning is a horrendous way to be ill, and it is never worth the risk.

8. **Play music.** Music makes cleanup efforts more fun. Put on an album, and force yourself to focus on the work for its entire length, before taking a break.

9. **Get help.** Big cleanups can be miserable, depressing jobs, as well as very physically demanding. Friends can offer moral support. Additionally, people to help you move things can make a big difference. In addition to saving you the physical effort of hauling a lot of stuff, managing people can help you to focus and persist in making progress on the work. Hire a couple high school kids for ten bucks an hour, and make them do the heavy lifting. Or, if you can afford it, hire a professional cleaning service.
   Much of the work in a major cleaning/reorganizing endeavor is psychological, and just that is exhausting. Delegating some of the physical work can help you get through it.

10. **Forgive yourself for getting rid of things of value.** Donate what you can, but don't avoid throwing things away at the expense of your psychic health. Order has value too. If a mess is really out of hand, your first priority is to restore it to a livable state. Making a financial donation to a conservation charity might help you feel that the karmic scales are coming back to balance, when you are in a position where you really need to throw a large amount of stuff away. But your priority must be to get your life back. If going into this, you know that there are some items that might have worth to someone else, deliberately manage its donation. Some organizations might pick up furniture and other items, but they might only do "pickup runs" in your area just once a month, so this needs to be coordinated.

11. **Schedule a party.** Invite people to a party in two months from when you commit to a major cleanup effort. This will help force you to keep at it and to prioritize your efforts in creating a positive and efficient living space. It's particularly a good idea to throw a party after you move, to force you to get out of your boxes and arrive at a new semblance of life for yourself. A potluck is a good idea, to reduce the amount of work and cost you'll need to expend, during what is likely a difficult time in your life. The fun of it will do you good.

Once an area is organized, protect it. Don't let even one little thing get out of place. The goal is to spread the new wave of organization outward, rather than letting the old habits of allowing chaos to creep back in.

A major cleanup effort is a project, so manage it like one. Write out the scope of your intensions, with clear objectives. Create a mess breakdown structure, dividing up your catastrophe into manageable components. Organize it based on thoughtful time estimates. Anticipate risks, and delegate tasks. Resource it appropriately.

This is how to make anything succeed.

CLOSING THOUGHTS

Some of us romanticize the benefits of life among the chaos of many intense objects, all in easy reach and plain view. We say that we like to have our stuff close at hand, and the skyscrapers of towering paperwork become invisible, after a while. If we measure our productivity objectively, however, the data shows that people work more efficiently and with less stress when their environment is orderly.

If your goal is to minimize the time you spend switching gears, mentally, and doing perfunctory and unnecessary tasks, such as searching for important papers, then living and operating in a precise, organized environment will help you focus on the important activities that only you can do.

It's an ongoing effort. I certainly am far from perfect in this regard, but I know that as I improve at this dimension of life, many things become easier and better.

PRACTICE

Vampire Analysis and Removal Matrix

Sit at your desk, scan your surroundings, and list the ten closest objects to you that you haven't used for the past two weeks—objects that make a more negative than positive contribution to your life. Why are they haunting you? Do you see a broken flute you bought at a garage sale for only $5, or an artifact from a failed romance, an obsolete computer, or even toxic waste, like an old can of paint or a burned-out fluorescent light bulb? Create a chart, and for each vampire object, list the following information:

1. When it was last used

2. When you next expect to use it

3. Where its ideal location should be and any strategies you have to get it there (donate, sell, throw out, etc.)

4. A rating of how easy it is to dispose of, from 1 (easy) to 10 (hard).

Confirmed	Vampire Object	Date Last Used	Date Next Used	Ideal Location/ Disposal Strategy	Ease of Disposition

FIG. 10.13. Vampire Removal Matrix

Then, analyze the objects for "Date Next Used," and if it is not within the next month or so, mark that it is a confirmed vampire. Then, dispatch all the items on this list that are confirmed in order of easiest to most difficult to move along. When you have rid yourself of all vampires, make a new list. When you can, expand your vision beyond your project office walls. Keep going until the entire, infinite universe is tidy and organized. Wave, when you get to my office.

Organization Project

Choose a physical area of your life, and organize it. Ideally, this will be your office, but it could be just part of your office or another dimension of your life, such as your desk or your supply closet, or your attic, or the room where you teach private students. First, consider the purpose of this space, and itemize what belongs there. Then, remove everything, so that you can start with a blank slate. Then, put it back together, so that it operates with ideal efficiency.

CHAPTER 11

Creativity and Problem Solving

In this book, we have been looking at very methodical, predictable approaches to work, designed to uncover 100 percent of issues associated with work, cost requirements, risks, and so on. The majority of these approaches have been no-nonsense, business-first, predictable, and assessable. They are time tested, well researched, and fairly well respected. They will predictably yield high quality results.

A limitation of many of these prescriptive, methodical tools is that their results are based upon the quality of the work previously done—*deductive* reasoning, where actions are based on the evidence at hand. Consider, for example, using a work breakdown structure in risk analysis. We have our list of deliverables, and then we can use a risk breakdown structure to methodically consider various dimensions of our product and areas of likely risk. What if, however, our WBS or RBS is somewhat incomplete? What if something off the wall happens? The deductive process might not yield something important. Robots getting tricked by humans is one of the great recurring themes of science fiction, and we need to make sure we're on the right side of that equation.

And so, we now must embrace some chaos.

In this chapter, we will focus on more out-of-the-box approaches to work, such as encouraging brainstorming, which might reveal possibilities that relying too heavily on the data in front of us might exclude. These are the techniques of creative problem solving. This is not to say that we haven't been using tools creatively up to this point. Rather, we will be focusing on techniques that unleash the power of our subconscious senses of intuition in hopes that it will yield additional value.

OBJECTIVES

By the end of the chapter, you will be able to:

- define and clarify problems

- generate many potential solutions to problems via many brainstorming techniques

- evaluate and prioritize possible solutions

- implement solutions into your project management approach

- organize reusable solutions as a rules and procedures handbook or an FAQ

PUTTING CREATIVITY TO WORK

Musicians often have an intuitive sense of the many different ways that the brain works. That's among the key reasons why many of us advocate for music to be included in general education. Few other fields deliberately combine the physical, conscious, subconscious, pragmatic, and emotional parts of the brain. To a musician, it is simply common sense that preparing for a concert involves practicing scales, studying formal structures, physical exercise to create muscle memory, channeling spiritual inspiration, historical research, meditating, caring for instruments, taking a break, and living a full life, all to solve the common problem of achieving expressive depth. That's how we roll, over here.

Bringing this same kind of mindset to project management and problem solving might seem forced, but it's not, really. The complicating factor is that an individual in a predicament is likely to settle on the first likely solution that comes to mind. That's a survival skill: the shark is coming towards us, so we swim away in a panic, without weighing other possibilities first.

Individuals sometimes achieve success that way, but the universe has a different model for achieving success: launching many possibilities, and then seeing which ones gain traction—more like the musician's whole-brain-investment approach. While it might seem tragic that just one out of a thousand hatched sea turtle eggs might grow up to become an adult sea turtle, if they all survived, in short time, the oceans would have only sea turtles in it, and soon after that, even the sea turtles wouldn't exist because their food would have been consumed. Their numbers would keep increasing until their resources ran out, and then they would die.

The system is a bit brutal, from the perspective of 999 out of 1,000 sea turtles, but ultimately, effective, and the same approach is essentially effective in problem solving generally. In truth, while swimming away from the shark seems like the best thing to do, sharks can swim faster than people can. Punching it in the eye or gills might actually be better ideas. (Punching it in the nose is actually not likely to be effective, in the case of a shark attack, but thanks for suggesting it.)

Ideally, when confronted with a problem, we want to generate many potential solutions to it, and then methodically determine which is likely to be most effective. That's the one we should go with. The principle is not unlike cross-footing in accounting, where you test your work by approaching it from different directions. The multitude of approaches is healthy for the whole system.

Again, musicians do this automatically, in certain contexts. Give them a theme, and they'll improvise endless variations. For whatever reasons, when those same musicians are confronted with non-music-related problems, such as a club owner refusing to give them a gig, they tend not to consider a multitude of potential solutions. They'll go into fight/flight mode, and instantaneously execute the first idea that seems good enough. Swim away, or punch the shark in the nose, rather than consider alternatives that might be more effective, despite being less orthodox.

Creativity is often associated with artistic creation rather than generally with all dimensions of life. However, since the 1940s or so, there has been some good research designed to capture the same fire that artists have seen as self-evident, and apply it more universally, such as in business, and thus, in project management. Revolutionary thinkers such as advertising executive Alex Osborne (who coined the term "brainstorming") and Dr. Sidney J. Parnes have developed formal systems for creative problem solving that slow down these processes, and formalize them, and turn them into ways of addressing problems that similarly reach the different dimensions of thinking we are capable of.

PROBLEM-SOLVING SYSTEMS AND TOOLS

The architecture of problem solving is actually much like that of project management. The problem is like the project vision: the ultimate reason for the work that is to follow. Then there is a bunch of planning that accompanies the solution, and then the solution gets implemented. Some approaches to project management actually equate projects with problems, and begin with the question, "What problem does your project solve?"

There are essentially four stages of the problem-solving lifecycle:

1. Problem Identification

2. Solution Generation

3. Solution Evaluation and Refinement

4. Implementation

Just like project management, there are many systems that have been developed based on this, each with their own products for sale, logos, and t-shirts. One of the best is "Creative Problem Solving" or CPS, based on the work of Osborne and Parnes, and many of the ideas discussed here have roots in their research.

Let's consider each step of problem resolution, and some of the tools and techniques used to complete them.

PROBLEM IDENTIFICATION

Problem solving begins by identifying and articulating exactly what the issue is that you are trying to address. A *problem* is a circumstance that requires attention.

In CPS, they like to use positively constructed prompts to help clarify what the issues are, and to help you hone in on exactly what the issue is that you need to resolve, suggest asking:

I wish...

Wouldn't it be great if...

The answers to these questions launch and frame the whole process, just like our project vision statement framed the project management process. The goal is to develop an awareness of the problem, to define exactly what we are trying to resolve, and to uncover the essential desire to be fulfilled by the solution.

"I wish the band was tighter." "Wouldn't it be great if our concerts were sold out?" "I wish that we could record more easily." "Wouldn't it be great if we had a full-time bass player?"

Asking the simple question, "What do you wish for?" can be a profound start to a discovery process.

The overall process is:

1. Someone has a vague sense that things aren't right. "The band just isn't going well."

2. They get asked, "Well, what do you wish was different?" (perhaps by a helpful project manager). To this, they answer, "Eh, I wish we just had more momentum and were getting more gigs."

3. We drill down, trying to uncover a more specific articulation of the problem.

When you arrive at the problem you want to focus on, write it as the introduction to any exercises that follow, to maintain focus. "I wish we were getting more gigs."

Five Whys

The *five whys* approach to problem identification comes from quality control procedures developed by the Toyota Motor Company. It digs deep in one spot, in order to help clarify what the problem might be.

Simply, when confronted with a problem, ask the question "why?" At the answer, ask "why" again. Keep doing this until you get an answer that seems right, or perhaps indicates one person's responsibility, or strikes a clear nerve in the person you are interrogating, indicating you have struck close to the truth—to the heart of what the problem really is.

Here's how it might work.

Problem: I wish we were getting more gigs.

Why aren't we getting more gigs?

> **Answer 1:** Club owners just don't return our calls.

Why?

> **Answer 2:** They don't think we're right for their clubs.

Why?

> **Answer 3:** Because they have a distorted idea of what we're capable of.

Why?

> **Answer 4:** Because our website isn't easy enough for them to see how we fit.

Why?

> **Answer 5:** Because we're a bunch of @!!*& amateurs at Internet marketing, and don't really know how to design this right!!!

Possible Clarification of the Problem: We need a more effective website!

Sometimes, you will need a greater or fewer number of "why" rounds to arrive at a problem's core, but five is often about right.

Whereas simply asking someone what they wish for is likely to feel like a healing and vibrant inspiration session, the five whys is useful for helping people confront ugly truths, which they might be avoiding. It can come across as confrontational. And you might find that this technique leads you around in circles, too, if the person you are questioning doesn't want to play along. That can be revealing, too....

In any case, the five whys can help you uncover some elusive truths—clarifying problems, and sometimes revealing solutions. It can also lead you to adopt a single, incorrect conclusion! If you keep this potential risk in mind, it can be a useful technique. Repeating it a few times, from different angles, might give you more rounded and accurate results.

SOLUTION GENERATION

The solution generation phase is where the true creative energy is unleashed. Here, the goal is to create a very large number of possible answers to the question:

"In what ways might I do..."

There are four things to point out about this sentence. First, notice the word "ways." It's plural, designed to inspire multiple possibilities. The word "might" implies that we are not committing to a certain direction, as the goal here is to open wide the gates to multiple possibilities, and not settle on one. "I" clarifies that we are taking responsibility for the upcoming action. And finally, "do" clarifies that we are going to be taking action, here.

The goal here is *divergent* thinking: the creation of a very long list of potential solutions, for evaluation later. Of course, it is essential to evaluate all ideas. But by isolating the idea generation phase from the idea evaluation phase, we are encouraging the creation of a greater number of possibilities.

An essential process of solution generation is brainstorming. Traditional brainstorming is the generation of a large list of ideas. There are many ways that brainstorming can be conducted, ranging from ultimately free to closely constrained. It can be done by one person alone or by a group; generally, around six people is considered an ideal. There are some generally accepted ground rules for maximizing how productive brainstorming sessions can be, and in group situations, it is helpful if they are enforced by a facilitator.

Some guidelines for brainstorming:

1. A great quantity of ideas are generated. Hundreds, even.

2. Ideas are all written down, sometimes by a designated scribe.

3. Criticism of ideas is deferred to a later stage of the process, and absent from the idea generation process.

4. Ideas are framed in positive terms; participant communication is positive and encouraging of each other and of the project.

5. Far-fetched ideas are particularly encouraged.

6. Building ideas off of other ideas is encouraged.

7. Particularly creative or extroverted participants should make space for others to participate fully.

Every idea is recorded, transcribed without judgment. The idea is to get a vast, multi-faceted, well-rounded set of possible approaches to addressing the issue. Outlandish ideas are encouraged. While off-the-wall ideas in themselves might not indicate well-targeted solutions, their presence can result in other ideas that will be effective, even if those other ideas are in reaction against the crazy one. Sometimes, viewing opposite solutions to what will work can help us see an unusual effective solution.

Here's a scenario. A band is rehearsing a song, and it isn't coming together. They decide to have a brainstorming session about why. It might go like this:

Question: Why do we sound so awful playing this song?

Keyboard:	It's not gelling.
Vocalist:	Bass and drums don't sound like a cohesive unit.
Bass:	Drummer can't keep time.
Drums:	Bass player is an idiot.
Bass:	Oh yeah? [Dumps drink on drummer's head and goes home.]

Better, if we keep to the rule of always phrasing everything as a positive. Remember the tip about framing the problem in a positive light:

Question: In what ways might we make our performance of this song better?

Keyboard:	Find a way to make it gel.
Drums:	Bass and drums find a way to sound more like a unit, perhaps physically facing each other.
Guitar:	Schedule rehearsals only on days when I'm not playing so much beforehand.
Vocalist:	Simplify the groove.

Drums:	Speed it up.
Bass:	Slow it down.
Drums:	Simplify the keyboard comping, and feature the guitar more, maybe more guitar volume.
Keyboard:	Try a guitar distortion pedal, to give his solo prominence and lead the groove.
Drums:	Replace guitar strings? Or amp?

At this point, the guitarist might have a realization. He'll say, "No, my strings are fine, and I only have one amp. But my wah-wah pedal might sound great on this!" None of the cluster of suggestions regarding the guitar sound might be exactly correct, as the guitarist knows that the strings and his instrument are really fine for the occasion. But he might consider some related solution, based on other types of feedback.

Here's another brainstorming session, this time on a potential theme to tie a collection of songs together.

Question: What theme should we use for our next album?

Keyboard:	Love
Bass:	Unrequited love
Drums:	Hate
Guitar:	Unrequited hate
Vocalist:	Lost freedom
Bass:	Penguins
Drums:	Unrequited hatred of penguins
Guitar:	A journey through an Arctic wasteland, confronting the freedom we've always been searching for, but now wondering if we'd be better off reassessing our life priorities and choosing mundane love instead of this abyss of hope.

Progress! Yes, the penguins were a silly idea, but in reaction to it, the others found a concept that could serve as a grandiose, sweeping idea that seems compelling enough to carry a major creative work.

Different personality types will tend to contribute differently to brainstorming sessions. Some will suggest similar ideas to what has come up before, evolving from them. Some will deliberately suggest sharply contrasting ideas, usurping the direction it is going. Some will be inclined to synthesize other ideas. Someone will say a lot of fluffy ideas, and then someone else might say just one that will become the obvious solution. A variety of these thinking types makes for a productive session.

While the facilitator of a brainstorming session should be careful not to close down the spirit of collaboration, he or she can prune or guide it, requesting more tangible concepts, or more customer-benefit-focused concepts, or otherwise directing the ideas.

Tracking all the ideas can be challenging, and it is helpful to have a dedicated scribe, whose job is simply to write everything down, preferably on a large whiteboard, large enough so that everyone can see it. Keeping it visible will help spur new ideas and avoid repeats.

Some people are more creative in private. After a public brainstorming session, you can type up the ideas, distribute them, and then solicit an additional round via email.

Brainstorming can be useful for generating many ideas and for building a cohesive team. However, social relationships and psychological tendencies can come into play during these sessions that actually serve to reduce certain types of creativity, rather than increase them. For example, if you have a team member who is particularly good at generating ideas but also very polite, he or she might hold back, so as not to overly dominate the discussion. The net result in this circumstance is that potentially good ideas are not being articulated. Also, some people might be relatively shy and tend to avoid contributing the outlandish ideas that are often the sparks for the best solution-finding.

Seeing brainstorming as a series of processes, both private and public, can help with this. Also, brainstorming in computer chat systems can help unleash more ideas. This can reduce some of the logistical hindrances of a brainstorming session, such as the need for one person to write fast enough to capture the ideas of a verbose group.

This is a very free form of brainstorming. Let's look at some more structured ones.

The 6-3-5 Method

The 6-3-5 method is a structured brainstorming technique designed (by Professor Bernd Rohrbach) to provide more connected results, and with greater participation from everyone in the group. The numbers stand for:

- 6 people in the session
- 3 ideas
- 5 minutes

A chart is constructed that looks like this.

PROBLEM: WHAT MIGHT WE DO TO GET MORE GIGS?			
	1	2	3
Forrest			
Mike			
Sue			
Raj			
Merlin			
Don			

Everyone gets a copy, and underlines his or her own name. The five-minute timer starts, and then everyone writes just three ideas next to their name only. The round ends when the time is up or everyone is ready to move on. After round 1, Sue's sheet might look like this:

PROBLEM: WHAT MIGHT WE DO TO GET MORE GIGS?			
	1	2	3
Forrest			
Mike			
Sue	Release a recording	Redo the website	Volunteer
Raj			
Merlin			
Don			

Similarly, at the end of round 1, Forrest's chart looks like this:

PROBLEM: WHAT MIGHT WE DO TO GET MORE GIGS?			
	1	2	3
Forrest	Win competition	Do TV commercials	Network
Mike			
Sue			
Raj			
Merlin			
Don			

Then, they pass their sheets to the next person on the list. Sue gives hers to Raj. Forrest gives his list to Mike, Don gives his list to Forrest. The timer starts again, and then everyone writes down an idea based on the ideas that came before it. At the end of round 2, Raj has added a comment to each of Sue's answers.

PROBLEM: WHAT MIGHT WE DO TO GET MORE GIGS?			
	1	2	3
Forrest			
Mike			
Sue	Release a recording	Redo the website	Volunteer
Raj	Include a cover song, to get more Google hits	Get a Facebook page for the band	Play for free at friends' parties
Merlin			
Don			

After round 3, Sue's sheet might look like this:

PROBLEM: WHAT MIGHT WE DO TO GET MORE GIGS?			
	1	2	3
Forrest			
Mike			
Sue	Release a recording	Redo the website	Volunteer
Raj	Include a cover song, to get more Google hits	Get a Facebook fan page for the band	Play for free at friends' parties
Merlin	Jazz standards album	Improve search engine optimization for words like "party" and "wedding"	Give out coupons, when we play for free
Don			

...and Forrest's looks like this:

PROBLEM: WHAT MIGHT WE DO TO GET MORE GIGS?			
	1	2	3
Forrest	Win competition	Do TV commercials	Network
Mike	Battle of the bands	Get on cable TV	Do band Facebook page
Sue	Host our own concert series	Make a video for YouTube	Send email to everyone we know advertising next gig
Raj			
Merlin			
Don			

In six rounds and half an hour, 108 ideas will be generated by this process. Everyone has an equal voice, and the ideas are developed.

You can certainly vary the parameters here: 7 participants, 4 ideas, 8 minutes; 10 ideas, 5 participants, 1 minute. It's an easy, structured way to perform team brainstorming.

SCAMPER

SCAMPER is another structured brainstorming technique (attributed to Bob Eberle and Alex Osborne of the Creative Problem Solving Institute). In this checklist-style framework, the brainstorming session is guided to focus on coming up with ideas that are based on types of logical deviations.

SCAMPER is an acronym, and you'll see variations of exactly what it stands for:

S = Substitute

C = Combine (or Change)

A = Adapt (or Add)

M = Magnify (or Modify or Minimize or Mega/Mini)

P = Put to Other Uses

E = Eliminate

R = Rearrange (or Reverse)

In round 1 of a SCAMPER process, potential solutions to the issue are considered with emphasis on the principle of "Substitute." What are some of the potential substitutions in our scenario that could happen?

Again, let's take "What might we do to get more gigs?" as an example problem. Considering the big picture of getting gigs, consider how *substituting* one idea for another might lead to some possible solutions.

Substitute:

What if we *substitute* the type of gigs we have been looking for?

- Instead of just wedding gigs, we might start trying to get sweet sixteen parties, or bar gigs, or clog dances.

- Instead of paying gigs, we might try getting some volunteer gigs.

- Instead of "gigs," which are one-off jobs, we could try getting recurring jobs, like opening for a band on tour, or being the Friday night house band for a club.

- Instead of "us," we might consider teaming up with another artist or band that would be more of a draw.

So, we are taking the concept of "substitution" and applying it to all dimensions of our current gig-getting mechanism.

Then, round 2, we brainstorm considering the word "Combine."

Combine:

- We might occasionally combine our band with the church choir, to get more visibility.

- We might combine our offer to play a wedding reception with an offer for just Forrest to play solo classical guitar at the cocktail hour.

And so on.

SCAMPER is good at uncovering logical connections that might have been previously elusive.

Forced Connections

In forced-connection brainstorming, we juxtapose ideas or attributes of our own scenario that might not obviously go together, to see if they inspire any insights. It is like SCAMPER except that we provide our own categories of topic to consider.

For example, we might chart a number of issues we know are related to our work, and then see how they interrelate to our work. Say, we can think of four dimensions of our work that might affect how to get more gigs: our booking agent, pricing, repertoire, and website. Start by making a list of the essential issues that seem to relate to this problem. (Coming up with this list might the result of another brainstorming session.)

Then, chart them in rows and columns, look at each intersection point, and brainstorm what solutions come to mind, based on each pair. It's similar to what we did earlier with the risk analysis chart (figure 7.3).

Problem: How might we get more gigs?

	Repertoire	Website
Booking Agent	Is our agent enthusiastic about our music?	Is our agent's contact info on the site?
Pricing	Should we pay for the rights to record more covers?	Should we pay more for a better site?

There are various iterations of this technique of forcing connections. One that works well if you have a lot of criteria is the *Circle of Opportunity*, designed by Dr. Eugene O'Loughlin, which involves setting up a circle, with numbers on it, like a clock. At each number, you write down a feature of the problem you are trying to solve.

Start with the list of problem features.

Problem: How might we get more gigs?

Problem Features:

Band	Fans	What's fun?
Repertoire	Wedding Planners	Business Savvy
Website	Booking Agent	Performance Vibe
PR Kit	Price	Network

Then set these features around the clock, to look like this:

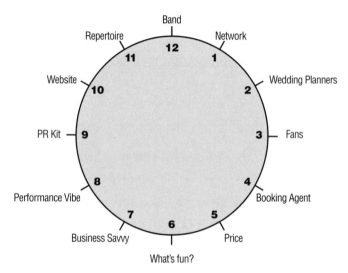

FIG. 11.1. Problem Features

Then, instead of looking at all 144 possible pairs of criteria (which would take a long time!), randomly choose two numbers between 1 and 12. You could use twelve-sided dice, or tear up twelve scraps of paper and put them in a hat, or scratch off the item at the 1:00 position and roll two six-sided dice twice. But somehow, get two random numbers from all the available positions, and then consider the terms. Say that the first random pair of numbers we first choose are 3 and 11, Fans and Repertoire.

Consider the problem statement: What might we do to get more gigs, related to fans and repertoire?"

Then, ask two questions. First, what issues does this combination bring to light?

Fans and Repertoire

Do fans like our repertoire?

Do they know what our repertoire is?

Does our repertoire match their needs?

Are we keeping current with what our fans are into?

Then ask, "Do these issues relate to our problem?"

> Are we not getting gigs because our music is out of touch with what people want to hear when we play the gigs we've been trying to get?

Try another round. Say, 4 and 7: Booking Agent and Business Savvy. What does this combination bring to light?

Booking Agent and Business Savvy:

> Do we need a booking agent?

> Do we have the business savvy to get a booking agent?

> Does our booking agent have the business savvy to get us better gigs?

> Is our booking agent coming across as too aggressive a business guy to talk to the places where we want to get gigs?

And then, "How does this affect our problem?" All of these answers are self evident, in terms of how they might relate.

Forced connections are a way to look into your process, to see what flaws of connection might exist. These juxtapositions of concepts can bring to light ideas that you might not have considered previously. Again, looking at problems from multiple directions can help you maintain the quality and control of how you interpret data.

Cause and Effect Diagramming

Another way of considering the current workings of your project is the *cause and effect diagram*, also called an *Ishikawa* or *fishbone* diagram. It accomplishes similar goals as forced connections, but is a little more methodical and builds more related kinds of connections, similar to 6-3-5 brainstorming. Originally, this approach comes from automobile manufacturing, where it is often used in quality control. Like the five whys, it can help identify problems, as well as solutions.

In this fish-like chart, we consider various dimensions of our predicament, trying to isolate all factors that resulted in something smelling, well, fishy.

Start with the problem, in the head of the fish, and the spine of the fish stretching across the page, leading to it. The "spine" represents all the events that contributed to the circumstance.

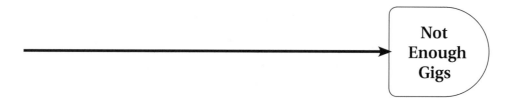

FIG. 11.1. Cause and Effect 1: Articulate the Problem

Then, the main causes of the problem are indicated using lines pointing to the spine. You might have some causes in mind, but to prime the brainstorming pump, you might decide to use standard categorical labels, such as Music, People, Processes, Objects. These are the primary ribs of the fish. You can have more than four ribs, if additional categories seem relevant.

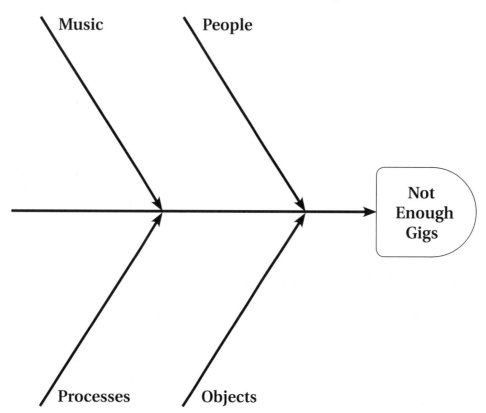

FIG. 11.2. Cause and Effect 2: Categories of Factors

Then, brainstorm the contributing factors to these main causes, and point to the ribs. And so on. It stops looking like a proper fish at this point, but it can be useful, nonetheless, in tracing the contributing factors of your problem.

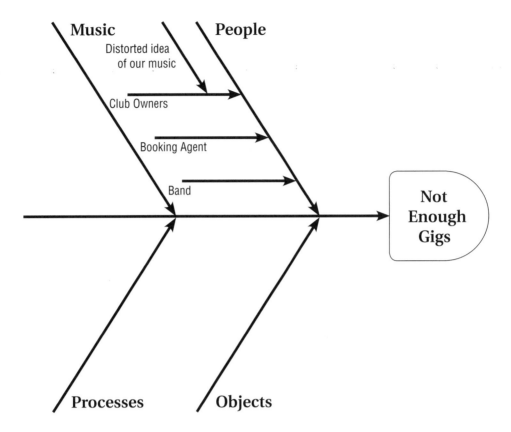

FIG. 11.3. Cause and Effect: Issues Related to Categories

Mind Mapping

Mind mapping is a creative diagramming technique that helps clarify our thoughts. Similar to the five whys and fishbone analysis, it helps drill down deeply into a problem, and like brainstorming, it can cast a relatively wide net. It is very flexible. You might use it when trying to get your head around a complex body of information, like planning a creative work, or starting a business. It can be useful as a preliminary step for planning a work breakdown structure.

Thought diagramming has been around since Ancient Greece, and maybe earlier, in various forms. Our work breakdown structure chart is a kind of hierarchical thought-diagramming technique. Building on the simple tree diagram, Tony Buzan codified a popular approach that incorporates colors and graphics, which add more creative and sensory dimensions to the process, and it has spawned many related products (such as software) and systems. It's flexible, though, and you should feel free to adapt it to your own sensibility. Some of the Buzan's essential practices:

Guidelines for Mind Mapping:

- State the problem in the center of the page, and enclose it in a shape.

- Itemize the large-scale component parts or ideas related to the main problem, drawn using thick, curved lines, each labeled in a different color.

- Labels can be text or graphics.

- From each leg, draw sub-legs that indicate component parts, drilling down into ever-finer detail, with ever-narrowing lines. Maintain the unique color for each tree, but also use color to make further logical distinctions, if it is helpful.

- If you see two inter-connected items that you want to link, use a broken line.

- Group related ideas that you want to consider by drawing a cloud around them.

Here is a completed mind map I drew when I was planning this very chapter. My purpose here was to get all my thoughts down, regarding the various topics and subtopics. It's not organized sequentially, or grouped in a way that ultimately translated perfectly into the resulting chapter, but at that point in the authoring process, I found it helpful.

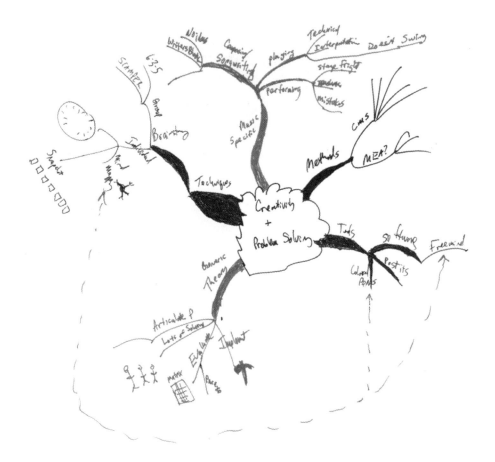

FIG. 11.4. Mind Map of This Chapter

Sure, it's a mess! It's essentially my focused doodles, late at night, sitting in bed with a few colored pens (accompanied by my snoring dog and reading wife) and a clipboard, while I tried to wrap my head around what was an elusive constellation of ideas, for me. Real life, man! The point here is drilling down and figuring stuff out. Many software products exist that will let you create graphically slick mind maps, such as iMindMap, created by MindMap's creator.

Personally, I usually prefer scribbling with my pens, because I can draw my own pictures without being limited by the software's constraints. My resulting images are unique and memorable. However, it is also nice to be able to present something to others more legibly, so iMindMap is useful for demonstration, such as the one that follows.

To create a mind map, begin by articulating the problem in the center of a page.

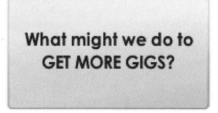

FIG. 11.5. Mind Map: The Problem

Then draw the main components of the problem leading out from it, in thick, curved lines, each in a different color (showing up gray, here, so use your imagination).

FIG. 11.6. Mind Map: Main Components

Next, develop each of these legs in finer detail. Add pictures, in order to draw more dimensions of your brain into the process, and thus create more ideas.

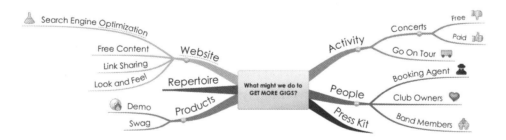

FIG. 11.7. Mind Map: Details with Icons

One nice thing about software, vs. pens, is that you can edit the diagram, if you want to change things around. This can make it easier to draw lines and clouds to connect and group related ideas.

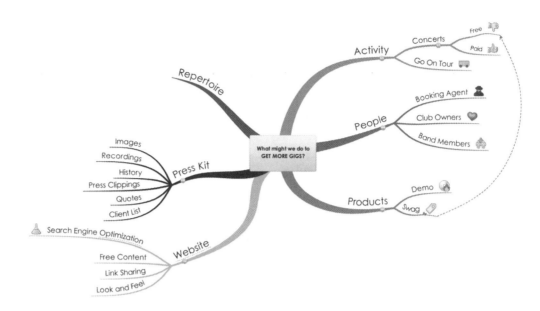

FIG. 11.8. Mind Map: iMindMap Software Enables Easy Rearrangement

Here's another one of my hand-drawn mind maps, this time, for the chapter on contracts, insurance, and so on. One might argue that my own cheesy diagrams are no better than the cheesy icons that come with mind-mapping software. It's generally faster to do a quick doodle that is exactly what you have in mind than it is to search a computer library for the right dingbat, so that's another reason why some people prefer the hand-drawn approach—even though your average first grader could probably come up with something that looks a bit more polished than my own drawings....

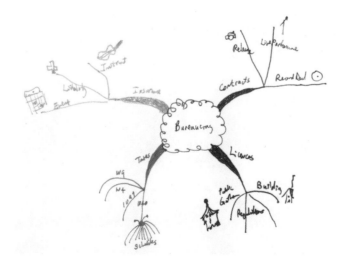

FIG. 11.9. Mind Map of Bureaucracy Chapter

Mind mapping is a convenient way to make sense of the clutter of ideas banging around inside of your head. Even if it doesn't lead to any actual solutions, the process is often a helpful intermediate step between idea generation and solution evaluation. It also helps clarify the central issue and its contributing factors.

Snapshots

Another technique for organizing a large number of creative ideas is to lay it out so that you can see a snapshot of the project, all at once. I sometimes do this following mind mapping or other brainstorming sessions, particularly when the problem I am addressing is to make sense of a large creative work, such as a book, lesson, composition, or album.

To create a snapshot of a complex idea, write each topic or idea on an individual sheet of paper, and lay it out on a long counter or on the floor of a room, so that you can see the whole work before you at once, as if it is a snapshot. Here's a picture (in fact, a photographic snapshot!) of my over-arching snapshot I made while I was writing this chapter. Each page is a topic, pulled from the mind map. In addition, there are some other add-ons here: books I want to remember, print-outs of Word files that contain related writing that I want to incorporate, and so on. Now, the ideas from the mind map are sequenced. When it's all laid out, I will stand back, look at the whole work at once, and consider issues of sequence, comprehensibility, relative timing, and so forth. I move the paper around, make notes on them about content or other things I want to remember, and occasionally tear parts of pages apart and redistribute the fragments. You can see the mind map of this chapter in the bottom left. You are there!

FIG. 11.10. Snapshot of This Chapter

When starting a new project, if I am just beginning and don't really have many ideas, I sometimes begin by laying out blank pages that in total represent the right amount of content for that work. For an online lesson, I will start with twenty blank pages, as I know that I want my ultimate deliverable to be somewhere between eighteen and thirty pages long, and twenty is a good place to begin. Next, I'll fill in certain dimensions of it that I know it must include. For online lessons, the first page is an introduction, the last page is a recap, and before the last page is the assignment. Often, I have an interview on page 2. There will predictably be one discussion and two or three assignments. I will label these pages, where they are likely to occur. Then, I can see that instead of twenty pages of content to develop, I really only have to write about twelve, to start. So, the process is more manageable, and I am also less likely to forget to write one of the standard pages.

As an editor, I use this technique to untangle large blocks of writing that are either wandering or have a lot of redundancy. This is common in live interview transcripts, where the topics discussed aren't in an order that makes sense for a final presentation. I will print out the draft and spread it out like this so that I can see it as a snapshot. Then, I'll read it, and in the margins, summarize the topics being discussed. Finally, I'll look at my margin notes and construct a major revision based on that. It's a way to escape the ordinary linearity in which text tends to come.

- As a composer, I often spread out music to see a snapshot of the work's over-arching form. I can fast-forward through the piece in my mind very quickly and consider the overall proportions and dramatic narrative.

- As a songwriter, I've used this to consider sequences of songs in an album or set. With many songs visible simultaneously, it is convenient to scan them quickly for the typical considerations of key, tempo, theme, and so forth.

In these snapshots, the order of topics or components can be easily rearranged and evaluated. Similarly, random configurations can be considered. Mix up the pages into a random order, lay them out, and see what the universe suggests. This is another way to make forced connections. Stravinsky did it in a process he called "scissors and paste." He'd cut up a score, rearrange the components by chance, paste them back together in the new form, sing it through, and consider the result. If the chance ordering had a certain magic to it, it could become permanent. If it didn't work, he'd try again. That is the source of some of his inventive juxtapositions of ideas. And this doesn't take a thing away from him as a thinker; judging the chance idea to be musically effective requires extraordinary insight. It's just one of the methods to his madness.

Excursions

When ideas stop flowing, it's helpful to take a break, and during or after these breaks, your subconscious might synthesize the best ideas together and reveal to you the best thought that's happened yet.

Great ideas come in the shower, or while we're trying to fall asleep, or while we're driving. This is no accident. It's how the brain works, and so it is to be encouraged during the idea generation process. If you are facilitating a group brainstorming session, keep it short, and break it up into multiple sections.

A hot shower, a cup of coffee, yoga, meditation, a good night's sleep, a vacation skiing in Aspen. Beethoven frequently spoke of his love for taking long walks. These are all ways to change the way your mind is operating, and letting different dimensions of it come into the service of our problem-finding process. We understand the brain so little, in some ways, but we can often set it in motion to do good work despite that fact.

You might have noticed an odd object on my snapshot counter:

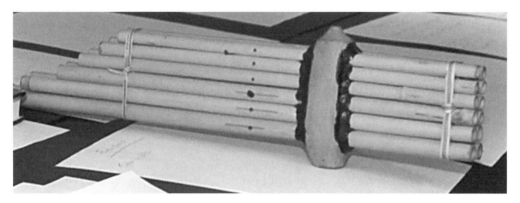

FIG. 11.11. Khene

Resting on my Excursions topic page (right here!) is a Southeast Asian instrument called a *khene* (pronounced "can"), which I bought from a street vendor in Luang Prabong, Laos. I certainly don't know how to play it, but it is one of my favorite office toys, and if I need a very quick excursion away from what I'm doing, I might blow on it a bit, to make some noise and shake up my concentration. It requires a lot of breath, and if you've ever tried practices such as yoga, you know how closely tied that is to energy level, and how we think and feel. This instrument smells really good, too, like cedar (I think, from the resin making the resonating chamber airtight).

For a more dramatic excursion, you can take a walk or improvise on the piano for a while. The point is to get away from the work, let your mind work in a different mode, so that ideas can gestate. You will then return from the excursion more refreshed and creative than before.

My favorite office extension (and occasional conference room):

FIG. 11.12. Maple Lane in Harvard, Massachusetts

SOLUTION EVALUATION AND REFINEMENT

Once you have generated a list of potential solutions, it becomes time to consider and evaluate them. Here, we explore the reality of what we can make happen. Often, brainstorming sessions are seen as self-contained processes, perhaps resulting in a list to be considered at a later date (which often never comes). By making follow through steps a formal part of your process, we get tangible benefit out of the creative power that we just unleashed.

After brainstorming, we want to know what will happen if we try the various candidate ideas. We want to choose a solution that is most likely to be effective in addressing our situation. The way to do this is by establishing a set of acceptance criteria and measuring each concept against it. In CPS, the standard questions to ask are, will it/could it address the requirements?

A ground rule, especially if you are reviewing potential solutions as a group, is to stay positive and open to finding the very best solution proposed—even if it is something that feels alien to how it's usually done. Our natural tendency, as discussed, is to go with the first reasonable solution that comes to mind. That might not be the best, though, so there is benefit in having someone facilitate the solution evaluation process who is not necessarily closely tied to the issue.

Back to our problem: What might we do to get more gigs?

What are our criteria for an effective solution? Perhaps, something like:

> Will it be:
>
> Affordable
>
> Reliable
>
> Practical
>
> Timely
>
> Easy

Come up with five or so criteria to rate your solutions, and then create a matrix: criteria as columns, potential solutions as rows. Your matrix might look like this:

Problem: In what ways might we get more gigs?

Solutions	Affordable	Reliable	Practical	Timely	Easy
Hire a booking agent					
Redesign the website					
Add better SEO to the website					
Update the PR kit					
Do a new demo					
Improve our song selection					
Get more testimonials					
List more quotes on the website					
List more clients on the website					
Talk to club owners in person					
Diversify what kinds of gigs we'll take					
Volunteer					
Play at friends' parties to get experience					
Hand out coupons					

Then, rate each potential solution. Perhaps, use a scale of 1 (doesn't meet the criteria at all) to 5 (meets the criteria magnificently). Go down each column, rather than across each solution, so that you can deliberately disrupt your brain's ability to create a pattern and unfairly bias a potential solution. Maybe, now your graph looks like this:

Problem: In what ways might we get more gigs?

Solutions	Affordable	Reliable	Practical	Timely	Easy
Hire a booking agent	2	5	2	5	4
Redesign the website	2	3	2	2	1
Add better SEO to the website	3	3	2	2	2
Update the PR kit	2	3	3	3	2
Do a new demo	2	3	1	1	1
Improve our song selection	3	3	1	3	1
Get more testimonials	5	3	4	4	4
List more quotes on the website	5	3	4	4	5
List more clients on the website	5	3	4	3	5
Talk to club owners in person	4	5	3	3	3
Diversify what kinds of gigs we'll take	4	4	3	2	2
Volunteer	1	4	2	2	1
Play at friends' parties to get experience	2	2	5	5	2
Hand out coupons	3	3	5	3	3

How to Analyze a Matrix

There are essentially two approaches to analyzing these results.

1. You could total the scores for each potential solution and compare them. This will show you which ones have the most consistent strong showings.

2. You could count how many 5's you've got for each solution. A 5 indicates a really extraordinary fulfillment of the criteria—a real star in a certain dimension, though the solution might also be problematic in some way(s). Such a score might highlight a strong option that would get screened out using just the total score, were the turkeys to get it down, but with some adjustment, it might be a good choice.

Here's a matrix showing both types of interpretation. The solutions are sorted by the overall score, to help clarify the difference in evaluation schemes.

Solutions	Affordable	Reliable	Practical	Timely	Easy	Total	Stars
List more quotes on the website	5	3	4	4	5	21	2
Get more testimonials	5	3	4	4	4	20	1
List more clients on the website	5	3	4	3	5	20	2
Hire a booking agent	2	5	2	5	4	18	2
Talk to club owners in person	4	5	3	3	3	18	1
Hand out coupons	3	3	5	3	3	17	1
Play at friends' parties to get experience	2	2	5	5	2	16	2
Diversify what kinds of gigs we'll take	4	4	3	2	2	15	0
Update the PR kit	2	3	3	3	2	13	0
Add better SEO to the website	3	3	2	2	2	12	0
Improve our song selection	3	3	1	3	1	11	0
Fix the website	2	3	2	2	1	10	0
Volunteer	1	4	2	2	1	10	0
Do a new demo	2	3	1	1	1	8	0

Now, we've got a prioritized list. If we were going to try the top two solutions, we would immediately see the benefit of having the secondary analysis, tracking the 5s, as the second and third items on this list have the same overall score, but the one in the third position is actually more outstanding in certain respects than the second.

How many solutions we will ultimately try could well relate to how easily they might be implemented.

Also, remember the Pareto Principle: 80 percent of the value is going to be found in the top-ranked 20 percent of the priorities. This list has fourteen items, so the top three or so are likely to result in 80 percent of the value of trying all of these solutions combined.

Knowing all this, you might be tempted to reword some of your brainstorms to make the chart work out better. One of the surprises here might be how well "hire a booking agent" fared. It rated number 4 (excluded by Pareto), but also shows two extraordinary ratings. I say, go for it, and see if you can compensate for its limitations. Cheat a bit, and combine getting testimonials and clients together as one task, like "Update the website with clients and their testimonials." That could actually combine all three top choices, and since they all are considered very easy, it seems like a reasonable maneuver. That will push two additional promising ideas up to the top 3, and thus, perhaps allow them to be considered more thoroughly.

If you have a vast number of brainstorm ideas to get through and not enough time, you could instead do a quick scan, considering impact and probability of being adopted, and thus winnow down the list to be more manageable. Then, do the full matrix on just the likeliest candidates.

Solutions	Impact	Probability that we'll do it
Hire a booking agent	X	X
Redesign the website	X	
Add better SEO to the website	X	
Update the PR kit		
Do a new demo		
Improve our song selection		
Get more testimonials	X	X
List more quotes on the website	X	X
List more clients on the website	X	X
Talk to club owners in person	X	X
Diversify what kinds of gigs we'll take	X	
Volunteer	X	
Play at friends' parties to get experience		
Hand out coupons	X	X

Sorted:

Solutions	Impact	Probability that we'll do it
Hire a booking agent	x	x
Get more testimonials	x	x
List more quotes on the website	x	x
List more clients on the website	x	x
Talk to club owners in person	x	x
Hand out coupons	x	x
Fix the website	x	
Add better SEO to the website	x	
Diversify what kinds of gigs we'll take	x	
Volunteer	x	
Update the PR kit		
Do a new demo		
Improve our song selection		
Play at friends' parties to get experience		

See how they compare:

Five Criteria	Two Criteria
List more quotes on the website	Hire a booking agent
Get more testimonials	Get more testimonials
List more clients on the website	List more quotes on the website
Hire a booking agent	List more clients on the website
Talk to club owners in person	Talk to club owners in person
Hand out coupons	Hand out coupons
Play at friends' parties to get experience	Redesign the website
Diversify what kinds of gigs we'll take	Add better SEO to the website
Update the PR kit	Diversify what kinds of gigs we'll take
Add better SEO to the website	Volunteer
Improve our song selection	Update the PR kit
Redesign the website	Do a new demo
Volunteer	Improve our song selection
Do a new demo	Play at friends' parties to get experience

At the top, where it matters the most, the two lists are not entirely unlike each other. (Remember, on the two-criteria list, all items with two X's are equal.) So, the initial screening can work reasonably well, particularly for a first pass.

IMPLEMENTATION

Once you arrive at some ideas that seem likely to successfully address the problem, the ideas have to be optimized so that they will have the best chance possible of succeeding. They need to become grounded in the real world before us, rather than remaining abstract pipe dreams. This mirrors the project management process of creating a work breakdown structure.

In CPS, they take each solution and ask the standard questions: Who, What, Where, When, Why, and How, in an effort to start evolving that solution into an actual plan.

In our example, we've arrived at the following possible solutions to our problem that seem the strongest:

- Update the website with clients and their testimonials.

- Hire a booking agent

- Talk to club owners in person

Take each one, and run the gamut of questions:

Update the website with clients and their testimonials.

- *Who* can help us do this? (The Web master, and our happiest clients.)

- *What* would make it stronger? (More quotes, and more buzz around the quotes.)

- *Where* is this likely to make an impact? (On the Home page, and on communications with prospective clients.)

- *When* should we do this to have the most impact? (Ongoing, so that the site always has something new, but especially before next month, when we are likelier to get a bounce in traffic.)

- *Why* is this going to help? (Because it will inspire confidence in us and reassure potential new clients that we are experienced.)

- *How* many ways can we use this to the best advantage? (Besides good advertising, the quote clients might feel more of a bond with us, and thus create more word of mouth. Asking for quotes is a way to reconnect with our most fruitful relationships, and that might lead us to more work.)

Then, move on to the next possible solution.

Launching the Solution

When the solution is figured out, the next step is to build a plan, and then launch it. By now, you know all about building implementation plans!

The big question is this:

How will you move your plan forward today?

This is the "Next Action" question. If you are guiding a team in solution-finding, don't let them leave your meeting without committing an answer to this question. Before the problem-solving process ends, a task needs to be added to someone's system that will move the solution forward.

Otherwise, the likelihood goes way up that *nothing* will get done, despite all of your fine thinking about the problem.

ORGANIZING SOLUTIONS

Some solutions are reusable. There's some approach to doing work, and once you figure it out, that solution can be used again by you, by your project team, by your customers, or even by your successor. Some ways to do this are:

- Rules and Procedures Tools
- Frequently Asked Questions (FAQ) Lists
- Technical Documentation
- "Help"

These can be helpful transitional mechanisms between the project phase of a product's life and the business-as-usual phase. During quality control testing, some issues might come to light that will be good candidates for this. These mechanisms can help your ongoing activities run more smoothly and improve your completed project's chances for success.

While developing comprehensive technical documentation and help systems are generally significant projects in themselves, and a bit beyond the parameters of what project managers typically do, let's take a closer look at rules-and-procedures handbooks and FAQs.

Rules and Procedures Handbook

A handbook of rules and procedures can be a convenient way to store codified systems.

The term *rule* is used in two ways. It can indicate a trigger and an action: "If more than an inch of snow is predicted, we communicate about whether rehearsal is cancelled."

It can also mean a law, or an approach to doing things, such as grammatical style decisions: "Always use serial commas."

A *procedure* is a set of actions, and they are often triggered by rules.

To cancel a rehearsal, Raj emails the whole group, and then we confirm it by using use the following telephone tree:

> Raj calls Merlin
>
> Merlin calls Sue
>
> Sue calls Forrest
>
> Forrest calls Mike
>
> Mike calls Don
>
> Don calls Raj

Rules:

- If the person you call doesn't answer, leave a voice mail saying rehearsal is cancelled, and that you will call that person's assigned caller. Then call the next person.

- If you miss a call and someone has to then make your assigned call, you owe the person who made the call for you a fancy hot coffee drink at Wired Puppy.

Some of the types of procedures to include in the Rules and Procedures handbook:

1. Contact information for the team

2. Emergency procedures

3. "Who to Call" list, indicating the right contacts to reach out to for various recurring issues: computer tech support, building operations, contacts at key vendors, knowledgeable people in the organization about key issues, etc.

4. Technical information, such as how to send a fax

5. Systems for handling certain types of work, such as how to process requests for updates

6. Communications plans, such as who must confirm changes of project scope, or who receives notifications that new prototypes are available for review

7. Checklists, particularly for quality control

8. A style guide of how you will handle certain types of grammatical and format considerations in all your published materials. It is a great help for maintaining consistency, and stating rules for house style can greatly reduce the amount of required communication and work a project will entail.

The style guide might be a separate document, depending on your work. At Berklee Press, we actually maintain two separate style guides: one for notation, one for text. We also reference a style guide used by the PR department of Berklee College of Music, which has some different information, more related to branding (say "Berklee College of Music," not "The Berklee College of Music") than how to handle music terminology (capitalize mode names, such as *Dorian*, but lowercase scale names, such as *blues*). And finally, we start the whole thing off by saying that we defer to the current edition of the *Chicago Manual of Style* and the *Harvard Dictionary of Music* for all such style choices, except the instances listed in our own guide.

Set up your rules and procedures handbook like a real book, or even create and print an actual bound book. Organize the contents by subject area, approaching the organization process as you would a work breakdown structure.

Include a table of contents. Include a list of people who should get a copy whenever it gets updated.

You might maintain several of these for different types of team members. Personally, I have three: one for my own work, one for my editorial assistants, and one for my authors. We maintain the style guide separately, as it gets used by all of the above, plus various vendors (freelance proofreaders, graphic designers, etc.). If there are multiple versions, try to minimize keeping the same information in multiple places, as it becomes easy to forget to update them somewhere.

FAQ Development

A *frequently asked questions* list (FAQ) is a system of questions and answers. They are common on websites aimed at customer support, but are also helpful in certain types of work settings, either replacing or supplementing a rules and procedures book. They serve as catch-alls for random questions that might otherwise be difficult to organize. Sometimes, they evolve to become rules and procedures handbooks.

You might have a simple one-page FAQ list, posted where a type of worker can reference it. For example, here's a simple FAQ you might provide to a concert hall stage manager, backstage.

Stage Manager FAQ
Who should I call for emergencies?
Building operations: ext. 1234
Police/Fire/Ambulance: 911
House Manager: ext. 4321
Who has the keys?
Building operations (ext. 1234) has all door keys except for:
Sound Closet: Jack: cell number xxx-xxx-xxxx.
Grand piano: Stage Manager Cabinet, black ring
Percussion Cabinet: Stage Manager Cabinet, gold ring
Green Room: Stage Manager Cabinet, green ring
When should I ring the warning buzzer?
Standard is to ring it 10 minutes before they begin playing and then again 3 minutes before. Dim the lights 30 seconds before.
Before the 3-minute buzzer, contact the House Manager to confirm that he or she is ready. The house manager must signal the 3-minute warning.
Note: If the buzzer doesn't work, blink the house lights three times instead, and call Building Operations to request that it gets fixed.
What must be done after the concert?
- Check the roster to see if a morning setup is required, and if so, make sure that gets done.
- If no morning setup is required, clear the stage completely, including chairs, stands, risers, sound equipment, instruments, and all other objects.
- Sweep the stage using sweeping compound.
- Green room is broom clean.
- Audience chairs need to be in the upright position, and any trash should be removed. Leftover programs should be recycled. (Note: the custodian will clean the audience area more thoroughly.)
- All lights get turned off except switch 16.
- The grand piano gets locked and covered.
- Confirm that the piano, percussion, and green room keys are in the stage manager cabinet.
- Contact building operations, if necessary (e.g., anything that requires repair, bulbs are burned out, etc.).
- The house doors get locked.

For more involved FAQs, a standard format is to set the categories of questions upfront, and then the actual questions separately, organized with a numeric system to make tracking individual points easier.

Concert Hall FAQ
1. House Manager
2. Ushers
3. Stage Manager
    3.1. Who should I call for emergencies?
    3.2. Who has the keys?
    3.3. When should I ring the warning buzzer?
    3.4. What must be done after the concert?
4. Stage Hands
5. Building Operations
6. Performers

Below that (on a webpage) or on separate pages, each question gets answered, just like the simple version, but keeping with the numbering scheme.

Design FAQs (and rules-and-procedures handbooks) for easy information retrieval. The FAQ format has been a bit co-opted by marketing people, which makes it very easy to find fluffy, non-helpful FAQs, mostly containing questions that nobody would really ask, and then answers that are geared towards product positioning. Silly stuff. But a clear, on-target FAQ can be a useful way to reduce confusion, minimize perfunctory communication, and help projects run more efficiently. They are also a way to encourage corporate memory and make the results of extensive problem-solving efforts durable, permanently implementing them as part of operations.

CLOSING THOUGHTS

Ideas are often the easy part of solution finding. Follow-through tends to be the missing link. As musicians, we know that the inspired, carefree, creative part of music is unfortunately just a small part of what goes into its production. Most of our task, as musicians, is concentrated, detailed, formal organizational work—setting up the context for inspiration to live and breathe, but relatively little time with the spark itself. So it is with creativity in a business context, as well. Administration is required to harness the sparks.

The way to put your creative ideas to work is by integrating them into a system as part of your planning process. Otherwise, they tend to dissipate into the wind. But by considering idea review and implementation as part of your creative work, you will give your madness its best chance of achieving tangible results.

PRACTICE

1. Use a brainstorming technique to generate a list of 50 to 200 potential or existing problems that could arise in your project, or perhaps strategic needs that it has. Try to engage others in this exercise, if you can.

2. Evaluate and select the three likeliest problems.

3. Brainstorm solutions to these problems/needs using a different method or tool than you used in step 1. Again, use your project team, if possible.

4. Evaluate and select the best solution.

5. Refine your solution, in terms of Who, What, Where, When, Why, and How, and create a report describing your answers to these questions, just for that one potential solution.

What can you do today to move your solution forward?

CHAPTER 12

Closure

Officially ending a project involves first confirming that it's really done and then preparing it and its associated resources for the future.

How cleanly this all works out varies tremendously. Some projects obviously end, with deliverables sewn up nicely and neatly. Other projects seem destined to go on forever, with certain proponents resisting the final signoff.

Any ending can involve some psychological baggage, but a healthy attitude is to hold onto the idea that this project gave you experience that will make the next project you do even better.

In this final chapter, we will look at various dimensions of closing out projects. Besides being helpful for when projects end, some of these procedures can also be useful for whenever a major phase of a project ends, and keeping up with end-of-phase tasks in this way can relieve some pressure at the very end of the project.

In these discussions about how to end, I hope you become inspired about new ways to begin.

OBJECTIVES

By the end of the chapter, you will be able to:

- confirm that the necessary work is truly done, including punch lists and closing out contracts and invoices

- complete post-creativity tasks, such as archiving, distribution, finalizing paperwork, and required communications

- organize lessons learned and relationships gained to make future projects easier, by maintaining templates and analyzing the project for reusable objects

- release project resources, and make sure all relationships end on the right foot

CONFIRMATION OF DELIVERABLES: PUNCH LISTS

There's done, and then there's done.

The primary execution phase of the project might have an obvious conclusion. You play a concert, and the curtain comes down. The postman delivers a box of CDs or books, or other products, smelling fresh and new in their shrink-wrap.

Creating the primary deliverable, though, is likely not the only work specified in your work breakdown structure. It might be the most important milestone, but there are likely some other dimensions of the work to complete, beyond the main deliverable. In project management terms, perhaps some of these become "business as usual," rather than part of the project itself. The project might be to create a music-related app, and then you have to provide customer support, for example. You can consider the project officially finished while customer support for it continues. However, there might be truly project-related tasks that will continue for a while. When you receive that final product, there might be a distribution list of people who get a free sample, and you, as the project manager, might be responsible for doing that.

After a quick victory sniff of that shrink-wrap, it's time to confirm that the project is truly done. This means checking all the deliverables listed in the scope statement, and confirming that they have been done.

A *punch list* is a final, comprehensive listing of all outstanding issues. It's a good way to formalize the very end of a project, or a phase, and helps prevent a process of endless revision, with draft after draft. They are particularly common in the construction industry (where they are sometimes called "snag lists"). The builder gets everything as good as possible and then does a formal walk-through with the client and project manager, generating a list of details to be addressed: that electrical outlet switch plate is cracked, that wall needs touch-up paint, this window is stuck, that pile of wood scraps needs to be removed. Everyone agrees that the punch list represents the last of the work to be done, and perhaps signs it. Then, as the items get addressed, they punch a hole next to each item (traditionally, with a nail; you can just check a box, if you are more of a refined sort).

These are particularly helpful for ends of project phases, as well as for the whole project. For example, finishing the mixing phase of an album, a producer (i.e., project manager) and an engineer might sit down together, when they have a mix that is practically done, and generate a list of every single outstanding issue. They can call it the "Final Punch List," have all parties sign it, and agree that no further changes will be made, after these. Signing it adds a formality to it, which can help focus people's attention on performing very thorough final reviews. Then, they must forever hold their peace. Or perhaps, pay more.

To prepare a punch list, review the scoped deliverables against what was created, focusing on specifications for quality. Examine every dimension of every deliverable, preferably with more than one person. If you are making a recording, check it on multiple sound systems—ideally, listening to it and then listening to a commercially released recording that you think is good that's in the same genre. A/B them: check one, then the other, then the first again, then the second, making sure that yours is okay. Itemize any issues.

The work breakdown structure can be a good starting point for making a punch list, but omit any items that don't require attention. The punch list is a list of issues. Be sure to add other items to it, as well, beyond what you find on the WBS, which won't have the required level of specificity.

So, a portion of the WBS might look like this, for an album:

1. Album
    1.1. Music
        1.1.1. Songwriting
            1.1.1.1. Song 1
            1.1.1.n. Song n…
        1.1.2. Demo Recordings
            1.1.2.1. Song Demo 1
            1.1.2.n. Song Demo n…
        1.1.3. Mixed Recordings
            1.1.3.1. Song 1
            1.1.3.n. Song n…
        1.1.4. Final Master
    1.2. Packaging
        1.2.1. Art
            1.2.1.1. Photography
            1.2.1.2. Booklet Layout
            1.2.1.3. ….

A punch list based on this that you might make for the mix engineer (1.1.3.) would look like this:

Complete	Issue
	1. Song 1
	Make bass louder throughout
	Omit "pop" at 2:04
	2. Song 2
	Add 1 more second between tracks 2 and 3
	3. Song 4
	Use take 3 of guitar solo at 1:34 to 1:54

FIG. 12.1. Punch List for Mix Session

You will probably have other deliverables besides the primary one. There could be invoices, reports, copies of essential graphics, archives, and so on, that all need to be addressed, as well as the primary thing you are creating. This end-of-project review should ferret out all the remaining work.

It is the closing step that confirms that your work is truly done.

ASSESSING SUCCESS

When the deliverables are set and the deadline pressure is relieved, it's time to reflect on how well the project went. The goal here is to improve at doing projects in the future, rather than beat yourself up over what you did wrong.

Consider each of the constraints, and write a report on how well you accomplished each. Quantify your answers. Don't just say, "We exceeded the budget." Write down exactly where, and by how much. The purpose of this report is to give information to someone in the future who is doing a similar project and wants to understand what you learned. That person might be you.

The three constraints:

1. **Quality.** Was the quality what you hoped it would be? Where did it fall short, and why? Next time, how can you avoid sacrificing quality? How will you implement this strategy?

2. **Cost.** Did you come out over or under budget? What was more expensive than you anticipated? Has this project created financial problems that must be explicitly addressed? Are there any outstanding invoices, either for money due to us or money that we owe to others? Are reliable mechanisms in place that will ensure that these invoices get paid?

3. **Time.** Did we make all the deadlines? Did certain types of work require more time than anticipated? Did we do an accurate job of assigning dependencies? Of analyzing risks?

Then, ask, did we fulfill the scope required by the original plan, or did we have to sacrifice some dimension of the original vision? Why? Should we create a new project to complete missing scope items in this one? Does the lack of some dimension of the specified scope require us to take action? For example, if our project was to design a new type of headphones and we decided not to manufacture them in pink (as originally scoped), as well as black, was there a stakeholder counting on the pink version that needs to be notified of this change?

In addition to assessing the deliverables, also assess the resources you used. How was the studio? How were the team members? Would you use them again? Recommend them to others? Blacklist them because they were so horrible? How will you implement these findings, so that your next project will benefit by this experience?

MAINTAINING INSTITUTIONAL MEMORY

Besides asking and answering these questions, actually implement better practices for future projects while you are cleaning up from the last one. This helps you create *institutional memory.* You create new systems and practices based on your experiences. This helps you evolve as a project manager and it helps whatever organization you are part of as well.

In the previous chapter, we saw how to create several mechanisms that help preserve institutional memory: FAQs, rules and procedures guides, checklists, and others. Let's discuss a few more.

1. Templates

2. Databases

3. Archives

Templates

Templates are reusable tools for starting tasks that let you begin new work without starting from scratch. Many kinds of work have templates. In crafts and manufacturing, shapes are used to make other shapes, like molds, stencils, and so on.

Many kinds of software have built-in templates, and for those that don't, you can simply create a file that you name "template" and replicate it.

Templates can dramatically speed up the work process. In notation software, for example, you can set up templates that have essential formatting done for common types of notation. If you often arrange for a wind ensemble, you can set up a blank wind ensemble score as a template. Rather than figuring out the layout each time you begin creating a new project, you extract a template from a finished score that would work as an effective model, and then begin the new project, not with a blank slate but with a lot of work already done.

A work breakdown structure is a great candidate for turning into a template, if you do the same type of project multiple times. If those structures were new to you at the beginning of this course, you probably created one for the first time, say for a recording, or a concert, or some other kind of work that you are likely to do multiple times. Certain information on it will only be relevant for your current project. But much of the information will probably be relevant to your next project.

The closure phase of your project is a perfect time to turn your WBS or any other documents into a template, to help speed up your process next time around.

To create a template, save your file as a new document, perhaps with the word "Template" in the file name (like, "CD_WBS_Template.doc"). Then, erase all information that is obviously only applicable to the specific project recently completed. Keep the rest: the dependencies, the time estimates, and so on.

Here's a template for a Finale music notation file of a blues progression in bass clef. If it seems likely that we'll be doing more blues notation in bass clef, having a template like this as a starting point could save some time in the future.

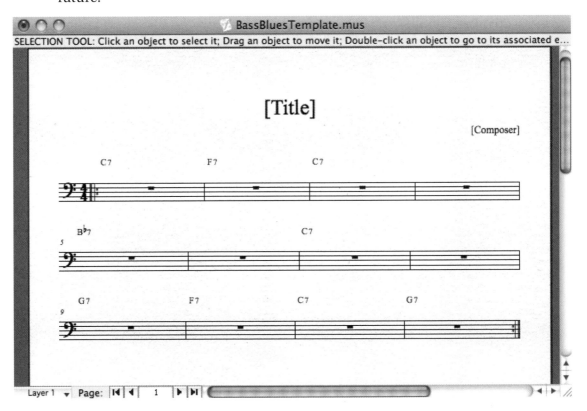

FIG. 12.2. Finale Template for Bass Clef Blues

What else did you create that could be useful in a future project? Contracts? Invoice forms? Pro Tools sessions?

Review all the contracts and tools you created, and look for opportunities to reuse things. This can save you a lot of time, and it can also help you maintain quality. Now, fresh from the work, these issues are clear for you in a way that they might not be later, when you begin a new project, so the project closure phase is a really good time to develop or refine templates.

Similarly, it's the right time to maintain templates that you might already be using. You might realize that for an information-gathering form that you've used for years, you really need certain information that wasn't on the template, but you expect to need it in the future—for example, an emergency contact number. You might decide on a new house publishing style for how to present a word, such as "website" instead of "Web site." You might update a timing estimate for a task so that you don't run late again.

Some features on templates eventually become obsolete. For a really long time, telex machines were standard ways to communicate in many corporate settings, and templates might include prompts to list telex addresses. Now, while it is still occasionally used, it has been mostly superseded by email and fax (which is also in decline). Any forms or templates you see that request a telex address should probably be updated, unless that's really a preferred way to communicate.

So, during project closure, review the templates you used, and see if there are any improvements to be made.

Databases

Databases are a great way to store information that can be helpful to future projects. A *database* is a type of software tool that stores information. If a Microsoft Word document is like a sheet of paper, then a database is a stack of cards, often with links to other stacks of cards. A program that creates databases, such as Access® or Filemaker®, is called a "database management system" (or DBMS). The files it creates are called databases. In common parlance, people tend to call DBMSs "database programs" or just "databases."

A contact manager program is a kind of simple database. Each item in it is in the same format, with information of the same type. Everyone has a name, street address, home phone number, and so on.

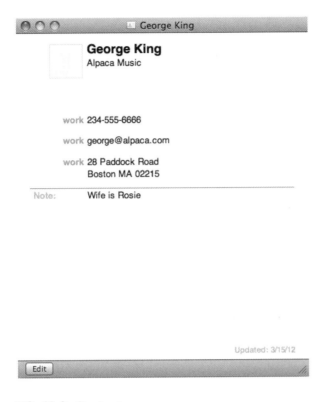

FIG. 12.3. Contact

You can make more customized and sophisticated databases with programs such as Filemaker. To give you a simple idea of what they can do, say that in your contacts management software, you have several people who work for the same company. Then the company moves. In most products, you will have to change every single employee's work address to the new location. With a more customizable product, you could set it up so that there are two related tables, one for addresses and one for people. Instead of the full corporate address in each contact, simply naming the company would link to the address database, and grab the address from there. This way, when the company relocates, you only need to update the corporate address once, because it is only stored once. This is referred to as "minimizing redundancy," and it helps speed up data entry and maintain accuracy, in addition to easing maintenance.

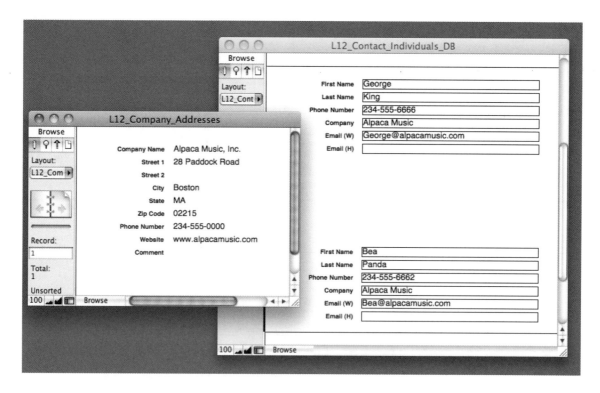

FIG. 12.4. Relational Database Tables

This can get very complicated really fast, if you want it to, but you can certainly just keep databases as simple, flat files (i.e., single unlinked tables), and they can be a great way to store information. You might maintain a database of products, or expenses, or how much time various tasks took, or hotels, or what gear you have, or any other kinds of information, as a means of storing information collected from your project. Databases are searchable, and this helps track information over time.

One database that I created and like a lot is one of sales reports that I get for all Berklee Press products. Every week, I get a comprehensive listing. By loading these into a database, I can track a book's sales over many years. When someone pitches us on a new product, I can search the database, to see how similar products have fared, historically, which can help inform the decision about which new projects to accept.

Database programs are very flexible, searchable, and infinitely useful means of storing information, and thus, building institutional memory.

Archiving

A project archive is like a time capsule/care package you send to your future self or others in your organization. Besides giving you what you need to reprint or otherwise recreate a project, the archive can provide essential historical information: actual costs, required task durations, who the team was, how effective they were, what facilities and vendors were used, and so on. When you prepare a project archive, the goals are to make retrieval of the vital information as easy as possible. This includes weeding out everything that isn't relevant: marked up drafts, for example. If there are a lot of pages, they should be organized into subfolders.

Some of the most critical components of a good archive are as follows:

1. **Archive index.** For each project in an archive, maintain a conspicuous index page that has critical information, including information about product versions, if that's relevant. Sometimes, you will print a short run of something for a first printing, catch and correct a few errors, and then release a second printing. Five years later, it may be helpful to know that. Include a tip about how to distinguish what the most recent version is, like "2007 version has blue cover, not green." An explanatory memo of various details might be appreciated to anyone who accesses the archive. For example, you might indicate where other files are stored, or more detailed thoughts about what a revision should include.

2. **Content files.** For recordings, books, artwork, and so on, it is essential to include all digital files, so that the project can be republished and/ or revised later. Include Pro Tools® sessions, InDesign® files, Word® files, PDFs, and all other final versions of the work. If you want to include draft versions, be sure to label what's a draft and what's the final. It's safer to just include the finals. (You don't want to create a second edition of something based on files that have not been updated.)

   Content files are probably the most critical component of your archive, and I recommend that content files be archived in at least three different locations, and on two different forms of media. At Berklee Press, we maintain four archives. One set is on a server, one set is with our distribution partner (Hal Leonard Corp.), one set is in a set of file cabinets on site, and one set is at a SECRET location. I've found that the server archive has been indispensable, because on very rare occasions, the CD archives eventually failed, for some reason. Maybe they were copied improperly, or maybe defective discs were used. (Always double-check CD archives before assuming that they were burned properly.)

3. **Copy of the actual final product.** Along with the paperwork and digital files, keep a published copy of the file in an archive. This might fit in a file cabinet, but if you are designing instruments, it might not. Somewhere,

you need to keep a pristine version. If you release multiple editions of a project, maintain a copy of each one you produce, and clearly mark them, if it isn't obvious which is which.

4. **Project plan.** This includes all planning and strategic documents. The most useful ones are the budget-to-actual financial report, the work breakdown structure, the scope statement, and information about resources (team, facilities, gear, punch lists, etc.).

5. **Contracts.** Some contracts have implications for many years, or decades, and keeping them all on file is essential. They might be confidential, so a relatively public project archive might not be the place for them, but they need to be somewhere. I've seen situations arise where we wanted to publish a new edition of a long out-of-print product (i.e., make some easy money), but couldn't do it because the likely owner of the contract died, and nobody could find the contract. Forty or fifty years ago, when that contract was probably signed, whoever was in charge was not keeping formal archives (or if they did, that archive is now lost —understandable, because the office moved at least six times since then). Rather than risk a potential lawsuit, in the event that the rights weren't as we would expect, the reprint project was shelved, and so everyone misses out.

6. **Project summary statement.** A project summary statement is like a letter to whoever is searching through the archives for information. It is a brief assessment, discussing how well the goals were met, what obstacles or unexpected events affected the project, how well it stayed within the projected budget and timing, and any other information that might be of use to someone doing something similar. Assume that anyone might read this document. Rather than, say, "Fred was a real jerk, and I'll never work with him again," you might do better to couch this information somehow, perhaps in a grid showing relative performance of all the team members. In other words, present the information in a depersonalized way that wouldn't make you uncomfortable if, say, Fred is the one who winds up digging through the archive and happens upon it.

There might be other information you want to keep, such as correspondence, final drafts, and so on, and it's better to keep too much rather than too little. Just make the above easy to find.

Consider how the archive will be used. Rarely, they will be used as evidence in lawsuits. Almost never. Their real purpose is to inform future work: new products, clarifications of contracts, employee performance evaluations, retrospectives on past accomplishments, and so on. Anything that distracts from that should probably be removed from the archive.

In truth, many archives are never used. But when they are, there is often an urgent, desperate need, with significant financial consequences if they are not in order, so try to keep your project archives in good shape.

FINALIZING PAPERWORK

We discussed how creating a punch list can help finalize the primary deliverable for the project. In addition to the primary deliverable, there are various other administrative components of project management that also have to be closed out, for the project to be truly complete. While a project manager is not necessarily in charge of completing these tasks, you might need to make sure that they are in a reliable system for them getting done.

Paying invoices is an important dimension of project work that the project manager needs to confirm happens appropriately. While actually writing the check might be the responsibility of an accounting department, the project manager is likely the face of the organization, as far as a vendor or service provider is concerned. Failure of the accounting department to promptly pay an outstanding invoice can disincline people from working with the project manager again. So, it's a good idea to make sure that this goes smoothly.

Some contracts specify mechanisms for releasing payments that might be relatively arcane to actually implement. For example, a composer agrees to provide music for use in a website, and his contract specifies that his first 50 percent is due two weeks after the producer accepts a rough cut of the music (confirming that it seems usable, with a bit more work) and the balance upon receipt of the final recording. The producer, then, must report to the accounting office regarding whether or not the deliverables are accepted. Otherwise, the composer won't get paid. So, the project manager needs to be familiar with all terms for payment such as this, and will probably be part of the contracting process. As part of closing out the project, it is a good idea to trace all points where invoices are paid—or submitted from the project organization—and then make sure that these payments were received, or that they are in a system that will ensure that they will be paid.

I recommend that you send all providers a friendly email, at the end of the project, thanking them for their work, and asking them to confirm that they received what they were due. It's a nice way to close out the relationship, and it can uncover administrative mistakes. Also, people are so unaccustomed to people in the business world actually looking out for their best interests that it helps to build relationships.

Stakeholder Notifications

When the project is done, some of the stakeholders need to be informed. They might be waiting for your final output, perhaps to use it as part of another project. They might be waiting for some of the resources tied up in your project to become available again. So, send them a note, with whatever information is relevant. A simple indicator that it is complete might be all that's necessary.

Distributing Completed Products

If the project results in a tangible deliverable, such as a recording, book, catalog, etc., there could be a long list of people who should get a free copy. Some of these distributions will be for relationship building, and others will be for truly functional reasons.

Maintain a list of people to whom you should send a copy. Depending on how expensive it is to provide this, the list will be longer or shorter, but free stuff is generally appreciated, and so I recommend that you give out as many freebies as you can afford.

Freebies can include:

- copies of a recording, whether the full CD or links to digital copies on a site such as SoundCloud or Bandcamp®.

- tickets (give at least two)

- invitation to an opening reception

People you might give freebies to can be broken down into two categories: those that are likely to result in sales and those that probably won't. Somewhere in the middle is the group of people that might somehow help your career as a result of knowing that you can bring something like this about, but aren't actually going to help you sell anything. It's helpful to keep these categories in mind as you distribute freebies.

Most Likely to Result In Sales

- Teachers who might use your product with their students
- Reviewers who might publish reviews (blogs, etc.)
- Store owners who might sell your product
- Libraries

Good for Professional Relationships

- Core stakeholders, particularly those who advocated for the project's creation
- Project team members

Nice to Give a Little Gift

- People who wrote marketing endorsements for it
- Friends and relatives

The list can grow pretty fast, and you have to be careful to watch the value of what you are giving away. The theory is that by giving it away for free, you get more people aware of it (and you), which then results in more sales. Giving away copies to your friends probably won't have any actual affect on sales. However, you can ask them to write positive online reviews for it at Amazon, Yelp, CD Baby, etc., and that might actually have an effect.

There might be a standard distribution list at your organization of whom to give new products. At Berklee Press, each new product we publish is sent to about half a dozen administrators on campus, plus the Berklee library and bookstore. I keep a checklist for this purpose, and then add names of additional people to it, customized for each product: blurb writers, certain teachers, authors who are currently writing other books that might be informed by this one, and so on. Tracking this helps me avoid forgetting anyone or giving people duplicates.

Resource Release

When the project is done, the resources committed towards finishing it are no longer required, and they can be used on other projects. Officially notifying the team and possibly other stakeholders that the project is done can help clarify this.

There's an old cartoon, and I wish I could find it for you, rather than describe it. It's in four frames. If you can find it and get me the reprint rights, I'd really appreciate it!

- Frame 1, two little boys are playing chess, staring at the board.

- Frame 2, they are still staring, but now they are teen-agers.

- Frame 3, they are middle aged, still staring. Same board, pieces in the same place.

- Frame 4, they are old men, with long beards, cobwebs connecting them to their chair and the floor, still staring. One says, "Aren't you going to move, already?" The other replies, "Oh, I thought it was your turn!"

So it goes, tying up resources. Formally announcing a project's end can help alleviate these bottlenecks. Tell the project team, and tell the stakeholders. Tell anyone else who might be waiting.

I'm mentioning several communications to the same group of people, but you should bundle them up, as you can, to minimize the number of separate emails you send to the same people.

Here are some of the considerations related to releasing resources. Essentially, what you are doing here is disbanding the project team.

1. **Team members are freed to work on other projects.** They no longer need to stand by, awaiting instructions. They should return all materials related to the project that they can. You want to avoid having outdated drafts circulating, such as rejected CD masters, as that can lead to confusion later on.

2. **Gear is returned.** If there are instruments, music stands, reference books, computers, effects pedals, sheet music, keys, laptops, cell phones, software license codes, or other items that were loaned or rented for the purposes of the project, they should get returned to wherever or whomever they belong.

3. **Computer permissions and security codes get updated.** Access to certain key data might only be appropriate during the life of the project. Project closure time is a good opportunity to consider and implement what the appropriate permissions structure is, in perpetuity.

MAINTAINING RELATIONSHIPS

In addition to simply disbanding the team, some relationship maintenance is likely necessary. Make sure that contact information is up to date. You might have received information (such as someone's cell phone number) in an email that should be stored in your contact management software. You also might want to keep track of the names of your team members' spouses or children, or other information that will help you remember details of your life and relationship. Personally, I have a terrible memory for such things, and I am very likely to forget how many children certain people have, even when I've worked with them for many years. I have to track such things in my contact management software. Birthdays, too.

Social media software, such as LinkedIn®, Facebook®, and the Berklee Music Network, are also good mechanisms for staying in touch with people. The more social sites, such as Facebook, can be a little awkward between business relationships, particularly when there is a subordinate to superior relationship. It is currently considered awkward, in business, for a superior to "friend" a subordinate, as it seems like an intrusion into their personal life. Similarly, it can be awkward for a subordinate to friend a superior. Schools often have policies against teachers and students friending each other. When a project ends, though, and the formal working relationships change, such relationships might feel better. I recommend keeping these social media ties professional, though. Facebook is really a fairly personal and intimate setup, for most people. Material gets posted by others in your circle that could be visible to all your contacts, including any clients that you happen to friend, and what others post might be counter to the brand image that your company wants to project. You don't want the fans of your heavy metal band to see a photo of you daintily sipping tea at the Ritz with your grandmother, giving your baby niece a bottle, for example. It's against your brand image.

So, build and encourage these networks, but be aware of how and when you are crossing the personal/business line. I strongly recommend professional-oriented sites, such as the Berklee Music Network, for this kind of permanent networking, over sites that encourage more sharing of your personal life. Your goal here is primarily to keep track of those whom you have worked with, and to see how they are evolving professionally, over the years, so that you can work with them again in the future. What cocktails your CD replication agent enjoyed at Mardi Gras is probably not so critical for you to be thinking about. And you almost certainly don't want to know the details of their political leanings. They are almost certainly not exactly like yours, and such exchanges of irrelevant information can easily damage professional relationships that really don't need to end.

ACKNOWLEDGMENTS

As a project manager, part of what you inevitably have to do is to create pressure in people's lives so that they deliver. People promise high and deliver low, and the project manager needs to reconcile what they are capable of with what they really must provide. This can result in some ruffled feathers. Frankly, it is extremely common for people in business to commit to doing things that are beyond their capability, and the project manager might be the first to find out what their actual limitations are. This can result in feelings of shame, defensive behavior, and a generally uncomfortable vibe.

At project closure, it's time to put all that aside, unless you really must make a big deal out of it (get someone fired, sue them, demote them, etc.). If everything is essentially cool, then set the relationship on course to be as positive as it can be.

As long as they delivered appropriately, thank them for their contribution, and try to crystalize all that's good about the relationship. Apologize for any miscommunication, and make them feel good about the project and their contribution.

It might be appropriate to have a celebratory event or give out awards, or bonuses, or distribute certificates, or even "I survived project X" t-shirts. Bonuses or other incentives might be part of the contract, or part of company policy, and so you should make sure that the mechanisms for such things are in place.

Having a debrief meeting might be helpful for certain key players, so that you can discuss what went right and what went wrong, in order to both learn from it. Set the tone for the meeting as a learning experience, not a blame-allocation session. Besides the specific information you get from such a meeting, you want the deliverable to be a relationship built on mutual respect, if not downright appreciation. You should leave it with a positive basis for moving forward with that person. Just like what you did with the project file, you're cleaning up your relationship with this person, and getting it set for later retrieval. You might not ever work with them again, but if you had a meaningful work relationship, it's helpful to continually develop your network.

You might get asked to provide recommendations for people you worked with in the past. While the project and their contribution are fresh in your mind, jot down some notes about the various team members, to help yourself out in case this becomes necessary later on.

REUSABILITY ANALYSIS

We discussed templates, earlier. Similarly, analyze the project documents with an eye towards reusability. If you developed a photo release agreement for the current project, then that would be a good candidate to put aside, in a more general location than the project folder, for future access. (Keep the original in the project folder.)

Agreements, contracts, databases, design templates, forms, distribution lists, job descriptions, want advertisements, spreadsheets, reports, and many other kinds of documents are potentially reusable (even if in heavily modified form). Consider what was generated in your project, and how to make them available to you and to your organization in the future.

Some of what you have created might be useful to others in your organization, so spread the wealth. First, clean them up, deleting any personal information. Make it easy for others to understand their worth and how to use them, even including an explanatory cover sheet, if appropriate.

Who would be the appropriate person to disseminate such things, organization-wide? That might be out of your own appropriate scope, but there is probably an appropriate department head, somewhere, who might like to know about the existence of certain kinds of documents or other tools.

PROJECT DESTINY

You might be done with your project, but what you have created might become the work of someone else, as part of a new project.

Whose responsibility or concern is it next? If you've created a product, once it exists, it needs to get advertised, sold, and supported. Those involved in such undertakings will likely appreciate insight from you and others intimately involved in the product's creation, regarding what its benefits are, how to use it, what problems it solves, and generally, how to describe its awesomeness. As part of project closure, a meeting with marketing or the delivery of some information might be helpful. You might be asked to draft some advertising copy, such as bullets articulating its benefits. The scope statement can be good inspiration for this; some of its text might be usable word-for-word in marketing contexts.

Similarly, your project might be destined to serve as part of a greater whole. You might be creating a program that adds to a larger curriculum, or a software component that will be integrated into a larger structure. There could be technical questions about it and how it works, worthy of a larger discussion with people in your organization that you've never worked with before.

Project closure isn't just about putting the project to bed, mothballing it, and hiding it in the attic. It's about preparing what you've created for its ongoing journey.

Consider:

- **Who can benefit by this project?** Customers? Co-workers? Other companies? How will they learn about it? Is someone else communicating with them, or do you need to perform some outreach?

- **Who will advocate for it?** Is there a team standing by, ready to hawk the wares you've created, or does that aspect of its lifecycle also fall to you?

- **What does it need to succeed and be useful?** Advertising? Reviews? Word of mouth? How will that happen?

- **What new projects might be possible as a result of this one?** Is this project really a proof/canary in the coalmine that will inform or evolve into a larger endeavor? If so, does a bridge need to be constructed for this to happen? Who needs to be notified?

As project manager, you are in the groove of being your project's primary advocate. By helping it along on its path, you give it the best chance of achieving its highest potential, so before you close that file drawer, consider how you can help move it along.

WHAT'S YOUR NEXT PROJECT?

When projects end, it's easy to fall into a kind of slump. Your time has been structured and clearly purposeful. There has likely been a swirl of activity surrounding you that might suddenly stop. This newfound lack of direction can be dispiriting.

The antidote to the post-project blues is to begin a new project before the old one has ended. At least, start thinking about what to do next, if not actively planning it.

From a practical perspective, you might have clear needs: adding to a product line, generating income fairly easily, or choosing among proposals. To select the right direction, draw up a matrix, such as the type we've been using in this book. Itemize your criteria, and see what best completes it. Analyze impact verses cost. Consider your life's projects as a portfolio, and consider what's missing. Even consider it in comparison with someone whose career you are trying to emulate in some way, and consider what types of projects they are doing in comparison with what you are doing. Are there lessons to be learned?

From a creative perspective, there are four typical directions for choosing what a next project will be. (And you could describe the same project as being in various relationships, but stay with me....)

1. **Similar.** In accomplishing the current project, you have developed unique expertise in how to get this kind of work done, and the next time through, it will be easier. To produce one concert requires a tremendous learning curve. The second concert you produce will require similar work: similar contacts, work breakdown structures, and even project team members. So, the next project you do might be another one that is similar to what you just accomplished. Say you just produced a bluegrass concert. Similar to this could be a folk music concert, or another bluegrass concert with different tunes or with a different band.

2. **Derivative.** Besides being merely similar to the project you've just done, you might do something truly derivative of it, in order to maximize some dimension of what you've done. Possible derivative projects from your bluegrass concert would be another bluegrass concert with the same artists on a different date, or with different tunes, or that same exact concert but on tour. You're trying to preserve what you can from the original project, while changing some dimension of it.

3. **Supporting.** Your next project might be something that will help support the project you just did. For example, you could produce a recording or concert DVD of the bluegrass concert.

4. **Contrasting.** You might prefer to find a uniquely different type of project to the one you just did, in order to balance out what you're doing in your career. You could be extreme in this, such as quitting music and becoming a chimney sweep (of the non-Mary Poppins variety). More likely, though, you will choose a contrasting project that keeps you in the general

ballpark of the career. For example, you might start a non-profit organization related to bluegrass, or folk music generally.

It's easy to get burned out. But the music industry offers so many different ways to participate that there is always something new and interesting to do.

How do you want to grow in your career? Hopefully, the next project you do will support that.

ELLIOT SCHEINER TALKS ABOUT JAMES BROWN

I will end this book with an inconvenient reality check. This story comes from the great recording engineer Elliot Scheiner, whose forthcoming book on music engineering I've had the honor of helping him to write. It throws a great monkey wrench into the traditional wisdom of teaching project management, and also reveals our unique predicament, as creatures of the music community who want to complete projects on time, within budget, on point, and to an excellent standard of quality. The story is about James Brown in a recording studio.

It would be difficult to argue that James Brown was ineffective at doing stuff. Compare him to the hundred billion or so other people who have walked the planet, and from my perspective, he accomplished more than most of us do. He certainly makes the top one percent. Besides his countless awards, hit songs, and so on, he defined one of the most influential musical styles of our time. He even redefined our conception of what a "groove" is. He's called the Godfather of Soul. He's a household name. Really, if you're looking for a model of someone who has completed a lot of projects successfully, you need not try to achieve more in life than did James Brown.

A project manager looking to run how a recording session will go will have some ideas about schedule and procedure, keeping a tight eye on the clock, and being ever conscious of the project's budget and how the proceedings of the session were supporting all these elements. There's that, and then there's real life. And to be effective in our search for management techniques that actually promise success, we have to start with real life, look at how great works have been created, and then map backwards our project management approaches from there, trying to make sure that we're developing effective systems and not just inconvenient bureaucracy to help us look busy.

The James Brown Session

So, Elliot was discussing how to talk to artists during recording sessions. I was hoping he'd reveal some neat how-to tips that we could write up as a tidy procedure in his book. Instead, he related this story.

I worked with James Brown in 1971, and it was one of the more interesting sessions I'd ever recorded. James Brown was an idol to me. I loved R&B music and the Motown and Memphis recordings. I was a staff engineer at the time when the office told me that I would be working with James Brown. I was really excited about having the opportunity.

We were in studio A2 at A&R. The band was comprised of mostly New York studio musicians, but two of them were formerly from Detroit: Andrew Smith on drums and Bob Babbit on bass. Fred Wesley was his band leader. It was the James Brown horn section with this New York rhythm section.

The band was all there before he arrived. I'd gotten sounds on everybody.

James walked in wearing a big fur coat. It was the dead of winter. He had two bodyguards with him.

He walked up to me and introduced himself, "I'm James Brown. Most people call me Mister Brown. You can call me James."

James dug into his pocket, took out a wad of bills, put five $100 bills down on the console, and said, "This is just so we get off to a good start. There's more where this came from." That was more than I was making in a week at A&R. That was like, oh my God! And at the end of the date, he gave me more. He also took care of my assistant.

We were recording "King Heroin," later released in two parts. Fred Wesley had come up with two 4-bar phrases, and everybody had a copy.

James was really interactive with the band. It was his first time working with most of them, except for the horns, so he was trying to tell everybody—mainly the drummer and the bass player—how to play and what he was expecting from them. And he eventually got it.

Once he got them to play those phrases, he danced around the room, as it was being recorded. He'd hold up his hand. One finger meant they were to play the first phrase until he told them otherwise. Two fingers meant they should play the second phrase.

The whole song was done that way. I don't remember how many hours we went or how long it lasted. It seemed like a long time because it took him a long time to get the players to play it the way he felt it. But he was out there, obviously for inspiration.

He would get angry, occasionally, and let the band know it. Everybody was frightened of the guy. He was such an overpowering personality.

That happens in a lot of cases. You go into the studio with someone whom you've idol-worshipped—who is your hero, who you've always wanted to work with. You want to do good for them, but you're frightened at the same time.

James was just totally into the session, and he wanted the players to be into it too. He was dictating how it would go, right on the spot: one finger, or two fingers.

I can't imagine what was going on in his head that prompted him to switch phrases. It was not a set amount of time for each phrase. I couldn't get any structure to this song. It was impossible to figure out. He would just change the groove, going back and forth.

Obviously, it worked for him. He was an unbelievable artist. And my job, as engineer, was to capture what he was doing while staying out of the way, so that he could create.

That, dear readers, is what effective project management looks like. Sure, one could whine that "King Heroin" wasn't one of James Brown's greatest hits. But considered in the grand scheme of all music ever created, the recording was a successful project. It was imagined, recorded, sold, and commented upon. Forty years later, people are still writing about it. Today, I Googled "King Heroin" and got over 100,000 hits. It was a meaningful step in James Brown's artistic output. Most art doesn't get that much traction.

The trouble with art, unlike most business endeavors, is that the metrics for success aren't as simple as, say, financial profit, or increased test scores, or measurable improvement in efficiencies. But one of the commonly required components for an endeavor to be considered a "project" is that it has a measurable success.

What does success look like, in a music project?

Many musicians go into a project without a clear concept of what their goals are, and this causes some existential angst. They chase the dream of recording an album, and then when the actual resulting sales are measured in the dozens, rather than the hundreds of thousands that they'd fantasized about, they see it as a failure and a sign that they are on the wrong path. Completing an album, though, is in fact an important success, if you're looking at the necessary evolution of artists. Some veteran songwriters say that the first twenty-five to fifty songs you write will be crap, so get them out of the way as quickly as possible, so you can get on with the actual good songs you'll write when you're more experienced. Recording songs is a way to complete their creation, so it's important. However, if you are using sales as your only metric, then you might, in fact, perceive low sales as failure. It ain't necessarily so.

So, part of the process, here, is having a realistic and mature sense of what the goals of a project are. Goals should be somewhat measurable, but you should also have a broad, overall life vision of what it is you are trying to accomplish, where you are in your development, and what appropriate goals should be. Perhaps, your resulting work will exceed these goals. That's great, but it's more important to be working towards something grounded in reality.

Our approach to project management must be grounded in business principles, so that we can actually get work done, but it must also allow for the less tangible dimensions of what we're trying to accomplish in our lives as music makers.

Some techniques are not reproducible. There's no way anybody would teach the approach that Elliot describes, above. Good luck "rinsing and repeating." It's too unique, and too individual to James Brown. It would never work for me, and probably not for you either.

So, if that's what a successful project looks like, how does formal project management fit into this crazy world?

In Elliot's words, "You have to be flexible, and able to work with artists in whatever way makes them comfortable and able to create."

It would be a mistake, here, to take this anecdote and draw the conclusion that this chaos was actually the method happening around the whole project. It's just a snapshot of one small dimension of the project: a bit of the "execution" phase. James Brown's antics during the session were one dimension of what happened to create the project. However, surrounding that anecdote is a lot more deliberate planning, which was necessary for the scene to be set where the magic could happen.

Someone had to envision what the recording would be. Depending on circumstance, that initial vision might be clearly or loosely defined, but at a point, it eventually has to come into focus—even if part of the definition is to encourage a relatively loose, free-form arrangement.

Then, the event must be scheduled. A recording date needs to be selected. Microphones need to be selected and set up, and backup musicians auditioned, contracted, and paid. James Brown needed to remember to stuff his wallet with cold cash, in order to create the atmosphere that his experience told him was necessary for him to create as he wanted to create. He needed to be able to flip out a few cool greenbacks to grease the young, impressionable engineer, so that this indispensable cog in the wheel would do anything to make the session a success. And to spread the legend.

After the session, the project needed to be mixed, mastered, promoted, delivered, and archived. Copyright forms needed to be filed so that the cash would continue pouring in for the next session date. And contacts made during that session needed to be entered into a Rolodex or little black book, so that more magic could be coordinated in the future.

Magic needs a managed context, and that's the project manager's job. Managing music projects seems to require more stretching of the imagination and tolerating more chaos than in some other industries, but that scaffold remains essential. Removing barriers to creativity and productivity are always part of the game—even in manufacturing physical products.

Another dimension of Elliot Scheiner's work, when he's not producing projects by top-flight artists, is a little business that he loves dearly: manufacturing high quality, hand-turned baseball bats (Star Bound Bats™, www.starboundbats.com). Many project management approaches are appropriate for making things like baseball bats. It's a relatively predictable path to project success. Of course, making the bats is a simpler proposition than making a company that profits by making the bats. But still, businesses that manufacture widgets have a reasonably well-established trajectory. Follow the well-trodden path, and you can probably make a profit in your widget business. If making hand-turned bats doesn't work, cut costs, diversify your offerings, improve your marketing, yadda yadda yadda.

There's much about music that isn't as controlled. However, that doesn't mean that there is nothing about it that isn't predictable. The big difference is in deliberately creating a space that allows for the magic to happen. Some approaches allow for this, but others don't, so as you research this topic of project management in other places, be aware that music projects are relatively sophisticated. Also, most project management approaches assume that the project team is a small part of a large, adequately resourced corporation, rather than an independent music ensemble or a church choir or a one-man-shop recording studio. Still, though, the formal modeling by professional researchers in project management can apply.

Most of the process of music-making isn't magic. The techniques we've been discussing here set the stage for the magic. It's the support mechanisms and logistics that allow the magic to happen. And these logistics can be overwhelming, to artists. Logistics out of hand can prevent the art from happening. But if it's all in place and well organized, then the vibe can be right, and your inner James Brown can dance around the studio, holding up his fingers, with everyone in the room simultaneously thinking he's crazy and being profoundly moved by his work.

CLOSING THOUGHTS

By the time the end of our project rolls around, we often just want to be done with it and hurry on to the next venture. Formal project closure procedures are often skipped, but that's at the detriment to future endeavors, and so I recommend allocating some time into closing them out in a way that will be helpful. Your future self will thank you for it.

And now, your project of reading this book draws to an end. Did you accomplish your goals, in reading it? Were you hoping to learn something that wasn't covered here? How will you learn that material?

How are you going to take what you found most useful in this book and then implement those practices into your own life? Without taking some deliberate action now, while it is fresh in your mind, you will forget much of it. By promptly systematizing the tools and techniques that you have learned here about project management, they will truly become yours, and your ability to manage projects will improve.

What will you do, today, to move it forward?

Thank you so much for reading this book. I hope that you got a lot out of it, and that it truly helps you in your career, creating more music. The world needs your participation, in whatever form that might be.

I wish you the very best of luck with it.

With warm regards,

—Jonathan Feist

PRACTICE

After your content is created, what clean-up work will need to be done? Consider all the elements discussed in this chapter (punchlists, reusability analysis, stakeholder notifications, etc.) and add them to your work breakdown structure. At what point will you truly be able to call your project "finished?" Articulate this, and then set your sites towards your next project. Consider both what it will be, and also, how you will bring the new project management skills you have learned towards that endeavor.

Scope Statement Sample: Emily's EP

PROJECT TITLE   VERSION/DATE

Emily's EP   DRAFT November 26, 2011

Summary

An EP of three original songs by Emily Peal, recorded with the Band of Skinny Men.

OBJECTIVES

We are doing this project to:

- fulfill our artistic desires to continually create and grow

- provide new music to people who appreciate what we do

- create an object to give to prospective record labels, booking agents, and others who might support our work

DELIVERABLES

- three original songs, presented by Emily to the band as lead sheets and rough recordings, to be arranged and developed in collaboration with the band during rehearsals in advance of the recording sessions

- original cover art as high-resolution digital file

- replication-ready CD pre-master

- 200 sales-ready copies of the completed EP

ACCEPTANCE CRITERIA

- Recorded songs will be artistically fulfilling and at a high standard of sound engineering
- EP replication pre-master will conform to Red Book standard
- EP will be separately mastered to optimize sound quality, loudness relationships, and transitions between tracks
- EP pre-master will have complete, error-free metadata including ISRC codes
- Album art will express spirit of this recording and the band generally
- Album art will be a high-resolution CMYK graphics file
- Album back cover will have a bar code

Exclusions

This project only includes the creation of a distribution-ready EP.

- It does not include sales, marketing, or distribution of the EP.
- It does not include the tour to support the EP.
- It does not include merchandise associated with the EP, beyond the replicated EPs themselves.

Constraints

Budget: See "Appendix A. Budget"

Item	Amount	Comment	Status
EP Packaging	$50 (self-packaging) $100 (sticker printing) $600 (artwork) $400 (CD replication) $1,150 Total		Secure
Mastering	$500	Separate from mixing	Not secure
Total	**$1,650**		Not secure

Milestones:

Item	Date	Status
Songs written		
Song demos (keyboard/voice) distributed to band		
Songs rehearsed and ready for recording		
Songs recorded		
Album rough mixed		
Listener Survey		
Album final mix		
Album mastered		
EP cover art approved		
EP replicated		

Assumptions

Item	To Be Validated By	Status	Mitigation Plan
Free recording studio time will remain available	Emily	Confirmed	Reconsider project
At least $2,000 in funding will be achieved	Emily	Open	Try alternative fundraising sites; postpone replication but not recording session
Our schedules will coincide to allow us to record for free	Emily, all band members, engineer	Open	If no date can be agreed upon, we will use substitute musicians for the recording

Dependencies

- Secured funding must precede setting the recording date.

- The songwriting must precede the art.

- The art must precede the creation of CD replication and all merchandise.

- This project and all merchandise must precede our planned tour.

Stakeholders

Distribution List	Name	Roles and Responsibilities	Status	Contact	Comment
•	Emily Peal	artistic director, songwriter, project manager, bandleader, writes songs, books venues	Confirmed	[add]	Approves all project decisions
•	Andrew	drums	Confirmed	[add]	
•	Mike	guitar	Confirmed	[add]	
•	David	bass	Confirmed	[add]	
	Aaron	mix engineer	Confirmed	[add]	
	Alan	mastering engineer	Pending	[add]	
	Secret Designs	illustrator	Confirmed	[add]	
		layout designer	Needed		
	Tammy	photographer	Confirmed	[add]	
	DiscMakers	replication house	Pending	[add]	
	Sample Audience	provide feedback on rough mix	Needed		

Recommended Reading

Allen, David. *Getting Things Done: The Art of Stress-Free Productivity*. New York: Penguin Books, 2001. The best $15 you'll ever spend.

Bargfrede, Allen and Cecily Mak. *Music Law in the Digital Age*. Boston: Berklee Press, 2009. An insightful and fairly comprehensive guide to understanding copyright law and the current legal state of the industry.

Cornell-Feist, Marci. *Board Meetings: A Guide for Charter Schools*. Harvard, MA: The High Bar, 2011. Okay, okay, this book is targeted at the niche market of charter school boards, and yes, my wife is the author and I'm the editor. But it is an excellent, concise guide to how to run effective meetings, good for all kinds of work, and I give it my highest (if, perhaps, slightly biased) recommendation. Money back guarantee....

Fraley, Gregg. *Jack's Notebook*. Nashville: Thomas Nelson, Inc., 2007. A delightfully creative and effective way to teach strategic thinking.

Gawande, Atul. *The Checklist Manifesto: How to Get Things Right*. New York: Metropolitan Books/Henry Holt and Company, 2009. Fun reading, especially for a book about checklists.

Halloran, Mark. *The Musician's Business and Legal Guide*, 4th Edition. Upper Saddle River, NJ: Pearson/Prentice Hall, 2008. Some good model contracts in this book.

Howard, George. *Music Publishing 101*. Boston: Berklee Press, 2005. A very concise and clear explanation of how the money flows.

King, Mike. *Music Marketing: Press, Promotion, Distribution, and Retail*. Boston: Berklee Press, 2009. A practical, informative guide to creating and managing music marketing campaigns.

Milosevic, Dragan Z. *Project Management Toolbox: Tools and Techniques for the Practicing Project Manager.* Hoboken, NJ: Wiley and Sons Inc., 2003. A useful, clear, very technical, and somewhat advanced collection of project management tools.

Norman, Eric S., Shelly A. Brotherton, and Robert T. Fried. *Work Breakdown Structures: The Foundation for Project Management Excellence.* Hoboken, NJ: John Wiley and Sons, 2008. Advanced and detailed, with great insights into best practice. Buy it now, put it on your shelf, and reference it when you have mastered all this other stuff and you want to get even more persnickety and organized.

Passman, Donald. *All You Need to Know about the Music Business,* Seventh Edition. Free Press, 2009. Excellent all-around book about the recording industry.

Project Management Institute, *A Guide to the Project Management Body of Knowledge (PMBOK Guide),* Fourth Edition. Atlanta, GA: Project Management Institute, Inc., 2008. The central repository for the most up-to-date research on best practice. This is the book that all the other project management books reference.

Ries, Eric. *The Lean Startup: How Today's Entrepreneurs Use Continuous Innovation to Create Radically Successful Businesses.* New York: Crown Business, 2011. A terrific book on one of the most useful micro-iteration processes.

Wynsocki, Robert K. *Effective Project Management: Traditional, Agile, Extreme.* Hoboken, NJ: Wiley and Sons Inc., 2011. A clear, end-to-end project management guide, primarily aimed at managing larger projects in a corporate context, but some very practical and thorough descriptions of the major standard tools.

ABOUT THE AUTHOR

Robert M. Hubert, Photographer

JONATHAN FEIST

Jonathan Feist is the editor in chief of Berklee Press, where he has helped bring over 150 commercial music products, including instructional music books, recordings, videos, and online courses, to a worldwide market since 1998. He is the author and instructor of two Berkleemusic courses: *Project Management for Musicians* (2012) and *Music Notation with Finale* (2002). He is also the co-author of two books: *Essential Songwriter* (with Jimmy Kachulis, Berklee Press, 2004) and the *Berklee Practice Method Teacher's Guide* (with Matt Marvuglio, Berklee Press, 2004). Jonathan is a composer and songwriter, and most recently released the album *Fantasy Monologue* (2010), where he served as songwriter and lead vocalist. He holds a bachelor's and master's degree in composition from New England Conservatory of Music. Read his blog at http://jonathanfeist.berkleemusicblogs.com.

To study this material in an online course and get personal coaching on your project, visit Berkleemusic.com. The course covers the material discussed in this book, but is expanded with interviews of music industry professionals, live online chats and other communication opportunities, interactive quizzes and animated demonstrations, weekly projects that get feedback from an instructure and classmates, and also a peer network of other project managers in the music industry. It is an excellent way to learn project management.

INDEX

Note: Page numbers in *italics* indicate illustrations or photographs.

STUDY PROJECT MANAGEMENT
with
BERKLEE ONLINE

Study Berklee's curriculum, with Berklee faculty members, in a collaborative online community. Transform your skill set and find your inspiration in all areas of music, from project management and music business to songwriting and music production, theory, orchestration, and everything in between. Build lifelong relationships with like-minded students on your own time, from anywhere in the world.

Discover Your Own Path At
Berkleemusic.com

More Fine Publications from Berklee Press

WOODWINDS

FAMOUS SAXOPHONE SOLOS
arr. Jeff Harrington
50449605 Book $14.99

IMPROVISATION FOR FLUTE
by Andy McGhee
50449810 Book $14.99

IMPROVISATION FOR SAXOPHONE
by Andy McGhee
50449860 Book $14.99

SAXOPHONE SOUND EFFECTS
by Ueli Dörig
50449628 Book/CD $14.99

ROOTS MUSIC

BEYOND BLUEGRASS
Beyond Bluegrass Banjo
by Dave Hollander and Matt Glaser
50449610 Book/CD $19.99
Beyond Bluegrass Mandolin
by John McGann and Matt Glaser
50449609 Book/CD $19.99
Bluegrass Fiddle and Beyond
by Matt Glaser
50449602 Book/CD $19.99

BERKLEE PRACTICE METHOD

GET YOUR BAND TOGETHER
With additional volumes for other instruments,
plus a teacher's guide.
Bass
*by Rich Appleman, John Repucci and the
Berklee Faculty*
50449427 Book/CD $14.95
Drum Set
*by Ron Savage, Casey Scheuerell and the
Berklee Faculty*
50449429 Book/CD $14.95
Guitar
by Larry Baione and the Berklee Faculty
50449426 Book/CD $16.99
Keyboard
*by Russell Hoffmann, Paul Schmeling and
the Berklee Faculty*
50449428 Book/CD $14.95

WELLNESS

**MANAGE YOUR STRESS AND PAIN
THROUGH MUSIC**
*by Dr. Suzanne B. Hanser and
Dr. Susan E. Mandel*
50449592 Book/CD $29.99

MUSIC SMARTS
by Mr. Bonzai
50449591 Book $14.99

MUSICIAN'S YOGA
by Mia Olson
50449587 Book $14.99

**THE NEW MUSIC THERAPIST'S
HANDBOOK – SECOND EDITION**
by Dr. Suzanne B. Hanser
50449424 Book $29.95

EAR TRAINING, IMPROVISATION, MUSIC THEORY

BEGINNING EAR TRAINING
by Gilson Schachnik
50449548 Book/CD $14.99

BERKLEE MUSIC THEORY – 2ND EDITION
by Paul Schmeling
50449615 Rhythm, Scales Intervals:
Book/CD $24.99
50449616 Harmony: Book/CD $22.99

BLUES IMPROVISATION COMPLETE
by Jeff Harrington
Book/CD Packs
50449486 B♭ Instruments $19.95
50449488 C Bass Instruments $19.95
50449425 C Treble Instruments $22.99
50449487 E♭ Instruments $19.95

**ESSENTIAL EAR TRAINING FOR THE
CONTEMPORARY MUSICIAN**
by Steve Prosser
50449421 Book $16.95

A GUIDE TO JAZZ IMPROVISATION
by John LaPorta
Book/CD Packs
50449439 C Instruments $19.95
50449441 B♭ Instruments $19.99
50449442 E♭ Instruments $19.99
50449443 B♭: Instruments $19.99

**IMPROVISATION FOR
CLASSICAL MUSICIANS**
by Eugene Friesen with Wendy M. Friesen
50449637 Book/CD $24.99

REHARMONIZATION TECHNIQUES
by Randy Felts
50449496 Book $29.95

MUSIC BUSINESS

THE FUTURE OF MUSIC
by Dave Kusek and Gerd Leonhard
50448055 Book $16.95

**HOW TO GET A JOB IN THE MUSIC
INDUSTRY – 2ND EDITION**
by Keith Hatschek
50449551 Book $27.95

MAKING MUSIC MAKE MONEY
by Eric Beall
50448009 Book $26.95

MUSIC LAW IN THE DIGITAL AGE
by Allen Bargfrede and Cecily Mak
50449586 Book $19.99

MUSIC MARKETING *by Mike King*
50449588 Book $24.99

**THE SELF-PROMOTING MUSICIAN –
2ND EDITION**
by Peter Spellman
50449589 Book $24.99

MUSIC PRODUCTION & ENGINEERING

**FINALE: AN EASY GUIDE TO
MUSIC NOTATION – 3RD EDITION**
*by Thomas E. Rudolph and
Vincent A. Leonard, Jr.*
50449638 Book $34.99

MIX MASTERS
by Maureen Droney
50448023 Book $24.95

PRODUCING & MIXING CONTEMPORARY JAZZ

by Dan Moretti
50449554 Book/DVD-ROM $24.95

PRODUCING AND MIXING HIP-HOP/R&B
by Mike Hamilton
50449555 Book/DVD-ROM $19.99

PRODUCING DRUM BEATS
by Eric Hawkins
50449598 Book/CD-ROM Pack $22.99

**PRODUCING IN THE HOME STUDIO
WITH PRO TOOLS – THIRD EDITION**
by David Franz
50449544 Book/DVD-ROM $39.95

**RECORDING AND PRODUCING IN THE
HOME STUDIO**
by David Franz
50448045 Book $24.95

UNDERSTANDING AUDIO
by Daniel M. Thompson
50449456 Book $24.99

SONGWRITING, COMPOSING, ARRANGING

ARRANGING FOR LARGE JAZZ ENSEMBLE
by Dick Lowell and Ken Pullig
50449528 Book/CD $39.95

**COMPLETE GUIDE TO FILM SCORING –
2ND EDITION**
by Richard Davis
50449607 ....$27.99

JAZZ COMPOSITION
by Ted Pease
50448000 Book/CD $39.99

MELODY IN SONGWRITING
by Jack Perricone
50449419 Book/CD $24.95

MODERN JAZZ VOICINGS
by Ted Pease and Ken Pullig
50449485 Book/CD $24.95

**MUSIC COMPOSITION FOR FILM AND
TELEVISION**
by Lalo Schifrin
50449604 Book $34.99

MUSIC NOTATION
Preparing Scores and Parts
by Matthew Nicholl and Richard Grudzinski
50449540 Book $16.95

MUSIC NOTATION
Theory and Technique for Music notation
by Mark McGrain
50449399 Book $24.95

POPULAR LYRIC WRITING
by Andrea Stolpe
50449553 Book $14.95

SONGWRITING: ESSENTIAL GUIDE
by Pat Pattison
50481582 Lyric and Form Structure: Book ...$16.95
50481583 Rhyming: Book $14.99

THE SONGWRITER'S WORKSHOP
by Jimmy Kachulis
50449519 Harmony: Book/CD $29.95
50449518 Melody: Book/CD $24.95

Prices subject to change without notice. Visit your local
music dealer or bookstore, or go to **www.berkleepress.com**

HAL•LEONARD® CORPORATION
7777 W. BLUEMOUND RD. P.O. BOX 13819 MILWAUKEE, WI 53213

1012